Carolyn Steele

A HISTORY
OF RECREATION

The End of the Fox Hunt

Painting of about 1780, owned by Dr. Wyndham B. Blanton. Courtesy of the Metropolitan Museum of Art.

A HISTORY OF RECREATION

America Learns to Play

SECOND EDITION

FOSTER RHEA DULLES

NEW YORK

APPLETON-CENTURY-CROFTS

Division of Meredith Publishing Company

Copyright © 1965 by
MEREDITH PUBLISHING COMPANY

All rights reserved. This book, or parts
thereof, must not be used or reproduced
in any manner without written permission.
For information address the publisher,
Appleton-Century-Crofts, Division of
Meredith Publishing Company, 440 Park
Avenue South, New York, N.Y. 10016

685-1

Library of Congress Card Number: 65-25489

Copyright © 1940 by D. Appleton-Century Company, Inc.

PRINTED IN THE UNITED STATES OF AMERICA
E 27782

TO
EDITH

PREFACE TO
THE FIRST EDITION

THE GROWTH OF POPULAR RECREATION IN THE UNITED STATES may be compared to a river—its course adapting itself to the nature of the country through which it flows, the main stream continually augmented by tributaries, and the river-bed itself ever growing both broader and deeper. In the early period of settlement it was little more than a thin trickle, forcing its way through a forbidding terrain, but with the eighteenth century it slowly gathered volume and flowed on quietly and steadily. The first half of the nineteenth century saw its course deflected into more narrow channels, and for a time the flow appeared to be almost checked, but after the Civil War scores of new tributaries swelled it to far greater size. The twentieth century transformed it into a riotous torrent, breaking through all barriers as it carved out fresh channels. Sometimes it appeared to sweep almost everything else aside, spreading in full flood over a vast territory.

This book is an attempt to trace the main course of this stream. Recreation is considered in its popular sense—the leisure-time activities that the American people have pursued over three centuries for their own pleasure. At all periods of history men and women have probably spent the greater part of their leisure in informal talk, in visiting and entertaining their friends, in casual walks and strolls, and sometimes in reading for their own amusement. But these more simple activities are hidden in the obscurity that shrouds private lives. Organized, public recreation has consciously been adopted as the basis for this record.

It has been found stupendously difficult to delimit its boundaries. There have always been leisure-time pursuits in which cultural and recreational motives are inextricably mixed, and in more recent years increasing emphasis has been placed on creative activities. In the main, the cultural and the creative have been ignored in this account of the people at play. Music and the dance are treated as entertainment, not art. Where religion, or rather the church, has impinged on the recreational scene, there is again no attempt to go beyond the surface implications of the popular enjoyment of the Sunday meeting or midweek Great and Thursday of colonial days, the frontier revival, the small-town church social of the 1890's, or the activities clustering about the institutionalized church of metropolis.

Even with these limitations recreation includes a wide category of amusements ranging from horseshoe-pitching to symphony concerts, from the circus to fox-hunting, from prize-fights to contract bridge, from lodge night to international polo. Throughout the book the emphasis has invariably been placed on those diversions or sports which have reached the greatest number of people. A century ago a shrewd foreign observer declared that democracy was too new a comer upon the earth to have been able as yet to organize its pleasures. America would be compelled in this field of activity, as in politics, to create everything fresh. How this challenge has been met is the basic question that has determined my lines of inquiry. Yachting has been largely ignored in favor of bicycling and motoring, the opera neglected to stress the importance of minstrel shows and vaudeville, and though the popular theatre of the mid-nineteenth century is described, the rise of the movies has forced the legitimate stage of the twentieth century into the background.

In view of the greatly increased leisure for the masses of people in the present day and the very real concern as to how it is being used, it is hoped that an account of changing trends in recreation during the past three centuries may prove of immediate interest. Two important factors, I think, stand out from the record. The first is the continuing influence of an inherent puritanism, both rising from and enforcing a dogma of work born of economic circumstance, which may be traced from the seventeenth century to the twentieth. Until recent times it has frowned severely upon what the early settlers called any "mispense of time." If to-day this attitude has somewhat changed, the American tradition still insists that amusements should at least make some pretense of serving socially useful ends. The businessman plays golf to keep fit for business; the woman's club emphasizes its educational program; and reformers would have all popular entertainment directed toward the establishment of higher cultural standards.

The second factor is the paramount influence on recreation of the gradual transformation of our economy from the simplicity of the agricultural era to the complexity of the machine age. No field of human activity has been more deeply affected by this change and the concomitant growth of cities. The machine has greatly increased the leisure of the laboring masses, and it has at the same time made life less leisurely. The traditional patterns of everyday living have been completely altered with an ever-growing need for play that can effectively compensate for the intensity under which we must work. If many of the forms of recreation that have evolved under these circumstances appear far from ideal, the question is nevertheless posed as to what the urban masses, granted the conditions of modern life, would be doing if they did not have their commercial amusements and spectator sports.

Entirely apart from the possible bearing on present-day recreation of the developments of the past, an account of three centuries of play also seems to throw as revealing a light upon how the American people have created the modern society in which we live as many records of more serious activities. Lord Lytton has somewhere stated that the civilization of a people is infallibly indicated by the intellectual character of its amusements. It is more and more widely recognized to-day that what a nation does with its leisure is oftentimes just as significant as how it either maintains itself economically or governs itself. This book is presented with the idea that on these grounds alone there is justification for surveying a phase of human activity which the historian often ignores.

The field is so broad that, with the best will in the world, it has proved impossible to treat many topics comprehensively. I have not tried to give a complete record of any single sport or amusement. The origins of diversions are generally traced in some detail, but once popularly accepted (the tributary joining the main stream), further developments have been noted only as incidental to the general expansion of recreation. Moreover, to write authoritatively of New England husking-bees and the concerts and balls of colonial Charleston; of sailing regattas in the 1830's and the trotting races of county fairs in mid-century; of archery and the roller-skating craze; of surprise parties and the popular melodrama of the 1890's; of automobile motoring, the movies, and radio; of softball and skiing; of jazz, crossword puzzles, and major-league baseball, would demand a familiarity with the social scene through three hundred years of American history which I would be the first to disclaim.

It has taken considerable courage even to attempt to plot a course. The mass of available evidence made a sampling process the only possible procedure. Where other writers have traced the history of some one form of amusement (for there is no comparable earlier book covering the whole subject), I have most gratefully availed myself of the fruits of their labor. The chapter notes and bibliography at the end of the volume will give some measure of my indebtedness. But so far as time and space have allowed, I have used the contemporary evidence of how the American people have amused themselves in their leisure time— the records contained in diaries, autobiographies, travel accounts, magazines, newspapers, playbills and posters, sports manuals and advertisements. I have selected whatever appeared significant, interesting, and sometimes amusing in order to present the kaleidoscopic scene as much as possible through the eyes of those who actually observed it. There can be no scientific exactitude about such a record. It is necessarily colored throughout, though

I have tried to restrain myself, by personal interests and enthusiasms—and also by personal blind-spots.

To acknowledge the aid and assistance I have received from various sources is but a poor return for these favors. The book would probably have never been written except for a fellowship awarded by the John Simon Guggenheim Memorial Foundation. I should also like to express my appreciation of the coöperation of Francis G. Wickware in assembling the illustrations, and of Janet Aaron in compiling the index. The manuscript has been patiently read and criticized by several co-workers or friends, among whom I am particularly indebted to John A. Krout; while the aid, encouragement, and practical assistance of Edith Dulles Snare and Marion Dulles are greatly responsible for whatever virtues the book may claim.

FOSTER RHEA DULLES

PREFACE TO
THE SECOND EDITION

IN THIS SECOND EDITION of *America Learns to Play*, I have not changed the material carrying the narrative up to 1900. However, the succeeding chapters dealing with the twentieth century have been partially reorganized, completely rewritten, and brought up to date. This has proved to be an exceedingly difficult task. What I referred to a quarter of a century ago as the incredibly broadened stream of popular recreation, has since the end of World War II expanded even more unbelievably. The development of television, the postwar revolution in sports, and the introduction of many new amusements have made the recreational picture even more crowded than it was in 1940. I have tried to bring into focus the more important elements in this postwar scene, but once again realize that its very diversity allows only a somewhat impressionistic treatment.

F. R. D.

CONTENTS

Preface to the First Edition . . . . *vii*

Preface to the Second Edition . . . . *xii*

Illustrations . . . . *xv*

1. "In Detestation of Idleness" 3
2. Husking-Bees and Tavern Sports 22
3. The Colonial Aristocracy 44
4. The Frontier 67
5. A Changing Society 84
6. The Theatre Comes of Age 100
7. Mr. Barnum Shows the Way 122
8. The Beginning of Spectator Sports 136
9. Mid-Century 148
10. Cow-Towns and Mining-Camps 168
11. The Rise of Sports 182
12. The New Order 201
13. Metropolis 211
14. World of Fashion 230
15. Main Street 248
16. Farm and Countryside 271
17. The Role of Moving Pictures 287
18. A Nation on Wheels 312
19. On the Air 327
20. Sports for All 344
21. The Changing Scene 366
22. The New Leisure 386

CONTENTS

Suggested Reading 399
Notes 401
Index 435

ILLUSTRATIONS

The End of the Fox Hunt . . . . *frontispiece*

FACING PAGE

Title-Page of King James I's "Book of Sports" . . . . . *on* 11
Bear-Baiting 24
Skittles 24
"The Hill Tops," a New Hunting Song 25
How to Mount a Horse . . . . *on* 32
The Square Dance . . . . *on* 38
Exotic Animals on Show in New England . . . . . *on* 41
Playbill of the Hallam Company of Comedians . . . . *on* 55
Shooting for the Beef 72
Joys of the Camp-Meeting 73
"Light May the Boat Row" 86
Dr. Rich's Institute for Physical Education 87
A Picnic on the Wissahickon 87
Female Calisthenics in the Pantalette Era . . . . . *on* 94
A Family Party Playing at Fox and Geese 96
The Dance after the Husking 96
Skating in Central Park, New York 97
A Society Audience at the Park Theatre, New York 106
Scenes from "Uncle Tom's Cabin" 107
Fanny Elssler in La Tarentule 116
Wonders of Barnum's Museum 117
First Appearance of Jenny Lind in America 126
Jim Crow 126
Christy's Minstrels 127
Barnum Enters the Circus Field 132
Circus Day in Chicago 133
Peytona and Fashion's Great Match 140
Lady Suffolk and O'Blennis 141
Boat-Race on the Charles River, Boston 144

FACING PAGE

A Great Foot-Race at Hoboken 144
The Great Fight for the Championship 145
A Yachting Club on Lake Erie 150
The Bathe at Newport 151
Sleighing in New York 156
A Home on the Mississippi 157
The Turkey Shoot 157
The Fashionable Singing Class 164
The Dance 164
Enter the Trick Horseman 165
The Hurdy-Gurdy House at Virginia City, Montana 174
Cow-Town Vaudeville 174
Bucking the Tiger 175
Cowboys in Town for Christmas 175
A Great Game for the Baseball Championship 186
The Game of Croquet 187
A Spring Meeting of the New York Archery Club 187
The First National Tennis Tournament at New Brighton . . 196
Washington Meet of the League of American Wheelmen . . 196
Yale Meets Princeton in Football 197
A Six-Day Walk for the Pedestrian Championship . . . on 200
Camping Out 202
The Great International Caledonian Games 203
Sunday "Social Freedom" in the Bowery 212
A Chicago Pool-Room on Sunday 213
Winter Amateur Athletic Meet at the Boston Athletic Club . . 222
The Bathing Hour on the Beach at Atlantic City 223
A Double Play to Open the League Season 223
Trotting Cracks of Philadelphia Returning from the Races . . 232
Fashionable Turnouts in Central Park 232
Baltimore Society Dances for Charity 233
When Wallack's Theatre Was New 238
Defense of the *America's* Cup 239
New York's First Coach 239
Polo at Jerome Park 244
The Social Side of Intercollegiate Baseball 245
Knights Templar in Conclave at Chicago 256

ILLUSTRATIONS

FACING PAGE

A Chautauqua Tent 257
The Lighter Side of Chautauqua 257
Program of a Typical Chautauqua Week . . . . . . on 259
Puck's Suggestion to His Religious Friends . . . . . on 268
A New England Straw Ride 274
A Grange Meeting in an Illinois School-House 274
The Day We Celebrate 275
The Country Fair 282
Jumbo 283
In the Days of the Kinetoscope 292
The Last Word in Picture Theatres 292
Incunabula of the Movies 293
New Toys for the Wealthy 314
Cars and Costumes of Pre-War Days 314
Vacationing on Wheels 315
The First Broadcasting Station 328
A Modern Television Control Room 328
Television Goes to the Golf Course 329
Pioneer Sportswomen 346
The Houston Astrodome 347
Factory Softball 362
College Basketball 362
Ski School in Vermont 363
Heat Relief at Coney Island 363

A HISTORY
OF RECREATION

chapter 1

"In Detestation
of Idleness"

THE SETTLERS WHO PLANTED THE FIRST ENGLISH COLONIES IN
America had the same instinctive drive for play that is the
common heritage of all mankind. It suffered no sea change in the
long and stormy crossing of the Atlantic. Landing at Jamestown,
Sir Thomas Dale found the almost starving colonists playing
happily at bowls in 1611.[1] * The first Thanksgiving at Plymouth
was something more than an occasion for prayer. Edward
Winslow wrote that among other recreations the Pilgrims exercised their arms and for three days entertained and feasted the
Indians.[2]

Against the generally somber picture of early New England
life may also be set the lively account of those gay and wanton
festivities at Merry Mount. To the consternation of "the precise
separatists, that lived at new Plymouth," the scapegrace followers
of Thomas Morton set up a May-pole, brought out wine and
strong waters, and invited the Indians to join them:

> Drinke and be merry, merry, merry boyes,
> Let all your delight be in the Hymens joyes,
> Joy to Hymen now the day is come,
> About the merry Maypole take a Roome.
> Make greene garlons, bring bottles out
> And fill sweet Nectar freely about.
> Uncover thy head and fear no harme,
> For hers good liquor to keepe it warme.[3]

---

* All numerical symbols throughout the text refer to source references to
be found in the notes at the end of the book. They may be ignored by the
reader not interested in such material.

3

They spent several days, in William Bradford's disapproving phrase, "dancing and frisking togither, (like so many fairies or furies rather,) and worse practises." [4]

It was from these beginnings that American recreation grew to the varied and full activities we know to-day. They naturally open any record that would attempt to trace its growth and expansion under the changing conditions of American life. But it would be placing a greatly exaggerated emphasis on these simple sports and festivities to imagine that they were everyday occurrences. The first settlers actually had very little time or opportunity to play. Harsh circumstance fastened upon them the necessity for continual work. In the strange and unfamiliar wilderness that was America, "all things stared upon them with a weather-beaten face." The forest crowded against their little settlements along tidewater, and they felt continually menaced by its lurking dangers. None knew when the eerie war-whoop of the Indians might break the oppressive silence. Starvation again and again thinned their ranks, and disease was a grim specter hovering over each household. Merely to keep alive in a land which to their inexperience was cruel and inhospitable demanded all their energy.

The ruling powers, whether north or south, Puritan or Anglican, consequently found it at once necessary to adopt the strictest regulations "in detestation of idleness," to the end of enforcing work and prohibiting all amusements. Sir Thomas Dale sternly forbade further bowling at Jamestown and decreed that any tradesman unfaithful and negligent in daily attendance upon his occupation should be "condemned to the Galley for three years." [5] Governor Endicott of the Massachusetts Bay Colony cut down the May-pole at Merry Mount, gravely warning the revelers for the future "to looke ther should be better walking," and prepared rigorously to enforce the General Court's law that "no person, householder or other, shall spend his time idly or unprofitably, under paine of such punishment as the Courte shall thinke meet to inflict." [6]

It was the paramount need of a primitive, pioneer society for the whole-hearted coöperation of the entire community that fastened upon the first Americans a tradition of work which still weighs heavily upon their descendants. The common welfare in those difficult and perilous days could not permit any "mispense of time." Those who would not work of their own volition had to be driven to it under the lash of compulsion. Religion provided the strongest moral sanction for every law suppressing amusements. It was one of the vital forces making for a life in which recreation for long played hardly any part. But in all the colonies there was this basic fact: if the settlers did not direct all their energy to their work, they could not hope to survive.

➤➤❳❲❮❮

VIRGINIA originally enacted laws fully as restrictive as those of New England.[7] The Assembly in 1619 decreed that any person found idle should be bound over to compulsory work; it prohibited gaming at dice or cards, strictly regulated drinking, provided penalties for excess in apparel, and rigidly enforced Sabbath observance.[8] There was, for example, to be no admission of actors "because we resolve to suffer no Idle persons in Virginia." [9] Court records show that offenses against these laws were dealt with severely.[10] It was only as conditions of life became somewhat easier that enforcement grew lax. Once the colony was firmly established and the need for incessant work began to lessen, Virginians were more generally permitted to make the most of whatever opportunities for recreation their expanding life presented.

In New England, where the stern rule of Calvinism condemned idleness and amusements for their own sake, the tradition that life should be wholly devoted to work ("that noe idle drone bee permitted to live amongst us" [11]) held its ground more firmly. The magistrates attempted to suppress almost every form of recreation long after the practical justification for such an unrelenting attitude had disappeared. The intolerance of Puritanism was superimposed upon economic necessity to confine life in New England within the narrowest possible grooves. Massachusetts and Connecticut banned dice, cards, quoits, bowls, ninepins, "or any other unlawful game in house, yard, garden or backside," singling out for special attention "the Game called Shuffle Board, in howses of Common Interteinment, whereby much precious time is spent unfruitfully." [12] They listed "common Coasters, unprofitable fowlers, and Tobacko takers" as idlers subject to immediate punishment. No smoker in Connecticut could "take any tobacco publiquely in the street, nor shall any take yt in the fyelds or woods." His indulgence in a habit generally condemned as time-wasting was limited to the "ordinary tyme of repast commonly called dynner." [13]

Throughout New England, local ordinances further ordered the constables to "search after all manner of gameing, singing and dancing" and to report "disordered meetings" even when they were held in private homes.[14] John Cotton had condoned dancing under certain circumstances, reserving his disapproval with possible justification for "lascivious dancing to wanton ditties, and in amorous gestures and wanton dalliances," but his successors admitted no such subtle distinctions. The Devil was responsible for all dancing, and especially "Gynecandrical Dancing or that which is commonly called Mixt or Promiscuous Dancing of Men and Women." [15] When the Massachusetts General Court learned that the custom of dancing at weddings was growing up, it flatly decreed that there should be no more of it, then or at any other time.[16]

The theatre was of course absolutely prohibited. Connecticut was prepared to adjudge as common rogues and serve fifteen stripes on the bare back to any one who should attempt to "set up and practice common plays, interludes, or other crafty science." Boston on one occasion refused permission for an exhibition of tight-rope walking "lest the said divertisement may tend to promote idleness in the town and great mispense of time." [17]

These laws represented a determination to promote industry and frugality; they also reflected the Puritan concept of the evil inherent in any frivolous waste of time. In one instance there was a curious conflict between these two motives. Toward the close of the period of the Great Migration, the popularity of the midweek church meeting, known as the Great and Thursday, began keeping many of the country people from their work. "There were so many lectures now in the country," John Winthrop wrote in 1639, "and many poor persons would usually resort to two or three in the week, to the great neglect of their affairs, and the damage of the public." [18] Here was one of the few breaks in the harsh routine of daily life that the early settlers experienced, a social function when there were no others. And while the lecture itself might be wearisome and dreary, at least for those to whom Calvinistic theology was not always completely absorbing, it offered a chance for neighborly gossip after the service and for the pleasure of seeing offenders against the Puritan code properly punished—placed in the stocks or whipped at the cart's tail. Consequently the colony's theocratic rulers found themselves in a difficult quandary. Attendance at these meetings could not be prohibited: it hardly fell under the head of idle or frivolous amusement. None the less it represented, from a utilitarian viewpoint, a serious "mispense" of time.

It was first ruled, to prevent waste of a whole day, that lectures should not begin before one o'clock. Then the ministers were urged to hold fewer midweek meetings. And finally the order went out that the church assemblies should ordinarily break up in time to enable people who lived a mile or two off to get home before dusk. Nothing could be permitted that in any way would impair the spirit expressed in William Wood's dictum that aside from everything else "all New England must be workers in some kind." [19]

No such reason could be advanced to justify the vehement efforts of magistrates and elders to compel that strict observance of the Sabbath which they had made one of the cardinal articles of their stern faith. Religion stood its ground without economic support. The Lord's Day was to be wholly devoted to pious reflection upon the bounties of an all-wise Providence. Puritanism did not admit the idea that this one day free of work might possibly be enjoyed for itself.

Virginia had forbidden Sunday amusements in the early years of settlement. The laws of that colony, as applied by Governor Argall in 1618, made the penalty for failure to attend church service imprisonment in the guard-house ("lying neck and heels on the Corps of Gard ye night following and be a slave ye week following") and strictly banned any Sabbath-day dancing, fiddling, card-playing, hunting, or fishing.[20] But while these laws soon fell into abeyance, New England's holy zeal in trying to turn the day into one of vacuous melancholy was not abated.

The strict prohibition of any Sunday labor, travel, or recreation was supplemented by specific bans on "all unnecessary and unseasonable walking in the streets and fields." [21] Application of this law was graciously limited to children over seven, but the Massachusetts General Court gave warning that this by no means implied that "we approve of younger children in evil." [22] In Connecticut the town of New London found occasion to hale John Lewis and Sarah Chapman into court "for sitting together on the Lord's Day, under an apple tree in Goodman Chapman's Orchard." [23] And there is the well authenticated case, cited by Charles Francis Adams, of the New England minister who refused to baptize children born on the Sabbath in the belief that they had been conceived on the Lord's Day, only to be confounded when his wife gave birth to Sabbath-day twins.[24]

-->>><<<-

WHY HAD Puritanism developed such an intense disapproval of sports and games, popular amusements? Where had its stern insistence upon the sanctity of the Sabbath come from? In part these ideas stemmed from the religious dissenters of fourteenth-century England. The revolt of Wycliffe and the Lollards against the worldliness of the Anglican Catholic Church had been directed against all those diversions which the Church of that day freely countenanced. They symbolized in the eyes of these reformers the triumph of evil impulses over truly spiritual values; they could have no place in consecrated lives. But there was also a social bias, a class-conscious protest, in this condemnation of pleasure. The Lollards came from the lower classes—poor, hardworking, struggling to improve their position. They resented the pleasures of the rich—the landed nobility, the dissolute court circle, and the wealthier classes in the towns. It was an easy rationalization of this natural feeling to condemn as sinful the amusements they could not themselves enjoy.[25]

Some two centuries later the Puritans found themselves in very much the same position. They too were a party of reform, condemning the worldliness of the Church and damning as sinful many of the pleasures that the Church countenanced. They too resented the amusements of the more wealthy, leisured classes, making a moral issue of their discontent. These two influences, spiritual reform and economic envy, can never be disentangled. They were both present in the sixteenth and seventeenth centuries, and they have been present in every later-day manifestation of the Puritan spirit. The popular conception of this attitude is expressed in Macaulay's often quoted phrase that the Puritans forbade bear-baiting, not because of the pain it caused the bear, but because of the pleasure it afforded the spectators. But it was rooted in the belief of a people who could not afford to waste time (they were dominated by their middle-class ideals of money-making, getting ahead) that any frivolous use of it was inherently sinful.

There was nothing in the original Calvinistic creed to justify the stern attitude that the Puritans assumed. John Knox once came upon Calvin himself playing at bowls, on a Sunday. So sincere a Puritan as Milton expressed again and again the most lively appreciation of all the joyous aspects of life in Merry England—the sports and games, the holidays

When the merry bells ring round,
And the jocund rebecks sound,
To many a youth and many a maid,
Dancing in the chequered shade.

But as the Puritans struggled to bring about the reforms they thought essential, they grew more and more scornful of the way of life of those who opposed them. Their disapproval of the moral laxity of the leisured classes of society soon covered all their diversions. Their foes jeered at them. On the anvil of persecution, disapproval was hammered into fanatical intolerance.

One of the most bitter sources of conflict between the Puritans and James I revolved around sports and Sabbath observance. Compulsory church attendance was a general rule in the early seventeenth century—not a Puritan invention; but after service the day was often given over to recreation—rough-and-tumble sports, morris-dances, interludes. Obsessed by an Old Testament interpretation of the meaning of the Sabbath, the Puritans took it upon themselves to condemn utterly this carefree enjoyment on the Lord's Day. There should be no sports or games, no dancing or interludes, no amusements whatsoever. They ascribed to God rules for keeping His day holy which were entirely born of their own intolerance.[26]

King James took up this challenge. In 1618 he issued a pronouncement, since known as the Book of Sports, declaring it to be the royal pleasure "that after the end of Divine Service, our good people be not disturbed, letted, or discouraged from any lawfull Recreation; Such as dauncing, either men or women, Archeries for men, leaping, vaulting, or other harmless Recreation, nor from having of May-games, Whitson Ales, and Morris-dances, and the setting up of Maypoles and other sports therewith used. . . . But withall We doe accompt still as prohibited all unlawfull games to be used upon Sundayes onely, as Beare and Bull-baiting, Interludes, and at all times in the meaner sort of people by Law prohibited, Bowling." [27]

THE KINGS

MAIESTIES
Declaration to His
Subiects,

CO *N* CE R *N* I *N* G
lawfull Sports to
be vſed.

LONDON
Printed by BONHAM NORTON,
and IOHN BILL. Deputie Printers
forthe Kings moſt Excellent
Maieſtie.

M.DC.XVIII.

Title-Page of King James I's "Book of Sports"
London, 1618. Courtesy of the New York Public Library.

These were among the pastimes that Englishmen, and among them many of the prospective settlers of Jamestown and Plymouth, Maryland and Massachusetts Bay, were accustomed to enjoy. King James would have encouraged them by annulling Sabbath bans. "For when shall the common people," he asked, "have leave to exercise if not upon the Sundayes and Holidays, seeing they must apply their labour, and winne their living in all working days?" Nevertheless, when their day of power came in England, the Puritans had the Book of Sports publicly burned by the common hangman.[28]

In America, as we have seen, the Puritans took an equally intolerant stand. They had sought out the New World to escape persecution, abandoning the program of reform at home to found a Utopia across the seas. They were determined that here there should be no trace of worldliness. "God hath sifted a nation," William Stoughton declared, "that he might send choice grain into this wilderness." [29] Among these chosen people the pagan festivities, the licentious plays and spectacles, the violations of the Sabbath, the generally dissolute ways which were bringing ruin on England, would not be tolerated. There could be no evil in Zion. From the moment of their first landing on the shores of New England, the leaders of this seventeenth-century exodus set themselves implacably against the slightest infringement of their austere code.

So long as these ideals were allied with the practical necessities of life, so long as the condemnation of idle sports and games conformed to that paramount need for day-long labor on which the very survival of the early settlements depended, Puritanism served the colonies well. The strict rule of magistrates and ministers, for which they generously acknowledged the inspiration of God, emphasized the importance of work during a period when any turning aside toward an easier life might well have doomed New England. This debt to Puritanism is a primary fact in American history. But the rulers of Massachusetts Bay and Connecticut, unlike those of the other colonies, became more and more strict in their insistence upon these rigid rules of conduct as their economic justification gradually lessened.

Suppression became a fetish of the Calvinist mind in the New World. Having convinced themselves that all idle pursuits were a Satanic trap to lure the godly from the path of duty, strict followers of the New England way could no more tolerate frivolity than heresy. Their conscience would not let them enjoy worldly pleasures themselves; it would not let them permit others such enjoyment. The compulsion was equal in either instance. On Christmas Day of 1621, when the greater number of Plymouth colonists had gone about their usual tasks, Governor Bradford was shocked to discover a group of newcomers to that godly community "in the streete at play, openly; some pitching the barr and some at stoole-ball, and such-like sports." He promptly took away their "implements," telling them that while it might be against *their* conscience to work on Christmas, it was against *his* conscience that they should play.[30] New England's magistrates took it upon themselves to control with conspicuous zeal every activity of the people given over to their moral and spiritual guidance. When an opportunity to interfere in any way with other people's lives presented itself, they joyfully answered the still, small voice of duty.

->>><<<-

THE ATTITUDE of one member of this ruling hierarchy is graphically portrayed in the intimately self-revealing diary kept by Samuel Sewall in the last decade of the seventeenth century and opening years of the eighteenth.[31] Magistrate and elder, Judge Sewall was continually busy with moral problems, counseling others on what they should do and sorrowing over their departure from the narrow path of righteousness. "I was grieved," we find him writing a friend on one occasion, "... when I heard and saw you had drunk to excess; so that your head and hand were rendered less useful than at other times. ... I mention this that you may believe I write not of prejudice, but kindness; and out of a sense of duty as indeed I do." Another time, when a party of revelers were drinking the Queen's health with too much enthusiasm, he went out in the middle of the night to remonstrate with them. They refused to go home. He took down their names in his little book—or rather, as he tells us, "not knowing how to spell their names, they themselves of their own accord writ them." [32]

Sewall thoroughly approved when Cotton Mather "struck at the Root, speaking against mixt Dances." He maintained an obdurate stand against the scandalous suggestion of allowing play-acting in Boston and vigorously combated the idea of any holiday festivities: "I took occasion to dehort mine from Christmas-keeping and charged them to forebear." When a dancing-master named Francis Stepney attempted to hold classes, he took a leading part in seeing that they were immediately prohibited. With testy ill-humor he noted "the great disorder in the town" when the English introduced the old sport of cock-skailing, or throwing sticks at a cock. "Jos. Mayhem carries a cock at his back, with a Bell in's hand, in the Main Street," he wrote scornfully; "several follow him blindfold, and under pretence of striking him or's cock, with great cart whips strike passengers, and make great disturbance." [33]

Nevertheless he had his own simple pleasures. He thoroughly enjoyed good food and wine: his diary bears frequent witness to his fondness for "rost Beef and minc'd Pyes, good Cheese and Tarts," and he had a special liking for black-cherry brandy with a lump of sugar in it. His appreciation of nature was surprising. We find him noting happily that "the Singing of Birds is come," and of seeing "Six Swallows flying together and chipering very rapturously." Another time he speaks of walking in a friend's orchard and getting quiet enjoyment out of "pushing Catterpillars off the Appletrees." It is also suddenly revealing to find in the memorable account of his courtship of Madame Winthrop the passage where he tells his lady that he came to see her only every other night for fear he would drink too deep draughts of pleasure—"She had talk'd Canary, her kisses were to me better than the best Canary." [34]

Other diversions more generally centered about the good judge's religious life. He often went to service, gladly riding several miles to the Great and Thursday at some outlying town, taking his wife, or perhaps his mother-in-law, on the pillion behind him. He led what went for singing at his own meeting-house. There were only a few mournful repetitive tunes in the Puritan repertory, to which were sung such strange distortions of the Psalms as

> Within their mouths doe thou their teeth
> break out O God most strong,
> Doe thou Jehovah, the great teeth
> break, of the lions young.

'I set York tune and the congregation went out of it into St. David's in the very 2nd. going over," Sewall wrote in his diary one day. "This seems to me an intimation and a call for me to resign the precentor's place to a better voice. I have through the Divine long suffering and favor done it for 24 years." [35]

This upright man found real enjoyment in seeing punishments properly administered, whether it was a whipping or a hanging, and he had that morbid preoccupation with death which was one of the most unpleasing of Puritan characteristics. He took a melancholy pleasure in serving as a pall-bearer at funerals, making a great collection of the gloves and rings with which custom decreed the pall-bearer should be rewarded. He was always happy to undertake this congenial task—unless he disapproved of the deceased's morals. But the obsession with death found most startling expression in his account of how he spent one Christmas. One of his daughters had recently died. Sewall passed the day in the family tomb: "I was entertained with a view of, and converse with the coffins. . . . 'Twas an awful yet pleasing Treat." [36]

→»)«←

IN THESE varied pleasures—spying upon one's neighbors, upholding public morals, going to church meetings, morbidly contem-
plating death—the Puritan leaders might find some compensation
for the amusements of which they deprived themselves. But they
could not possibly satisfy the needs of the humbler members
of the community whose instinct for play could not so easily be
eradicated. Even when these men and women in the ordinary
walks of life were wholly in sympathy with the rule of the
church, it was not enough for them to attend service and go to
funerals. And increasingly large numbers of New Englanders
were not Puritans. During the Great Migration even, between
1630 and 1640, only some four thousand out of sixteen thousand
arrivals in Massachusetts Bay were church members. The rigid
requirements for membership made it entirely possible for a
majority even of the non-members to be in sympathy with the
church, but nevertheless there was a dissident element in the
colony from the very first. And it steadily grew as more and
more people poured into New England whose motives for
seeking the New World had nothing to do with religion.

In their zeal to maintain godliness, to enforce general con-
formity with their own principles of conduct, the magistrates
failed signally to take this group into consideration. Whatever
may be said for the first generation of Puritan leaders, their
successors' inability to recognize the need of the people as a
whole for a freer outlet to the normal urge for recreation was
continually adding fuel to the discontent of the non-Puritans.
They began to consider the restraints imposed upon them an
intolerable burden. Worn out by the endless work on their little
farms, discouraged by poor harvests, fearful of famine, plague,
or Indian attack, they had to have some release for pent-up
emotions, some way to forget the world.

Many of them—and this was true not only in New England
but in all the colonies—found it in drinking. The tavern sprang
up as naturally as the meeting-house, and the conviviality of the
tap-room met a genuine need. They came of good drinking stock,

these New World pioneers, and the early lack of malt and spirituous liquors had been for a time a great cause for complaint. It is revealing to find how proud one godly minister was because he had learned to drink water, and to note another worthy writing home that while he did not yet prefer water to good beer as some professed to do, "any man would choose it before Bad Beere, Wheay, or Buttermilk."[37] Nevertheless the Puritans did not allow any pernicious habit of water-drinking to take hold. Beer and cider were soon plentiful; rum became a New England staple. The taverns and ordinaries everywhere offered an engaging selection of drinks to gratify every taste.[38]

Drunkenness was a frequent consequence of their growing popularity. The early records show many cases of fines, confinement in the stocks, and public whippings for an overindulgence which the lower classes (the indentured servants, the apprentices, the laborers) could hardly avoid with rum at two shillings a gallon. Sometimes the penalty of public scorn was administered. "Robert Cole, having been oft punished for drunkenness," John Winthrop reports in his history of Plymouth (an anything but isolated case even for that sober community), "was now ordered to wear a red D about his neck for a year."[39]

The increase in drinking and its attendant evils was largely due to the lack of other entertainment and to the promotion by tavern-keepers of what was a very profitable business. By the middle of the seventeenth century the General Court was compelled to recognize that it had created a serious social problem. "How has Wyne and Cider, but most of all Rum debauched Multitudes of People," exclaimed the redoubtable Increase Mather. Viewing the fearful circumstances into which Connecticut had been brought, Cotton Mather somewhat later declared somberly that "the consequences of the affected Bottel, in that Colony, as well as in ours, are beyond Imagination."[40]

Many other instances might be cited to show the extent to which tavern drinking took the place of other amusements in these days of Puritan repression. One law deplored the growing custom whereby on pretext of going to midweek church meetings, men and women rode from town to town "to drinke and revell in ordinarys and tavernes." An irate clergy thundered the warning that "the Riots that have too often accompanied our Huskings have carried in them fearfull Ingratitude and Provocation unto the Glorious God." [41]

It may well be noted, however, that it was not in New England but in what has so often been called Cavalier Virginia that an attempt was made in the seventeenth century to enforce prohibition. For all his alarms, even Increase Mather accepted the need for taverns to sell liquor. "No sober Minister," he declared, "will speak against the Licensing of them." [42] But an Assembly dominated by Nathaniel Bacon passed a law, in 1676, taking their licenses from all taverns in Virginia except those at Jamestown and at the two main ferries on the York. These privileged ordinaries were permitted to sell beer and cider, but otherwise a fine of one thousand pounds of tobacco was to be imposed on any one who sold "any sorte of drinke or liquor whatsoever to be drunke or spent in his or their house or houses, upon his or their plantations." [43]

It was not only in drinking that New England was breaking through the bonds of Puritan restraint. The diary of Samuel Sewall itself affords graphic evidence of the revolt against repression. Its accounts of the pageantry of Joseph Mayhew, parading through the streets of Boston with cock and bell; of attempts to stage plays and hold dancing-classes; of the celebration of Christmas festivities, all reveal a departure from the original severity of life in New England.

This is shown also in many of the laws that the magistrates found it necessary to pass after the middle of the seventeenth century. They are fully as indicative of what certain elements in the growing towns of New England were actually doing as of what their rulers were determined they should not do. Laws on the statute books often have this paradoxical significance. The future student of twentieth-century legislation will be quite justified in assuming that our prohibition laws reflected the popularity of drinking quite as much as they represented an authoritarian attempt to impose a dry régime. In the same way, much of the legislation of early New England forbidding tavern sports, card-playing, and dancing throws a penetrating light on how a very considerable number of the people were spending such free time as they had. Not the rulers and magistrates, but the everyday people of the Puritan world.

This is illustrated in successive edicts with respect to observance of the Sabbath. We learn from the statute books that on Saturday and Sunday young people were more and more freely taking "liberty to walk and sport themselves in the streets and fields... and too frequently repair to public houses of entertainment and there sit drinking." [44] Finally it even became necessary to forbid, on Sunday and in the neighborhood of meeting-houses, "all shouting, hollowing, screaming, running, riding, singing, dancing, jumping, winding horns or the like." [45] Here are glimpses of a Puritan Sabbath oddly at variance with copy-book and historical legend. Some of the youths and maidens of old New England, for all the insistence of the godly that the Sabbath should be a day of peace and quiet, appear to have utilized it for a little restrained hell-raising in vociferous protest against the laws.

Indeed, at no time after the very first years of settlement was the New England scene actually as devoid of all amusements as it is so often said to have been. The Puritans have been depicted as a "crowd of sad-visaged people moving duskily through a dull gray atmosphere"; their social life has been termed "bare and spiritless beyond the possibility of description." [46] But this is to take at their face value the repressive edicts of the magistracy. It ignores the place in New England's life of the large number of its settlers who were non-Puritan in their sympathies and who could hardly be compelled by magisterial fiat to accept the idea that pleasure was synonomous with sin.

Those two stern guardians of public morals, Increase and

Cotton Mather, had no doubts as to what was happening in the closing years of the seventeenth century. The iniquities of the younger generation were causing the glory of the Lord to depart from New England. "How many there are amongst us whose Fathers in coming into the Wilderness, designed nothing but Religion," declared Increase. "But *they* are for another Interest. Their Hearts are not but for the World. . . . That there is a general defection in New England from Primitive Purity and Piety in many respects is so plain that it cannot be denied." Cotton labored under no such restraints in characterizing the age. "Some of our Rising Generation," he stated, "have been given up to the most abominable Impieties of Uncleaness, Drunkeness, and a Lewd, Rude Extravagant sort of Behaviour. There are the Children of Belial among them, and Prodigies of Wickedness." [47]

The Mathers often found evil in what another age would freely condone. Many of their "prodigies of wickedness" would to-day go unrecognized under such a description. Their fierce onslaughts against the rising generation reflected a bitterness at their own departing glory as well as at the departing glory of the Lord. At the same time it was inevitable that reaction to the stern rule Puritanism attempted to impose should in some cases lead to extremes. For in forbidding so many forms of normal recreation the elders and magistrates had only served to confuse moral values. When they instituted such strict laws as to forbid, according to one traveler in Connecticut, "even a harmless Kiss or Innocent merriment among Young people," [48] they were asking for trouble. Human nature could not be flouted with impunity, even by professed men of God.

➤➤〉〈〈➤

PURITANISM failed to eradicate the early Americans' natural urge for play. It brought on the inevitable revolt against attempted suppression of human impulses. Nevertheless it left a deep imprint on the mind of New England. And for all the growth of more liberal ideas as the power of the clergy and magistrates declined, some part of the old intolerance lingered on. The northern colonies were always more restricted in their diversions than the middle colonies or the South.

The spirit of Puritanism still has an important influence on our recreational life. Conditions have so greatly changed that our whole idea of leisure-time activities has been completely transformed. The suspicion with which church and state three centuries ago viewed all diversions in their common "detestation of idleness" has given way to the active encouragement and promotion of every form of healthful amusement. But there is certainly more than a trace of the old Puritanism, whatever other factors in a capitalistic society may enter the picture, in an attitude which so often views the increase in present-day opportunities for recreation as the "problem of leisure."

chapter 2

Husking Bees
and Tavern Sports

A S THE ECONOMIC SECURITY OF THE LITTLE COMMUNITIES THAT
stretched along the eastern fringe of America from Maine
to South Carolina gradually increased, colonial life took on many
new aspects. The opening of the eighteenth century marked a
far departure from the first days of settlement. The South had
almost completely broken away from earlier restraints; New England's outlook was beginning to broaden. The colonists generally
sought out and developed opportunities for recreation they had
not before had time to enjoy. Among the common people, the
great mass of yeomanry who made up nine-tenths of the population, the English love of games and sports was reasserting itself.
An eager welcome was accorded all possible amusements.

It is not always easy to discover just what form this recreation took. The short and simple annals of the poor are no more
revealing on this phase of their life than of other aspects. But
there is sufficient evidence to show that they found many ways
to enjoy themselves. And the common experience of colonial
farmers in hunting and in shooting contests, in simple country
sports, in the communal activities of training days and barn-
raisings, played its part in the welding of a nation. These phases
of colonial recreation more truly reflect the life of eighteenth-
century America than the social activities of Boston's wealthy
merchants, the dancing assemblies of New York, or the fox-
hunts of Virginia.

Rural life in New England was still hard and laborious. It was
back-breaking to induce crops to grow in that stony soil. Nevertheless there were compensations which other farming com-

munities in this country have not always enjoyed. The original settlers had taken up their land in townships, close to one another, with communal pasturage for their stock. And the town had its meeting-house, its tavern, and later its town hall. The people from the surrounding countryside could easily gather for their Sunday church services and midweek lectures; they could meet on more festive occasions at the tavern. There was no isolation in the life of colonial New England comparable to that in the Middle West a century and more later when the pioneers of the prairie states were so widely scattered on their far-separated quarter-sections.

The middle colonies, despite their large trading towns, were also a primarily agricultural community. But in addition to farms comparable to those of New England, there were the great estates of the Dutch patroons along the Hudson, and in Pennsylvania and western New York many rough frontier settlements. Conditions were more varied than in New England, and the population with its infiltration of Scotch-Irish and Germans much more mixed. Consequently we find amusements and diversions greatly restricted in some sections and in others freely enjoyed. The influence of Dutch Calvinists and Pennsylvania Quakers was offset by the greater liberalism of other groups in the population.

In the South highly distinctive economic and social conditions prevailed. While the land to a great extent was held in small farms during the seventeenth century and the staple crops of tobacco or rice were grown by as independent and self-respecting a yeomanry as that of the North, the growth of slavery with its substitution of Negro labor for white indentured servants wrought a gradual transformation during the next century. It led to the creation of large plantations which made it more and more difficult for the small farmers to maintain their position. Slave competition, exhaustion of the soil, and lower prices for tobacco drove many of them to the new lands in the west and tended to reduce those who remained near tidewater to the status of poor whites. Nevertheless the southern yeomanry continued to make up the bulk of southern population, sometimes themselves owning one or two slaves with whom they worked in the tobacco fields. Their rôle in colonial life was still an important one.

Recreation for this class corresponded in many respects to that of the comparable class in the North. But the farms were more widely separated, without centralizing townships as in New England. The small planters often led a more lonely life. On the other hand, a warmer climate and more productive soil made possible greater leisure, while the institution of slavery, tending to deprive work of the nobility with which the Puritans clothed it, was a further influence contributing to an easy-going attitude in the use of this leisure.

→»)«‹←

Now THAT the early Americans were beginning to feel at home in field and forest, hunting and fishing could be enjoyed as sport. The wealth of game drew out the townsman as well as the farmer, the New Englander as well as the Carolinian. Deer were plentiful everywhere, and the wild-fowl so numerous that account after account describes flocks of wild turkeys or pigeons darkening the skies. Moose ranged through the still unbroken forests of New England; wolves preyed upon the outlying settlements of Connecticut; bear and panther were hunted in the backwoods of Virginia, and buffalo could be found in the western parts of South Carolina.

"Bears, Deer, Beavers, Otters, Foxes, Racounes (almost as big as a Fox, as good meat as a lamb) Hares, wild cats, musk rats, Squirrels (flying and other sorts) and Apossumes of the bignesse and likenesse of a Pigge of a month old..." reads Ralph Hamor's list of early Virginia's game. "Eagles, wild Turkeys (much larger than our English), Cranes, Herons (white and russet), Hawks, wild pigeons (in winter beyond number or imagination, myself have seen three or four hours together flocks

Bear-Baiting

English tavern sports transplanted in America. From *The Sporting Magazine,* London, 1795 and 1801.

Skittles

"The Hill Tops," a New Hunting Song

The first sporting picture in an American periodical. *Royal American Magazine*, 1774.

in the air, so thick that even they have shadowed the sky from us), Turkey Buzzards, Partridges, Snipers, Owls, Swans, Geese, Brants, Ducks, and Mallards, Divers, Shel Drakes, Cormorants, Teale, Widgeon, Curlews, Puits, besides other small birds, as, Blackbird, hedge sparrows, oxeies, woodpeckers, and in winter about Christmas many flocks of Parakertoths. . . . For Fish—the Rivers are plentifully stored, with Sturgeon, Porpasse, Base, Rockfish, Carpe, Shad, Herring, Ele, Catfish, Perch, Flat-fish, Trout, Sheepshead, Drummers, Jarfish, Crevises, Crabs, Oysters and diverse other kinds." [1]

Farmers of Massachusetts and Connecticut enjoyed squirrel hunts, went out often after raccoons and also banded together to hunt wolves. In New London ten to forty men met together every autumn to beat up the swamps and kill these "pernicious creatures."

There was a great deal of fishing. John Rowe, an enthusiastic angler, noted in his diary a day's catch of five dozen large trout— "extraordinary sport." It had been vouchsafed religious approval in Joseph Seccombe's discourse "utter'd in part at Ammauskeeg-Falls, in the Fishing-season, 1739." "If I may eat them [fish] for Refreshment," this worthy divine contended, "I may as well catch them if this recreate and refresh me. It's as lawful to delight the Eye as the Palate." [2] Even Cotton Mather fished. Samuel Sewall tells of the time when the stern old Puritan went out with line and tackle and fell into the water at Spy Pond, "the boat being ticklish."

Long Island was a veritable fish and game paradise. New Yorkers "went out a shooting" regularly at the opening of the century, as the journal of the Reverend John Sharp reveals,[3] and somewhat later we find the sport lending an element of considerable hazard to the lives of the island's settlers. In 1734 a woman was shot accidentally when taken for a fox. "The fatal mistake," reads the old record, "was occasioned by her wearing an Orange Brown Wast-Coat. The man is in a very melancholy condition." The newspaper account of the incident advised shortsighted hunters to go farther west where their mistakes might not be so costly.[4]

"They have hunting, fishing and fowling, with which they entertain themselves in an hundred ways," Robert Beverly wrote of Virginians.[5] The farmers joined in moonlight excursions after opossum as they have done ever since, but a far more exciting sport was hunting the wild horses which ranged through the backwoods. In the Carolinas deer were hunted on horseback, the planters taking a stand and having their beaters drive the deer past them. Sometimes such expeditions were held at night, the huntsmen well fortified with brandy and accompanied by Negroes carrying pans of burning charcoal to serve as flares. In 1784 they were made a misdemeanor because of the inadvertent slaughter of so many cows and horses.[6]

How general hunting was in the South is shown in a statement in George Alsop's seventeenth-century account of life in Maryland: "For every Servant has a Gun, Powder and Shot allowed him, to sport withall on all Holidays and leasurable times...."[7]

-»» ««-

ALTHOUGH they were relatively rare, gatherings at training days and elections, at country fairs, corn-huskings, and barn-raisings, provided welcome breaks in the monotony of farm life. Folk-dancing and folk-music were enjoyed on these occasions, with the singing of the popular English ballads which were being hawked through the countryside, even of Massachusetts, as early as 1680. There were sports—shooting at a mark, foot-races, wrestling matches—and a great deal of convivial drinking. "Possibly this leafe may last a century," reads an entry for October 14, 1766, in the diary of Nathaniel Ames, a young man living in Dedham, Massachusetts, "and fall into the hands of some inquisitive Person for whose Entertainment I will inform him that now there is the custom amongst us of making an Entertainment at husking of Indian Corne whereunto all the neighboring Swains are invited, and after the Corn is finished they, like the Hottentots, give three cheers or huzzas, but cannot carry in the husks without a Rhum bottle. They feign great exertion, but do nothing until the Rhum enlivens them, when all is done in a trice; then, after a hearty meal about 10 at night, they go to their pastimes." [8]

There is a somewhat unpuritanic record of certain of these pastimes in a poem of another countryman, Jacob Bailey, probably written when he was teaching school at Kingston, New Hampshire, about 1755:

> The chairs in wild disorder flew quite round the room.
> Some threatened with firebrands, some brandished a broom,
> While others, resolved to increase the uproar,
> Lay tussling the girls in wide heaps on the floor. [9]

It was the custom at the "frolic scene," as is well known, for the young man who might find a red ear of corn to claim a kiss from whatever damsel he chose. On one occasion—it was in a day when strict Puritan supervision was responsible for the story being spread on the town records—difficulties arose over the interpretation of this genial law of the husking-bee. James Chicester found a red ear and promptly kissed Bette Scudder. But the young lady objected and somewhat bluntly told him she "would whip his brick." In the ensuing scuffle Goody Scudder came to her daughter's defense, and the unfortunate James was fined twelve shillings for his temerity. [10]

Quite different is the story of Sarah Tuttle, similarly honored by one Jacob Murline. "They sat down together," we learn again from the court records, "his arm being about her, and her arm upon his shoulder or about his neck, and hee kissed her and shee kissed him, or they kissed one another, continuing in this posture about half an hour." This was too much for the elders, and Jacob was hailed before the magistrate on a charge of "inveigling" Sarah. But Sarah promptly owned up that there had been no inveigling: she had wanted to be kissed. The shocked magistrate thereupon denounced her for a "Bould Virgin," and although she demurely acknowledged her error, expressing the hope that

"God would help her to Carry it Better for time to come," a heavy fine was imposed.[11]

The flirtations and love-affairs of young people naturally suggest the curious custom of bundling, widely prevalent in New England and Pennsylvania. Its origin was supposedly found (although the custom has also been noted among other peoples) in the premium placed on heat and light in those early days of settlement when the whole family had to roll up together in front of the open fire on cold winter evenings. A visitor could be offered only such hospitality as the house afforded, and consequently bundling became among country people a natural and accepted form of courtship. Andrew Burnaby, writing as late as 1775, describes how the young folk in a home he was visiting got into bed together—"but without pulling off their undergarments, in order to prevent scandal." On a tour through Pennsylvania at the close of the century, John Bernard also noted the custom under the name of "tarrying." He reported that in extending the hospitality of her bed it was customary for the girl to take the thoughtful precaution of "confining her petticoat to her ankles." [12]

Bundling was not always as safe as these measures would suggest. The approving Mr. Burnaby wrote that pregnancy was "an accident that seldom happens," but at times all precautions failed. In the case of engaged couples, however, public disapproval of premarital relations was tempered, even in the strictest circles, by the desirability of large families in a primitive farming community. Marriage expiated all guilt. In 1722 there was nothing out of the way in a Harvard student society's publicly debating "Whether it be Fornication to lye with ones Sweetheart (after contract) before Marriage?" [13]

Nevertheless bundling of itself certainly did not imply any improper relationship. It was perhaps the eighteenth-century equivalent of the buggy drive of the next century, or of the evening automobile ride of our present age. Abigail Adams refers casually to it in several of her letters. There is a comfortable description of bucolic life in Royall Tyler's play *The Contrast:* "twenty acres of rock, the Bible, Tabitha, and a little peaceable bundling." A young Connecticut girl gaily records in her 1775 diary how sister Ellen bundled "till sun about 3 hours high," adding

> If I won't take my sparks to bed
> A laughing stock I shall be made.[14]

-》》》《《《-

"THEIR DIVERSIONS in this part of the Country," wrote Madame Sarah Knight, as that "fearfull female travailer," journeyed through Connecticut in 1704, "are on Lecture days and Training days mostly: on the former there is Riding from town to town. . . . And on Training dayes the Youth divert themselves by Shooting at the Target, as they call it, (but it very much resembles a pillory,) when hee that hitts neerest the white has some yards of Red Ribbin presented him, which being tied to his hattband, the two ends streaming down his back, he is led away in Triumph, with great applause, as the winners of the Olympiack Games." [15]

No less a one than Judge Sewall used to attend training days in Boston, where upwards of a thousand men would gather on the Common to drill, practise markmanship, and then celebrate the day in more lively fashion. "Go to prayer. March down and shoot at a mark," was his usual laconic description of this great event. But he also records that on one occasion he presented his company, as a prize for marksmanship, with a pike headed and shod with silver, which he supposed would stand him some forty shillings. On another he had the entire company to his house and treated them with bread, beer, and wine syllabub. A third time, after some recent bereavement, he gives a pathetic picture of marching sadly off to muster: "I put on my mourning rapier, and put a black ribbon in my little cane." [16]

The celebration of training days, as of election days and court days, almost invariably ended in a general descent upon the local tavern. There was no other occasion when colonial neighbors so

much enjoyed passing around a friendly bottle. At the opening
of the eighteenth century, Cotton Mather was already thundering against "Training Days become little other than Drinking
Dayes," but though his voice reached throughout New England,
it was more and more ignored. And going south, through the
middle colonies into Virginia and the Carolinas, it would have
been hard to say whether there was more or less drinking. There
is, for instance, the evidence of Ebenezer Cook, from his
memorable "Sot-Weed Factor," which relates the traveler's experience on seeking out the tavern on a Maryland court day:

> A Herd of Planters on the ground,
> O'er-whelmed with Punch, dead drunk we found.[17]

Country fairs drew crowds of merrymakers. The social gatherings in New England were more likely to be associated with
useful communal work—house-raisings, sheep-shearings, log-
rollings, or husking-bees; but Virginia more naturally had meetings where there was little pretense of utility and a wide variety
of diversions. Here was in evidence more of the spirit of Merry
England than Puritans could easily express—horse-racing, chasing
a greased pig, dancing on green lawns.

An advertisement in the *Virginia Gazette* for October, 1737,
tells of some of these sports and the prizes offered for them. It
was proposed that a pair of silver buckles be wrestled for; that a
pair of handsome shoes be danced for; that a hat of the value of
twenty shillings be cudgeled for; that a violin be played for by
twenty fiddlers; that a quire of Ballads be sung for by a number
of songsters; and "that a pair of handsome Silk Stockings of one
Pistole value be given to the handsomest young country maid
that appears in the field." In the case of the songsters it was
announced that they would be allowed "liquor sufficient to clear
their wind pipes," but the advertisement closed with the admoni-
tion that "as this mirth is designed to be purely innocent and void
of offence, all persons resorting there are desired to behave themselves with decency and sobriety." [18]

Still another colonial holiday was the college commencement. At Harvard, Yale, and Princeton, graduation exercises drew not only "a vast concourse of the politest company" to listen to the day's oratory and debates, but also crowds of simple country folk who made the occasion one for horse-racing, games, dancing, and drinking. "Fe-o, whiraw, whiraw, hi, fal, lal, fal, lal, lal, de lal dal, a fine song: commencement is over whiraw I say again whiraw whiraw," wrote one exuberant graduate of Nassau Hall who would appear to have confused those phases of commencement intended for the student body with the more general celebration of the day.[19]

At Harvard too the exercises did not always conform to the expected academic traditions. The day's activities were satirically recorded early in the eighteenth century:

> Some spend the Time at Pins (that toilsome Play)
> Others at cards (more silent) pass the Day.
> In rings some Wrestle till they're mad outright,
> And then their Antagonists they fight.

> On Horses some to ride full Tilt along
> Are seen; while on each side a Numerous Throng
> Do gaze. . . .
> Others (as brutish) do propagate their Kind:
> Where amorous Lads to shady Groves resort,
> And under Venus with their Misses sport.[20]

The colonial colleges had to change the date of commencement in order to prevent the occasion from turning into too festive a celebration. Nassau Hall shifted it from autumn to spring in the hope that their planting and sowing might keep the farmers at home.

→>>><<<-

THESE FÊTE-DAYS were not the only occasion for sports. "This is to give Notice," reads an announcement in the *Boston News-Letter* of August 22-29, 1715, "that at Cambridge on Wednesday the 21st day of September next, will be run for, a Twenty Pound

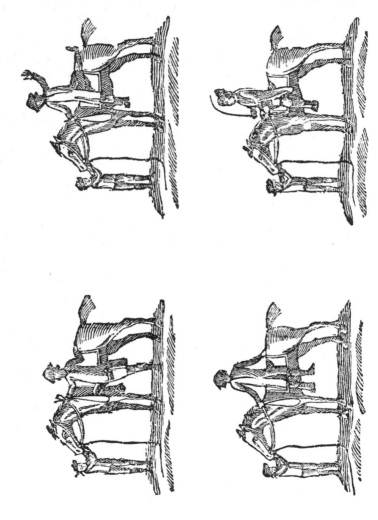

How to Mount a Horse

Philip Astley, *The Modern Riding Master*, Philadelphia, 1776.

Plate, by any Horse, Mare or Gelding not exceeding Fourteen and half hands high. . . ." [21] There are many records of cockfights —"fought cocks in the Town House" is one surprising entry in the diary of a Salem resident in 1744—and also of New England bull-baitings and bear-baitings.[22] But while members of the Puritan communities appear to have enjoyed these spectacles, they were much more common in the South than in the North. Activities in which the people themselves could take part were the more general rule in Massachusetts and Connecticut. Sleighing was a favorite winter diversion; in the summer men and boys went swimming. Many accounts refer to cricket, "bat & Ball," and football.[23]

"The place we went to was a Town call'd Rowley, where most of the inhabitants had been Clothiers," John Dunton wrote during his New England travels in 1686; "but there was that Day a great game of Foot-Ball to be play'd with their bare feet, which I thought was very odd; but it was upon a broad Sandy Shoar, free from Stones, which made it more easy. Neither were they so apt to trip up one anothers heels and quarrel, as I have seen 'em in England." [24] A century later William Bentley also speaks of football as being played by the fishermen of Marblehead. "The bruising of shins," he adds to his account, "has rendered it rather disagreeable to those of better education, who use a hand ball, thrown up against an house or fence instead of the Foot Ball, which is unfriendly to clothes as well as safety." [25]

In New York the influence of the Dutch settlers made bowling the most popular pastime, and on the basis of Sabbath-day regulations forbidding certain amusements during the hours of service (not for the entire day as in the case of New England), there were "Dancing, Card-playing, Tick-tacking [a type of backgammon], Playing at ball, at bowls, at ninepins; taking jaunts in Boats, Wagons or Carriages." [26] Another regulation, passed in the days when New York was still New Amsterdam, prohibited picking strawberries on Sunday, and it would seem to merit description as a Long Island sport.

"Such abundance of strawberries is in June," Daniel Denton wrote, "that the fields and woods are dyed red; which the country people perceiving, instantly arm themselves with bottles of wine, cream and sugar, and instead of a coat of Mail every one takes a Female upon his Horse behind him, and so rushing violently into the fields, never leave them till they have disrobed them of their colors and turned them into the old habit." [27]

Winter brought out many skaters, a sport for which the Dutch again were primarily responsible. Ice carnivals, where the tradespeople set up little booths selling liquor and sweetmeats, were held with racing and hockey. The children coasted; in Albany regulations had to be passed for the protection of pedestrians.[28]

In the southern colonies the stratified social order based on the ownership of large plantations sometimes led to the drawing of class lines in sports activities. While the diversions of the semiannual fair at Williamsburg in the middle of the eighteenth century were apparently open to all comers, Sir Francis Nicholson had in 1691 instituted a more exclusive series of athletic games. He offered prizes "to be shott for, wrasttled, played at back-swords, & run for by Horse and foott," but expressly provided that "all which prizes are to be shott for and played for by the better sort of Virginians only, who are Batchelors." [29]

One of the earliest records of horse-racing, which was to become Virginia's most popular sport, also has this undemocratic note. A tailor was fined in 1674 for "haveing made a race for his mare to runn with a horse belonging to Mr. Mathew Slader for twoe thousand pounds of tobacco and cash, it being contrary to law for a Labourer to make a race, being a sport for Gentlemen." [30] But the interest of every Virginian—"almost every ordinary person keeps a horse," wrote a traveler early in the next century [31]—made it impossible to restrict racing to the gentry. Entirely apart from the fashionable meets at Williamsburg or Annapolis, with their expensive trophies and heavy betting, it became a universal feature of country life. The wealthy planters might have their blooded horses and imported stock, but the small farmer was ready to make a match with his own riding horse anywhere and any time. Quarter-racing (an informal quarter-mile match) was a leading village sport, one visitor noting on occasion how the course was lined with a "motley multitude of negroes, Dutchmen, Yankee pedlers, and backwoodsmen." [32]

Cock-fighting was another pastime distinctive of plantation life, far more popular than in New England. Its pitched mains attracted spectators of all ranks, plantation owner, poor white, and Negro slave hovering together over the pit. "The roads as we approached the scene," wrote a northern visitor, "were alive with carriages, horses, and pedestrians, black and white, hastening to the point of attraction. Several houses formed a spacious square, in the center of which was arranged a large cock-pit; surrounded by many genteel people, promiscuously mingled with the vulgar and debased." He was enthusiastic over the beauty of the cocks and their amazing gameness, but it was too much for him: "I soon sickened at this barbarous sport, and retired under the shade of a widespread willow." [33]

Many of the visitors to the southern colonies, both those from the North and those from Europe, were shocked by the rôle that horse-racing and cock-fighting appeared to play in the lives of the people. They seemed to have time for nothing else. "The Common Planters," Hugh Jones wrote in 1724 with some asperity, "don't much admire Labour or any other manly exercise except Horse racing, nor diversion, except Cock-Fighting, in which some greatly delight. This easy Way of Living, and the Heat of the Summer make some very lazy, who are then said to be Climate-struck." [34] At the close of the century the Marquis of Chastellux was even more critical. "The indolence and dissipation of the middling and lower classes of white inhabitants of Virginia," he declared, "are such as to give pain to every reflecting mind. Horse racing, cock fighting, and boxing matches are standing amusements, for which they neglect all business." [35]

→»«←

OTHER AMUSEMENTS common to all the colonies were those associated with the taverns. The bans upon unlawful games imposed by the Puritans have already been noted as indicating diversions which the colonists in New England surreptitiously enjoyed even in the seventeenth century. In later years there was a progressive relaxation in the enforcement of these rules. Instances may be found in which the licenses granted innkeepers still prohibited all cards, dice, ninepins, and shuffle-board, but open advertisements in the colonial newspapers may be set against obsolete statutes. The tavern was a social center, primarily for drinking, but also for all manner of popular pastimes.[36]

"In most country towns," John Adams wrote of New England in 1761, ". . . you will find almost every other house with a sign of entertainment before it. . . . If you sit the evening, you will find the house full of people, drinking drams, flip, toddy, carousing, swearing."[37] There were not as many towns to support taverns in the South, and the isolation of the plantations made people of all classes so eager to entertain chance travelers that keepers of ordinaries complained that their business was one hardly worth following. Nevertheless they could always be found at the county-seats and at the frequent ferry crossings.

An advertisement in the *New England Courant* for April 30, 1722, announced that a public house in Charlestown, Massachusetts, had tables for those who "had a Mind to Recreate themselves with a Game of Billiards."[38] Alexander Macraby singled out what he thought a vile practice in the taverns of New York: "I mean that of playing backgammon (a noise I detest) which is going forward in the public coffee-houses from morning till night, frequently ten or a dozen tables at a time."[39] Dicing was even more popular, fines for playing it having to be imposed upon apprentices, journeymen, servants, and sailors. In Virginia a traveler speaks of finding planters at cards and ninepins even in the early morning hours.

Shooting matches, a favorite amusement of the colonial farmer north and south, were often held at the local tavern. With an

eye to trade the landlord would put up prizes, generally the
fowls that were used as marks. He could count on a tidy profit
from the drinking which was such an essential part of the event.
"There will be a Bear, and a Number of Turkeys set up as a
Mark next Thursday Beforenoon," reads an advertisement of
one such contest, "at the Punch Bowl Tavern in Brookline."[40]

In addition to providing games and also serving as headquarters for cock-fights and animal baitings, the tavern was a
popular place for country dances. It was not only the colonial
aristocracy who danced in the eighteenth century. This diversion
was enjoyed by all classes. Although Puritan prejudice was never
entirely dissipated, the rôle of ordination balls in Connecticut
social life indicates how much the attitude had changed. The
tavern-keeper's bill for one of these affairs included seventy-
four bowls of punch, twenty-eight bottles of wine, and eight
bowls cf brandy.[41] At the close of the century a contemporary
historian declared that dancing had become "the principal and
favorite amusement in New England; and of this the young
people of both sexes are extremely fond."[42] Its hold upon the
South may be illustrated by the will of Charles Carter. He carefully stipulated, in 1762, that his daughters should be "brought
up frugally and taught to dance."[43]

Country people did not dance "la minuet de la cour, with the
gavet," or "la minuet ordinaire with pas grave," so popular with
the gentry. Their dances were jigs and reels, gay and boisterous,
the square dances still known in rural communities. They
amazed one sophisticated observer in the South. "These dances
are without method or regularity," he wrote. "A gentleman and
lady stand up, and dance about the room, one of them retiring
and the other pursuing, then perhaps meeting, in an irregular
fantastical manner. After some time another lady gets up, and
then the first lady must sit down, she being, as they term it, cut
out. The second lady acts the same part which the first did, till
somebody cuts her out. The gentlemen perform in the same
manner." He added ungraciously that "in this they discover

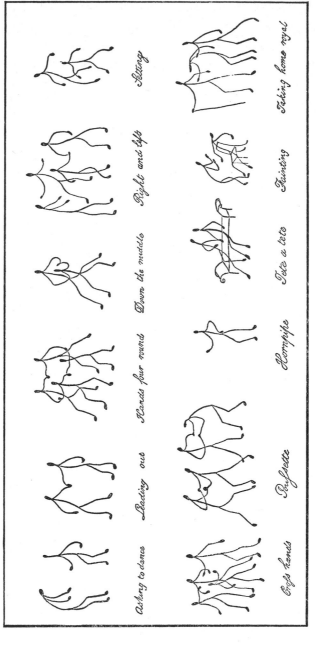

The Square Dance
The Port Folio, 1817.

great want of taste and elegance and seldom appear with the grace and ease which those movements are so calculated to display." [44] To another traveler the "latitude of shuffle" and alternate pursuit of lady and gentleman in these country dances appeared to test "at every turn the respective strength of their sinews." [45]

The music might be a small orchestra of flute, viol, and spinnet, as provided by Benjamin Parker for the dance-hall in his tavern at Medford, Massachusetts. It was more generally furnished by an ancient fiddler or Negro slave with strumming banjo. Farm boys and girls, in leather jerkins and homespun gowns, asked only that the tune be lively. Often they danced until dawn, and sometimes they appear to have spent all their substance on the flips and toddy so obligingly sold by the tavern-keeper. There is a plea in one colonial paper respectfully asking those who had attended a recent dance "to pay the honest fiddler for his trouble and wearing out of his strings, for he gathered but 12d. among the whole company." [46]

Occasionally a traveling performer—acrobat, tight-rope dancer, juggler, the exhibitor of a learned dog or sapient pig—appeared at the tavern to provide the villagers with amusement of a quite different sort. It was a rare event. Such entertainment was seldom found except in the larger towns. Nevertheless there were some forerunners of the traveling wagon shows which in another century were gradually to evolve into the circus.

A wild animal always proved a popular exhibition in town or country. The earliest notice of one appears somewhat mysteriously in Samuel Sewall's diary, in 1714: "May 12. In a piece of Gazett, mentioned, a large Dromedary seven foot high, and 12 foot long, taken from the Turks at the Siege of Vienna, to be sold." [47] Was this dromedary actually in America? If so, it must have been an appalling apparition as it soberly paraded through the twisted lanes of puritan Boston at the opening of the eighteenth century. A few years later a lion was taken on tour throughout the northern colonies, royally caged in an ox cart.

His progress may be traced from Boston to Philadelphia. Somewhat later he appears again in New London, having in the meantime been as far north as Albany. Nor did he neglect Long Island. The *New York Gazette* in May, 1728, stated in its announcement of the Jamaica fair, "It is expected that the Lyon will be there to be seen." [48]

There was a white bear on tour in 1733—"a sight far preferable to the Lion in the Judgment of all Persons who have seen them both"—and also "a very strange & Wonderful Creature called a Sea Lion." One advertisement tells of a "wild animal lately brought from the Mississippi, called a Buffalo," and another of what must have been a monkey—"a creature called a Japanese about 2 feet high, his body resembling a human body in all parts except the feet and tail." The first elephant to visit America was brought from Bengal by Captain David Crowninshield in 1796. It was immediately taken on tour, the Reverend William Bentley looking it over while on exhibition at Salem. He recorded in his diary that the elephant could pull out the cork and drink a bottle of port.[49]

More ambitious showmen than these wandering animal trainers staged various exhibits from elaborate panoramas to acrobatic performances. They reached the village tavern even more rarely than the peripatetic bears and lions, but their appeal was to the same class in colonial society. Their shows were for the common man. Again Samuel Sewall's diary provides one of the earliest records of such entertainment. The magistrates had trouble, in 1687, with a tavern-keeper who set aside one of his rooms "for a man to shew tricks in." He was persuaded of the error of his ways ("he saith seeing 'tis offensive, he will remedy it"), and the disciplinary meeting broke up with singing the ninetieth psalm.[50]

Apparently more successful was the exhibition, possibly the first advertised in a colonial newspaper, of a "curious and exact Modell of the Czar of Muscovia's Country seat, near Moscow." "Tis the most Ingenious and Compleat piece of Workmanship of

To the C U R I O U S.

To be ſeen at Major Leavenworth's Stable, oppoſite Mr. Lothrop's, State-Street,

Two C A M E L S,

Male and Female, lately imported from

A R A B I A.

THESE ſtupendous Animals are moſt deſerving the Attention of the Curious, being the greateſt natural Curioſity ever exhibited to the Public on this Continent. They are Nineteen Hands high; have Necks near Four Feet long; have a large high Bunch on their Backs, and another under their Breaſts, in the Form of a Pedeſtal, on which they ſupport themſelves when lying down; they have Four Joints in their hind Legs, and will travel Twelve or Fourteen Days without drinking, and carry a Burden of Fifteen Hundred Weight; they are re-·markably harmleſs and docile, and will lie down and riſe at Command.

Price of Admittance for a Gentleman or Lady, NINE-PENCE *each.*

- - - - - - - - - - - - -

[*Abraham was old and well ſtricken in Age: And the Lord had bleſſ'd Abraham in all Things. And Abraham ſaid unto his eldeſt Ser-vant of his Houſe, that ruled over all that he had; Thou ſhalt go unto my Cuntry, and to my Kindred, and take a Wife unto my Son Iſaac. And the Servant took Ten Camels, of the Camels of his Maſter, and departed; and went to Meſopotamia, unto the City Nahor. And he made his Camels to kneel down without the City, by a Well of Water, abthe Time of the Evening, even the Time that Women go out to draw Water. Pure Wiſdom directed the Servant, and ſucceeded him in obtaining the Conſent of the Parents, Brethren and Kindred of* REBECCAH, *that ſhe ſhould go to the Land of Canaan, and become the Wife of* ISAAC. *And they ſent away Rebeccah, their Siſter, with her Damſels, and her Nurſe, and Abraham's Servant, and his Men, and they rode upon the Camels.*   GEN. xxiv.]

Exotic Animals on Show in New England

An advertisement in *The Connecticut Journal,* June 30—July 7, 1790.
Courtesy of the American Antiquarian Society.

this Nature that ever was exposed in Europe or America," its happy proprietor announced in the *American Weekly Mercury* for August 1-8, 1723, inviting the good people of Philadelphia to see it "at Mr. Oliver Galltry Perriwig Maker in the Market Street near the Old Prison." [51]

Mr. and Mrs. Dugee delighted many an audience in mid-eighteenth century. The gentleman member of this team could dance on the stiff rope with iron fetters on his feet; his lady could hold six men standing on her ample breast while lying stretched out between two chairs. She was known as the Female Samson and had performed her unusual feat before H.R.H. the Princess Dowager of Wales.[52] Another acrobatic family brought their act to a stirring climax with the star performer "turning round with swift motion, with seven or eight swords' points at her eyes, mouth and breast, for a quarter of an hour together, to the admiration of all that behold the performance." [53] In Boston a Mr. John Childs announced his plans "to fly off of Dr. Cutler's Church." A few days later the *Gazette* stated that "as the performances led many People from their Business, he is forbid flying any more in the Town." [54]

In the latter part of the century there were also exhibitions of "philosophical optical machines," "magick lanthorns," and on one occasion "a very large moving Mashene or Land and Water Skip." [55] After the French Revolution the democratic followers of Mr. Jefferson applauded heartily the affecting spectacle of the guillotining of Louis XVI—"performed to the life by an invisible machine without any perceivable assistance." It reached its climax, as advertised for a performance at the Sign of the Black Bear in Philadelphia on November 21, 1794, when "the head falls in a basket, and the lips, which are first red, turn blue." [56]

→»}«←

HUNTING and fishing, the sports and games associated with farm festivals, shooting matches and horse-races, country dances, the amusements of the colonial tavern with its convivial social atmosphere and pleasant tippling—these were the characteristic forms of recreation for the colonial yeomanry during the eighteenth century. The sports and games were largely those which their forefathers, or they themselves, had once enjoyed in England. The scene depicted in a sixteenth-century poem addressed to Queen Elizabeth would not have been altogether unfamiliar in eighteenth-century America:

Now, when their dinner once is done, and that they well have fed.
To play they go; to casting of the stone, to runne, or shoote;
To tosse the light and windy ball aloft with hand or foote;
Some others trie their skill in gonnes; some wrastell all the day;
And some to schooles of fence do goe, to gaze upon the play;
Another sort there is, that doe not love abroad to roame,
But, for to passe their time at cardes or tables, still at home.[57]

Yet in many instances colonial amusements had been greatly modified by passage overseas, as were all English institutions transplanted to the New World. The training days and election days, with their democratic atmosphere and general participation in sports, were a product of the new environment, and the barn-raisings and husking-bees grew out of the special circumstances of colonial life. The universal popularity of hunting, with the premium placed upon markmanship as exhibited at shooting matches, was even more directly a frontier phenomenon. In their outdoor recreation the colonists turned from masques and wakes, church-ales and morris-dances, and also from such spectator sports as the animal baitings of eighteenth-century England, to the more homely diversions of a life largely shaped by pioneer conditions.

For a time the Great Awakening exerted a repressive influence, but in general there was increasingly less evidence in the eighteenth century of that puritanic condemnation of all amusements which had characterized the early period of settlement. Recreation played an important rôle in colonial life, and it was taking on distinctively American forms.

chapter 3

The Colonial Aristocracy

LET NO TRIFLING DIVERSION, OR AMUSEMENT ... ; NO GIRL, NO gun, no cards, no flutes, no violins, no dress, no tobacco, no laziness, decoy you from your books." [1]

Writing this stern injunction in his diary, a young man starting life in Braintree, Massachusetts, in the 1750's, a young man destined to be the second President of the United States, was guarding himself against what he considered the growing laxity of the age in which he lived. For in his attitude toward amusements, in his discipline of himself, John Adams was very much the Puritan. The changes that had come over the habits of New England, and especially of what had become the New England aristocracy, were a cause for his anxious, although probably not prayerful, concern.

He was highly scornful of the fashionable vogue for frivolous and idle diversions. "Let others waste their bloom of life at the card or billiard table among rakes and fools." Nor could he tolerate the ball-room: "I never knew a dancer good for anything else." He did not go so far as to "conclude peremptorily against sending sons or daughters to dancing, or fencing, or music," but he declared emphatically that he would rather they should be "ignorant of them all than fond of any one of them." [2]

But John Adams was swimming against that strong tide which we have already seen beating against the crumbling rock of Puritan intolerance. The simple country folk of New England were asserting their right to play, the more wealthy and leisured class was even less restrained by earlier prejudice. Prosperity induced a more liberal attitude, and the barriers which once

44

had blocked almost all worldly pleasures were being let down. An advertisement in the *Boston Gazette* in 1767 took "Persons of Fashion" severely to task for their unashamed attendance at plays, balls, assemblies, and card parties.[3] It was a voice crying in the wilderness after Puritan ideals of conduct which no longer commanded popular sanction.

Thirty years after John Adams' troubled reflections, changes along still more liberal lines are reflected in the diary of John Quincy Adams describing his life at Newburyport. He too suffered from the New England conscience. "I go but little into company," reads one entry which might well have appeared in his father's diary, "and yet I am not industrious. Indolence, indolence, I fear, will be my ruin." Nevertheless Mr. Adams allowed himself many pleasures of which his father would hardly have approved.

"Rather dissipated the whole day," we find him writing on one occasion; "could not study with the proper attention, and indeed gave the matter up in the afternoon. At about seven o'clock we met at the dancing hall, and from that time till between three and four in the morning we were continually dancing. I was unacquainted with almost all the company; but I never saw a collection of ladies where there was comparatively so much beauty. Two or three gentlemen got rather over the bay; but upon the whole the proceedings were as regular and agreeable as might be expected." [4]

He appears to have enjoyed female society, with that condescending air which came so naturally to an Adams. One day the entire afternoon was "employ'd in rigging for the ball," and he spent the better part of the evening in the company of "a young lady with a beautiful countenance, an elegant person, and (I am told) an amiable mind." He called on her the next day and learned to play quadrille. But it was also about this time that he confided to his diary that "there are very few young ladies who talk and yet preserve our admiration." [5]

A popular fashion of that day—as of a good many days since—

obliged young women at an evening party to play on the harpsichord, or the new pianoforte, and to sing to their own accompaniment. This bored John Quincy Adams extremely, especially
the long preliminaries before the musician would allow herself
to be persuaded to perform. "We had some very agreeable and
entertaining conversation," he wrote once, "but singing soon came
on the carpet, and then the usual nonsense succeeded." Parlor
games—for they too have a hoary antiquity—were even worse.
Mr. Adams found himself forced to play "start; what is it like;
cross questions; I love my love with an A." One evening it was
pawns: "A number of pledges were given all 'round, and kissing
was the only condition upon which they were redeem'd. Ah!
what kissing! 'tis a profanation of one of the most endearing
expressions of love." [6]

There are also references in the diary to sleigh rides, noisy
walks, serenades until three in the morning, evenings of whist.
One day was spent in reading, shooting birds, and flute-playing.
An amiable young man, Mr. Adams, enjoying what had come to
be accepted as the normal pleasures of society in a small New
England town.

-》》《《-

IN NEAR-BY BOSTON, social life was at once gayer and more
sophisticated even in the middle of the eighteenth century. If
there were still vestiges of Puritan restraint, they were not very
much in evidence—less so than in the next century. English
visitors found the atmosphere little different from that of other
American cities. As early as 1740 one of them was both surprised
and delighted to discover the Bostonians not quite as sad-visaged
as he had apparently been led to expect. "Notwithstanding plays
and such like diversions do not obtain here," he wrote, "they
don't seem to be dispirited nor moped for want of them, for
both the ladies and gentlemen dress and appear as gay, in common, as courtiers in England on a coronation or birthday. And
the ladies here visit, drink tea, and indulge every piece of gen-

tility to the height of the mode and neglect the affairs of their families with as good grace as the finest ladies in London." [7]

In this same year an assembly was established. For all of Puritanism's disapproval of dancing, teachers had been available for the young ladies and gentlemen of Boston from some date prior to 1716, an advertisement in the *News-Letter* of that year announcing lessons in "all sorts of fine works, as Feather-work, Filigre, and Painting on Glass . . . and Dancing cheaper than ever was taught in Boston." [8] An assembly, however, was an innovation. Our observer noted that the ladies who attended it "are looked upon to be none of the nicest in regard to their reputation; and it is thought it will soon be repressed, for it is much taken notice of and exploded by the religious and sober part of the people." [9] He overestimated their influence. Four years later it was reported that "assemblies of the gayer sort are frequent here, the gentlemen and the ladies meeting almost every week at concerts of music and balls." [10] In mid-century another visitor declared that they "consisted of 50 Gentlemen and Ladies and those the Best Fashion in Town."

The record of the visit of this latter traveler, Captain Francis Goelet, gives an unusually gay picture of a Boston enlivened both by the rise of a mercantile class and by the presence of a royal governor and his staff. He ferreted out its amusements with commendable perseverance. "Where very merry" is the constant refrain of the accounts of his lively escapades—evenings with the ladies at whist and with the gentlemen over wine, excursions to country taverns for dinner and dancing.

"After haveing Dined in a very Elegant manner upon Turtle, &," Captain Goelet reported of one party at which some forty gentlemen had gathered at a Mr. Sheppard's, "Drank about the [sic] toasts, and Sang a Number of Songs, and where Exceedingly Merry until 3 o'clock in the morning, from whence Went upon the Rake, going past the Common in Our Way Home, Surprised a company of Country Young Men and Women with a Violin at a Tavern, Danceing and Makeing Merry, upon our

Entering the House they Young Women Fled, we took Possession of the Room, having the Fiddler and the Young Men with us with the Keg of Sugared Dram, we where very Very Merry, from thence went to Mr. Jacob Wendells where we were Obliged to Drink Punch and Wine, and about 5 in the morning made our Excit and to Bed." [11]

On the eve of the Revolution there were two assemblies in Boston, one for those with Tory leanings, another the Liberty Assembly. The letters of a young lady loyalist declare that the former was reputed to be the best in America.[12] There are frequent references in the diary of John Rowe, friend of John Adams, to brilliant balls and very good dancing. An account in the diary of William Pynchon of the festivities in Salem during the holiday season of 1783 seems wholly modern.[13] Nothing could afford more striking illustration of how times had changed since Cotton Mather fumed over "wanton Bacchanallian Christmases," petulantly rebuking young people who might attend "a Frolick, a revelling Feast, and a Ball, which discovers their corruption."

Card-playing, especially whist, had won its way into almost complete favor. Custom-house records of imports of cards from England fully substantiate references to it in diaries and travel accounts. "The inhabitants of Boston," the Marquis of Chastellux wrote just after the Revolution, "are fond of high play, and it is fortunate perhaps that the war happened when it did, to moderate this passion, which began to be attended with dangerous consequences." [14] The Revolution had far-reaching social effects, but it is surprising to find this French observer discovering one of them to have been the curtailment of the gambling fever in one-time Puritan Boston.

Attempts to introduce the theatre resulted in one of the few victories of those still true to earlier traditions. It was not until the very end of the century that the stage was officially tolerated. When some English actors tried to put on a play in 1750, there was a small riot, and the Massachusetts General Court sternly reaffirmed its traditional ban on "public stage-plays, interludes, and other theatrical entertainments, which not only occasion great and unnecessary expenses, and discourage industry and frugality, but likewise tend generally to increase immorality, impiety, and a contempt for religion." [15]

Now and then something very closely approaching theatricals took place in the guise of public readings or moral lectures, and amateur performances were presented quite openly. The diary of Nathaniel Ames, both as a Harvard student and a resident of Dedham, has frequent references both to attending such plays and to acting in them. To his notice of a performance of *Tancred and Sigismunda,* on April 8, 1760, he adds, "We are likely to be prosecuted." [16] But, still active in these theatricals twelve years later, he reported on April 20, 1772, that "the Farce called The Toy Shop was acted ... before a numerous audience of the most respectable Inhabitants of the First Parish in Dedham both male and female." [17]

Concerts took the place of the theatre to a certain extent. Various musical instruments—virginals and spinets, violins and bass viols, flageolets, flutes, and hautboys—were being imported in 1716 by the organist of King's Chapel in Boston. In another fifteen years, to judge from an advertisement in the *News-Letter* by a Mr. Pelham, who was also a dancing-master and tobacconist, public performances were being given with an admission fee of five shillings. Soon thereafter the approval of the selectmen (although they were careful to make it clear they did not wish to establish any "president") was obtained for a concert in Faneuil Hall. By the 1760's concerts were a regular feature of the social calendar. [18]

The wealthy merchants who had taken the place of the Saints in the social hierarchy of New England fully recognized and thoroughly enjoyed the pleasures of this world. Their recreational life did not include commercial amusements, nor did it extend to active sports. In some respects it was typified by those impressive dinners which everywhere brought colonial society together—tedious except for the gaiety inspired by fine old Madeira and good New England rum. But its limitations were those of the age. Boston in the latter half of the eighteenth century may still have had that atmosphere of sobriety and decorum which has generally distinguished it, but its citizens knew how to amuse themselves.

-»»«<-

THE SOCIAL LIFE of the colonial aristocracy in the middle colonies was seen at its gayest in New York. Philadelphia was noted for its dancing assembly, its exclusive fishing parties on the Schuylkill, and the epicurean banquets given by its prosperous citizens. It had its concerts and its theatre—also its horse-races and its cock-fights for all the disapproval of the Quakers. But the lively little town of some twelve thousand inhabitants at the lower end of Manhattan Island was by mid-century a pressing rival of Boston and Philadelphia "in its fine buildings, its opulence, and extensive commerce," [19] and the superior of either Puritan or Quaker capital in amusements and entertainment. Trade with the West Indies, supplemented by the important side-line of privateering against the French, had created a class of pleasure-loving citizens of both wealth and leisure whose social life was given a further fillip by the presence of the officers of the English garrison.

They might best be seen, these leaders of colonial society, as they paraded of a late afternoon in the fashionable district about Hanover Square, dressed in the latest London mode. The gentlemen were resplendent in powdered wigs, varicolored coats, lace and ruffles, the young dandies wearing silver-hilted small swords and ostentatiously taking snuff from jeweled boxes. New fashions in hooped petticoats, vivid creations in bright scarlet or glistening green, featured the dress of the women. "One cannot but be troubled," wrote a correspondent of the *New York Mercury*, "to see so many well shaped virgins bloated up, and waddling up and down like big bodied women." [20] Sedan-chairs were carried through the streets by Negro slaves. Occasionally Lieutenant-Governor de Lancey drove by in his gilded chariot, drawn by four white horses, or Abraham de Peyster in his silver-trimmed coach, with liveried outriders in blue coats, yellow capes, and yellow small-clothes.[21] There were marked social distinctions in New York, as there were throughout the colonies. Luxurious display had an important rôle in the world of fashion.

The carriages of the gentry were usually bound for their estates out on the Bowery road or even farther afield in Harlem, and excursions by chair or chaise to near-by country taverns had a great vogue among the socially elect. Ladies and gentlemen were assured of being entertained at these resorts "in the genteelest manner," with rich foods, imported wines, and music. Turtle feasts, the terrapin washed down with well-aged Madeira, and fashionable picnics were held on the banks of the East River.

"Thirty or forty gentlemen and ladies," a traveler in 1760 noted, "meet and dine together, drink tea in the afternoon, fish and amuse themselves till evening, and then return home in Italian chaises... a gentleman and lady in each chaise. In the way there is a bridge, about three miles distant from New York, which you always pass over as you return, called the Kissing Bridge, where it is part of the etiquette to salute the lady who has put herself under your protection." [22] It may be added that the visitor, Andrew Burnaby, found the ladies of New York handsome and agreeable.

"Their Diversions in the Winter," Madame Sarah Knight commented, "is Riding in Sleys about three or four Miles out of Town, where they have Houses of entertainment at a place called the Bowery; and some go to friends houses who handsomely treat them.... I believe we mett 50 or 60 slays that day—they fly with great swiftness and some are so furious that they'le turn out of the path for none except a Loaden Cart." [23] Describing one such party in 1768, Alexander Macraby says that the sleighs were preceded by fiddlers on horseback, and the company drove to a country inn "where we danced, sung, romped and eat and drank and kicked away care from morning till night." [24]

Toward the close of the century Long Island was drawing an increasing number of pleasure-seekers, the ferries being busy every pleasant summer afternoon. Hempstead and Salisbury Plains attracted fashionable crowds to the horse-races which had been held there every season since 1665. "Upwards of seventy chairs and chaises were carried over the Brooklyn Ferry the day before," the *Weekly Post-Boy* reported after one race meeting, "besides a far greater number of horses." [25] In the years immediately preceding the Revolution the stables of imported thoroughbreds built up by a number of wealthy New Yorkers gave a wide fame to Salisbury. "These plains were celebrated for their races throughout all the Colonies and even in England," a London race book stated in 1776. "They were held twice a year for a silver cup, to which the gentry of New England and New York resorted." [26]

Other sports enjoyed at least occasionally by wealthy New Yorkers are indicated by contemporary references to pleasure boats, shooting matches, cork swimming-jackets, "gouff clubs," and (as advertised by James Rivington in 1766) "battledores and shuttlecocks, cricket-balls, pillets, best racquets for tennis and fives. . . ." [27] Cock-fighting, to say nothing of animal baitings, had its devotees among the aristocracy as well as among the common people. The diary of the chaplain of the English troops makes frequent references to the mains he attended: "Prayers, visited at night ye fighting cocks," or "I was late at ye fighting cocks." [28]

Balls and assemblies, card parties and evening frolics, were greatly enjoyed. The diary of Elisha Parker in 1747 records his being invited to both the Old Assembly and the Young Assembly.[29] The newspapers always noted the great occasion of the Governor's Ball. "The night was passed in the general satisfaction," stated one such report, "without the least incivility offered or offence taken by any one, which is scarce to be said on the like occasions." In 1762 sixty-nine couples attended a lavish ball given by Sir Jeffrey Amherst which was adjudged the "most elegant ever seen in America." [30]

William Livingstone, later to be governor of New Jersey, has left a record of waffle frolics. When one such entertainment included cards and a magnificent supper, he expressed his surprise that so luxurious a feast should be given this humble name. The evening concluded, he further noted somewhat cryptically, with *"ten sunburnt virgins lately come from Columbia's New-foundland,* besides a play of my own invention . . . kissing constitutes a great part of its entertainment." [31]

New York had its concerts. One for the benefit of Mr. Pachelbel, harpsichord player, was advertised in 1735; weekly performances, with both professional and amateur instrumentalists, were being given in the 1760's, and in the period just before the Revolution there was a great deal of musical activity. It is interesting to trace through these days the career of Mr. Herman Zedwitz, successively concertmaster at "Hull's Assembly Rooms, at the Sign of the Golden Spade," chimney-sweep, and a traitor to the patriot cause.[32] Band music was played at the Vauxhall Gardens kept by Samuel Francis, later steward of General Washington, and open-air concerts were given three times a week at the garden of the Kings Arms.

A more distinctive feature of the city's recreational life was the theatre. New York gave an early welcome to the stage, although just how early cannot be definitely stated. Its historians have had an agreeable time progressively moving farther and farther back the probable occasion of the first American theatrical performance. They may yet arrive at the landing of the Jamestown settlers aboard the *Susan Constant.* For it was a practice early in the seventeenth century for sailors aboard English ships to hold amateur theatricals, and as early as 1607 a Captain Keeling, of the East India Company, reported a showing of *Hamlet* aboard the ship *Dragon.*[33]

However that may be, there is definite evidence of a certain Richard Hunter's petitioning the legislature of New York for a license to act plays about 1699; the English actor Anthony Aston (arriving "full of Lice, Shame, Poverty, Nakedness, and Hunger") has left on record that he was playing in the colonies in 1703-04; there is notice of a performance of *The Recruiting Officer* in New York on December 6, 1732; and seven years later *The Adventures of Harlequin and Scaramouche, or The Spaniard Trick'd,* was staged at Mr. Holt's Long Room with a prologue beginning "This gen'rous Town which nurs'd our infant Stage." [34] If no one of these isolated references to the stage is accepted as marking the real beginning of New York's theatrical history, the *New York Gazette or Weekly Post-Boy* records the brief and somewhat inglorious season ("they met with small encouragement") of a company of comedians, believed to have been a troupe headed by Thomas Kean and Walter Murray, which moved upon New York from Philadelphia and gave a series of plays in the winter of 1749-50.[35]

Three years later a band of professional actors headed by Mr. and Mrs. Lewis Hallam arrived. They had reached this country in 1752 by way of the West Indies and had already acted for almost a year in the South, but their reception in New York was only moderately enthusiastic. They soon returned to the richer harvests to be gleaned in Jamaica. There Lewis Hallam died, his widow married David Douglass, and soon afterwards the reorganized troupe, now known as the American Company of Comedians, made a second and more successful venture to the American mainland. From 1758 until the Revolution forced their temporary withdrawal, they played before colonial audiences from Albany to Charleston.

New York's first permanent theatre was the John Street, opened in 1767. It was a small house, seating perhaps three hundred, and drew its audiences from both the aristocracy and the less polite members of society. The presence of the former is attested by advertisements warning patrons to send their servants by four in the afternoon to reserve their places for them, and to set their carriages down with the horses' heads facing up John

By a Company of COMEDIANS,

At the New-Theatre, in *Naffau-Street*,

This Evening, being the 12th of *November*, will be prefented,

(By particular Defire)

An *Hiftorical Play*, call'd,

King RICHARD III.

CONTAINING

The Diftreffes and Death of King *Henry* the VIth; the artful Acquifition of the Crown by *Crook-back'd Richard*; the Murder of the two young Princes in the Tower; and the memorable Battle of *Bofworth-Field*, being the laft that was fought between the Houfes of *York* and *Lancafter*.

Richard,	by	Mr. Rigby.
King Henry,	by	Mr. Hallam.
Prince Edward,	by	Mafter L. Hallam.
Duke of York,	by	Mafter A. Hallam.
Earl of Richmond,	by	Mr. Clarkfon.
Duke of Buckingham,	by	Mr. Malone.
Duke of Norfolk,	by	Mr. Miller.
Lord Stanley,	by	Mr. Singleton.
Lieutenant,	by	Mr. Bell.
Catefby,	by	Mr. Adcock.
Queen Elizabeth,	by	Mrs. Hallam.
Lady Anne,	by	Mrs. Adcock.
Duchefs of York,	by	Mrs. Rigby.

To which will be added,

A Ballad FARCE call'd,

The *DEVIL TO PAY.*

Sir John Loverule,	by	Mr. Adcock.
Jobfon,	by	Mr. Malone.
Butler,	by	Mr. Miller.
Footman,	by	Mr. Singleton.
Cook,	by	Mr. Bell.
Coachman,	by	Mr. Rigby.
Conjurer,	by	Mr. Clarkfon.
Lady Loverule,	by	Mrs. Adcock.
Nell,	by	Mrs. Beccely.
Lettice,	by	Mrs. Clarkfon.
Lucy,	by	Mifs Love.

PRICES: BOX, 6f. PIT, 4f. GALLERY, 2f.

No Perfons whatever to be admitted behind the Scenes.

N. B. Gentlemen and Ladies that chufe Tickets, may have them at Mr. Parker's and Mr. Gaine's Printing-Offices.

Money will be taken at the DOOR.

To begin at 6 o'Clock.

Playbill of the Hallam Company of Comedians
November 12, 1753, in their first New York season.

Street; that of the latter by notices requesting the gallery gods not to throw eggs on the stage.[36] Admission ranged from three to eight shillings, however, and the colonial theatre was primarily class entertainment. On one occasion a mob broke in on a performance of *The Twin Rivals* and sent the audience flying as a protest against such extravagance while there was serious distress among the poor.[37]

It was at this theatre that the first American comedy to be regularly produced, Royall Tyler's *The Contrast,* was staged on April 16, 1787. One of its characters, prototype of the country yokel in the big city, describes the playhouse. "As I was going about here and there, to and again, to find it," Jonathan says, "I saw a great crowd of folks going into a long entry that had lanterns over the door.... So I went right in, and they showed me away, clean up to the garret, just like a meeting-house gallery. And so I saw a power of topping folks, all sitting around in little cabins, just like father's corn cribs; and there was such a squeaking with the fiddlers, and such a tarnel blaze with the lights, my head was near turned." [38]

Jonathan was none too comfortable in the gallery, but accommodations for "the power of topping folks" were not much better. The two little rows of boxes and the pit were furnished only with hard wooden benches. Heat for the cold winter nights came from a large stove in the foyer, but the wiser members of the audience brought their own foot-warmers. Candles provided the lighting, often dripping on the powdered wigs of those in the boxes. Although the audience were supposed to keep their seats, the management repeatedly complained in public notices that "gentlemen crowd the stage and very much interrupt the performance."

Staging and scenery were primitive. When the green curtain was raised on the sharp blast of a whistle, the audience saw a few painted flats and a backcloth. Stagehands were liable to appear at any moment to shift the flats or to snuff a candle foot-light—if one of the actors had not in the meantime broken off his lines to do it himself. The performance was Elizabethan in its simplicity, but colonial audiences were not over-critical.

The play was the thing. The American Company of Comedians included in its repertoire not only all the Shakespearean plays, but the best of Elizabethan and Restoration comedies and popular ballad-operas. Its principal offerings were tempered by farces played as afterpieces. At the John Street Theatre the social world of colonial New York saw *Richard the Third, The Beggar's Opera,* and *Venice Preserved; Hamlet, The Beaux' Strategem,* and *She Stoops to Conquer; Flora, or Hob in the Well, The Mock Doctor,* and *High Life Below Stairs.*[39]

-->>><<<-

IN THE SOUTHERN colonies, social life was even more varied and colorful than in the prosperous cities of the North. The planters rode to hounds through the lush countryside of Virginia and Maryland in blue coats and scarlet waistcoats; they went to horse-races and cock-fights, betting heavily in so many pounds of tobacco or so many slaves; and they flocked to Williamsburg, Annapolis, or Charleston for the most festive social seasons anywhere in America. Washington Irving, in his *Life of George Washington,* describes how the young ladies of Maryland rode to the assembly at Annapolis in scarlet riding-habits thrown over their satin ball dresses, kerchiefs drawn about the great masses of their puffed and pomaded hair, and after dancing through the night rode home again in the shadowy dawn.

Through their immense holdings of lands and slaves, the planters had acquired wealth which set them off completely from the yeomanry of tidewater and the small farmers of the back country. Tobacco, rice, and indigo had been transmuted into riches, and the southern aristocracy seized upon every possible opportunity for diversion. They were not bothered by the puritanic soul-searching which sometimes still inhibited New England's wealthy merchants. They did not care whether their amusements were inspired by God or the Devil.

"Indolent, easy and good-natured," was Andrew Burnaby's characterization; "extremely fond of society and much given to convivial pleasures." [40] Somewhat later the Marquis of Chastellux caustically declared that the young men were all gamblers, cock-fighters, and horse jockeys—"to hear them converse, you would imagine that the grand point of all science was properly to fix a gaff and touch with dexterity the tail of a cock while in combat." [41] The planters were not the cavaliers of southern legend, but they lived the life of the English aristocrat on their great plantations, the life of the fox-hunting country squire, just as fully as circumstances would permit. It was the most leisured and pleasure-loving society America has ever known—and it produced some of the country's greatest political leaders.

One of the most engaging descriptions of this life is contained in the diary of Philip Vickers Fithian, a young northerner who acted as tutor for the children of Colonel Robert Carter at Nomini Hall, in Westmoreland County, Virginia. A serious-minded young man (he had studied for the Presbyterian ministry at Nassau Hall), Fithian was somewhat disturbed by the gaiety of the society into which he was thrown—"the Balls, the Fish-Feasts, the Dancing-Schools, the Christenings, the Cock-fights, the Horse-Races. . . ." [42] He could not approve an attitude which placed so high a premium on pleasure and amusement that even the Sabbath was largely given over to diversions. It troubled his Calvinistic conscience that every one should look festive and cheerful on the Lord's Day.[43]

His diary tells of race meets at Richmond where the stakes on a single race were £500, and of cock-fights which created the wildest excitement both in the Great House and in the slave quarters. It records a gala occasion with boat-racing on the Rappahannock, and afternoons with the gentry bowling on the green at Nomini Hall. The generous southern hospitality of Colonel Carter, guests being always present at a table luxuriously supplied with all the varied produce of the plantation and a wealth of wines and liquors, greatly impressed him. And it seemed that the women of the South rode about as freely as the men in their visits to neighboring plantations. "Almost every Lady wears a red Cloak," Fithian reported wonderingly, "and when they ride out they tye a red handkerchief over their Head and face." [44] He thought at first that the toothache was epidemic throughout Virginia.

Nomini Hall was a musical household. One day Fithian came home about candle-light to find "Mrs. Carter in the yard seeing to the Roosting of her Poultry; and the Colonel in the Parlour tuning his guitar." There were many evenings when the Colonel was so disposed—music was his "darling amusement"—and the tutor took part in many informal concerts. Colonel Carter had a harpsichord, a forte-piano, a German flute, and a harmonica. The latter, of course, was not our modern mouth-organ. It was an instrument invented by "Mr. B. Franklin of Philadelphia... being the musical glasses without water." Fithian declared that its virtues "far exceed even the swelling Organ." [45]

Of all the diversions of the plantation, the one that most intrigued this conscientious northerner with his Presbyterian scruples was the dancing. There were not only regular classes for the children, Mr. Christian coming over to Nomini Hall after giving his lessons at Mount Vernon, but frequent formal dances. During the Christmas holidays there was talk of little else than "the balls, the Fox-hunts, and fine entertainments."

"The assembly was remarkably numerous; beyond my expectations, and exceedingly polite in general," Fithian wrote of one affair to which he was somewhat unwillingly taken. But while not even Mr. Christian could persuade him to take up dancing himself, he greatly enjoyed watching it, especially the jigs, reels, and country dances—the company "moving easily, to the sound of well-performed Music, and with perfect regularity, tho' apparently in the utmost disorder." He would spend most of the evening wandering about, looking in occasionally at the people in the drawing-rooms drinking and playing cards. Little escaped his observant eye: "There was A short pretty stump of a girl. A

young Spark seemed to be fond of her; She seemed to be fond
of him; they both were fond, & the Company saw it.... The in-
sinuating Rogue waited on her home, in close Hugg too, the
moment he left the Ball-Room." [46]

On this first occasion Fithian at length became anxious to get
away, yet he could not help being drawn back again and again.
"The ladies were dressed Gay and splendid, & when dancing,
their skirts & Brocades rustled and trailed behind them!" With
what seems to have been a somewhat un-Presbyterian eye, he
noticed that Miss Betsy Lee was "pinched up rather too near" in
a long pair of the new-fashioned stays which permitted "scarce
any view at all of the Ladies Snowy Bosoms," and described
Miss Priscilla Hale as "a slim, puny silent Virgin.... I dare say
from her Character that her Modesty is invincible." He had left
his own love in the North. It was she whom he always had in
mind when the gentlemen drank their toasts to the ladies of
Nomini Hall. So after a time Fithian wandered out to walk alone
through the woods. He sadly took out his penknife and "carved
Laura's much admired Name upon a smooth beautiful Beech
Tree." [47]

→>≫×≪←

THE FIELD sports which were such a distinctive feature of plantation life are illustrated in a somewhat better known diary, that
of George Washington. This typical southern gentleman was a
great rider and huntsman. He was proud of his horses, his pack
of hounds (Pilot, Musick, Countess, Truelove), and his imported
fowling-pieces. His riding-frocks, waistcoats of superfine scarlet
cloth and gold lace, his elegant buckskin breeches, were all specially made in England. Diary entries under the heading "Where
and how my time is spent" bear frequent witness to the days he
"went a ducking" or "a Fox hunting in the Neck." During January and February, 1769, for example, he rode to hounds fifteen
times, one week on six successive days. [48]

Washington was equally enthusiastic about social activities, especially dancing. His diary usually records attendance at the balls and assemblies at Williamsburg, Annapolis, or Alexandria with the brief note, "Went to the play and Ball." On February 5, 1760, there was an occasion which inspired more extensive comment: "Went to the Ball at Alexandria, where Musick and Dancing was the chief Entertainment. However in a convenient Room detached for the purpose abounded great plenty of Bread and Butter, some biscuits with Tea, and Coffee which the Drinker of could not Distinguish from Hot water sweetened. Be it remembered that pocket handkerchiefs served the purpose of Table Cloths & Napkins and that no apologies were made for either. I shall therefore distinguish this Ball by the Stile and Title of the Bread and Butter Ball." [49]

The proprietor of Mount Vernon, whose innate dignity has been translated in terms of dull stuffiness for so many generations of schoolboys, quite evidently preferred the wines more generally served at colonial assemblies to the pallid refreshment of weak coffee. But the dancing itself was the lure that drew him even to bread-and-butter balls. One wonders, recalling the marked contrast in his attitude toward social pleasures to that of the man who was to be so closely associated with him in later years, at what point John Adams may have finally admitted that there might be a good dancer who was also good for something else.

Another Virginia planter who thoroughly enjoyed the various aspects of the South's recreational life was Thomas Jefferson. "From the circumstances of my position," he once wrote, "I was often thrown into the society of horse-racers, card-players, fox hunters...." It was not said in disparagement. He thoroughly enjoyed the victory of a favorite horse and being in at the death of a fox. Even greater was his fondness for music—"the favorite passion of my soul"—and there were few more zealous dancers at the fashionable balls in the Raleigh Tavern at Williamsburg. In his young days Jefferson once wrote a friend of his conception of the ideal life: "Get a pole chair and a pair of keen horses, practice the law in the same courts, and drive about to all the dances in the country together." [50]

The colonial South had another amusement in the theatre. It was there the Hallams had first landed, and nowhere did the American Company of Comedians find more appreciative audiences. It was a part of the English tradition this aristocratic society encouraged. Plays were staged not only at Williamsburg, Annapolis, and Charleston, but at Hobb's Hole, Port Tobacco, Upper Marlborough, and other little villages where the near-by planters could congregate. As the players moved on from town to town, many of the audience followed them. In the season of 1771-72 we find Washington attending the play four times at Annapolis and four times at Williamsburg during the fall, and then seven times at Williamsburg and four times at Annapolis in the spring. The total cost of his tickets for these performances of the Hallams (as well as a waxworks exhibition and a puppet-show) came to £17.[51]

Amateur theatricals are recorded in Virginia as early as 1665, when a play "commonly called Ye Bare and Ye Cubb" was put on; Williamsburg had a theatre in 1716, perhaps the first in America, and there is notice of a performance of Otway's *Orphan* in Charleston, South Carolina, in 1735. The Murray and Kean troupe toured the South after playing in Philadelphia and New York. But it was the Hallams, giving their first American performance at Williamsburg on September 15, 1752, that introduced the theatre to the South, as well as to the North, on something like a permanent basis.[52]

Advance notices in the *Virginia Gazette* told of the Hallams' pending performances. Scenes, costumes, and decorations were entirely new, giving every assurance that the audience could count "on being entertained in as polite a Manner as at the Theatre in London." *The Merchant of Venice* was played first, and a few days later *Othello*. Governor Dinwiddie took the royal family of the Cherokee Nation to the latter performance. So convincing was the players' acting that the chieftain's consort could hardly be restrained from ordering "some about her to go and prevent their killing one another." [53]

Possibly the most brilliant dramatic season of the American Company was that at Charleston, the social and cultural capital of the South, in 1773-74. "All seems at present to be trade, riches, magnificence and great state in everything; much gaiety and dissipation," a northern visitor, Josiah Quincy, Jr., wrote that year.[54] And well he might. The visiting players gave over a hundred performances, their repertoire including no less than fifty-eight different offerings. Eleven of Shakespeare's plays were staged, eight of Garrick's, and almost all the popular ballad-operas of the day.[55]

->>><<<-

THE CENTERS of society—Boston, New York, Philadelphia, Williamsburg, and Charleston—were so widely separated that there was little contact among the aristocracy of the different colonies. The lack of roads, and the miserable condition of such roads as there were, constituted a barrier to pleasure travel which even wealth could not easily overcome. One might journey by boat, at considerable expense, but by coach or stage it was an experience not many people willingly undertook. In few respects have conditions of life so greatly changed as in the broadening of our horizons through modern means of transportation.

Nevertheless there were occasional instances of touring the colonies, and for such hardy travelers, with the proper letters of introduction, an entrée into society was provided through the various social and sporting clubs found in every city. In the next century Alexis de Tocqueville was to note an unusual peculiarity of Americans whenever public pleasure was concerned: an association would be formed "to give more splendor and regularity to the entertainment." [56] This tendency already had expression in the colonies through the social clubs which met at the taverns and coffee-houses for conversation and drinking.

On a trip north in 1744, Dr. Alexander Hamilton of Maryland

was entertained at the Physical Club and Withered's in Boston;
in the Philosophical Club at Newport (where he was unduly
surprised "to find that no matters of philosophy were brought
upon the carpet"); and at the Hungarian Club in New York—
"after supper they set in for drinking, to which I was averse, and
therefore sat upon nettles." [57] On visiting Philadelphia, Andrew
Burnaby wrote of the "Colony in Schuylkill" whose members "divert themselves with walking, fishing, going up the water, dancing, singing, conversing, or just as they please." [58] In Annapolis
the Tuesday Club met every week, serving at its dinner only one
dish of "vittles" and no liquor after eleven. Charleston had its
well-known Jockey Club (as did Annapolis) and a Monday
Night Club, while Savannah enjoyed a Quoits Club.[59]

Another meeting-ground for colonial society was Newport,
Rhode Island. "It is made the resort every summer," Robert Melville, the governor of Granada, wrote in 1765, "of numerous
wealthy inhabitants of the Southern Colonies, and the West
Indies, seeking health and pleasure." In the eight years from
1767 to 1775, indeed, the pioneer society column of the *Newport
Mercury* listed some four hundred summer visitors.[60]

The amusements of these vacationists included the assemblies,
card parties, and concerts that characterized their social activities
at home. The *Mercury* carried notices of the availability of Mrs.
Cowley's long room for dancing, with a "separate genteel Apart-
ment with card-tables and a good Fire," and of an "Entertainment
of Musick every Monday, Tuesday, Wednesday and Thursday,
to be given by Mr. Henry Hymes." Newport also offered outdoor
dances and evening promenades, driving in chaises, beach races
of the famous Narragansett pacers, turtle dinners on Goat Island,
and excursions on "the new pleasure-boat, Liberty." [61]

David Douglass even brought the American Company to Newport in a daring theatrical invasion of New England. No more
sympathetic audience was likely to be found in all America, but
there remained the fact that geographically at least Newport was
within the precincts of Puritanism. A performance to be given

at the King's Arms Tavern on June 10, 1762, was therefore announced as a moral dialogue. The sole object of the entertainment, it was carefully explained, was to depict "the evil effects of jealousy and other bad passions.... Proving that happiness can only spring from the pursuit of Virtue." Mr. Douglass himself would represent "a noble and magnanimous Moor," Mr. Hallam take the part of a "young and thoughtless officer," while Mrs. Morris would be cast as a "young and virtuous wife, who, being wrongfully suspected, gets smothered (in an adjoining room) by her husband." The dialogue was to conclude at ten-thirty "in order that every spectator may go home at a sober hour, and reflect upon what he has seen, before he retires to rest." [62]

What could be more conducive to morals? What could offer less offense to the puritan conscience? But there were Calvinists in Rhode Island who had heard of *Othello,* who had heard of Shakespeare. They knew the theatre for the Devil's handiwork which it really was. A few performances were given in Newport, the company even ventured to Providence, but the Rhode Island Assembly soon took decisive action. There would be no more theatrical performances, on penalty of £100 fine for every actor.[63] Newport continued to flourish as a summer resort, but it had to get along without its theatre.

->>><<<-

ON THE EVE of the Revolution the Continental Congress proposed to curtail the amusements of the colonial aristocracy. One of the articles of the "Association" of 1774 called upon the several colonies to "discountenance and discourage every Species of Extravagance and Dissipation, especially all Horse Racing, and all Kinds of Gaming, Cock Fighting, Exhibitions of Shows, Plays, and other expensive Diversions and Entertainments...." [64]

It is interesting that these amusements should have had a sufficiently wide vogue to warrant such action; it is interesting to speculate upon the possible motives behind this drastic ban. Was it an expression of popular discontent with an extravagant way of life which contrasted too sharply with the simple, frugal, hard-working life of the colonial yeomanry? Was it the sign of an inherent Puritanism in the attitude of the New England delegates at the Continental Congress which was outraged by the frivolity of the rich planters of the South? The Revolution had its social as well as its political aspects. It was an attack upon economic privilege at home as well as upon political control from abroad. This resolution voiced a protest which may well have reflected the stirrings of a new class consciousness in colonial America.

In any event, the local committees of correspondence and the Sons of Liberty, representing the masses rather than the classes, took it upon themselves to enforce the resolution. Horse-races were effectively prohibited, the American Company of Comedians compelled to leave for the West Indies, and balls and assemblies were on occasion broken up by radical agitators. The recreation of merchant and planter was rudely interrupted even before war broke out, and not until well after the Revolution could a restored society again enjoy a social life in any way comparable to that of the middle of the eighteenth century.

chapter 4

The Frontier

APART FROM THE MAIN STREAM OF AMERICAN RECREATION, fitting into no general pattern, were the amusements of the frontier. They maintained their place in our national life for almost a century after the establishment of the Republic. New developments affecting other phases of social activity did not touch them. But the frontier during these years was being pushed farther and farther westward, changing in place if not in spirit. And once civilization had caught up with it—on the slopes of the Alleghenies, in the valley of the Mississippi, on the Great Plains —the natural restraints of a more conventional way of life quickly spelled the decline of many of the pioneers' rough and boisterous diversions.

At the opening of the nineteenth century, travelers in Ohio brought home vivid accounts of the "dram-drinking, jockeying, and gambling" that characterized the frontier. They told tall tales of barbecues and backwoods balls where home-distilled whisky stood ready at hand in an open tub, a drinking-gourd beside it. The women sometimes drank toddies; the men took theirs straight:

> Hail Columbia, happy land,
> If you ain't drunk, I'll be damned.

Some three decades later, when this pioneer country had become a state proudly boasting close upon a million inhabitants, Frances Trollope was visiting Cincinnati. "The only rural amusement in which we ever saw the natives engaged," she wrote, "was eating strawberries and cream in a pretty garden about three miles from town." [1] So rapidly did the new West progress from its tumultuous beginnings.

The story was a similar one everywhere. The Federalist period found the western pioneers enjoying very much the same diversions from the backwoods of New York to those of Georgia. Twenty years pass, and the environment has so changed that the life of these early days is almost legend, but the same scenes are being reënacted on the new frontier in the Ohio Valley. Two more decades, and this western border is pushed beyond the Great River; soon the trails to Oregon and California will be opened up. And finally the latter half of the nineteenth century will witness settlement of the prairie states, the establishment of the cow-towns of Kansas and Wyoming, the mining-camps of Colorado and Nevada. Here again the exuberant spirit of the early frontier, with even more riotous emphasis on its drinking and gambling, will flare up and then die away against the colorful background of Abilene or Virginia City.

In this new western country a nation was being born. Its settlers were not transplanted Englishmen, but largely men born on American soil and imbued with American ideals. They poured forth from the older states in successive waves, these pioneers whose restless steps led them continually toward the setting sun. Hunters and trappers, carrying lightly their long rifles, blazed the forest trails; land-hungry settlers followed in their wake with ax and plow to clear the land and build their log-cabin homes; and at last the artisans and mechanics and tradespeople drove over the widening trails in lumbering Conestoga wagons to transform the scattered frontier outposts into thriving towns.

Life in this virgin territory was on a more generous scale than life had been on the shores of the Atlantic at a similar stage of development. Distances were greater, the vast forest lands more impenetrable, the rivers longer and deeper. With land trails more difficult of passage than ocean routes, the first settlers in trans-Appalachia were actually more cut off from civilization than the founders of America had been from their homeland. They were freer from restraining influences; circumstances compelled them to be more independent and self-sufficient. With no overseas trading companies sending them supplies, buying their products, exercising control over their activities, the western pioneers recognized no authority except of their own choosing.

They came from all ranks of contemporary society: there were the amiable and the virtuous, in the approving phrase of Timothy Flint (hopefully distributing copies of "The Swearer's Prayer" to Pennsylvania teamsters), and the scoundrels and wastrels singled out by Timothy Dwight. The pioneers of the new West, that is, comprised a cross-section of society in the older states just as the colonial settlers had represented all social elements of seventeenth-century England. But experience in America had given them a new approach to life. They were tougher and more adaptable. They were not the men to starve when fish and game were plentiful. They had expansive theories of democracy and a strong belief in the equality of man. They had an individualism which would not permit them to settle together in close little towns comparable to those of New England in the early days of settlement. Each man was prepared to hew his own way through the world.

Their recreations reflected their environment. They had no more leisure than the first settlers in America; they had less opportunity for social gatherings. The frontier offered a lonely and hard life. But when the craving for companionship could no longer be ignored, when the need for amusement had to be satisfied, there were no artificial constraints or polite conventions about the pioneer celebrations. Here were no self-constituted magistrates attempting to regulate manners and morals or to enforce rules against the "mispense of time." In so far as earlier traditions affected the pioneer attitude, the liberal influence of the early French settlers in the Mississippi Valley outweighed that of Puritan New England. In a spirit of full democracy, the frontiersmen intended to enjoy themselves when they met at their log-rollings and barbecues and camp-meetings. The repressive influence of the more civilized East would soon reach them, but for a time the pioneers lived their own life.

They drank the raw, stinging whisky of the country with even more gusto than their colonial forebears; they gambled with greater abandon over horses and cards. The sports and games that marked their infrequent social gatherings were always rough, and sometimes brutal. When they met on some festive occasion, they danced through the whole night. They had no thought of observing Sunday quiet and decorum. As the frontier stretched ever farther westward, they boasted that the Sabbath would never cross the Mississippi.

->>|<<-

IN THE FIRST DAYS of settlement the frontiersman was seldom seen without his rifle, generally a long and heavy single-barreled flintlock; his otter-skin bullet pouch, with its string of patches; his powder-horn; and his "iron hook to tote squirrels." Often a pack of mongrel dogs crowded his moccasined heels. The colonial settler with his Old World background had hardly known how to handle his gun; the ways of the forest were entirely strange to him. These later pioneers were thoroughly at home on its narrow, winding trails; they were hunters before everything else.

The wealth of game along this new frontier was even greater than that of the Atlantic seaboard. In his *Memorable Days in America*, William Faux relates that there were times when the flocks of wild pigeons roosting on the trees sent them crashing to the ground amid "a scene of confusion and destruction, too strange to describe, and too dangerous to be approached by either man or beast." [2] The dead pigeons would be gathered up by the cartload—which is recorded as an illustration of the game available rather than of the sport of hunting.

Competitive squirrel hunts are often mentioned in travel accounts. On one occasion two competing teams of four men each returned at nightfall, the one with 152 squirrels and the other with 141. Another time two thousand tails were brought home as trophies. The record was perhaps that announced by the *Kentucky Gazette* in May, 1796. It reported that a party of hunters "rendezvoused at Irvine's Lick and produced seven thousand nine hundred and forty-one Squirrels killed by them in one day." The frontiersmen were such crack shots, as Audubon and many others have testified, that they could kill a squirrel by barking it—firing so close to it that the squirrel would fall to the ground stunned by the concussion, without actually being touched by the bullet.[3]

Wolf drives and ring hunts were also features of pioneer life. An army of men and boys from near-by settlements would form a vast encircling line of huntsmen around an area of perhaps forty square miles. Gradually they would close in the circle, driving ahead of them all the game they could scare up. When at last the ring was so small that the harried animals began to try to break through, the signal of a huntsman's horn would start a wholesale slaughter. Guns would be used as long as this was reasonably safe, and then clubs, pitchforks, any available weapon. At one such hunt, some sixty bear, twenty-five deer, one hundred turkeys, and even larger numbers of smaller animals and gamebirds were reported to have fallen before the enthusiastic hunters.

Pride in marksmanship made shooting matches of all kinds even more popular than they had been in the colonies. They were an institution along the entire border at the close of the Revolution, and they followed the frontier westward, bequeathing to more settled communities in the East rifle clubs and trapshooting. It was no longer customary to shoot at a live mark, a staked fowl or animal, and take it off as the trophy. Targets were more generally used, and a "beeve" or a barrel of whisky was often the prize.

Entrants in one of these contests would pay twenty-five cents for each shot, each man supplying his own target, a cross marking the bull's-eye or a center nail. Rules of procedure would be carefully agreed upon (such as the allowance for an offhand shot as opposed to shooting with a rest) and an impartial board of judges selected. To the marksman who most often hit the bull's-eye, or drove his center nail in farthest, custom decreed award of the hide and tallow of the beef animal for which they were shooting; to the second highest scorer went choice of the animal's hindquarters; third, the remaining hindquarter; fourth, choice of the forequarters; fifth, the remaining forequarter; while the man in sixth place would be entitled to the lead in the tree on which the targets had been set up.

"This is one of our homely amusements," wrote Colonel Davy Crockett. "Each man takes a part, if he pleases, and no one is excepted." Side bets generally enlivened the match, Davy Crockett declaring that he would "never bet anything beyond a quart of whisky upon a rifle shot—which I considered a legal bet, and a gentlemanly and rational amusement." [4]

A more hazardous type of shooting match, which John Bernard mentions as popular in the western parts of the Carolinas early in the century, was "shooting the tin cup." [5] We are told that it meant literally shooting a tin cup off a man's head at thirty paces for a prize of a quart of whisky. Mike Fink, the legendary hero of the Ohio keel-boat men, was to become the great champion at this sport. The redoubtable Mike is said never to have missed until the sad occasion when "corned too heavy . . . he elevated too low." He shot his man through the head, and it was the resentment of the victim's friends at such inexcusable carelessness that finally brought to a violent end the last of the great rivermen.

Racing was almost as universal an amusement as shooting matches, a characteristic feature of every pioneer celebration. Every owner of a horse was confident of its prowess and eager to match it against all comers. And for the entire community the race offered a chance to bet. America has always had its race meets, from colonial days to the present, but the informal, spontaneous quarter-racing of the countryside was for long a far

Shooting for the Beef

Painting by George Caleb Bingham, 1850. Garvan Collection. Courtesy
of the Metropolitan Museum of Art.

Joys of the Camp-Meeting

Lithograph by Kennedy and Lucas after a painting by A. Rider. Courtesy of Harry T. Peters.

more general sport. It followed the frontier from the Atlantic seaboard to Wyoming and Arizona. In the early days of settlement in the valley of the Ohio, there were races of every kind. Lively accounts tell of all Pittsburgh turning out in that city: the local course lined with an excited crowd; the betting, drinking, and occasional fisticuffs; the sudden rush to the rails as the cry rang out, "To horse, to horse!" [6]

The importance of physical strength in pioneer life gave a fresh interest to other traditional colonial sports, and also accounted for new variations of the older events. Throwing the long bullet, hurling the tomahawk, and flinging the rail were added to the usual foot-races, jumping contests, and wrestling matches. In place of the old sport of quoits—at which Chief Justice Marshall had been a club champion—the homely pastime of pitching horseshoes became a favorite game. It was to remain one for the next century, a typically American amusement.

Andrew Jackson was reputed to be a champion at throwing the long bullet—a sport which involved throwing, or slinging from a leather strap, an iron ball of several pounds weight in such a way as to make it roll through a marked goal. Abraham Lincoln won wide fame for his weight-lifting and wrestling prowess. Reminiscences of the latter's contemporaries recall that the awkward country boy, so strong that he could pick up a whisky barrel and drink out of the bung-hole, was among the most active in the sports of the little town of New Salem, Illinois. His friends were always ready to back him against all comers. One time he failed them. He was matched against a local wrestling champion, and for all their efforts neither man could get a fall. Lincoln recognized his equal: "Jack, let's quit. I can't throw you—you can't throw me." [7]

Mark Twain has written of a rough-and-tumble fighter of the western country somewhat more confident of himself. "Whoooop! I'm the old original iron-jawed, brass-mounted, copper-bellied corpse-maker from the wilds of Arkansaw!" this shrinking violet announced as he challenged all comers. "Look at me! I'm the man they call Sudden Death and General Desolation! Sired by a hurricane, dam'd by an earthquake, half-brother to the cholera, nearly related to the small-pox on the mother's side! Look at me! I take nineteen alligators and a bar'l of whiskey for breakfast when I'm in robust health, and a bushel of rattlesnakes and a dead body when I'm ailing. I split the everlasting rocks with my glance, and I squench the thunder when I speak! Stand back and give me room according to my strength! Blood's my natural drink, and the wails of the dying is music to my ear! Cast your eye on me, gentlemen, and lay low and hold your breath, for I'm 'bout to turn myself loose." [8]

Sometimes these frontier bouts ended very close to Sudden Death. All holds were allowed, and kicking, biting, punching, and gouging freely permitted. "I saw more than one man, who wanted an eye," one traveler reported as he crossed the border into Kentucky, "and ascertained that I was now in the region of 'gouging.'" [9] Another judged the respectability of the inns at which he was forced to put up by whether mine host still had his ears.

"Very few rounds had taken place," runs a vivid account of one fight, "before the Virginian contracted his whole form, drew up his arms to his face, with his hands closed in a concave, by the fingers being bent to the full extension of the flexors, and summoning up all his energy for one act of desperation, pitched himself into the bosom of his opponent.... The shock received by the Kentuckian and the want of breath brought him instantly to the ground. The Virginian never lost his hold; fixing his claws in his hair and his thumbs in his eyes, he gave them an instantaneous start from their sockets. The sufferer roared aloud, but uttered no complaint. The Kentuckian not being able to disentangle his adversary from his face, adopted a new mode of warfare. He extended his arms around the Virginian, and hugged him into closer contact with his huge body. The latter, disliking this, made one further effort and fastening the under lip of his mutilator tore it over the chin. The Kentuckian at length gave out, on which the people carried off the victor, and he preferring a triumph to a doctor ... suffered himself to be chaired round the grounds as the first rough and tumbler." [10]

While this record bears the mark of a lively imagination, the brutality reflected in such fighting was perhaps only natural in a frontier community. It was also shown in the popularity of cock-fighting and gander-pulling. Lincoln attended cock-fights, as had George Washington before him, and William Herndon has left a fragmentary description of one such affair. "They formed a ring, and the time having arrived, Lincoln, with one hand on each hip and in a squatting position, cried, 'Ready.' Into the ring they toss their fowls, Bap's red rooster along with the rest. But no sooner had the little beauty discovered what was to be done than he dropped his tail and ran." [11]

Whether Lincoln had a wager on Bap's disappointing game-cock is not revealed, but if the story had been told of Andrew Jackson, we could have been sure of the betting. As a young man in North Carolina, he was known as "the most roaring, rollicking, game-cocking, horse-racing, card-playing, mischievous fellow, that ever lived in Salisbury." The earliest document found among his personal papers is a memorandum: "How to feed a Cock before you him fight Take and give him some Pickle Beef cut fine...." [12]

More surprising to find in these early years are the occasional instances of cricket-playing reported by some travelers. Wherever settlements were made by English immigrants in the nineteenth century, this sport was introduced. They played it on the open fields of the settled East; they played it on the little clearings of this new western country. William Faux noted it in Kentucky in 1818, and both John Woods and Richard Flower report it as a sport in Illinois a year later. [13] The Chicago of 1840, where foot-races, boating, and quoits were also general diversions, had three cricket teams. Here was fertile ground for the introduction of baseball in the middle of the century. [14]

→»«←

BEES and frolics, which had become so universal a feature of American folk life, were often the occasion for sports and games, for informal horse-races, and for frontier dances. One English visitor came to the conclusion that Americans could not do anything without a frolic. "They have husking, reaping, rolling frolics, &," he wrote; "among the females, they have picking, sewing and quilting frolics." [15] Their most general characteristic appears to have been their enthusiastic drinking. They had changed from colonial days in only one respect, the substitution of whisky for rum.

The log-rolling was perhaps the most typical of these gatherings. A settler taking up land in the West had a hard task clearing his ground. He would first girdle the trees on the plot he expected to plant, cutting a wide circle in the bark to kill them, but when he finally cut them down, he had to have help to roll the huge logs into piles for burning. Neighbors from miles around came to aid in this work, and the log-rolling was made a holiday spree in which whole families—wives and children—took part.

Dinner was a gargantuan feast: a barbecued beef or hog, roasted in a deep hole lined with hot stones; quantities of buffalo steaks, venison, baked 'possum or wild turkey; and always hominy, corn dodgers, and wheatcakes fried in bear's oil. After dinner and general sports, the climax of every gathering was a dance. The men and women of the frontier loved to dance. It was a favorite amusement everywhere, singled out by traveler after traveler surprised to find such rollicking gaiety in the gloomy shadows of the deep western forests.

There were no formal rules of etiquette for the backwoods ball, no costumes in the latest mode of London or Paris. Deerskin hunting-jackets, leggings, and moccasins for the men; for the women, homespun dresses of linsey-woolsey and worn shoes which they had perhaps carried in their hands on the long walk along forest trails. As for the dances themselves, "None of your straddling, mincing, sadying," wrote Davy Crockett, "but a regu-

lar sifter, cut-the-buckle, chicken flutter set-to. It is a good wholesome exercise; and when one of our boys puts his arm around
his partner, it's a good hug, and no harm in it." [16]

Virginia reels, country jigs, shakedowns, were the order of the
day, danced on the forest floor as the fiddler made the catgut
screech through the night air and the pine knots flared against a
full moon. Some one called the numbers:

> First lady to the right, cheat and swing,
> Ladies do so do, and gents you know.
>
> Gents hands in your pockets, backs to the wall,
> Take a chaw of tabacker and balance all.

Well into the morning the backwoodsmen danced: every now
and then a halt for a "bite and a swig," but the violins always
called them back to their wooded ball-room.

"Every countenance beamed with joy," wrote Audubon, lyrically describing a Kentucky barbecue in 1834, "every heart
leaped with gladness; no pride, no pomp, no affectation were
there; their spirits brightened as they continued their exhilarating exercise, and care and sorrow were flung to the winds. During each interval of rest, refreshments of all sorts were handed
round, and while the fair one cooled her lips with the grateful
juice of the melon, the hunter of Kentucky quenched his thirst
with ample draughts of well-tempered punch." [17] He too describes the racing and shooting at a mark, the tables heaped
with food and the ready barrels of Old Monongahela.

On the sod-house frontier soon to be opened up beyond the
Mississippi, dancing became as popular as it had been in the
Ohio Valley. There was always a great scarcity of women for
the holiday balls, and the young men would scour the prairies
looking for partners. They would ride in to the dance with
young girls or grandmothers, it little mattered, perched on the
saddle behind them, calico dresses neatly tucked in, sunbonnets
swinging in the wind. On one mid-century occasion no less than
two thousand people gathered at Brownsville, Nebraska, for a

Fourth of July barbecue and dance. The buffalo, venison, oxen, sheep, hogs, and pigs slaughtered were said to have been "enough to have fed the whole territory." Another time a New Year's dance at Lecompton, Kansas, found the ladies dancing on the open prairie in mackinaws and overshoes. Dinner, brought in by hunters, was served in tents pitched by a roaring fire. For a frolic at Blue Springs, Nebraska, a special committee caught one thousand pounds of catfish.[18]

They danced the scamperdown, double shuffle, western swing, and half-moon:

> Grab your honies, don't let 'em fall,
> Shake your hoofs and balance all.

A deep pull from the little brown jug; the men would swing their partners until they kicked the ceiling—if there was any ceiling. Faster, faster, the old fiddler would sway over his precious instrument, and heavy boots stamp on the hard ground floor. Receptions, and assemblies, and cotillions were just over the horizon. This was still the frontier. Another swig from the little brown jug; call out the numbers:

> Ringtailed coons in the trees at play:
> Grab your pardners and all run away.

Weddings and infares provided other bright spots in pioneer life. On the occasion of the former, the day usually started with the groom's friends escorting him to the bride's house, on horseback, in solemn procession. But the moment the party came in sight of their destination, they would be off on a mad race to be the first to arrive. For custom decreed a prize for the winner—a whisky bottle affectionately known as Black Betty. Once the ceremony itself was performed, this bottle circulated briskly, and the party took care of itself.

The wedding guests had a friendly obligation, however. They put the newly married couple to bed, with the crude jokes and good-natured ribaldry typical of the frontier. Then, as the evening grew gayer and the whisky flowed more freely—"Where is Black Betty, I want to kiss her sweet lips"—they would thoughtfully send up drinks with uproarious shouted toasts: "Here's to the bride, thumping luck and big children."

The horse-play was sometimes rough. Uninvited guests might try to cut off the manes and tails of the wedding party's horses; they sometimes attempted to set up a pair of horns on a pole near the house as a subtle reflection on the bride's chastity. To interrupt the ceremony just as the minister started to read the service by letting loose so noisy a serenade that he could not be heard, or even to try kidnapping the groom, was a popular sport. The charivari or "shivaree," that noisy concert in which no instrument was more effective than a horseshoe and a sugar-kettle, in time became so regular a feature of frontier wedding celebrations that the bride's family had always to stand ready to buy obstreperous serenaders off with more liquor.[19]

The story is told that Lincoln once almost broke up a wedding party. He was not invited, perhaps as the result of some earlier feud, to a double ceremony in the Grigsby family, and he arranged with a confederate for a sensational revenge. When the grooms were escorted to their respective bridal chambers, they found themselves with the wrong brides. Lincoln then went on to add insult to injury by writing a scandalous version of the whole affair—"The Chronicle of Reuben." The consequences are obscure: a renewed feud, a general fight, and Lincoln waving a triumphant whisky bottle over his head and shouting that he was "the big buck of the lick." [20]

The accounts of this incident may be embroidered, for nothing was more typical of the frontier than the telling of tall tales. At every frolic, as well as at trading-posts, about camp-fires, on the decks of flatboats, and at the village taverns, the pioneers whiled away hours with story and anecdote. In no other part of the country has talk played a larger rôle in popular diversion. There grew up in the West a wealth of legend and folklore, at once realistic and wildly exaggerated, which was American to the core. Stories of Daniel Boone, Kit Carson, Davy Crockett, or some even more mythical figure as Mike Fink, Paul Bunyan, or Jim Henry, are still a delight to an age far removed from that which gave birth to them.

There were the traditional tales of mighty hunters, of wonderful marksmanship, of the great feats of the rivermen. A host of popular legends developed about "the ugly man" (Lincoln himself could have filled this rôle) who became a western folk hero. It was related of Davy Crockett that his grin had such a paralyzing effect that he could bring down raccoons without either powder or shot: he merely grinned at the 'coon and it would fall at his feet. One day his grin failed to work. The raccoon appeared glued to the tree. But Davy finally discovered that it was his eyes rather than his ugliness that had failed him. There was no raccoon, merely an unusual knot in the oak-tree . . . and he had grinned all the bark off it!

A story of the western plains, not of the forest, describes a part of the country where the atmosphere was so rarefied that the sound of one's voice would be thrown back from a mountain several hundred miles off. It took six hours for the echo to return. Making camp for the night, Jim Bridger would turn toward the mountain and shout at the top of his voice, "Time to turn out!" He could then roll up in his blankets, confident that the echo would awaken him at daybreak.[21]

->>X<<-

ANOTHER OUTLET valve for men and women who had so few chances to escape their loneliness was the camp-meeting. Its primary purpose was to work a spiritual regeneration among those who attended it, to point the path of salvation from the ungodly ways fostered by the rough life of the pioneer country. The Methodist circuit-riders warned of fire and brimstone for all those who indulged in the frontier amusements of dancing, card-playing, horse-racing, gambling, and drinking. But at the same time the camp-meeting was an occasion which often provided exciting entertainment. The crowds, the intoxication of revivalist oratory, the hymn-singing, all contributed to an emotional release from the cares of everyday life which had every aspect of hearty recreation.

"Vast numbers are there from curiosity and merely to enjoy the spectacle," wrote one observant visitor. "The young and the beautiful are there with mixed motives, which it were not best severely to scrutinize." [22]

When a meeting was announced, the people would gather from miles around, many of them undertaking a several-days journey. The countryside would present the appearance of a general migration. From the more settled communities heavy ox carts carrying whole families would bump over the rough plank roads. Lonely men and women from isolated cabins in the depths of the forest threaded their way along trails seldom pierced by the light of the sun. At the appointed place, usually some clearing on the edge of the woods, near water, they would make camp. Tents were pitched, a platform built for the preachers, and sometimes benches set up for the huge audience which would crowd the enclosure. The meeting would last perhaps a week, with continual services. It was a gigantic community picnic.

"Large fires of timber were kindled," reads the description of one such meeting, "which cast a new lustre on every object. The white tents gleamed in the glare. Over them the dusky woods formed a most romantic gloom, only the tall trunks of the first rank were distinctly visible, and these seemed so many members of a lofty charade. The illuminated camp lay on a declivity, and exposed a scene that suggested to my mind the moonlit gambols of beings known to us only through the fictions of credulous eyes. The greatest turmoil prevailed within the fence, where the inmates were leaping and holding together with upward looks and extended arms. Around this busy mass, the crowd formed a thicker ring than the famous Macedonian phalanx; and among them a mixture of the exercised were interspersed. . . . The sublimity of the music served to give an enchanting effect to the whole. . . . It had been thought proper to place sentinels without the camp. Females were not allowed to pass into the woods after dark." [23]

The manifestations of the Holy Spirit were strange and wondrous as the shouting, gesticulating, hair-tearing revivalists warmed to their vehement attacks on the Devil and all his ways. "It was supposed that no less than three hundred fell like dead men in a mighty battle," Peter Cartwright, a Methodist circuit-rider of wide fame, reports of one meeting in his autobiography; "and there was no calling of mourners, for they were strewed all over the camp ground: loud wailing went up to Heaven from sinners for mercy, and a general shout from the Christians, so that the noise was heard afar off." [24] Another witness tells of "twenty thousand persons tossed to and fro like the tumultuous waves of the sea in a storm, or swept down like trees of the forest under the blast of a wild tornado." [25]

Nor was falling beneath the power of God the only hysterical response to the flaming oratory of the camp-meeting. Other accounts tell of the Holy Laugh and the Holy Dance, of people barking like a flock of spaniels, of great crowds uncontrollably seized by the jerks. "No matter whether they were saints or sinners," Cartwright wrote another time, "they would be taken under a warm song or sermon, and seized with convulsive jerking all over, which they could not by any possibility avoid, and the more they resisted the more they ·jerked. . . . I have seen more than five hundred persons jerking at one time in my large congregations." [26]

In bringing men and women together, especially young people, under such circumstances, the camp-meeting had its dangerous aspects because of the intense emotionalism it stirred up. The placing of sentinels about the ring of camp-fires was a common practice, but with all precautions there were many camp-meeting babies. William Herndon has a story of a young couple at a camp-meeting in the Lincoln country. "Slowly and gracefully they worked their way towards the centre," he writes, "singing, shouting, hugging and kissing, generally their own sex, until at last nearer and nearer they came. The centre of the altar was reached, and the two closed, with their arms around each other, the man singing and shouting at the top of his voice

> "I have my Jesus in my arms
> Sweet as honey, strong as bacon ham." [27]

Whether an active participant or an interested spectator, it is not difficult to understand why the frontiersman found the camp-meeting an exciting experience. A drunken spree at barbecue or log-rolling could hardly rival taking one's place on the "anxious bench," mingling one's hallelujahs with those of a thousand other frenzied converts, or joining in the Holy Dance as some inspired preacher called the tune. A revival was something for the pioneer to look forward to as he swung his heavy ax to clear another half-acre or hoed at his stubborn cornpatch. Conversion might of course limit his other amusements, but it was not necessary, as he must often have thought on his exhausted journey home, to stay saved for very long.

chapter **5**

A Changing Society

IN THE OPENING DECADES OF THE NINETEENTH CENTURY, THE American people throughout the eastern parts of the country were enjoying very much the same recreations as they had in colonial days. The Revolution had marked a distinct break in many customs, especially for the wealthier classes, but old threads of activity were quickly picked up. Writing about 1821, Timothy Dwight singled out the principle amusements as "visiting, dancing, music, conversation, walking, riding, sailing, shooting at a mark, draughts, chess, and unhappily in some of the larger towns, cards and dramatic exhibitions." [1] Social life had a relative simplicity, and popular diversions conformed to familiar patterns.

But new winds were blowing. The turbulent, expansive years of the first half of the century were to usher in changes in recreation as far-reaching as those in any other department of the national life. The country was going through the first phase of its transformation from a simple agricultural community into a highly complex urban society. New means of amusement had to be found to replace those from which increasingly large numbers of persons were cut off by the very circumstance of city life. The rise of a working class imbued with the pervasive ideals of Jacksonian democracy created a demand for popular entertainment which had hardly been felt in colonial days.

The trend toward urbanization and the growth of a factory population were to continue in later years at a greatly accelerated pace. It was the novelty of these developments, crowding people together in living conditions entirely new to America, that gave

84

them their importance in this period. Between 1800 and 1850 the proportion of the population living in urban communities of more than 8,000 tripled, representing in the latter year twelve per cent of the total. Some of the little colonial towns had become real cities. In mid-century New York had a population of more than 500,000, Philadelphia of over 300,000, and there were six other cities with more than 100,000 each.[2] Still small by to-day's standards, they nevertheless gave rise to a serious problem. What was to be the recreation of the new urban democracy which could no longer look to rural sports and informal country pastimes for relaxation? Some substitute had to be found to meet a demand growing greater every year because of the indoor confinement and monotonous routine of so much city work.

"Democracy is too new a comer upon the earth," wrote a shrewd foreign observer, Michael Chevalier, in 1833, "to have been able as yet to organize its pleasures and amusements. In Europe, our pleasures are essentially exclusive, they are aristocratic like Europe itself. In this matter, then, as in politics, the American democracy has yet to create every thing fresh." [3]

The answer to this challenge was the gradual growth of commercial amusements, the beginnings of what has now become a vast entertainment industry. But for many years during this difficult period of transition, recreation appears to have been more limited than at any other time in our history. The general shift from active to passive diversion did not make for a normal, healthy adjustment, and not until after the Civil War was this balance redressed by the rise of organized sports. New forms of recreation, moreover, found all the moral forces of the age arrayed against them. Whatever their actual value as a relief from the tedium of everyday life, they generally stood condemned.

A renewed emphasis upon the importance of work was one of the most telling repressive influences. The spirit of the times was expressed in the preamble of a New Hampshire law: "All young countries have much more occasion to encourage a spirit of industry and application to business, than to countenance schemes of pleasure and amusement." And this attitude was strengthened and intensified by a revived Puritanism which again provided a moral sanction for the disapproval of recreation. It was in 1839, however reminiscent of 1639 it may seem, that public speakers everywhere were preaching the doctrine upheld by one prominent lecturer who sententiously declared, "We tolerate no drones in our hive.... The sweat-drops on the brow of honest toil are more precious than the jewels of a ducal coronet." [4]

The intolerance of the seventeenth century, rather than the liberalism of the eighteenth, swayed public opinion. It was the dark period of Victorian repression. For the recreational scene actually to broaden under these circumstances, as it eventually did, was proof of an underlying need on the part of the American democracy which could not permanently be left unanswered. It was the expression of an unconscious determination in the pursuit of pleasure which had even stronger roots than Puritan tradition.

->>><<<-

THE OPPORTUNITY to develop the boundless resources of a continent, the need to build up trade and industry in order to assert our economic as well as our political independence, afforded very real justification for a return to the gospel of work. Without our national response to this opportunity the material development of the country would have been substantially slowed up. But it was equally true that continual application to business, with increasing concern over its profits, greatly narrowed the horizon of the average American. He became obsessed with a mania for making money. "In no country are the faces of the people furrowed with harder lines of care," wrote one sympathetic observer. "In no country that I know is there so much hard, toilsome, unremitting labor: in none so little of the recreation and enjoyment of life. Work and worry eat out the heart of the people, and they die before their time.... It is seldom that an

"*Light May the Boat Row*"

Lithographed cover of a music sheet of 1836. Courtesy of the New York Historical Society.

No 159 Crosby, near Bleeker St. New York.
ESTABLISHED FOR THE PROMOTION OF HEALTH
BY MEANS OF SYSTEMATIC PHYSICAL TRAINING.
JOHN B. RICH, M. D. PRINCIPAL.

Dr. Rich's Institute for Physical Education

About 1850. J. Clarence Davies Collection, Museum of the City of New York.

A Picnic on the Wissahickon

Engraving by Rawdon, Wright and Hatch after a drawing by William Croome. *Graham's American Monthly Magazine,* 1844.

American retires from business to enjoy his fortune in comfort.
Money-making becomes a habit. He works because he has always
worked, and knows no other way." [5]

The Almighty Dollar cast its long shadow over the land. With
depressing unanimity the host of English travelers who examined
American democracy in the 1830's and 1840's found us too absorbed in work's daily routine to recognize any other phase of
life. Never has criticism on this score been more general or persistent. Frances Trollope, Basil Hall, Thomas Hamilton, Frances
Wright, and Charles Dickens—they all rang the changes on the
same tune. Our only pleasure was business, our only amusement
making money. Arriving at New Orleans at the time of that city's
colorful Mardi Gras, Sir Charles Lyell breathed a sigh of relief
to find at last some signs of gaiety in the United States. "From
the time we landed in New England to this hour," he wrote, "we
seemed to have been in a country where all, whether rich or poor,
were laboring from morning till night, without ever indulging
in a holiday." [6]

Frances Trollope's observations were colored by her snobbish
scorn of the crudities of American life, but with all proper allowance for prejudice her repeated complaints of how dull she
found this country carry conviction. "We are by no means as gay
as our lively neighbors on the other side of the Channel," she
wrote, "but compared with Americans, we are whirligigs and
teetotums; every day is a holiday and every night a festival." She
concluded that Americans must somehow not have the same
need of being amused as other people—"they may be the wiser
for this, perhaps, but it makes them less agreeable to a looker-
on." [7]

Dickens was greatly depressed by a point of view which not
only left no time for normal recreation, but gave a businesslike
efficiency to activity outside the counting-house as well as within
it. Among the people he encountered at boarding-houses and
hotels, in stage-coaches and on steamboats, there were always the
same rush and hurry. We may look back upon life a century ago

as having had infinite leisure, but it was already marked by quick drinks and quick lunches. The American meal-hour horrified Dickens: "No conversation, no laughter, no cheerfulness; no sociality, except in spitting; and that is done in silent fellowship round the stove, when the meal is over. Every man sits down, dull and languid; swallows his fare as if breakfasts, dinners, and suppers, were necessities of nature never to be coupled with recreation or enjoyment; and having bolted his food in a gloomy silence bolts himself, in the same state." [8]

Our English visitor wandered forth from his hotel to observe the habits of the frenetic dollar-chasers of New York. "But how quiet the streets are! Are there no itinerant bands; no wind or stringed instruments? No, not one. By day are there no Punches, Fantocinne, Dancing Dogs, Jugglers, Conjurers, Orchestrinas, or even Barrel-organs? No, not one. Yes, I remember one, one barrel-organ and a dancing monkey, sportive by nature, but fast fading into a dull, lumpish monkey of the Utilitarian school. Beyond that, nothing lively; no, not so much as a white mouse in a twirling cage.

"Are there no amusements? Yes, there is a lecture room across the way, from which that glare of light proceeds, and there may be evening service for the ladies there thrice a week, or oftener. For the young gentlemen, there is the counting-house, the store, the bar-room. . . ." [9]

-»>«<-

THE MORAL APPROVAL given this attitude served the same end as had Puritanism's support of the early colonial laws in detestation of idleness. The reawakening that succeeded the skepticism and apathy of the close of the eighteenth century made the period one of intense religious interest, and nowhere was it more strongly manifest than in its influence on recreation. A new generation of spiritual leaders took up arms against any broadening whatsoever of the field of amusements. They preached the sinfulness of idle pleasure with a fierce intolerance. Their prohibitions were most effective among those who actually had little chance to enjoy many diversions, again demonstrating the close relationship between reform and economic environment; but they affected all classes. The influence of the church largely determined the public attitude.

The full force of religious disapproval was thrown against the struggling theatre. President Dwight of Yale flatly declared that "to indulge a taste for playgoing means nothing more nor less than the loss of that most valuable treasure the immortal soul." [10] The church generally condemned commercial amusement, whatever its form, as "the door to all the sinks of iniquity," an attitude clearly revealing its complete failure to realize that a people growing further away from the simpler pastimes of an agricultural civilization had to have some substitute for them. As late as 1844 Henry Ward Beecher singled out for attack, with a vitriolic bitterness reminiscent of Cotton Mather, the stage, the concert-hall, and the circus. He made no distinctions. Any one who pandered to the new taste for entertainment was a moral assassin. The fate awaiting this enemy of society was certain: "As borne on the blast thy guilty spirit whistles towards the gates of hell, the hideous shrieks of those whom thy hand hath destroyed, shall pierce thee—hell's first welcome." [11]

The pulpit's wholesale denouncement of pleasure was more typical of New England, but other parts of the country also felt the heavy hand of puritan repression. The evangelical churches everywhere banned the race-course and all games of chance, forbade card-playing in whatever guise, and disapproved severely of dancing. Nineteenth-century Presbyterians, Baptists, and Methodists, gathering thousands of converts into their folds as they went south along the mountain ridges and then spread westward into the Mississippi Valley, reimposed many of the prohibitions of seventeenth-century Calvinists. In some sections the Middle West was to become more New England than New England itself.

In these circumstances another phenomenon of seventeenth-century life was repeated in the growing towns and cities of nineteenth-century America. The saloon and grog-shop became more than ever the workingman's club as urban life cut him off from other emotional outlets. Heavy drinking was a widely prevalent habit. It played a rôle fully as important as it had in colonial days, and had more serious consequences. It was the common belief of English visitors that a man could get drunk twice in America for sixpence—and usually did.[12]

In their efforts to suppress intemperance the reformers made no attempt to find a substitute for the saloon. Anne Royall once argued that establishment of theatres might be the means of saving the people "from the effects of an evil which seems to threaten their morals with a total overthrow,"[13] but no one listened. The church easily fell in with the attitude of the merchant-manufacturer class, whose sole objective was to get as much work as possible out of its employees. The theory here was that drinking was the result of idleness, and consequently long hours of labor should be maintained for the sake of the wage-earners' moral welfare. They should not be allowed time for anything else. Spokesmen of religion turned a deaf ear to labor's contention that the intolerable burden of a twelve- or fourteen-hour day compelled some "excitement fully proportioned to the depression," which under existing circumstances could be found only in drinking. They gave full support to the new order of industrialists in upholding "the wholesome discipline of factory life."[14]

Nor was there any toleration of recreation on the one day in the week on which workers were free. The old issue of Sabbath observance was revived. At the close of the eighteenth century a marked weakening of Puritan restrictions had taken place. Even in Boston travelers reported that the townspeople had in great measure lost "that rigidity of manners and vigilant way of keeping Sunday" which had formerly characterized New England.[15] But as the nineteenth century progressed, many of the old bans were reapplied. No sports or games were allowed on the Lord's

Day, let alone public amusements. Travel was no longer permitted. In many states even the Government mails were stopped. Public opinion, if not actual laws, decreed church attendance as the only permissible Sunday activity.

"In 1800," Emerson Davis wrote in mid-century, "good men slumbered over the desecration of the Sabbath. They have since awoke." [16] This simply meant that on this count the harsh rule of the Puritans was firmly refastened upon the country—"all was solemn and drear. Laughter was considered irreverent." [17] It has taken almost a century for Sunday bonds to become sufficiently relaxed to sanction normal recreation.

Deprived of support from the more responsible elements of society because of the church's attitude, public entertainment often fell into the hands of those who on occasion did not hesitate to pander to the lowest order of popular taste. This in turn aroused further opposition to commercial amusements. The vicious circle continued until social leaders began to recognize the importance of recreation in the national life, accepting the fact that in what was becoming an urban society, it necessarily had to be organized, and often placed on a commercial basis.

->>)<((-

ANOTHER FACTOR serving at times to discourage the growth of amusements as such was a nation-wide cultural reawakening which affected all classes. The 1830's and 1840's were an age of intense activity along many lines. American thought was going through a period of ferment which was expressed by a keen and active interest in things of the mind and spirit. New concepts of democracy, of humanitarianism, of the brotherhood of man, were in the air. Among the factory workers there was often strong disapproval of the recreational use of even such little leisure as they commanded because of an unusual sense of civic responsibility.

When labor urged the reduction of the working-day from the prevailing twelve and fourteen hours to ten, it did not assert any claim for time to play. "All men have a just right, derived from their creator," a resolution of the Journeymen Carpenters of Philadelphia stated in 1827, "to have a sufficient time in each day for the cultivation of their mind and for self-improvement; Therefore, resolved, that we think ten hours industriously employed are sufficient for a day's labor." "Let the mechanic's labour be over when he has wrought ten or twelve hours in the long days of summer," reads another piece of propaganda, "and he will be able to return to his family in season, and with sufficient vigour, to pass some hours in the instruction of his children, or in the improvement of his own mind." [18]

With this strong feeling of the importance of self-education and widespread interest in intellectual matters, a great vogue developed for public lectures. The lyceum movement, bringing public speakers to every town throughout the country, spread rapidly. It was started in 1826. Five years later a national organization was formed with some nine hundred local lyceums.[19] They provided a platform for speakers on every conceivable topic—history, philosophy, and geology; women's rights, prison reform, insane asylums; temperance and abolition. Sir Charles Lyell was astounded in the 1840's to find the general public rushing to the lecture as they might formerly have done to a play; Philip Hone observed with amazement that in New York the craze had left the theatres flat on their backs.[20]

Many of our foreign visitors spoke of the workingmen audiences at these lectures. They were especially noted in New England, and one of the most striking instances of cultural enthusiasm was found at the cotton-mills of Lowell, Massachusetts. Its atmosphere was far from typical of most manufacturing towns, and even here the roseate picture drawn by foreigners was greatly exaggerated. Nevertheless, the great majority of the workers were self-respecting country girls, serious and intelligent. Their attitude may be taken as a symbol of the zest for knowledge.

"In Lowell reading is the only recreation," wrote Michael

Chevalier; [21] Professor Peabody of Harvard found his lecture-room crowded with factory operatives who laid aside their books only to take notes on his talk; [22] and Dickens, visiting the city in 1842, was impressed by three facts: "Firstly, there is a joint stock piano in a great many of the boarding houses. Secondly, nearly all the young people subscribe to circulating libraries. Thirdly, they have got among themselves a periodical called The Lowell Offering." [23] This publication exuded the factory town's lofty spirit. There was the story of Abby's first year in the mills: "She gratified no feeling but a newly awakened desire for mental improvement, and spent her leisure hours in reading useful books." [24]

In many instances the public crowded the lecture-hall with less elevated motives than self-education. George Combe, lecturing on the popular fad of phrenology, freely admitted that "entertainment and excitement, as much as instruction," drew the crowds that nightly attended his lectures in Boston.[25] And there was even less pretense of culture in the audiences that gathered to hear the ever-popular spiritualists, hypnotists, mesmerists, psychometrists, hydropathists. . . . A woman speaker advertised a lecture on animal magnetism in which she would painlessly draw the teeth of any person who so desired, and a lecturer on mesmerism promised to operate on the entire audience and produce a variety of results in trance and catalepsy. This was clearly entertainment as much as concert-hall or theatre. Philip Hone considered it of an even lower order, but commented philosophically, "the people will be amused."

Nevertheless the serious purpose that lay behind this vogue for lectures was their important feature. It reflected the idealistic belief that in a democracy all citizens should be able to take an intelligent part in the conduct of government. They should be educated to fulfil their social obligations. Self-improvement was not a selfish goal: it was a responsibility of citizenship. In the awakening desire of democracy to play a full rôle in public affairs, the need for a wide diffusion of knowledge seemed implicit.

Female Calisthenics in the Pantalette Era

The Casket, 1832.

In considering popular lectures, in this or other periods, it is never possible to draw a hard and fast line between education and entertainment. In most cases both elements were present. The lecture craze of the 1840's, however, had the full support of all those who felt it was sinful to use leisure solely for enjoyment. For that reason it was an important phenomenon both in itself and because of its retarding influence on the growth of amusements which could make no cultural claims.

->>>‹‹‹-

THE STATUS of women in the social life of the nineteenth century also had a very definite bearing on recreation. Prevailing concepts of the proper relationship to be maintained between the sexes were a barrier which, apart from all other considerations, prevented the natural development of many forms of diversion. They gave an atmosphere of artificial restraint to ordinary social functions. For long they made it almost impossible for men and women to enjoy together any outdoor activities. And it was not only that there was less freedom in social intercourse than there is to-day. Popular ideas on the delicacy of females—a basic canon of the mid-nineteenth century—and an almost morbid prudery meant a more restricted life for women than in the eighteenth century. In colonial days they had been able to enter far more fully into both the work and the recreation of men. They took part in the farm festivals and holiday celebrations; they enjoyed as spectators if not as actual participants whatever amusements were available. But now women were more and more condemned to a life separate and apart.

It was a man's world, with its tremendous emphasis on work and getting ahead. Young people were allowed great liberty. "They dance, sing, walk and run in sleighs together, by sunshine and moonshine," wrote Frances Wright, "without the occurrence or even the apprehension of any impropriety." [26] But this dispensation was short-lived. "Once married," another contemporary observer reported, "the young lady entirely changes her habits. Farewell gaiety and frivolity." [27] Whatever their position in society, women were expected to devote themselves wholly to the duties of domestic life. Visitors from abroad often singled this out as a bizarre and unexpected aspect of the American scene. The sparkling Fanny Kemble found it impossible to conform to such a narrow tradition after her own American marriage. Frances Trollope was incensed at an attitude which so closely restrained those of her sex.

If they had any leisure, the ladies took up embroidery, painting on glass or china, and waxwork—with commendable perseverance and devastating results. But they kept indoors, and everything else, including health, was sacrificed to incredible standards of proper female decorum. Viewing the results, Thomas Hamilton mourned that "at one or two-and-twenty, the bloom of an American lady is gone, and the more substantial materials of beauty follow soon after. At thirty the whole fabric is in decay, and nothing remains but the tradition of former conquests." [28] Delicacy became the hall-mark of gentility, the sign and symbol (as the Chinese mandarin's long finger-nails) of freedom from manual labor. It was not, indeed, a general characteristic. By far the larger number of women could not afford delicacy: their household work would not permit it. But it was the goal toward which they all aspired, and the dominant male encouraged it. It contributed to his own sense of importance and established social status.

The few attempts that were made to persuade women to take outdoor recreation illustrate this general attitude even more pointedly. In mid-century there was a revival of skating which brought out thousands to country ponds and city rinks. During twenty-seven days of good ice in one season, over two hundred thousand skaters were estimated to have visited the lakes of New York's new Central Park; excursion trains daily carried from a thousand to fifteen hundred Boston enthusiasts to Jamaica Pond.[29] It was urged as a suitable sport for both sexes. But the female skater was advised in one such appeal to take fast hold

A Family Party Playing at Fox and Geese

Drawing by Winslow Homer. *Ballou's Pictorial Drawing-Room Companion*, 1857.

The Dance after the Husking

Harper's Weekly, 1858.

Skating in Central Park, New York

Painting by Johann M. Culverhouse, 1865. J. Clarence Davies Collection, Museum of the City of New York.

of the coat tails of her gentleman partner, for then, "if he was a dextrous glider, and she maintained a firm position, a gay time she could have of it enjoying all the pleasure without incurring any of the fatigue of the exercise." [30]

One English visitor who greatly missed feminine society as he traveled about America, Captain Basil Hall, reported sadly that he had positively never once seen "anything approaching within many degrees to what we should call a flirtation." His lively wife confirmed his impression that there was "a great separation between the ladies and gentlemen in society here." They found few women at the theatre in New York or at the race-track in Charleston; even at dances, hardly possible without some recognition of females, the two sexes "appeared to be entire strangers to each other." At a country fair at Brighton, Massachusetts, only nine women were counted in a crowd of several thousand. Captain Hall heard some music and rushed excitedly to the spot. "What was there?—four men dancing a reel." [31]

He was taken to task, however, by a dissenting English observer for the conclusions he drew from this incident. James Stuart explained the absence of women at the Brighton Fair. "For very obvious reasons," he pointed out quietly, "it would be reckoned a breach of delicacy in Britain for ladies to attend cattle-shows." [32]

The prudery of the period to which Queen Victoria has lent her unblemished name may be interpreted as both cause and consequence of this failure of men and women to associate more naturally in their everyday life. When modesty and decorum were carried to such lengths that an English book of etiquette adapted for publication in the United States could state "that, in America, female delicacy has become morbid," [33] one could hardly expect society to be as lively and gay as it had once been. It is not necessary to take overseriously such tales as Captain Marryat's account of his visit to the home of Edward Everett, where he found a statue of the Apollo Belvidere carefully draped and the legs of the piano "in modest little trousers, with frills at the bottom of them." [34] One may largely discount Mrs. Trollope's amazing stories of flounces painted on immodest sign-post milk-maids, the ostracism of a man who used the word "corset" in mixed company, and the consternation of the young girl in a boarding-house who, unexpectedly encountering a member of the other sex, ran from the room screaming "A man! A man! A man [35]!" Nevertheless the artificial restraints growing out of such prudishness had a depressing effect. Men could not help feeling more at ease when alone with other men. Recreation lost something which only the participation of women could give it.

-»»«<-

THESE WERE the influences which served to make the American scene so dull in the first half of the nineteenth century. Seriousness of purpose was heightened by strong religious feeling; the average man locked himself in his office and his wife in his home. But the forces let loose by the growth of cities and the rise of a new working class could not be withstood. The demand of the urban democracy for amusements to take the place of the rural pastimes they could no longer enjoy was too insistent. Mrs. Trollope notwithstanding, the American people had the same need for being amused as the people of any other nation. The development of new forms of entertainment could not be permanently stayed for all the prejudice and opposition of those social forces which disapproved of them.

So it was that this period of repression was actually marked by the beginning and gradual expansion of popular amusements which have ever since played an increasingly important part in our recreational life. The first half of the nineteenth century witnessed the growth of the theatre as entertainment reaching out to all classes of people. It saw the beginnings of variety, minstrel shows, and the circus; the establishment of amusement parks, public dance-halls, concert-saloons and beer-gardens; a revival of horse-racing and the rise of other spectator sports. By the Civil War the nation was in the midst of those far-reaching changes in the recreational scene which were a natural corollary of the broader social changes through which it was passing.

The new amusements may not have been as healthful and innocent as those they replaced. They were generally something to be watched rather than enjoyed through active participation. But in opposing them so indiscriminately the confused reformers of the day were combating something essential for a society shaped by nineteenth-century industrialism. Despite prejudice and opposition from so many quarters, a new America, a fumbling, often inept democracy, was feeling its way toward a fuller, more satisfying life for the masses of its people.

chapter 6

The Theatre
Comes of Age

IN SPITE OF THE DISAPPROVAL OF THE STRONG RELIGIOUS FORCES of the day, the theatre was forging steadily ahead after 1800. It was attempting to establish itself by pleasing all classes, and with this end in view the playhouses of the period welcomed everything on their hospitable stages with delightful indiscrimination. A century ago the same house might advertise Junius Brutus Booth in *Hamlet* on one night, the "Original, Aboriginal, Erratic, Operatic, Semi-Civilized and Demi-Savage Extravaganza of Pocohontas" on the next, and on the third an equestrian melodrama with a cast of circus performers playing on horseback. A single evening often produced almost as varied theatrical fare, *Macbeth*, a daring French ballet, and perhaps such a popular and rowdy farce as *My Young Wife and the Old Umbrella*, making up the program. The theatre, that is, was a democratic institution, playing a rôle which in later years it largely surrendered, first to the vaudeville stage and then to the moving picture.

The trend was steadily away from Shakespeare and toward more farce and variety. But the function of the theatre before the days of vaudeville, let alone those of the movies, made this natural. "The rapid increase in population in newly formed cities," wrote an observant visiting actor, William Davidge, "produces a style of patrons whose habits and associations afford no opportunity for the cultivation of the arts." [1] When the craze for lectures in the 1840's drew off the theatre's more sophisticated patrons, there was even greater need to meet the populace's demand for undiluted entertainment. "Opera and burlesque, the melodrama and the ballet," sighed one critic, "have literally swallowed up the

100

legitimate drama. ... We are not a theatrical people." [2] But this was a prejudiced view. In its growth and development in these years the theatre was merely reflecting those diverse and contradictory impulses which animated American democracy in its awkward age.

-->>)(((-

UPON THEIR RETURN from exile after the Revolution, the English actors who had introduced the theatre to America struggled against heavy odds. There was always puritanic prejudice, but for a time colonial traditions also led to the theatre's being vigorously attacked as an aristocratic, un-American institution. It was declared an enemy of true republican principles, a foe to democracy. The giddy ideas of the stage could not be reconciled with the virtue which was the true basis of the freedom so lately won on revolutionary battlefields. And it undermined public morals. "At present," shouted an irate speaker in the Pennsylvania legislature, "play-writers are held at liberty, when they wish to throw their audiences into fits of laughter, to make a smutty joke, throw the ladies into confusion, and give the jessamies a chance of tittering to show their teeth." [3]

Nevertheless the theatre quickly gained a foothold. It could not hope to win full popular approval with the church thundering against it as the Devil's workshop, but before the close of the eighteenth century it had at least broken through official prohibitions which might have completely barred it. After long debate the battle may fairly be said to have been won when the newly built Chestnut Street Theatre opened in Philadelphia in 1794 with the legend carved over its door, "The Eagle Suffers Little Birds to Sing." In the meantime the old John Street Theatre, soon to be replaced by the first Park Theatre, had won a popular following in New York, and after furtive ventures into the dangerous territory of Boston under the guise of moral lectures, the theatre was even admitted within the sacred precincts of Puritanism. [4]

For some two decades these three cities were almost the only ones supporting the stage, and in each instance a single playhouse dominated the scene. Only gradually was the theatre able to extend its scope and become a national institution.

Albany had a surprisingly long theatrical tradition, John Bernard managing the company there at the opening of the nineteenth century. Near-by Rochester was hardly as hospitable. "It is really astonishing to think that the trustees of so respectable a village," its newspaper declared in 1828, "should permit such a disorderly place as the theatre." In New England we find a troupe of Boston players visiting Salem in 1792, but its theatre languished and died, for the townspeople "found it a much more profitable mode of spending their time and money, to hear lectures on interesting and useful subjects." James Silk Buckingham reported a theatre as far afield as Bangor, Maine, in 1840, commenting, however, that as in all provincial towns it was not attended by the better class of people.[5]

The South was far more receptive, as it had been in colonial days. Before there were any real playhouses in New England outside of Boston, theatres had been established in all the principal southern cities from Baltimore to Savannah. The West too was cordial. Soon after the War of 1812 a company of players brought together by Samuel Drake, an English actor who had been playing with Bernard's company in Albany, made its adventurous way to Kentucky by wagon and flatboat. Soon what was still the pioneer country of trans-Appalachia was dotted with theatre towns.[6]

The theatrical circuit by the fourth decade of the century is illustrated by the tour of Tyrone Power, the Irish comedian. From his first engagement at the Park in New York, now the country's amusement capital with half a dozen playhouses, he went to Philadelphia, where he played at the Chestnut Street and the Walnut Street. Then he went to the Tremont in Boston. Starting on a southern tour, he visited Baltimore, Washington, Alexandria, Charleston, Savannah, and Columbus. There were engagements also at New Orleans, Mobile, and Natchez, and back again in the North somewhat later, at Albany.[7] These were the more accessible theatres. Those in St. Louis and Cincinnati were also important, and before mid-century the roster included cities as far west as Dubuque, Iowa. In all, more than fifty established stock companies scattered throughout the country marked the theatre's half-century advance.[8]

An outstanding characteristic of the playhouses of this period, in contrast to theatres of the legitimate stage in the twentieth century, was their immense size. The second Park Theatre in New York, opening in 1821, provided accommodations in its great yawning pit, three tiers of boxes, and top gallery for 2,500 persons; the Bowery, bursting upon a startled world a few years later with all the magnificence of gas-lights, held 3,500; and in another decade the Broadway advertised seats for 4,000. Theatres in other cities were not quite as big as these New York houses, but they too were far larger than the average to-day.[9]

They were large because of the theatre's appeal to the masses, and, once built, their very size forced them to cater more and more to the general public. The amusement business acted on the principle of volume production at a low cost. When the first Park Theatre opened at the close of the eighteenth century, admission prices were $2.00 in the boxes, $1.50 in the pit, and $1.00 in the gallery. Before the second Park closed its doors fifty years later, these prices had been reduced to 75 cents, 50 cents, and 37½ cents. The more general scale in the 1840's was a 50-cent top and gallery seats for 12½ cents.[10]

Under these conditions the theatre could not in any sense constitute the comparatively select entertainment it had been in colonial days and has subsequently become again through the growth of other forms of commercial amusement. It was taken over by "our sovereigns"—as the conservatives now fearfully designated those whom they had formerly complacently dismissed as "the people of no importance"—in a spirit of militant democracy. Writing of the theatres even in conservative Philadelphia, an English traveler pointedly observed that they were "not much frequented by the more opulent and intelligent classes, but sustained by the middle and humbler ranks." [11] Society might remain ensconced in the boxes, where "elegant and well-dressed females" could look disdainfully down on the crowd below, but it was the common man who ruled the show. At Mitchell's Olympic in New York the pit was exclusively reserved every Saturday afternoon for newsboys and butcher-boys. [12]

The theatre's democratic appeal is further illustrated by the popular interest shown in favorite actors, especially by the excitement occasioned when some player offended the public. The most sensational instance of this was the famous Astor Place riot in 1849, which grew out of the bitter feud between Charles Macready, the English tragedian, and Edwin Forrest, favorite of the American stage. The populace translated a professional quarrel in terms of English aristocracy versus American democracy, rallying to Forrest's defense in behalf of their "almighty independence." New York was plastered with posters calling upon workingmen to decide the issue: "We advocate no violence, but lawful rights." Influenced by such appeals, a Bowery mob stormed the theatre where Macready was playing; the troops were called out to restore order, and before the affair ended, twenty-two persons had been killed and a large number wounded. [13]

The size of the buildings and the character of the audiences combined to make the early nineteenth-century theatre a somewhat appalling place according to modern standards. It had few of the comforts to which the polite audiences of to-day are accustomed. Women stayed away quite as much on these grounds as from moral prejudice. Nor could one always be certain that the performance would be allowed to proceed in peace. Although Astor Place riots might be exceptional, special police had always to be on hand to preserve order. Theatre-going a century ago had about it certain adventurous aspects which are now lost.

The cold was a great discomfort in winter. Wood-burning stoves in foyers could not adequately heat such huge, barnlike structures, and though box-holders still brought their own char-coal foot-warmers and the entire audience kept on coats and hats, there was no really satisfactory way of keeping comfort-able. The audience slowly congealed, and the actors almost literally froze. The various lighting systems were also a hazard. Candles dripped and sputtered; oil lamps hung in immense chan-deliers smoked unmercifully; and when gas-lights were intro-duced, it was long before they became anywhere nearly satisfac-tory. Curtains and scenery were constantly catching on fire, and theatres burned down with distressing regularity—thirty-three were wholly or partially destroyed by fire, including the Park and the Chestnut Street, between 1798 and 1852. The old Bowery burned down no less than four times in seventeen years. The worst conflagration of the period was the burning of the theatre in Richmond, Virginia, in 1811 with the loss of some seventy lives—a catastrophe interpreted by the pious as a judgment of God.[14]

There were no really comfortable seats anywhere in the house. The boxes were "like pens for beasts," reads a contemporary description of the Park.[15] The benches with which they were fitted were no more than scantily upholstered boards with nar-row, shoulder-high backs, and they were so closely crowded to-gether that their occupants could hardly move. Mrs. Trollope has a lively description of the gentlemen trying to get comfort-able. Their postures were "perfectly indescribable," she wrote; and then added somewhat cryptically, "heels higher than the head, the entire rear of the person presented to the audience." It was also this observant visitor who noted a lady in a box at the Chatham in New York, "performing the most maternal office possible." [16]

The pit was far worse than the boxes, with its backless benches set in serried rows on the rough, unswept floor. Women were not generally allowed in this section. What is now considered the choice part of the theatre would be crowded with a conglomerate mass of men who left on their hats, took off their coats, and made themselves at home with complete disregard of the more polite amenities. The habit of standing on the benches and spitting into the boxes or on the stage was deprecated, a writer in the *New York Herald* satirically approving the custom at Niblo's, where a gentleman could place his hat on the floor and have it serve "as a spittoon for three men behind him, who ingeniously spit over each other's shoulders." [17] The audience moved about freely, there was a constant cracking and crunching of peanuts, and a rank odor of onions and whisky rose like a miasmic cloud. "The place was pervaded by evil smells," the description of the Park states, "and not uncommonly in the midst of a performance, rats ran out of the holes in the floor and across into the orchestra." [18]

The top gallery was shared by toughs, Negroes, and prostitutes. Their sections were railed off, and to add to the congeniality of the surroundings there was usually an adjacent bar. Approval or disapproval of the play was most vociferously expressed in these upper reaches of the theatre. In his letters to the *Morning Chronicle* at the opening of the century, Washington Irving commented feelingly on the gallery barrage of apples, nuts, and gingerbread, and its continual stamping, roaring, hissing, and whistling.[19] The police kept what order they could, but in the more popular houses it was a difficult task—especially when some insulted actor broke off his lines to step to the front of the stage and tell "the dirty blackguards" just what he thought of them.[20]

Conditions in what was commonly called the "third tier" were in part responsible for the continued opposition of church-goers to the stage. They were no less condemned by the better managers. William Dunlap—actor, manager, playwright, historian— vehemently protested when the Federal Street Theatre in Boston allotted this special section of the theatre to "the unfortunate females," as he gallantly characterized them, "who have been the victims of seduction." [21] With almost puritan restraint Noah Miller Ludlow strictly barred both liquor and prostitutes from

A Society Audience at the Park Theatre, New York

Water-color by John Searle, November, 1822. Courtesy of the New York Historical Society.

Scenes from "Uncle Tom's Cabin"

Lithographed poster with manuscript alterations. Courtesy of the New York Historical Society.

his theatre in St. Louis.[22] Edmund Simpson made the same experiment in New York but lost so considerable a part of his
clientele that he had to restore to the third tier its privileges.

The newspapers often took occasion to condemn these customs, but their disapproval was aimed at the ladies' display of
"their meretricious attractions, before the very faces of the chaste
part of the audience," rather than at their presence in the theatre.
In an editorial on September 19, 1838, the *New York Herald*
reported that eighty-three of "the most profligate and abandoned
women that ever disgraced humanity" had been freely mingling
the night before with the virtuous and respectable at the Park.
It urged the citizens of New York not to take their wives and
daughters to this theatre. It was a disgrace to society. The management could hope to win back popular favor only "by con-
structing a separate entrance for the abandoned of the sex." [23]

In the smaller towns, conditions differed very markedly from
those in the large cities. Their theatres could not expect patronage comparable to that in the more sophisticated urban communities, and circumstances often compelled the staging of
performances with crude, makeshift scenery which made heroic
demands upon the ingenuity and imagination of both cast and
audience. An old warehouse or barn might be temporarily converted into a theatre by the erection of a stage, installation of
some benches, and provision of a few makeshift properties and
an improvised curtain. Often a shop or a tavern dining-room
served even more informally for strolling players. Joseph Jefferson, barnstorming through Illinois in its pioneer days, described
one performance in an old barn where moonlight and candles
provided a dramatic atmosphere for the production of *The
Spectre Bridegroom.* Another time his company built its own
theatre—a shaky structure with "the appearance of a large dry-
goods box with a roof." A young lawyer named Abraham Lincoln
defended the players on this occasion against the town's attempt
to impose an exorbitant license fee.[24]

Traveling players on the western circuit experienced one of

their greatest difficulties in finding the supers necessary for a chorus. Ludlow tells of an early performance of Sheridan's *Pizarro* before an audience of four hundred keel-boat men and foundry workers in Pittsburgh at which the ceremony of the Virgins of the Sun presented an acute problem. Pittsburgh offered no virgins—Ludlow carefully explains that of course he means theatrical virgins—and it finally became necessary to fall back on an old Irish cleaning woman and the property man. They came on the stage draped in cotton gowns and gauze veils, and they were doing very well indeed until a piteous groan came from the audience, "Oh! what virgins!" There was an immediate outburst. The play could not go on until the manager stepped to the front of the stage and rebuked the audience for insulting actors who had come so many miles to entertain them.[25]

Further brilliant inspiration in providing supers is related by Sol Smith, another pioneer of the western circuit who formed a partnership with Ludlow. Again it was *Pizarro*, and twenty-four Creek Indians were engaged to play the parts of the Peruvian soldiery. They were given 50 cents apiece and a glass of whisky —unfortunately, paid in advance. When their cue was given, the Indians broke into a war-dance with the greatest enthusiasm. As they leapt about the stage brandishing tomahawks and yelling at the top of their voices, the frightened virgins of the cast fled precipitantly to their dressing-room. The Indians had driven every one off the stage and demolished the Temple of the Sun before they could be quieted down.[26]

→»)«←

EXCEPT in a few of the houses in the larger cities, the stock companies making up the American theatre were for the most part composed of casual collections of actors and actresses whose histrionic deficiencies appear to have been monumental. They seldom knew their parts completely, although the frequent changes of plays and scant rehearsals provided some excuse for this; they were as apt as not to disregard all stage business; and in keeping with a memorable tradition of the dramatic profession they often came on quite drunk. The diverting journal of Harry Watkins, a strolling player of the 1850's, reports that after reading his part over three or four times, he often went on stage knowing as much as any one in the cast. Another journal entry speaks of "winging a part," or going on in complete ignorance of it. Drunkenness often led to dramatic quarrels. There was the occasion in Louisville, also related by Watkins, when the leading lady chased one of the actors off the stage with a spear. When he tried to return, she renewed the attack with a screw-driver, dramatically screaming, "You son of a bitch, die!" [27]

The theatre was really sustained by a handful of stars who played engagements of varying lengths in the eastern cities and then took to the road. They completely dominated the stage. Often there was barely time for a rehearsal with the local stock companies which supported them, and the star went blithely ahead almost regardless of other members of the cast. "I'm not much of a judge," commented one member of a Philadelphia audience at a performance of *King Lear* by James Wallack, "but I should think he was a damned fine actor for he played this piece all by himself." [28]

In the first decades of the century these stars were primarily English actors: George Frederick Cooke, Edmund Kean, the elder Charles Mathews, Charles Kemble and the delightful Fanny Kemble, William Charles Macready, and Junius Brutus Booth. Only very slowly did American actors begin to rival them. But by mid-century native talent had won enthusiastic recognition. The melodramatic genius of Edwin Forrest made him the country's foremost tragedian, James H. Hackett swung into popular favor with his comic Yankee rôles, and the American-born Edwin Booth was starting on his memorable career. The entire country was immensely proud of Charlotte Cushman, an actress whose emotional power carried her to dramatic heights unscaled by her contemporaries. There were others: Henry Placide, John Gilbert, E. L. Davenport, William Warren, Jr., James E. Murdoch, the young Joseph Jefferson. . . . A theatrical tradition was being firmly established.

The temperamental eccentricities of many of the stars, their arrogance, their frequent drinking, their disregard of conventions, clothed them with a fatal fascination for the theatre-going public. But these habits also brought down on their heads the horrified attacks of all custodians of public morals. The stars gave the theatre its artistic standing, but they also made far more difficult the slow process of winning approval for the theatre in the country at large.

Cooke was an unregenerate drunkard; Kean was involved in scandals which finally led to his being hissed off the stage; the records of Forrest's unsavory divorce case were spread over the pages of the country's newspapers; and the drunken brawls of Junius Brutus Booth, the preludes to his repeated fits of insanity, won him nationwide notoriety.

Booth's managers were at times compelled to resort to every possible stratagem to get him on the stage in a reasonably sober condition. They would take him out for long carriage drives just before a performance, lock him in his hotel room, or dose him with vinegar. When he escaped their vigilance, there was no telling what might happen. Sometimes he would stagger through his part, his voice hardly audible; at other times he would give a brilliant performance which would bring down the house. On one occasion he could not be found. A thorough search of the city's bars finally led to his discovery, very drunk, a good half-hour after the curtain should have gone up. The audience was going wild. Booth rushed on the stage, shaking an infuriated fist at the galleries. "Shut up!" he yelled. "You shut up out there and in ten minutes I'll give you the god-damnedest King Lear you ever saw in your life!" The story is that he did, and a delighted audience was with him from his opening line.[29]

The plays necessarily conformed to the taste of a democratic audience. Shakespeare was the favorite vehicle of the stars—they would condescend to play few other parts—and the theatre-going public appears to have hugely enjoyed the dramatic and fervid oratory, "the rant and cant," which marked their acting of the great tragedies. It was an age of oratory, of theatricalism. The actors were the rivals of Clay, Calhoun, and Webster, and they had to outdo them at their own trade. It must have been an experience to see and hear Forrest as King Lear. "Played it, Sir? Played it?" this redoubtable actor exclaimed when complimented on how he had acted the rôle. "By God, I *am* King Lear." [30] But while Shakespeare was a great drawing-card among all classes, the public demanded above all else change and variety. Programs were shifted so frequently, and so many different plays were given, that when an entire season's repertoire is considered, Shakespearean drama did not actually fill a very large place.

A single theatre might present more than a hundred different plays in one season (the St. Louis theatre gave no less than one hundred and fifty-seven in the season of 1839), and few of them would have as many as three or four performances. The bill changed almost every night. Under such circumstances sixty-five performances of Shakespeare in Philadelphia's three theatres during the season of 1835 far exceeded performances of plays by any other single dramatist. Eighty-three productions of *Richard III* over an eight-year period made it the most frequently presented of all dramas. When Forrest actually played *Macbeth* for twenty consecutive nights at a New York theatre in 1853, he set up a phenomenal record.[31]

The public enjoyed the stars in these rôles, but the domination of the individual actor is responsible for the overemphasis always placed on the Shakespearean tradition. The more general run of plays provides a clearer indication of popular taste. Hundreds of thoroughly second-rate comedies, farces, and melodramas, now happily forgotten, innumerable musical shows, extravaganzas, and burlesques, were the theatre's real stock in trade. There were plays hastily adapted from novel or story, crudely concocted by managers or actors for a single perform-

ance. Watkins tells of writing a five-act drama in eight days—
"the last two days I suffered a great deal of pain." [32]

Even when Shakespeare was presented, the principal play did
not stand alone. Other entertainment was interpolated between
the acts—specialty dances, popular music, jugglers, acrobats, or
even trained animals. And the whole performance invariably
concluded with a farce. As the Prince of Denmark wandered off
the stage, the clown came on; the echo of Othello's threats was
a comic song; and Lady Macbeth washed her frenzied hands
only to provide the cue for a French danseuse. When the Hallams had invaded New England almost a century earlier, their
Shakespearean performance had concluded at ten-thirty so that
"every spectator may go home at a sober hour, and reflect upon
what he has seen." Not so these audiences of the new democracy. They did not want to be kept awake pondering over Hamlet's soliloquies or Desdemona's wrongs. They couldn't take their
Shakespeare straight; they demanded a chaser.

Booth played *Hamlet* at the Boston Museum in a program also
including Miss Avila and Master Phillipa in a Pas Hongrois and
the new farce *Village Gossip*. A performance of *Much Ado about
Nothing* with Clare Fisher was followed by a musical farce in
which the leading lady returned to sing "Oh! Brave Rub a Dub."
Romeo and Juliet, with a comic clog-dance as an entr'acte, was
followed on occasion by the double bill of *Oh! Hush* and *The
Good Looking Fellow*. A performance of *Richelieu* with Edwin
Forrest was enlivened by a "grand pas de deux" and a "national
descriptive melange" between acts, the performance then closing
with *The Double Bedded Room*.[33] The early nineteenth-century
audience got its full money's worth at the theatre—a good fifty
cents' worth of lively entertainment. The program of main
feature, several shorts, and a comedy pointed the way to the
modern movie program. So did the occasional double feature.
The theatre of the 1840's reached out to very much the same type
of audience.

Apart from Shakespeare, few of the plays constituting the theatre's principal offerings have survived even in memory. They were largely English in origin, or adapted from the German of such a popular playwright as Kotzebue. American dramas were a long time in coming, and those written in this period hardly deserved to last. For the excellent plays with which the colonial theatre had supplemented Shakespeare, there was substituted a miscellany of largely worthless trash. *The Lady of Lyons* and *Richelieu,* both by Bulwer-Lytton, were popular; Sheridan Knowles' *The Hunchback* was a favorite; and a number of plays specially written for Forrest—*The Gladiator* and *Metamora, The Last of the Wamponoags*—had a wide vogue. Mrs. Anna Cora Mowatt struck a new note with her comedy of manners *Fashion;* Dion Boucicault started the long list of his popular dramas with *London Assurance,* and in mid-century came *Our American Cousin,* which Lincoln was seeing on the fatal night of his assassination. Even more typical of this day were such plays as the historical romance *The Green Mountain Boys of 1776;* the French adaptation *Adeline, or The Victim of Seduction;* the old farce of *High Life below Stairs;* and the exciting melodrama *Nick of the Woods:*

> Hold, murdering villain! Richard Braxley, forbear!
> Now, Rowland Forester, I defy thee!
> Monster, hold. . . .
> Behold thy promised bride. Consent to make her mine or down yon boiling cataract I'll hurl her to destruction. . . .

Shakespeare's greatest rival, however, was probably John Baldwin Buckingstone, the prolific author (one hundred and fifty plays) of *The Pet of the Petticoats* and *A Kiss in the Dark.*

No one of these plays ever had a run comparable to those achieved to-day by scores of modern productions. It was *The Drunkard, or The Fallen Saved,* with a record of some one hundred and thirty performances at the Boston Museum in 1844, that inaugurated the more modern custom of an unchanging bill over any considerable period.[34] Its highly moral treatment of the universal topic of temperance (Watkins almost killed himself with his realistic interpretation of delirium tremens), made a tremendous appeal to those pious elements of society who usually condemned the theatre as a subversive influence undermining morals.

Even more important in winning new converts to the theatre, a landmark in the gradual breaking down of religious prejudice against the stage, was *Uncle Tom's Cabin*. Its dramatic version —its many dramatic versions—toured the country with phenomenal success in the 1850's. Performances were given by troupes of Tommers in villages and hamlets where a play had never before been seen. Its exploitation of antislavery sentiment brought thousands of persons to the theatre who justified their attendance by devotion to what the *Herald*, assailing the play as a firebrand, called the "pestilent principles of abolitionism." [35] After the Civil War there was a revival of *Uncle Tom's Cabin*. It became a classic of the stage, performed more times than any other American play; and Uncle Tom, Little Eva, Simon Legree, became a part of our national folklore.

→»><«←

As THE CENTURY advanced and theatre audiences became more and more plebeian, various specialty performances with an even wider popular appeal increasingly overshadowed serious drama. The hodgepodge of entertainment in which acrobatic acts and farces lightened Shakespearean tragedy gave way to a new differentiation in programs. The legitimate stage and wholly popular entertainment were at last divorced. There was a franker appeal to "the blood and thunder taste of the lower half million" by producers whose sole goal was to chalk up large box-office receipts.

One such type of performance coming down from an early day was the equestrian drama. It was soon to merge with traveling menageries and country road shows to form the modern circus, but throughout the first half of the century there were

many heroic spectacles in which troops of horses clattered noisily
on and off stage at even the most aristocratic houses. The great
size of the stage made this easily possible, and there was continuous rivalry among the managers in presenting more and
more elaborate spectacles. They crowded the background with
precipices, waterfalls, forest groves, lakes, terraces, palaces, and
castle walls. The scenery was always advertised as being of the
most gorgeous description, the dresses extraordinarily costly,
and the stage machinery the most complicated and expensive yet
devised.

Consider the stage directions of the prologue of *Putnam, or
The Iron Son of '76:*

The Vision

*Slow music. Three quarters dark. Ethereal firmament filled with
silver stars. Eagle flying in the air, to ascend, looking down upon a
lion couchant, on trap to descend. The goddesses discovered in various groups bearing blue wands with silver stars. God of War on small
Roman chariot, to descend. Goddess of Liberty on trap in small Roman
chariot, to descend.*

In the more serious business of the play, Putnam is continually
dashing about the stage on horseback, guns and drums keeping
up a terrific uproar in the wings. Finally he leaps a gate, falls
on the stage covered with blood:

CLARA. Dear Uncle, you are wounded!
PUTNAM. A mere flea bite! Arm boys, arm; the white skins and red
    skins are upon us! The war kettle boils! Three cheers, and upon
    them! [36]

In 1803 the grand pantomime of *La Fille Hussar* was performed in New York with real horses—"never before attempted
in America." A few years later Philadelphia went wild over
Timour the Tartar, an exciting drama in which the heroine,
mounted on her splendid white charger, "ran up the stupendous
cataract to the very height of the stage." During the depression
year of 1837 the immensely popular *Mazeppa, or The Wild*

Horse, was playing to standing-room only in New York with "Mr. Cook's unrivalled stud of horses, amounting to fifty in number." [37]

Even Shakespeare was put on horseback with a neat blending of classic drama and the circus. *Henry IV* was staged as a mammoth spectacle, *Richard III* performed with the principal characters mounted. Toward the close of its long career the Park attempted to remain loyal to its traditions and at the same time profit from a broader appeal by staging what it called a Tribute to Shakespeare. Neither Forrest nor Macready nor Booth was the star attraction, but the famous southern equestrian C. J. Rogers, assisted by twenty-one riders in correct and superb costumes. To the delight of his audience Mr. Rogers impersonated on horseback, among a number of other less distinguished horsemen, both Falstaff and Shylock.[38]

Quite a different and surprisingly popular show was the ballet. The first arrival of a troupe of French dancers in the 1820's caused a sensation. Many contemporary accounts bear witness to the consternation of even veteran theatre-goers. "I was at the first presentation," Achille Murat wrote. "The appearance of the dancers in short dresses, created an astonishment I know not how to describe. But at the first pirouette when the short petticoats, with lead at the extremities began to mount and assume a horizontal position, it was quite another matter; the women screamed aloud and the greater part left the theatre; the men remained, for the most part roaring and sobbing with ecstasy, the sole idea which struck them being that of the ridiculous." [39]

Audiences quickly became more sophisticated. Even in Boston the ballet was a great success, a contemporary reporting that "the more outré the dancing, the more applause." When the divine Fanny Elssler arrived in the 1840's, her triumph was a milestone in theatrical history. Her sensational dancing of La Cracovienne and La Tarentule became "all the rage—all the mania—all the talk." "The grace, the beauty, the purity, the hue of innocence and virtue which surrounded the highest and most

MAD.^{LLE} FANNY ELSSLER,

IN

La Tarentule

Pr. 50 cts

Fleetwoods Lithog.

NEW YORK. Published by FIRTH & HALL, No 1 Franklin Sq.

Lithographed cover of a music sheet of 1840. Courtesy of the American
Antiquarian Society.

Wonders of Barnum's Museum

Wood engraving by Waters and Son after a drawing by Edward A. Hall. Courtesy of Harry T. Peters.

classical order of dancing," rhapsodized the *New York Herald,* "was never presented here in so marked and distinct style." [40]

The lamentations of outraged prudes did not stay for a moment her triumphal tour about the country or prevent her from being invited to sit in the chair of the Speaker of the House of Representatives.[41] "The good newspapers rail dreadfully at the bad people who will go to see her," Philip Hone noted in his diary, ". . . but the more they rail the more people won't mind them. Nothing is more ridiculous than these abortive attempts to stem the current of public opinion in relation to the people's amusement." [42]

The 1840's also saw the growth of a new type of burlesque and musical travesty, the forerunners of to-day's topical revues, which delighted both the newsboys at Mitchell's Olympic Theatre and the more fashionable audience at Brougham's Lyceum. Everything was burlesqued: Shakespeare in *Much Ado about a Merchant of Venice,* the dancing of Fanny Elssler in *La Mosquito,* and grand opera in *Lucy Did Lamm Her Moor.* Elaborate extravaganzas were staged, such as *Pocahontas* with its lusty chorus:

> Well roared, indeed, my jolly Tuscaroras
> Most loyal corps, your King encores your chorus.

A revue centered upon the marital customs of the Mormons had an even greater success. The Bowery Amphitheatre made a sensation with *The Revolt of the Harem.* Over the horizon was *The Black Crook* (it was to run at Niblo's for sixteen months when first staged in 1866 and was thereafter revived again and again until the close of the century) and the rage for what were already being called leg shows.[43]

This trend in theatrical entertainment inevitably awoke new opposition to the stage and served in some part to offset the approval it was winning among former foes by the production of such plays as *The Drunkard* and *Uncle Tom's Cabin.* When some of the managers went a step further still and staged a series of *tableaux vivants* in which appeared "living men and women in almost the same state in which Gabriel saw them in the Garden of Eden," the godly were still more convinced that the stage was the Devil's workshop.

Advertisements of the Living Models assured the public that nothing would be shown that could bring a blush to the most chaste cheek, but with this concession to prevailing morals they went unashamedly ahead to stress the "beautiful symmetry" of the artists who would appear in "Psyche Going to the Bath" and "Venus Rising from the Sea." [44] Crowds flocked to the new attractions. The *Tribune* forcefully declared that "the majority go because of depraved taste rather than pure love of art"; the *Herald* stigmatized the audiences as "fashionable old rakes and ineffable scoundrels about town"; [45] but the fact remained that the classes as well as the masses found their senses agreeably titillated. Nothing could better illustrate the curious blend of prudery and prurience which characterized the period.

Finally the police were goaded into action and descended on one of the shows. There ensued a "scene of stirring interest" in the dressing-rooms, again to quote the *Herald*, "where some five or six well formed females were in the act of preparing for the next tableau. In one corner was seen a very fleshly lady dressed as Bacchus, studying her position on a barrel. Another beautifully formed creature, just drawing on her tights for the Greek Slave, and some of the others, were so dreadfully alarmed at the sight of the police with their clubs in hand that they seized up a portion of their garments in order to hide their faces, forgetting their lower extremities, thus making a scene mixed up with the sublime and the ridiculous." [46]

The girls were duly escorted to the police station (where a supper of roast turkey and wine was served to "cheer their souls"), and measures taken to prevent any further performances. Eventually they proved successful. In the *Sunday Mercury* in May, 1848, we find a plaintive correspondent sorrowfully asking what has happened to

Those nice tableaux vivants
Of beautiful young ladies, sans
Both petticoats and pants,
Who, scorning fashion's shifts and whims
Did nightly crowds delight
By showing up their handsome limbs
At fifty cents a sight. . . .[47]

A more important development was the production of variety
shows clearly foreshadowing modern vaudeville. By the middle
of the century every city had playhouses presenting varied programs of specialty acts designed solely for the entertainment of
the democracy. The theatrical advertising columns fairly bristled
with announcements of such performances. At Niblo's a program
featuring the celebrated Ravels, a band of pantomimists, acrobats, and dancers, was even advertised as "French Vaudeville."
Another playhouse was renamed the New Theatre of Mirth and
Variety. Its shows included "Elboleros, Cachuchas, Scotch flings
and Strathspeys," a selection of "the most astonishing feats of
Gymnastics and Contortions ever presented in this country," and
an act billed as "the Flying Cord by the unequalled Mr. Ruggles."
The whole performance, admission from 6¼ to 25 cents, was enlivened with music by the New York Brass Band.[48]

The program at the Franklin Theatre on one occasion included
Chemistry, French plays, Magic, Mesmeric Clairvoyance, beautiful and admired Astronomical Diagrams, and Diaphanous
Tableaux—a selection clearly designed to meet all tastes, including the educational. The popularity of infant prodigies was reflected on the variety stage, a featured act being the Bateman
children, aged six and eleven, who played in *Romeo and Juliet*
and *The Merchant of Venice*. Other shows paid less attention
to the vogue for culture. Ballad-singers, strong men (breaking
eighty-pound stones with their bare fists), burlesque dancers,
and companies of female minstrels were widely advertised. A
new costume suggested for women at this time was responsible
for the Bloomer Troupe, while a mysterious act sandwiched in

between the bloomer girls and the juvenile Shakespeareans was titled "Spirituall Nekings." As the variety theatre worked its way down through the free-and-easy concert-halls, the entertainment became more and more questionable. Free Sunday performances were given at the Melodeon, advertising "prettiest female attendants, best wines and segars and liquors." [49]

-»>»«<-

LEGITIMATE DRAMA was not entirely given up even though the theatres devoted to circus stunts and variety multiplied much faster than the more conservative houses. But mid-century critics gave the impression that it was forever doomed by such unashamed catering to a debased public taste through "senseless, absurd, inconsistent, tinselled, vulgar and immodest spectacles." None of them was more alarmed than the future poet of democracy. "Of all 'low' places," Walt Whitman stormily wrote in the *Brooklyn Eagle* of February 8, 1847, "where vulgarity (not only on the stage, but in front of it) is in the ascendant, and bad taste carries the day with hardly a pleasant point to mitigate its coarseness, the New York theatres—except the Park—may be put down . . . at the top of the heap." [50]

In so far as these attacks were justified, the reason could largely be found in the failure of the better elements of the population to give the theatre decent support. In a day when the stage was "indiscriminately voted immoral, irreligious, and what is much worse, unfashionable," as Philip Hone sharply declared,[51] there was very little the managers could do other than give the general public what it wanted. The survival of the theatre during the hard times that followed the panic of 1837, its success in riding out that financial storm, was largely due to this broadening of its popular appeal. It could not afford to be artistic or too fastidious.

It was really more firmly established, however, than the contemporary critics thought. Looking back upon the age that saw the great acting of Edmund Kean, Edwin Forrest, and Junius

Brutus Booth, of Fanny Kemble and Charlotte Cushman, as well as the equestrian melodrama, living models, and variety shows of the cheaper houses, writers on the theatre now declare that the second quarter of the nineteenth century ushered in a golden era in the history of the American stage.[52]

"Still does the Drama sit with the mob; still is Pegasus yoked with the ox," a contributor to the *Dial* declared in 1860.[53] Entertainment for the democracy was the theatre's primary function at a time when it was the only public diversion, as the *Southern Literary Messenger* stated, to furnish "entertainment to all classes." [54]

chapter 7

Mr. Barnum
Shows the Way

WHILE THE THEATRE CONTINUED TO BROADEN ITS POPULAR appeal, it faced the increasing competition of other forms of commercial entertainment. By the 1850's almost every city had a museum with a jumbled collection of curiosities, dead and alive, and a program of concerts and variety acts which could be seen for twenty-five or fifty cents. At scores of music-halls bands of black-faced comedians broke happily into the "Lucy Long Walk Around" or plaintively sang "Old Black Joe" as a phenomenal rage for minstrelsy swept the land. And into towns and villages from Maine to Georgia, westward to the Mississippi, rolled the red and gold wagons housing the properties of what was to become one of America's great institutions—the circus.

Phineas T. Barnum stands out as the leading figure of this period in amusing the populace. No struggle between dramatic standards and popular taste ever troubled the master showman of them all. He was not one whit interested in art; he was interested in entertainment. He recognized the potential market in the restless urban masses. With uncanny prescience he sensed what they wanted, or could be made to want, and gave it to them. He gave it enthusiastically, generously, lavishly—whether Jenny Lind, the country's pioneer baby show, or his Grand Colossal Museum and Menagerie. Nor did Mr. Barnum ever wait for his public to become bored; he believed in infinite variety. The Feejee mermaid gave way to General Tom Thumb, General Tom Thumb to the Bearded Lady, the Bearded Lady to Campagnolian Bell Ringers. His American Museum took in everything from trained fleas to panoramas of the Holy Land. James Gordon Bennett called him the Napoleon of Public Caterers:[1] he always provided a good show, and the eager, unsophisticated, amusement-hungry public of his day loved it.

Barnum represented democracy in public entertainment much as Andrew Jackson had represented it in politics. Government in the interests of the common man, amusements in the interests of the common man. No one did more to promote the leveling influence of popular recreation. The theatre had tried to compromise. It staged its equestrian dramas, its burlesques, its extravaganzas, but it was always trying to get back to Shakespeare, looking a little down its nose at the raucous taste of the lower half-million. Mr. Barnum was out to take the lower half-million into camp, and he succeeded because his methods were direct and simple. The democratic masses followed his lead as docilely as the Irish visitors at his Museum followed the sign "to the Egress"—and found themselves in the street. For though sometimes he outrageously fooled his public, put over elaborate hoaxes, they enjoyed it hugely.

It was all highly educational and strictly moral—the exhibitions in his museum, the strange curiosities touring the country under his sponsorship, the variety acts staged in his sumptuous lecture-room. When the old lady from Dubuque asked him when the service began, the great showman soberly told her that the congregation were already taking their seats. Spellbound country folk who delighted in his presentations of *The Drunkard* and *Uncle Tom's Cabin* would have been horrified at the suggestion that they had attended the theatre.

This skilful exploitation of the prejudices of his day was one of the secrets of Barnum's success. The gospel of work, the urge for self-education, religious disapproval of amusements, never hampered his activities. The theatre struggled against the spirit of the times. Barnum capitalized it. The "chaste scenic entertainments" of his lecture-room were generously staged for "all those who disapprove of the dissipations, debaucheries, pro-

fanity, vulgarity, and other abominations, which characterize our
modern theatres." [2] Not a thought would be breathed in his
museum, let alone act performed or word uttered, that could
bring a blush to the cheek of modesty. The Puritan in entertainment, Barnum proudly recorded that "even Shakespeare's dramas
were shorn of their objectionable features when placed upon
my stage." [3] He saw sermons in circus elephants and preached
them to the discomfiture of rival managers. No one better understood the temper of the Victorian era.

-->)(<(-

BARNUM's American Museum—it was in New York, but it had its
counterpart in other cities and its features were widely copied—
became a national institution in the 1840's. No out-of-towner ever
missed it; it was the delight of country visitors. They might occasionally have seen giants and dwarfs, jugglers and rope-dancers,
pantomimes and acrobats, but here under one roof was a wealth
of amusements (six hundred thousand curiosities) such as imagination could hardly picture. The visitor bored by the national
portrait gallery could watch the three living serpents of enor-
mous size being given their noonday meal. When he had exhausted the wonders of the model of Niagara Falls (with real
water from the new Croton Reservoir), he could have his fortune
told by the mysterious Madame Rockwell. There were statues of
scriptural characters and waxwork figures depicting the horrors
of intemperance; models of new machines and an anatomical
Venus; an ever-changing selection of panoramas, dioramas, cy-
cloramas, and georamas.[4]

Urban workers and country farmers were not the only visitors.
When a Canadian giant was exhibited, the aristocratic Philip
Hone, one-time mayor, made careful measurements of this
natural phenomenon, reporting in his diary that the 619-pound
monstrosity had ankles three feet five inches around. He went
repeatedly to see General Tom Thumb. Upon the midget's return from his triumphal foreign tour ("kissed by a million pairs

of the sweetest lips in Europe"), Mr. Hone proudly noted that Tom Thumb spoke to him by name.[5]

From the portals of the Museum went out scores of traveling exhibitions which gave Barnum his nation-wide fame. Some of them were authentic, some of them cleverly faked. There was no denying the genuineness of the giants and midgets. Possibly the bearded lady was a border-line case, although her whiskers were guaranteed "to put at a single glance all incredulity at defiance." But there were also Joice Heth, whom Barnum blandly claimed to have been the nurse of George Washington; the notorious Woolly Horse, supposedly captured by John C. Frémont; and in later years the famous white elephants of Siam.[6] Few people really cared whether the elephants owed their color to art rather than nature, even when the whitewash began to fade. No one minded being taken in by the Prince of Humbugs.

When exhibitions began to pall, Barnum experimented with melodrama and variety acts in his sumptuous Lecture Room. He was prepared to stage anything—so long as it was highly moral—and he gradually evolved a program with two and three performances a day which won his show-place still greater popularity. In midsummer of 1843 we find him advertising Chang Fong, the Chinese juggler; the inimitable Winchell, famous for "Droll, quizzical, mirth-provoking impersonations"; a knitting-machine run by a dog; and the Ethiopian Serenaders, with "six performers, each one of whom is a professor of music." [7]

The most spectacular triumph of Barnum's career—more notable than the European tour with General Tom Thumb—was his mid-century presentation of Jenny Lind. The country had never known anything comparable to the excitement evoked by the tour of the Swedish Nightingale. Fanny Kemble had won the heart of America in the 1830's, Fanny Elssler had swept all before her in the 1840's. Jenny Lind became the idol of millions who would not have anything to do with the stage. New York, Boston, Philadelphia, the South and the West, worshiped at her shrine.

"Not a day passes," wrote a contemporary diarist just before her appearance at Castle Garden, "without some article lauding her talents until Jenny Lind is in every mouth; Jenny Lind hats, Jenny Lind coats, cigars, oysters, etc., in short, everything is Jenny Lind. When she arrived on Sunday from England, thousands of people swarmed the wharf eager to glimpse the 'Divine Creature.' Her carriage to the hotel could hardly make its way through the dense crowds. At night she was serenaded, and by day the Irving House was besieged by men, women and children anxious to peek at her." [8]

The newspapers estimated these crowds milling about her hotel at thirty thousand. They reported a street fight growing out of a struggle to recover a peach-stone which she had supposedly dropped from the balcony; the enterprise of a speculator who had secured what was declared to be one of her gloves, charging twenty-five cents to kiss the outside of it, fifty cents the inside. A competition for a Jenny Lind prize song, won by Bayard Taylor, attracted seven hundred and fifty entries. "New York is conquered," the press agreed, "a hostile army or fleet could not effect a conquest so complete." "The excitement is of the hottest temperature," one paper declared. "It is universally conceded that Jenny Lind is the greatest woman, Barnum is the greatest man ... in the world." Tickets for the first concert were auctioned off at $225. Boston showed a supercilious scorn for such emotionalism on the part of New York—and was soon paying $625 for the first ticket at its own auction.[9]

It was inspired showmanship. Barnum knew his public and played upon its emotions with a sure touch. America had not seen Jenny Lind (no more had Barnum before she landed in New York), had not heard her, knew nothing of her. He publicized her beauty, her generosity, her goodness, so eloquently that he made her a heroine whom all America could take to its sentimental heart. The popularity of twentieth-century movie stars can hardly be compared with it. Accounts of Lindomania reaching the staid office of the London *Times* aroused deep con-

First Appearance of Jenny Lind in America

Castle Garden, New York, September 11, 1850. Lithograph by N. Currier.
J. Clarence Davies Collection, Museum of the City of New York.

Jim Crow

Thomas D. Rice on the fifty-seventh night of his sensational success at the American Theatre, New York, November 25, 1833. Contemporary painting in possession of the Museum of the City of New York.

Christy's Minstrels

Lithograph by Sarony and Major after a drawing by N. Sarony, 1847.
J. Clarence Davies Collection, Museum of the City of New York.

cern. If the American people could be so easily swayed by an appeal to their emotions, they would be at the mercy of the first political adventurer who attempted to exploit them.[10]

Accounts of her first appearance at Castle Garden state that seven thousand persons crowded the auditorium, and when Jenny Lind appeared on the stage, demurely dressed in white, the audience rose as one man to greet her with such prolonged cheering, handkerchief-waving, and clapping that it appeared doubtful if the performance could ever get under way. She sang "Casta Diva," Rossini's "I Turchi in Italia," the "Herdsman's Song," and the prize-winning "Greeting to America." Her success could not have been greater. "To Castle Garden," commented the *Tribune's* critic, "is reserved the sublime spectacle of a whole people, as it were, worshiping at the shrine of art. . . . Jenny Lind is evidently most herself and most inspired when she sings most *for all*." [11]

That was the symbol of her triumph. Barnum knew very well what he was about. He was not concerned with Jenny Lind's contribution to American music (although she paved the way for successful tours by many other singers and musicians) or with any other phase of her artistic career. He had sensed the new market for entertainment, a market which took in the masses of citizenry, and he supplied a popular product. He dressed it up in the sort of package that he knew would please American taste, and as he traveled about the country with his prima donna, he lectured alternate nights on temperance.

During her nine months' tour, visiting every major city in the United States, Jenny Lind gave ninety-five concerts. The gross receipts were $712,161, affording Jenny Lind $176,675 and Barnum (including expenses) $535,486.[12] Popular amusement paid; it was becoming big business. Nor did the American people criticize Barnum for his financial success. That he could make money out of offering them entertainment—whatever it was— endeared him even more to them.

→»《←

THE MINSTREL SHOWS which were so popular in the 1840's and 1850's were something far more than an amusing act incorporated in the program of a variety bill or occasionally presented at Barnum's Museum. They were a unique form of entertainment, thoroughly American in their inspiration, whose appeal was universal. The gay, rollicking walk-arounds, the sad, sweet notes of the sentimental ballads, the grotesque exaggerations and tall stories, the incessant cross-fire of shrewd jokes, were so native to the soil that the democracy crowded to hear them. The minstrels won instant popularity in New England, spread throughout the Middle West, and went to California with the gold-rush. Every city had several bands of black-faced comedians. Road companies playing in local halls or under canvas toured back and forth throughout the country. The most eminent in comedy or tragedy toiled with but slight reward, mourned an English actor, while "fantazias upon the bones, or banjo, have called forth the plaudits of admiring thousands." [13]

Minstrelsy made its formal bow before an unsuspecting public when Dan Emmett's "novel, grotesque, original and surpassingly melodious Ethiopian band, entitled the Virginia Minstrels," opened at the Chatham Theatre, in New York, early in 1843.[14] But it had had predecessors. The most popular (for the first black-face performer on the American stage is not known) was the Jim Crow act of the comedian Thomas D. Rice. From the first time it was given (the records variously stating it was at Louisville, Cincinnati, and Pittsburgh about 1829)[15] thunderous applause greeted the shuffling steps danced to the plaintive little song:

> Wheel about, turn about,
> Do jis so,
> An' ebery time I wheel about
> I jump Jim Crow.

It was as popular in New York and Boston as in the cities of the Mississippi Valley; it was a success in London. Joseph Jefferson was introduced to the stage by way of Jim Crow. Rice brought him on, aged four, in a bag and dumped him on the floor:

> Ladies and gentlemen,
> I'd have for you to know,
> I'se got a little darky here
> To jump Jim Crow.[16]

The vogue for this act had prepared the way for the real minstrel shows. Their success, one magazine declared, was "unparalleled by any popular exhibition that has ever been offered in New York." [17] Barnum early jumped aboard the bandwagon with his own Ethiopian Serenaders, but the most famous minstrel band was Christy's. Established at Mechanics Hall in New York in 1846, it gave its "unique and chaste" performance almost nightly for a period of ten years, drawing crowds which were always enthusiastic over the performers' tuneful songs, clever dancing, and engaging humor. At one time there were some ten minstrel shows playing simultaneously in New York; Boston had several companies; and Cincinnati was the minstrelsy center of the West. The Kentucky Minstrels, Bryant's Minstrels, the Nightingale Serenaders, the Washington Utopians, the Sable Brothers, Ordway's Aeolians. . . . Throughout the country—traveling "a world of belated railway trains, steamboat explosions and collisions, and runaway stage horses"—these blackface comedians sang and danced.[18]

From the moment the interlocutor gave his stentorian command, "Gentlemen, be seated," and the end-men, resplendent in gaudy full-dress suits, wide white collars setting off their heavily blackened faces, took their places, happy audiences sank back to revel in a show whose spontaneity removed it far from the artificialities of so much of the contemporary theatre. Mistah Tambo and Mistah Bones spoke the language of the people—for all their exaggerated dialect. Their jokes, timely and topical, were meant to be understood and laughed at by the man in the street. When they sang, it was a song all the world knew and could sing. Delighted audiences stamped and cheered when the minstrels swung into "The Essence of Old Virginnv" or "Old Dan Tucker":

> Old Dan Tucker was a fine old man,
> Washed his face in a frying pan,
> Combed his hair with a wagon wheel,
> Died with the toothache in his heel.

There were many other favorites: "Stop dat Knockin' at My Door," "Dandy Jim of Caroline," "Hard Times Come Again No More," "Big Sunflower," "Root, Hog, or Die":

> I'se de happiest darkee on de top ob de earth,
> I get fat as possum in de time ob de dearth,
> Like pig in a tater patch, dar let me lie,
> Way down in old Virginny, where it's
> Root, hog, or die. . . .[19]

The humor of the old-time minstrel show was rough and ready, although the essentially clean and moral atmosphere of the performance was one of its greatest assets. The jigs and fancy steps danced to tambourine and castanets were lively and amusing. But in its songs, minstrelsy had something genuine and enduring. While everything else about it was ephemeral, its music won a hold which it has never lost. It was for these black-face comedians, these knights of the burnt cork, that Stephen C. Foster wrote "My Old Kentucky Home," "Old Black Joe," "The Old Folks at Home," and "O Susanna." It was as a minstrel-show walk-around that "Dixie," written by Dan Emmett, won its popular vogue. Lincoln heard it at a performance in 1860. "Let's have it again!" he shouted from his box. "Let's have it again!" Within the year Lincoln was President and "Dixie" the battle-song of the Confederacy.[20]

Through its songs the minstrel show has won immortality, but in the form in which the nineteenth century so enjoyed it, it has almost completely faded away. The other types of popular entertainment developing in this period gradually expanded, or took on new shapes, but Mistah Tambo and Mistah Bones are to-day seldom seen. The limitations of minstrelsy were too marked. There was no room for the change and diversification that the public in time demanded. There were no women in the cast. As interest began to decline in the decade after the Civil War, the minstrels drew further and further away from the carefree, homely atmosphere of the plantation life they had tried to depict. It had always been fanciful rather than realistic— who can say to what extent the popular conception of Negro character was framed by minstrelsy, how influential it was in winning northern sympathy for the slave?—but the minstrels of the latter part of the century bore no relation whatsoever to the plantation blacks. When the slender thread that bound their performances to real life was snapped, their shows were doomed.

-->>><<<-

THE CIRCUS was another form of popular entertainment now gradually evolving. It did not spring full-panoplied upon the world, this dazzling combination of animal exhibits, equestrian performances, band music, and crude comedy. Nor was it a revival of those elaborate spectacles, marked by the cruelty of the gladiatorial contest, whereby the rulers of Rome had sought to quell the restlessness of the populace. The American circus, with all its distinctive features, was a native product. It was a combination of the little menageries and bands of itinerant acrobats which had put on their performances at the colonial taverns and the more sophisticated equestrian circuses which had been staged in city amphitheatres (the pit easily converted into a ring) since the close of the eighteenth century. It became primarily a traveling tent show, providing the rural population with an equivalent for the popular theatre and the variety-hall. It was one answer to the need for diversion of country people who found themselves isolated from the multiplying attractions of city life.

Among the traveling animal exhibits early in the century, the most ambitious was that of Hackaliah Bailey, of Somers, New

York. Soon after the War of 1812 he toured New England with
the famous elephant Old Bet. She created a tremendous sensation; everywhere crowds flocked to see her. To avoid giving a
free show en route, Bailey had to travel by night. But learning
that the elephant was coming the farmers lined the road with
huge bonfires, and Old Bet literally traveled in a blaze of glory.
Until she met her tragic end—shot by an irate Maine farmer
whose bigotry could not condone even the exhibition of an elephant—she had a spectacular success.[21]

It inspired other managers of traveling menageries. They
began to make more extensive tours, aided by the slow improvement of roads, and animal exhibits became a feature of village
entertainment. Barn shows were given, with admission usually
12½ cents, at which the farmers gaped wonderingly at strange
apparitions from another world. Contemporary notices tell of one
in Salem, Massachusetts, in 1816 at which a tiger, buffalo, and
dancing dogs were exhibited; of another in Lawrenceville, Pennsylvania, twelve years later with a bear, a wolf, a camel, and a
monkey.[22]

In this same period acrobats also began to join forces to travel
about the country together. These little groups of entertainers
would send a clown ahead to announce their coming with a few
antics on the village green (precursor of the circus parade), and
the performance would be given at night. Not in a tent. A piece
of canvas would be stretched about a small platform, the troupe's
wagons drawn up to serve as box seats at twenty-five cents
apiece; and tight-rope dancer, juggler, or sword-swallower would
go through his fascinating routine on a stage lit by flaring pine
torches.[23]

For long the menageries and the acrobatic troupes maintained
a separate identity. Sometimes they traveled together, the one
staging its performance in the afternoon and the other in the
evening; but there were two distinct shows. Gradually they
began to join forces. The proprietors of the menageries added a
few acrobatic performers; managers of the acrobats included ani-

Barnum Enters the Circus Field

Lithographed poster, about 1840. Courtesy of the American Antiquarian Society.

Circus Day in Chicago

Parade passing the Sherman House at Clark and Randolph Streets, about 1866. Lithograph by Jevene and Almini. Courtesy of the New York Historical Society.

mal exhibits. A more ambitious joint entertainment developed which was usually staged under canvas.

The country about Somers, New York, where Old Bet had had her start, became the headquarters for a number of these new rolling shows. They toured New England, worked their way south where warm weather gave them longer playing seasons, and gradually crept westward toward the frontier. But these pioneers of the circus had to be both enterprising and daring. Traveling conditions were still difficult, and in the rural districts the popular attitude was often severely disapproving. They had to perform miracles in meeting the problem of transportation, and they could combat prejudice only by continually stressing the supposed cultural features of their entertainment. It was long before a circus dared call itself a circus. It clung to the name menagerie which the pious approved, invariably advertising the performance as "a great moral and educational exhibition." It was perhaps from their early association with such shows that James Fisk and Daniel Drew, both circus men in their young days, learned the technique which stood them in such good stead in their later exploitation of a gullible investing public.

By the 1830's some thirty rolling shows were regularly touring the country. Buckley and Wick had eight wagons, forty horses, thirty-five performers, and a tent holding eight hundred people. Soon the Zoölogical Institute advertised forty-seven carriages and wagons, one hundred and twenty matched gray horses, fourteen musicians, and sixty performers. The parade had by now been introduced; the performers came to town to the blare of a brass band. Still it was not the real circus. There was no ring; there were no riding acts.[24]

The final step in the evolution of this institution, its merger with the equestrian shows of urban amphitheatres, took place just before mid-century. The popular appeal of riding and tumbling acts (President Washington had been an impressed spectator at John Bill Ricketts' indoor circus in the 1790's) naturally suggested an addition to the program of the traveling tent shows.[25] The more enterprising managers introduced a ring beneath the big top; the country as well as the city was treated to bareback riding and trick horsemanship. The thrills of equestrianism supplemented the lure of wild animals, and the circus as we know it to-day at last emerged in all its spangled glory.[26]

The Mammoth Circus of Howe and Mabie—"Greatest Establishment of its Kind in the World"—ventured as far west as Chicago in the 1850's, and there faced the unexpected competition of the Grand Olympic Arena and United States Circus. Van Amburg and Company's Menagerie—still advertising itself as "the only moral and instructive exhibition in America"—carried east and west its African ostriches nine feet high, its polar bears, and Hannibal, the world's largest elephant. Dan Rice, King of American Clowns, was earning $1,000 a week with his acrobatic nonsense; the famous Herr Driesbach was nonchalantly having his supper "at a table set in the den of his animals." Finally, in 1856, the Spaulding and Roger's Circus announced it would travel by railroad, nine special cars: "team horses and wagons won't do in this age of steam." [27]

Nothing could have been more democratic than the circus. Traveling what was still pioneer country, Edmund Flagg found the little village of Carkinsville, Illinois, "absolutely reeling under the excitement of the 'Grand Menagerie.' From all points of the compass men, women and children, emerging from the forest, came pouring into the place, some upon horses, some in farm wagons, and troops of others on foot." [28] Seeing a performance at Newport, Belle Brittan wrote: "Everybody went—all classes, ages, colors and conditions. There were as many as five thousand people there, all mixed up with the most democratic indiscrimination—Fifth Avenue belles sitting on narrow boards with their dresses under their arms, alongside of Irish chambermaids and colored persons of all sizes and sexes." [29]

Barnum now entered the circus field. It was not yet the Greatest Show on Earth, only a Grand Colossal Museum and

Menagerie, but nothing in the 1850's could rival it. General Tom Thumb was a first drawing-card; there was choice of all the freaks and curiosities of the American Museum, and a menagerie drawn from the four quarters of the earth. Barnum had chartered a ship, sent abroad for his own animals. It was an epochal day in circus history when his ten elephants, fresh from Ceylon, paraded up Broadway harnessed in pairs to a gilded chariot and amid the cheers of an immense crowd were reviewed by Jenny Lind from the balcony of the Irving House.[30]

chapter 8

The Beginning
of Spectator Sports

THE SAME PEOPLE WHO CROWDED PIT AND GALLERY AT THE country's early theatres, who made up the vast audience so cleverly exploited by Mr. Barnum, were also responsible for the beginnings of what are termed spectator sports. City crowds early developed that habit of watching others perform in the field of sport which has so often given rise to the charge that Americans are a nation of onlookers. It was a complaint more justified a century ago than it is to-day. "Society would drop a man who should run around the Common in five minutes," declared Oliver Wendell Holmes,[1] but thousands flocked to watch some one else run—to witness a horse-race, a boat-race, or a professional foot-race.

The failure of the increasing mass of urban dwellers, of whatever class, to get outdoors themselves did not mean that the American people had lost the Anglo-Saxon love for sports. The rise of cities had broken the traditional pattern of recreational life. Restrictions of time and space, the limitations imposed upon people crowded into small living areas without parks or open spaces, did not permit the familiar games and athletic contests of village life. And organized sports to replace these informal pastimes were a long time in developing, discouraged by those social influences which in every direction were holding up the normal expansion of recreation.

Nevertheless, the commercial amusements whose rise we have traced could not wholly satisfy the needs of men who unconsciously missed the wrestling match, the shooting contest, the foot-race, in which they themselves might have taken part or at

136

least watched their friends and neighbors. Theatrical entertainment did not offer the excitement of competition, of taking sides, of betting; it did not get one out of doors and into the open. A people whose attitude was greatly influenced by the traditions of a pioneering frontier life were restless under city restraints. Until they found the escape-valve of new sports for themselves, they eagerly took up the next best thing. If they could not play or compete, they could at least get the thrill of vicarious participation by cheering on their favorites from a grand stand.

Crowds ranging from twenty to fifty thousand, made up of all members of society, were consequently turning out as early as the 1820's for widely heralded horse-races, for the regattas held at cities along the Atlantic seaboard, and for the grueling five- and ten-mile races of professional runners. The available stands would be packed, the overflow spreading to every point of vantage. A contemporary newspaper reporting on a foot-race in 1835 declared that "it would have required the amphitheatre of Titus to have accommodated all." [2]

The eagerness for such amusements was a striking manifestation of changing times. "Every new attraction gathers its countless throng," an Englishman commented on visiting New York in 1842, "as if the people had no other occupation than sight-seeing, though it is well known that they are among the most constantly occupied and busiest people in the world." [3]

How explain this apparent paradox? The city crowd was composed of many elements quite unknown in that earlier period when virtually the entire population lived in the country. If a majority of all classes were employed in various mercantile and manufacturing pursuits, there were always large numbers unemployed or at least temporarily not working. Periods of depression threw men out of jobs; every city had its influx of immigrants and country boys looking for work which took some time to materialize even under the best conditions; and the seasonal nature of much employment accounted for a good deal of leisure despite the long hours of labor generally prevailing. Also, city life inevitably created a class of ne'er-do-well floaters and professional sport followers who swelled the ranks of the temporarily idle.

All this was new. It gave rise to many problems. These restless crowds, with so few opportunities for healthy recreation, made up the mobs through which democracy often attempted to assert its rights. The rougher elements hung around the bar-rooms. They frequented the so-called sporting-halls where cock-fights were staged, dogs pitted against each other, and "rat worries" held. They supplied the recruits for a sporting fraternity known as "the fancy" (from which the word *fan* is derived), as ready to bet on a yacht-race as on a back-room game of faro or chuck-a-luck. They furnished material for the city's notorious gangs. They populated the underworld. And while commercial sports were a far from adequate answer to problems created by the new conditions of urban life, they were at least better than saloons and pool-rooms for the army of discontented ready for anything that promised to satisfy their thirst for amusement.

In general, the sporting events of the period were professional affairs, put on, like any other form of public amusement, for profit. Proprietors of the resorts beginning to spring up on the outskirts of the new cities and owners of transportation facilities —stage-coaches, ferries, and, later, the railroads—were the pioneer sports promoters. Even before they erected grand stands and collected admission charges, they could make money by bringing large numbers of people together for any sort of race. There were the fares collected for ferry or omnibus service, and the profits from drinks and refreshments. The new sports were promoted much as the tavern sports of an earlier day had been, with the further aid of professional gamblers who would put up money purses for the chance to bet.

Barnum never applied his talents to this field, but he tells of one venture which reveals the indirect profits, entirely apart from possible admission charges, to be made from staging such outdoor performances. Happening to pick up a herd of about fifteen calf buffalo in the summer of 1843, he organized a great buffalo-hunt and western-sports spectacle which was to be held in New Jersey "on the extensive grounds and race course of the Messrs. Stevens, within a few rods of the Hoboken Ferry." It was. widely advertised that no admission would be charged, and in enthusiastic response to such an exceptional opportunity for a free show some twenty-four thousand persons crossed the Hudson to watch the sport. The buffaloes, as it turned out, were sick and frightened; they could hardly be goaded into any action at all. But the twenty-four thousand enjoyed their excursion nevertheless. Profits? "I had engaged all the ferry boats to Hoboken," Barnum wrote in his autobiography, "at a stipulated price, and all the receipts on the day specified were to be mine." [4]

-->>)(((<--

HORSE-RACING, with its traditions going back to early colonial days, was the first of the popular spectator sports. Widely prohibited in the early years of the century, it gradually came back into favor, and city crowds naturally turned to the highly organized meets which replaced the more informal rural races. New courses were established throughout the country, with enlarged grand stands for paying customers. The early impetus for racing had largely come from the desire of breeders to improve their stock, but a broader popular interest caused *The Spirit of the Times,* the most important journal devoted to the sport, to declare in mid-century that racing was now mainly, if not exclusively, intended for the public amusement.[5]

Every one went to the races, from the President (John Quincy Adams as well as Andrew Jackson) to newsboys. There was the gambling fraternity, referred to by *Frank Leslie's Illustrated Newspaper* as "this racing world—this huge agglomeration of gambling and fraud, of weakness and wickedness"; the fashionable race-track followers— "galaxies of beauty and booty"; and in addition thousands of everyday working people. The more straitlaced could never countenance racing: it was damned forever by the betting. But at the new Fashion Course things were so well managed that *Leslie's* stated in 1856 "that families can visit the races with propriety and have no fear of their sensibilities being shocked by improper exhibitions." [6]

The crowds that attended the Union Course on Long Island were the largest at any track. A series of North-South matches held there aroused a nation-wide excitement which drew visitors from all over the country. In 1823 a crowd variously estimated at from fifty to one hundred thousand, including some twenty thousand out-of-town visitors, turned out to see the famous race between Eclipse and Sir Henry which has come down in sporting annals as one of the great events of the century. It was for a purse of $20,000 a side, to be decided by two out of three four-mile heats. When the northern horse, Eclipse, won the final heat, the huge crowd went wild. "The air was now rent with shouts of extacy from the New Yorkers, and the press around the judges' stand for a short time was so great that nothing could overcome it." [7]

Later races drew almost as many spectators. When Fashion and Peytona met in 1845, a wide-eyed reporter from the *Herald* (which brought out extras between the heats) informed his paper that fifty thousand persons had crossed the East River by noon, while the roads were still so densely packed with omnibuses and hacks that many of the spectators would never get near the course.[8] Another time transportation facilities appear to have been even more seriously overtaxed. "The tens of thousands of the sovereign people who wished to see this race," a spectator wrote, "made their arrangements to go by railroad from the South Ferry, but the numbers were so great that the locomotives refused to draw. They balked and would not go ahead; the mob who had provided themselves with tickets, finding it was 'no go' became riotous, upset the cars, placed obstructions in the rails, and induced all sorts of violence." [9]

Racing flourished in all parts of the country except New England. The South and West were great centers for the sport.

Peytona and Fashion's Great Match

For $20,000, Union Course, Long Island, May 13, 1845, Peytona of Alabama winning in two four-mile heats. Lithograph by H. R. Robinson after a drawing by C. Severin. Courtesy of Harry T. Peters.

Lady Suffolk and O'Blennis

"The Old Gray Mare of Long Island" at St. Louis, 1851, in her nineteenth year still doing the mile in 2:33 to sulky. Painting by R. S. Hillman in the collection of Harry T. Peters.

And if the best-known courses after those of New York were at Washington, Louisville, Cincinnati, and New Orleans, other widely scattered tracks held race meets which became a distinctive feature of community life. Those at Nashville, Tennessee, drew immense crowds from all the western country. When Andrew Jackson's Truxton beat out Captain Joseph Erwin's Ploughboy, the future President declared there was on hand "the largest concourse of people I ever saw assembled, unless in an army." [10] The races of even the small towns beyond the Mississippi were drawing considerable crowds by the 1850's. The Wichita *Eagle* reported one at which over a thousand men were present—"besides some five carriage loads of soiled doves." [11]

Even more popular than running races was the distinctively American sport of trotting matches. In addition to their place on the schedules of all regular tracks, they had become by mid-century almost the most important feature of country fairs. Even New England welcomed this sport. At a trotting carnival and horse show held in Massachusetts in 1856 there was a daily attendance of thirty thousand, including "the very cream of the Boston population." [12] Thousands upon thousands who cared not a whit for running horses were eager spectators. Among others, such famous trotters of the period as Tacona, Lady Suffolk, and Flora Temple were known the length and breadth of the land; the most famous of sulky-drivers, Hiram Woodruff, was a national hero. As the record for the mile was progressively lowered to under 2:20 minutes, an English expert simply refused to believe it had been done. "I apprehend no horse ever did, or could trot over the measured English mile in that short space of time," he scornfully wrote. "From the extensive rapidity of his trot his feet would be apt to strike fire and set him ablaze." [13]

->>>«<-

Rowing and sailing regattas had a very unusual place in the life of the times. While many of the boat-races were for sweepstakes and involved heavy betting on the merits of the rival craft as well as rival crews, amateur contests brought out tremendous crowds which found them a thrilling spectacle. Members of the clubs that staged these events were of the wealthy class. The Castle Garden Amateur Boat Club Association was restricted, in the 1830's and 1840's, to "young men of the highest respectability, who were determined to combine with pleasure the utmost propriety of conduct." [14] Membership in the yacht clubs even more inevitably meant social position. But tradespeople and mechanics who could never expect to pull an oar in a racing-barge or hold the tiller of a sailing-yacht were perfectly free to watch their regattas. A race in Boston, calling out eighty-odd entries; a match between two lap-streak gigs from among Philadelphia's forty rowing clubs; the races of oarsmen in Baltimore, Charleston, New Orleans; a long-heralded contest between one of New York's eight-oared barges and a boat from St. John's, Newfoundland—all these events meant crowded water-fronts.[15]

In 1824 a boat-race in New York harbor for a $1,000 purse attracted a throng estimated by the *Evening Post* at fifty thousand. The victory of the winning *Whitehall* boat was acclaimed as a baseball world's championship might have been a century later, its crew appearing at the Park Theatre to receive a tremendous ovation.[16] Some years later a regatta of the New York Yacht Club, which was organized in 1844, found the harbor filled with excursion steamers and other craft, all with "densely packed masses of pleasure seekers," while the piers of lower New York, Jersey City, and Staten Island were crowded with "multitudinous and vociferous citizens." [17] In mid-century the fever spread to inland cities—Chicago, Pittsburgh, St. Louis— and regattas at such widely separated points as Portland, Maine, and Milwaukee, Wisconsin, were watched by twenty thousand to thirty-five thousand spectators.[18]

"The beauty and the fashion of the city were there," reads the description of a regatta at Louisville on July 4, 1839; "ladies and gentlemen, loafers and laborers, white folks and 'niggers,' steam-

boat cooks, scullions, cabin boys, mates, passengers, and captains, and all the paraphernalia of a city life on an Independence
Day, formed the constituent parts of the heterogeneous mass that
stood jammed and crowded upon the levee." [19] And that same
year a spectator at the annual regatta at Newburgh, New York,
wrote of how "the innumerable windows of the Warehouses and
Factories were crowded with ladies . . . every piazza and house-
top was stirring with animated beauty—the locks and steamboats,
and the rigging of sloops and schooners, were all crowded with an
indescribable mass of men, women and children of all ranks
and all ages." [20]

->>><<<-

THE FOOT-RACES were wholly professional events, and the runners
of the day (*pedestrians* as they were called) had large numbers
of followers who gambled heavily on their prowess. The races
were at first run through city streets, men on horseback riding
ahead to open lanes through the dense crowds of onlookers, but
their popularity soon led to their being moved to race-courses
where admission could be charged. Great excitement was aroused
in New York in 1835 by the offer of a $1,000 purse for any man
who could run a ten-mile course in under an hour. "Without
intending it by any means," wrote Philip Hone, "when I arose
this morning I found myself with Robert in the barouche, en-
veloped in clouds of dust . . . on the road to the race course,
jostled by every description of vehicle, conveying every description of people." He thought the total attendance approached
that at the race between Eclipse and Sir Henry, although it was
probably nearer twenty or thirty thousand. When one of the
nine starters completed the course in just under the stipulated
hour, the crowd went wild, while the winner jumped on a horse
and rode triumphantly around the track.[21]

Individual match races, growing out of challenges flying back
and forth among the professional runners, were most common.
"Thomas Wood, of East Cambridge," reads a typical announce-

ment in the new sporting journal, the *New York Clipper,* in 1856, "will run Joe Travis, three or five miles for $250 a side. Man and money ready at Adams Billiard Hall." There were scores of popular champions: Henry Stannard, the man who had run the ten-mile event in under an hour; William Jackson, the American Deer, who was disastrously defeated by the English runner John Barlow; the Welsh Bantam, the Worcester Pet, the Boston Buck, the Bunker Hill Boy.... Each "ped" had his own colors—a gaily hued shirt, and in one case red shoes tipped with blue.[22]

→»)«←

PRIZE-FIGHTING was not really a spectator sport in this period: "We are not yet fashionable enough," *Niles' Weekly Register* commented sarcastically, "for such things in the United States." [23] But despite the brutality which everywhere placed it under official ban, fights surreptitiously staged by "the fancy" were beginning to attract ever-widening notice. The champions were winning a popular following for all the disapproval voiced by the more respectable elements of society.

"The amusement of prize fighting," again to quote Philip Hone, that estimable diarist of so many phases of New York life, "has become one of the most fashionable abominations of our loafer ridden city. Several matches have been made lately. The parties, their backers, betters, and abettors, with thousands and tens of thousands of degraded amateurs of this noble science, conveyed by steamboats chartered for the purpose, have been following the champions to Staten Island, Westchester, and up the North River, out of the jurisdiction (as was supposed) of the authorities of New York; and the horrid details, with all their disgusting technicalities and vulgar slang, have been regularly presented in the *New York Herald* to gratify the vitiated palates of its readers, whilst the orderly citizens have wept for the shame which they could not prevent." [24]

There was no denying the brutality of old-style bare-knuckle fighting. It was as cruel as the gouging match of the frontier,

Boat-Race on the Charles River, Boston
Ballou's Pictorial Drawing-Room Companion, 1857.

A Great Foot-Race at Hoboken
Illustrated London News, 1845.

THE GREAT FIGHT FOR THE CHAMPIONSHIP.

John C. Heenan and Tom Sayers at Farnborough, England, April 17, 1860. Lithograph by Currier and Ives. Courtesy of the New York Public Library.

sometimes quite literally being a fight to the death. A contemporary account tells of one bout in which for almost three hours two bruisers "thumped and battered each other for the gratification of a brutal gang of spectators," until after being knocked down eighty-one times, one of them fell dead in the ring.[25] There was no science in this fighting: a pugilist's greatest asset was his ability to take punishment. With little thought of self-defense, his one object was to pummel the other fellow into unconsciousness.

Police regulations forced secrecy upon the promoters, and actual attendance at the bouts was consequently small. It was not until some time after gloves were substituted for bare fists and the Marquis of Queensberry rules had been adopted that prize-fighting was legally approved. When Yankee Sullivan and Tom Hyer fought their championship bout in 1849, they had to hold it in the woods on Maryland's Western Shore, having been driven away from the chosen site, Peel Island, by a boatload of militia. A few years later the fight in which Hyer lost the championship to John Morrissey was held under equally furtive circumstances, while the latter's successful defense of his title against John C. Heenan, "Benicia Boy," took place before two thousand spectators who had sailed over from Buffalo in three steamers to a point on the Canadian border.[26]

The growing attraction of prize-fighting, with its primitive appeal even for those who were shocked by its brutality, was graphically displayed on the eve of the Civil War in the universal interest aroused by Heenan's challenge of the English champion, Tom Sayers. Although he had not beaten John Morrissey, the latter's retirement from the ring left "Benicia Boy" undisputed champion, and the good wishes of all America followed him to England. His name was on everybody's lips—Concord philosopher and Nevada miner, New York newsboy and Ohio farmer. What were his chances? Could he stand up against Sayers? "Benicia Boy" himself was confident. *Vanity Fair* published his farewell:

I'll wind our colors 'round my loins—
The blue and crimson bars—
And if Tom does not feel the stripes,
I'll make him see the stars! [27]

The country breathlessly awaited the outcome. It was inde-
cisive. Historians of the prize-ring still quarrel over who might
have won if the crowd had not broken up the fight in the forty-
third round. But "Benicia Boy" was the hero of the day. *The
Spirit of the Times,* getting out an extra edition of one hundred
thousand copies with the first report of the fight, hailed him as
the world champion.[28]

Upon his return to this country Heenan began giving boxing
exhibitions. They drew the crowds that prize-fighting itself could
not command because of its illegality. In Boston some twelve
thousand persons turned out to see the champion, while a boxing
festival he staged at Jones Woods, outside of New York, attracted
thirty thousand.[29]

→»«←

THESE spectator sports of the first half of the nineteenth century,
harbingers of the tremendous development of this type of amusement in later years, were at best but a poor substitute for games
or athletic contests in which the spectators themselves might
have actively participated. But again it must be remembered
that city crowds a century ago had no ready means for getting
out into the country—either by street-car or automobile. Our
whole modern organization of sports, together with parks and
public playing-fields, was completely unknown. The idle city
worker who did not spend the afternoon at the race-track, watching a boat-race, or cheering his favorite "ped" was driven to some
indoor amusement. The habit of watching professional athletes
fastened itself upon the city dweller a century ago because he
had almost no other alternative for daytime recreation.

These spectator events nevertheless helped to make possible
the rise of modern organized athletics and the public participa-

tion of later decades. The interest in professional running in the 1840's provided the impetus for the growth of amateur athletic organizations in the 1870's. The crowds drawn to regattas created an ever-widening interest in rowing and sailing. The immense vogue for trotting matches inspired every horse-owner to see if he could not develop a champion; it crowded the roads, town and country, with drivers always ready for a "brush" with friend or neighbor. Even pugilism led in time to the development of boxing as a popular pastime for young men and boys. These activities of a century ago promoted the audience habit, but they also played their part in maintaining an interest in sports for themselves which was soon to have a phenomenal flowering.

chapter 9

Mid-Century

BY MID-CENTURY GREATER WEALTH AND MORE LEISURE MEANT broader opportunities for recreation among the well-to-do. They began to give increasingly elaborate balls and entertainments. When Charles Dickens landed in New York, the great Boz Ball—"the tallest compliment ever paid a little man, the fullest libation ever poured upon the altar of the muses," as Philip Hone described it—was attended by twenty-five hundred persons representing the world of society. The decorations were scenes from *Pickwick Papers,* and *tableaux vivants* were presented of *Nicholas Nickleby, Oliver Twist,* and *The Old Curiosity Shop.* Supper was enlivened with quantities of champagne. It was an occasion typifying a new measure of sumptuous display in American social life.[1]

There was also a growing enthusiasm for yachting, inspired by the memorable victory of the *America* in the first international cup race; an increasing vogue for driving in summer and sleighing in winter; and greater interest in field sports. Game-hunting had always been popular in the South. It had long been commended in Baltimore for drawing the young gentlemen of the town into the open fields "where no man ever contracted dyspepsia, or imbibed an ignoble passion." Wealthy eastern sportsmen—and visiting Englishmen—now went to the Far West to shoot elk and buffalo.[2]

More significant was the beginning of pleasure travel and the growth of summer resorts. New turnpikes and canals, the steamboat and the railroad, were working revolutionary changes in American life which affected recreation as well as business and

148

industry. In 1825 the appearance of a little booklet called "The Fashionable Tour" had signalized the new trend, and Timothy Flint declared that the better classes were carrying their desire for travel "to a passion and a fever." [3] It was soon possible for even the less well-to-do to undertake trips of which an earlier generation would hardly have dreamed. "There is scarcely an individual in so reduced circumstances," marveled one foreign visitor, "as to be unable to afford his 'dollar or so,' to travel a couple of hundred miles from home, in order to see the country and the improvements which are going on." [4]

The establishment of summer resorts came as a direct result of these improved means of transportation, and the fashionable world rapidly made them popular. It flocked to the new watering-places, turning what had been quiet little havens for invalids into bustling social centers. Nahant, near Boston, began to advertise "its sports and fare" for vacation visitors. Newport resumed its rôle of colonial days, attracting a larger and larger summer population until in mid-century the *New York Herald* disagreeably declared that "fashion, handmaid of vice, has set her seal upon the escutcheon of this town." New Jersey offered Cape May and Long Branch. New York had the most fashionable of all resorts of this period in Saratoga Springs, where

> Hotels of vast Extent at length arose,
> In whose capacious bosoms were receiv'd
> Of guests the copious streams, that hither flow'd
> From various regions. . . .[5]

Easterners were naturally in a majority among the visitors at these resorts, but every westerner with social aspirations labored under the necessity of staying for a time at one of them, and the wealthy plantation-owners of the South made a virtual hegira north every summer. Until the bitterness aroused over the slavery issue caused them to stay at home, at some such southern resort as White Sulphur Springs, some fifty thousand southerners were said to visit the northern states annually.[6]

Many of these visitors were not so much seeking rest or amusement as the establishment of their position in the social world. Resort life reflected the confused gropings of society toward a new order, and itself contributed to the decline of former distinctions. The elegant hotels at Saratoga or Newport attracted people who formerly would have vacationed in the country only at exclusive house-parties, and the socially ambitious saw their opportunity. "Hundreds, who, in their own towns could not find admittance into the circles of fashionable society," James Silk Buckingham observed in 1838, "... come to Saratoga where ... they may be seated at the same table, and often side by side, with the first families of the country." [7]

On the deep verandahs of the huge, sprawling Congress House or United States Hotel (accommodations for two thousand), on the neat gravel walks cutting across Saratoga's well-mowed lawns, might be seen "the fairest sample of the better class throughout the United States. ... What bustle, and display, and expense, and frivolity!" [8] The frock-coated Washington politician tipped his tall silk hat to modish ladies in billowing hoopskirts; the smart New Yorker in tight-fitting trousers and flowery waistcoat, inordinately proud of his curled whiskers, bowed to blushing southern belles in beribboned satin bonnets. "All the world is here," marveled Philip Hone on visiting Saratoga in 1839; "politicians and dandies; cabinet ministers and ministers of the gospel; officeholders and office seekers; humbuggers and humbugged; fortune hunters and hunters of woodcock; anxious mothers and lovely daughters; the ruddy cheek mantling with saucy health, and the flickering lamp almost extinguished beneath the rude breath of dissipation." [9]

Flirtation was a major amusement. The Courting Yard was an institution at Saratoga; White Sulphur Springs had its "Billing, Wooing and Cooing Society." There was not much else to do. Cards and backgammon, bowling and billiards were possible, but none of the outdoor sports to-day associated with the summer resort. Exercise was still unfashionable. There was not even

A Yachting Club on Lake Erie

Painting by an unknown artist, about 1870, owned by A. Hyatt Mayor.
Courtesy of the Metropolitan Museum of Art.

The Bathe at Newport

Drawing by Winslow Homer. *Harper's Weekly*, 1858.

the horse-racing of a later day. The gentlemen whiled away long
hours in smoke-filled bar-rooms over their gin slings, sangarees,
sherry cobblers, and mint juleps. The ladies were relegated to the
piazza, or possibly allowed an afternoon carriage drive. Nowhere
were the restraints of the Victorian era, the respect for female
delicacy, more rigidly observed. "Our amusements were simple
and distinctly ladylike," Eliza Ripley recalled of resort life at
Pass Christian, on the Gulf of Mexico. "There was no golf or
tennis, not even the innocent croquet, to tempt the demoiselles to
athletics." [10]

Two French visitors found this life unutterably dull. "People
rise early," Achille Murat wrote of Saratoga, "go and drink,
or make believe drink, of the water at the fountain; return to
breakfast in common; the papas and mamas are ready to die
with ennui all the day; the young ladies play music, the young
gentlemen make love to them; from time to time some excursion
is made in the neighborhood; in the evening comes dancing.
People are very soon tired of this sort of life.[11] Michael Chevalier
even more devastatingly summarized a day's program at Bedford
Springs. He wondered how its visitors could get any possible
satisfaction out "of gaping on a chair in the piazza the whole
day; of going arms in hand (I mean the knife and fork) to secure
their share of a wretched dinner; of being stifled in the crowd of
the ball-room during the evening, and of sleeping, if it is possible,
upon a miserable pallet in a cell echoing one's tread from its
own floor of pine boards." [12]

The evening hop or Saturday-night ball nevertheless made up
for a good deal of the day's deficiencies. The introduction of such
exciting new dances as the waltz and the polka had given the
ball-room a new popularity. Although there was shocked criticism from those who clung to puritanic traditions, the pulpit
holding forth bitterly "against the abomination of permitting a
man who was neither your lover nor your husband to encircle
you with his arms, and slightly press the contour of your waist," [13]
these importations won their way into society. The *New York*

Herald might rave about "the indecency of the polka as danced at Saratoga and Newport. . . . It even outstrips the most disgraceful exhibitions of the lowest haunts of Paris and London," [14] but the floor would be crowded on a Saturday night. The company whirled away the evening in grand style until it settled down to its midnight supper of champagne, ice-cream, and blancmange.

At the shore resorts there was one diversion that such watering-places as Saratoga lacked. This was sea bathing. Occasional references to it may be found in earlier days. A Mr. Bailey planned to institute "bathing machines, and several species of entertainment" at his resort on Long Island in 1794. [15] A few years later a hotel proprietor at Nahant advertised "a machine of peculiar construction for bathing in the open sea." [16] But not until much later were the first daring steps taken toward popularizing it as a sport for mixed company.

An early record of this is found in a description of Long Branch written by James Stuart in 1829. "Because of the swell," wrote the circumspect Mr. Stuart, "females are often afraid to venture into the sea with a female bathing woman, and on that account prefer the assistance of a man. This custom, which is very far from being general, has given rise to ill-founded stories of want of delicacy on the part of American females. The fact is, I believe, exactly as I have stated it, and the parties always go into the water completely dressed." [17]

A few years later a correspondent of *Frank Leslie's Illustrated Newspaper* described the costumes that accounted for Stuart's phrase, "completely dressed." "Some wear Bloomers, buckled nattily about the waists, with cunning little blue-veined feet twinkling in the shallow water," he wrote; "some are wrapped in crimson Turkish dressing gowns, and flounder through the water like long-legged flamingoes; and others in old pantaloons and worn-out jackets." Bathing-suits, it would appear, had not yet been invented, and after lunch there was a gentleman's hour, as our correspondent phrased it, "sans costume." [18]

Prejudice against mixed bathing gave way slowly. But soon visitors to Newport told of parties of ladies and gentlemen dashing out "hand in hand, sometimes forty of them together, into the surf upon the beach." They described with engaging enthusiasm how the men "handed about their pretty partners as if they were dancing water quadrilles." [19] "I do not believe," a writer in the *New York Herald* lyrically reported in 1853, "that Franconi's Hippodrome ever presents a gayer, more grotesque and animated scene than I witnessed. Hundreds of bathers, clad in garments of every shape and color—green, blue, orange and white—were gaily disporting before me, and within a few yards of my window. The blooming girl, the matronized yet blushing maiden, the dignified mamma, were all playing, dancing, romping, and shouting together, as if they were alive with one feeling. I noticed several ladies of admirable shapes. . . . Oh! ye happy waves, what a blissful destiny is yours, when you can enclasp and kiss such lovely forms." [20]

-»>)«<-

IN THE MISSISSIPPI VALLEY the flush times of mid-century were marked by a spirit of boisterous gaiety which held its ground firmly against the pressure of those civilizing influences curbing the old sports and diversions of the frontier.[21] The Great River was an artery for amusements as well as commerce. Palatial steamers made their perilous way back and forth between St. Louis and New Orleans, their passengers gaily dancing on the hurricane-deck and gambling in the saloon; gaudy show-boats— the *Snow Queen* or the *Fanny Elssler*—tied up every night at village landings, with uniformed bands announcing their coming, and traveling entertainers of every kind brought to the river towns dazzling visions of the outside world. Farce and melodrama, musical extravaganza, elaborate minstrel shows, were staged in the gilded concert-saloons. Less ambitious entertainers went from town to town by smaller steamer. Aboard one of them Thackeray saw a bearded lady who in shipboard life delicately concealed her hirsute growth beneath a red silk hand-kerchief.[22]

In the 1850's some two thousand professional gamblers were operating on the river boats.[23] There has always been a great deal of gambling in American life, from colonial lotteries to the present-day policy-game, but never has this major diversion flourished so mightily as in those booming days of the Mississippi Valley. Faro, monte, and chuck-a-luck were the favorite card games. Poker had been introduced by way of New Orleans and was soon to make its way still farther west. For those who wanted to lose their money with even less effort, the steamers had their full quota of three-card monte-throwers, dice-coggers, and thimble-riggers. The Mississippi River travelers do not seem to have ever caught on to the old shell-game.

"They'd just flutter them up like a flock of quail," one traveler wrote of the skilful way the gamblers handled their cards, "and get the aces, kings, queens, jacks and tens all together as easy as pie. A sucker had no more chance against those fellows than a snow-ball in a red-hot oven." [24] But it was not entirely skill. The professional gentlemen of chance freely availed themselves of the wares advertised by a certain Monsieur Grandine: "Advantage and Marked-Back Playing Cards . . . an exact imitation of the fair Playing Cards in use, and are adapted for bluff or poker, Seven-Up, Forty-Five, Euchre, Cribbage, Vingt-et-un, or Twenty-One, Loo. . . ." Monsieur Grandine was also obligingly ready to provide "sleeve machines" which held the cards in a most natural manner and allowed them to slip out perfectly noiselessly.[25]

The gamblers had a well recognized costume—black slouch hat, broadcloth coat, flowing tie, black high-heeled boots, white shirt elegantly frilled and ruffled, gaudy vest, and invariably a large diamond in the shirt-front and a massive gold watch and chain. They were the aristocrats of the river, making fortunes in fleecing the innocent, and then as promptly losing them at faro establishments in New Orleans. One of the best-known of them, George H. Devol, has left in his *Forty Years a Gambler on the*

Mississippi an engaging record of adventures which often involved hasty dives overboard when his victims discovered they had been tricked. Usually he was ready to defend himself. "I was always very stubborn," he admits, "about giving up money if any one wanted to compel me to do it." On one occasion his victim tried to call his bluff: "He took off his coat, and after he got it off he weakened, and picked up a big iron poker that lay by the stove. I pulled out old 'Betsy Jane,' one of the best tarantula pistols in the Southern country...." And so Mr. Devol kept his winnings.

Three-card monte always got them, ministers and all, this hardened soul declared. "I caught a preacher once for all his money, his gold spectacles, and his sermons. Then I had some of those queer feelings come over me ... so I gave him his sermons and specs back." [26]

Away from the river there were other amusements—political rallies, horse-races, dancing assemblies, the theatre, and traveling shows from eastern cities.[27] The local paper of one small Ohio town recorded the visit of Swiss bell-ringers, an exhibition of dissolving views by the aid of a magic lantern, "the inimitable Winchell," a panorama of the Mississippi Valley half a mile long and twelve feet high, "J. H. Green, Reformed Gambler, with card tricks," Joe Ginger's Minstrels, and "Moxon & Kemp's Great Eastern Circus, Five Nations, and a Steam Calliope drawn by forty horses." [28]

The moving panorama, exhibited not only in western towns but in eastern cities, was almost the equivalent of the later-day moving picture. The Mississippi Valley exhibition just noted toured the entire country, was advertised in New York as one of the great attractions of the age, and disappeared from the American scene only when it was taken abroad, to Europe and the Far East, for still further conquests. Many others were widely known: the "Classical Panorama of Roman History," the "Sacred Panorama of Pilgrim's Progress," the "Moving Mirror of the Overland Route to California." The long rolls of painted canvas were slowly unwound before admiring audiences as a lecturer described the background for the scene depicted. In the dioramas these scenes were made to change and dissolve into each other by means of cloth transparencies and complicated overhead lighting effects.[29]

On the sod-house frontier, opening up in Kansas and Nebraska, life was incredibly hard—bitter winters with sweeping snowstorms, summers of searing drought, devastating plagues of locusts, and always the terrible isolation of the prairies. Strongwilled settlers struggled against immense odds to build a familiar life against an unfamiliar background. But they early had their amusements. Lawrence, Kansas, had a bowling-alley within a few months of its being sacked in the free-soil struggle; the *People's Press* of Nebraska City declared a few years later that "the fever is now for billiards."[30] There was a theatre of sorts at Leavenworth in 1858 which welcomed to its boards a minstrel show, the New England Bards, a troupe of saxhorn players, and a circus.

Marked differences, of course, still existed between East and West, between the long-settled communities on the Atlantic seaboard and these rapidly growing states of the Mississippi Valley. But improved means of transportation and closer communications gradually promoted a uniformity in modes and manners which was directly reflected in amusements. Whatever was in vogue in commercial entertainment in New York or Philadelphia eventually made its way west; social life in western cities and towns aped that of eastern cities as much as it could; and as other forms of recreation developed on the seaboard, they were rapidly transferred to the Mississippi Valley and beyond.

⊢≫⋇≪⊣

THE SOCIAL LIFE of the South throughout the first half of the nineteenth century, and until the outbreak of the Civil War, is generally viewed through a haze of romantic glamour. The pattern is all too familiar: gay young couples dancing on the

Sleighing in New York

Lithograph by Nagel and Lewis, composed and lithographed by Theodore
Benecke, 1855. Courtesy of Harry T. Peters.

A Home on the Mississippi

Painting by an unknown artist, about 1850, owned by Mrs. Alice T. McLean. Courtesy of the Metropolitan Museum of Art.

The Turkey Shoot

Painting by Charles Deas, about 1836. Rutherford Stuyvesant Collection Courtesy of the Metropolitan Museum of Art.

colonnaded porches of the "big house" as moonlight floods through the magnolia trees; race meets and fox-hunts; barbecues and oyster suppers; the cool tinkle of mint juleps . . . and carefree, happy slaves singing spirituals as they picked the cotton that made possible this leisured, luxurious way of life.

With what acute nostalgia did Thomas Nelson Page, only one of a host of reminiscent southern writers, look back upon such scenes. Here is a gay picnic, carriages laden with "precious loads of lily-fingered, pink-faced, laughing girls with teeth like pearls and eyes like stars," and gallant riders bursting with southern chivalry "who would have thrown not only their cloaks but their hearts into the mud to keep these dainty feet from being soiled." The social life of Dixie? "It made men noble, gentle and brave, and women tender and pure and true. . . . It has passed from the earth, but it left its benignant influence behind it to sweeten and sustain its children. The ivory palaces have been destroyed, but myrrh, aloes and cassia still breathe amid their dismantled ruins." [31]

It is true that there were a grace and dignity, and at the same time a gay spirit, about life in the ante-bellum South which were swept away in the cataclysm of civil war. The comfortable mode of living and easy acceptance of everything that contributed to amusement had continued over from colonial days on the great plantations. "Leisure and ease are inmates of his roof," one northern visitor wrote of the southern aristocrat. "He takes no note of time. Your Yankee will take time by the forelock, and push business through. But a Southerner never heard of the 'old man with a scythe.'" And he went on to note that under these circumstances, so foreign to the bustling life of the North, recreation played a different rôle. Where life had a more definite pursuit, it was perhaps not so necessary—"but here, where one finds golden leisure, amusements are indispensable." [32]

Other records tell of these amusements. Henry Barnard, a young northerner visiting in a southern family, wrote home enthusiastically of the lavish hospitality at "Shirley," the plantation of Hill Carter on the James River.[33] Susan Dabney Smedes has depicted in glowing colors the life at "Burleigh," in Mississippi, with its music and dancing, charades and cards, riding and driving.[34] Herbert Ravenel Sass recalls the house-parties, the deer-hunts, the chivalric tournaments (costumed knights jousting with their ladies' colors on their sleeves), which enlivened the long, languorous days on South Carolina's rice plantations.[35] For the wealthy planters in all parts of the South, and especially in those states newly carved out of the western wilderness to grow the cotton which brought them such dazzling prosperity, life had a flavor in mid-century known to no other part of the country.

But it concerned only that small group at the apex of the pyramid that made up southern society. It was no more typical of Dixie than the crowded ball-rooms of Saratoga were representative of recreation in the North. What of the great mass of southern yeomanry, small farmers still working their own land? What of the poor whites, that pitiful class of "vagrom-men, idlers, and squatters, useless to themselves and the rest of mankind"? And what of the slaves? The majority of people in the South had little direct contact with the life of the great plantations. Nowhere were class lines drawn more rigidly; nowhere was there a greater gulf between the different strata of society.

The statistics of that "peculiar institution" on which southern life was based rudely shatter many legends. At the close of the ante-bellum period, some three-fourths of the white population had no proprietary interest in slavery whatsoever. They were humble folk, largely engaged in grubbing out a living on their own small farms, in bitter competition with the slave labor they could not themselves command. There were in all only some fifty thousand estates on which there were as many as twenty slaves. The entire planter class totaled but a quarter of a million among the South's eight million white population.[36]

The slaves and the poor whites—it is difficult to say which class should be considered as the lowest order of society—could enjoy only such amusements as their owners or abject poverty permitted them. In the case of the former, conditions greatly varied. They often went out with their masters on moonlight 'possum- and 'coon-hunts; they were among the spectators at horse-races and cock-fights. On many of the plantations they were given free rein on such festive occasions as holidays or weddings to enjoy themselves with music and dancing, with contests in clogging, cakewalks, and Charlestons. "To see a group of them on the floor," wrote an entranced northerner, "or on the lawn, beneath the shade of the China-trees, when

> Hornpipes, jigs, strathspeys and reels
> Put life and mettle in their heels

whirling in the giddy mazes of the dance with their buxom dulcineas, each seeming to vie with the other in dancing the most; it is one of the finest specimens of animated nature I ever gazed upon. . . . No restraint of the etiquettish ball-room . . . whew! They'd burst like steamers. . . . What luxury of motion, what looks—breathing and sighs! what oglings, exclamations and enjoyment! This is *dancing*. It knocks the spangles off your light fantastic tripping, and sends it whirling out of the ball-room." [37]

Sometimes a Baptist revival would induce the Negroes to forswear dancing and music—"I done buss' my fiddle an' my banjo, and done fling 'em away"—but there was no restraining them for very long. God could not blame them for such simple amusements. The Negro preacher explained it in his Christmas prayer:

> Des dance bekase dey's happy—like de birds hop in de trees,
> De pine-top fiddle soundin' to be blowin' ob de breeze. [38]

Wherever the master did not approve, however, there would be no dancing and no banjo-playing in the slave quarters, no time for hunting or fishing. In many instances the slaves were harshly or cruelly treated, deprived of much more than the opportunity to play. That is the other side of the picture of plantation life in old Dixie. But even where they were well taken care of and allowed such amusements as did not interfere with their work, there could be no real freedom for enjoyment. The pleasures of the slave were always wholly dependent on the will of his owner.

The poor whites had the leisure and freedom that the blacks so often lacked, but their leisure was born of complete poverty and unwillingness to work. They were the forgotten men in this thriving Kingdom of Cotton, isolated in the pine-barrens or the back-country mountain areas. The chronic disease that made them so lazy and apathetic, that drove them to become clay-eaters, was not then recognized as hookworm. Fanny Kemble sorrowfully characterized them as "the most degraded race of human beings claiming Anglo-Saxon origin that can be found on the face of the earth." [39] "Even their motions are slow, and their speech is a sickening drawl," wrote D. R. Hundley, a good Alabaman, "... while their thoughts and ideas seem likewise to creep along at a snail's pace. All they seem to care for is to live from hand to mouth; to get drunk ... to shoot for beef; to attend gander pullings; to vote at elections; to eat and sleep; to lounge in the sunshine of a bright summer's day, and to bask in the warmth of a roaring fire, when summer days are over." [40]

Here were amusements, perhaps, but the amusements of idleness and debility. They did not awaken in the dulled minds of the poor whites any zest for living. Among the slum outcasts of the industrial North might be found men and women for whom life offered as little as it did for these unfortunates. But there was this marked difference: the North was slowly awakening to the needs of its depressed classes; the South was blind to the degraded status of the poor whites.

Between the wealthy planter and the Mississippi hillbilly or Florida clay-eater there was an impassable gulf. The self-respecting southern yeoman, sometimes working in the fields side by side with a Negro slave whom he either owned or hired, had at least some opportunity. He might conceivably make his way into the planter class. But in his own life he had little contact with his social superiors. Susan Dabney Smedes recalled that the Christmas egg-nog party that was always given at "Burleigh" for the overseer and "other plain neighbors" was one of the few occasions when plantation life and that of the small farmers overlapped.[41]

For these people, bound to the soil and hard pressed to earn a livelihood, hunting and fishing were still the most universal recreation. They also had their occasional farm festivals—corn-shuckings and cotton-pickings enlivened by persimmon beer or jugs of whisky—and annual country fairs and militia musters. There were horse-races and cock-fights, sometimes a circus or other traveling entertainment. The latter were rare. In the little town of Tarboro, North Carolina, there was but one such show in 1832, and twenty years later only five—three concerts, an exhibition of curiosities, and a circus. Many of the frontier customs lingered on in the back country. Rough sports and heavy drinking vied with the camp-meeting.[42]

One pastime peculiar to this part of the country was gander-pulling. The Dutch settlers in New York had practised this sport, and there was to be a later variation of it on the western prairies, but here it had a much stronger hold among the common people. A well greased gander was strung head down from the overhanging bough of a tree. One by one the contestants, mounted on horseback, would ride full speed under the struggling bird, trying to seize it by its slippery neck as they tore by. The man who made off with the goose's head was declared the winner. A contemporary record describing gander-pulling in North Carolina declares that it was "anticipated with rapture by all bruisers either at fist or grog, all heavy bottomed, well balanced riders, all women who wanted a holiday and had the curiosity to see the weight and prowess of their sweethearts tried in open field."[43]

Augustus Baldwin Longstreet singles out dancing as a favorite amusement. In his *Georgia Scenes* he describes the dinner out under the trees, the old Negro sawing on his fiddle, the awkward farm boys and fresh-cheeked girls. It was all simple and wholesome. The women "used no artificial means of spreading their frock-tails to an interesting extent from their ankles. They had no boards laced to their breasts." As for the dances themselves, "none of your immodest waltzes; none of your detestable, disgusting gallopades." [44]

Sometimes there were plank dances. "You stand face to face with your partner on a plank and keep on dancing," a countryman explained to one visiting northerner. "Put the plank up on two barrel heads, so it'll kind of spring. At some of our parties— that's among common kind o' people, you know, it's great fun. They dance as fast as they can, and the folks all stand around and holler, 'Keep it up, John!' 'Go it, Nance!' 'Don't give it up so!' 'Old Virginny never tire!' ' 'Eel and toe, ketch a-fire!' and such kind of observation, and clop and stamp 'em." [45]

Diversions of this character represented the recreation of the people of the South more faithfully than the formal balls, the fashionable picnics, the chivalric tournaments of the planters. But the opportunities to enjoy them were few and far between. The common man had a hard time. For him the slavery that brought wealth and leisure to the aristocracy meant a more narrowly circumscribed life, greater toil, and even less chance than had the small farmers of the North and West for real amusement. Not for him the frosted julep on a shaded porch; he was busy picking cotton.

-»»)«(«-

Throughout the land, holidays were a great occasion in the mid-century years. In town and country, east and west, these infrequent breaks in a life which for the workingman might still mean twelve hours' daily labor for six full days a week were seized upon with a zest that this age can hardly appreciate. They meant far more than they do in a day when every weekend is free for recreation, and they were enjoyed in great crowd activities.

A parade almost invariably led off the day's festivities. Every one turned out—the militia companies in their handsome uniforms, the patriotic societies and political clubs, the volunteer firemen in glistening helmets and flaming red shirts. The generation of the 1850's was fascinated by parades; a band stirred urban crowds even more than it does to-day. At election time— and there was no more exciting holiday—the streets of every town and city would be filled with rival marchers. Torch-light parades added a new zest to the absorbing game of politics which neither young nor old could resist. On other occasions the crowds gathered to watch and cheer military parades with a fervor which was the essence of the period's intense nationalism. There was no artificiality, no regimentation, about the public demonstrations of the young democracy.

In the cities the parade was often followed by a mass-meeting or public banquet; in the rural areas there were picnics and barbecues to which the entire countryside flocked. Scores of aspiring Daniel Websters orated eloquently to the great crowds gathered on New England village greens; innumerable Davy Crlocketts attempted to spellbind their audiences as the oxen roasted at frontier barbecues. Hogsheads of punch or rum or whisky were consumed in toasts to the Universal Yankee Nation. Horse-races, impromptu sports, dancing to patriotic airs, were throughout the entire country a prelude to the night's fireworks displays.

The urban dweller also had his amusement park. The social world was being forced to share its near-by country retreats with working people. On a visit to Hoboken's Elysian Fields, Fanny Kemble was amazed to find the resort crowded with people from a quite different stratum of society from that of her own party. "Journeymen, labourers, handicraftsmen, tradespeople, with their families, bearing all in their dress and looks evident signs of well-being and contentment," she wrote, "were all flocking from their confined avocations into the pure air, the bright sunshine and beautiful shade of this lovely place." [46] There was no parallel in England to such a scene. It went far toward reconciling Miss Kemble to the crudities of American democracy. Children played on the swings, visited the bear dens, and enjoyed Punch and Judy shows as their parents picnicked and listened to the band music. The fastidious Samuel Dexter Ward noted "that there were a great many people here, male and female, but in my opinion few respectable ones." [47] The exclusiveness of an earlier day was gone.

Steamboat excursions enjoyed an immense popularity. Sir Charles Lyell noted that the passengers on Hudson River boats, on week-days as well as holidays, were very largely shopkeepers, artisans, and mechanics taking pleasure trips.[48] Horace Greeley, worrying over the $10 weekly budget of a New York workingman, wondered where he could get the money for his Sunday trip up and down the river to get some fresh air. Here was a new means of recreation, and the common man was taking full advantage of it.[49]

The *New York Herald* advertised dozens of holiday excursions for which the fare was never more than $1.00. One could cruise to Coney Island, already starting on its career as a popular resort, for fifty cents, visit the Lower Bay and Staten Island for twenty-five cents, and sail up river from the Battery to Harlem for twelve and one-half cents. Sometimes the excursions were organized by special groups. The Shamrock Benevolent Society and the Laborers' Union Benevolent Society had annual Independence Day outings. On one occasion the Thistle Benevolent Society gave a Grand Excursion and Cotillion Party aboard the steamboat *Robert L. Stevens* and an accompanying barge. The moonlight return down the river from West Point, the barge's deck cleared for dancing and the band playing gaily, rockets cutting their flaring paths of light across the sky, was a fitting climax to a day of enthusiastic festivities.[50]

Balloon ascensions drew great crowds. They may be traced back to the close of the eighteenth century, when President Washington was an eager spectator at Blanchard's stirring flights.

The Fashionable Singing Class

Leslie's Gazette of Fashions, 1862.

The Dance

Lithograph by E. B. and E. C. Kellogg, about 1852. Courtesy of
Harry T. Peters.

Enter the Trick Horseman

Lithographed poster of 1856. Courtesy of the American Antiquarian Society.

In the 1830's Charles F. Durant was charging fifty cents admission for "the inspiring spectacle" of his embarkation. As the band played, he distributed copies of an appropriate poetical address, stepped into the cage of his balloon, and, waving an American flag, started aloft to the booming of guns. Some years later John Wise had become the popular aeronaut. He provided twenty thousand seats at the scene of ascension, including in the price of admission souvenir watches and jewelry.[51]

Every place of entertainment in the cities would be filled on holidays. People crowded the open-air gardens to hear band music and watch the fireworks. In New York's City Hall Park scores of booths would be set up to cater to holiday needs. Here were roast pig and spruce beer, lemonade and boiled eggs, lobsters and mint juleps, myriads of pies and cakes. The band played, and again there were free fireworks.[52]

Public balls, the populace's equivalent for the assemblies and cotillions of society, were coming into favor. The popular clubs vied with each other in staging entertainments for which general admission might range from twenty-five cents to $1.00, the latter price usually including a gentleman and two ladies. Mr. Parker's ball at Tammany Hall, the Third Ward American Republican Ball at the Minerva Assembly Rooms, the Native American Ball at the Park Theatre, were New York affairs, but they had their counterpart in every town and city throughout the country.[53]

Less respectable were the dance-halls—"branches of Satan's den," the puritans termed them; the cheap variety shows, twelve cents admission with refreshments; the free and easy concert-saloons, which became especially popular in Philadelphia; and the beer-gardens where the growing German population was giving the country a taste for lager beer. These were the amusements already beginning to shock rural communities—the dreadful lure of the wicked city; but they were a part of the recreation of great masses of the people.[54]

Of all the holidays, democracy took over especially for its own the Fourth of July. On this day of all others it paraded with riotous enthusiasm, cheered itself hoarse, drank a thousand patriotic toasts; listened eagerly at banquets, barbecues, and picnics to the flamboyant oratory of an age which could get drunk almost as easily on words as on whisky; crowded the circus tent, museum, minstrel show, and popular theatre; overran the amusement parks and packed the holiday steamboat excursions; watched horse-races, sailing regattas, and pedestrian races; danced on the open prairie, at country taverns, and in crowded city dance-halls; fired off cannon and watched the sky redden with the fireworks of a nation still young enough, careless enough, exuberant enough, to take the keenest joy in this fervid expression of patriotism and high spirits.

The American people never indulge in a holiday? Too absorbed in money-making to let themselves go? The caustic English critics of the first half of the nineteenth century must have shut themselves into ivory towers on the Fourth of July. The crowd of ladies and gentlemen, loafers and laborers, white folks and "niggers," who jammed the Louisville levee to watch an Independence Day regatta; the two thousand people who gathered on the Nebraska plains for a barbecue and night-long dance, feasting on enough buffalo, venison, sheep, hogs, and pigs to have fed the whole territory; the holiday seekers overrunning the swings, flying deer, bowling-alleys, and target ranges of city amusement parks—were they too dull-spirited and depressed ever to enjoy themselves?

"It was remarkable for the general turn out of all classes, ages, sexes, and conditions," the *New York Herald* ecstatically reported of one Fourth of July celebration; "it was remarkable for the most splendid pageant ever displayed in this city since the war; it was remarkable for the extraordinary amusements and recreations of the day, not the least of which was the exhibition of the tall, the graceful, the majestic, the beautiful giraffes; and for the elegant display of beautiful women that grouped within the pleasure gardens of Niblo, at Vauxhall, at Castle Garden, at the Museums, at the Theatres, or at the Cotillion parties, in the numerous aquatic excursions in the evening." [55]

Not enjoy themselves? The American people were gradually breaking down the one-time exclusive barriers in the world of amusements. Michael Chevalier had declared democracy to be "too new a comer upon the earth to have been able as yet to organize its pleasures and amusements." It was doing so now, as he had advised, without regard to the aristocratic precedents of Europe. The gospel of work still gave a popular sanction to long hours of labor. Holidays were few and far between. Nineteenth-century puritanism continued to disapprove the theatre, dancing, card-playing, and many other amusements. But the common man's need for recreation was asserting itself.

chapter 10

Cow Towns
and Mining Camps

No ACCOUNT OF THE AMUSEMENTS OF THE AMERICAN PEOPLE would be complete without some record of the rough-and-ready life in that new West which was growing up during the troubled years that saw the rest of the country convulsed by civil war and then largely absorbed in the problems of Reconstruction. Its vivid story has often been told in western dime novel, melodrama, and moving picture. They have portrayed in lurid colors the roaring, wide-open days when drunken cowboys rode their horses into the saloons and shot out the lights, suave professional gamblers dealt out poker hands with guns on the table, and pistol-shots punctuated the dance music as flannel-shirted miners sported at hurdy-gurdy or honky-tonk.

It is true that the whisky-mill, the gambling-palace, and the dance-hall dominated recreation. There was little to amuse the solitary miner prospecting among the ravines and gulches of the Sierras, the cowboy riding the range or driving cattle north from the Texas plains. Their pleasures were almost entirely centered on their occasional visits to civilization. For six months or longer they worked hard, lived in the open, and never saw a woman. "When they hit the bright lights of some little town that looked like gay Paree to them, they just went crazy." [1] With silver dollars jingling in their pockets, crying to be spent, they needed only a haircut and shave, a new outfit of clothing, and a few drinks to be ready to go.

> Whoopee! drink that rotgut, drink that red nose,
> Whenever you get to town;
> Drink it straight and swig it mighty,
> Till the world goes round and round. [2]

Cowboy or prospector, they were all alike. "It is he that bucks at Monte; plays draw-poker; fights the tiger; patronizes the Hurdies; sings like a 'Washoe canary,'" Dan De Quille wrote of the western miner; "it is he who first sees the peep of dawn—through the bottom of a tumbler—through the same cocks his eye on the last smile of evening." [3]

→»«←

LIFE in the gold-fields of California during the feverish days that followed Forty-Nine has been graphically portrayed (discounting their sentimentality) in "The Luck of Roaring Camp" and "The Outcasts of Poker Flat." A few years later similar scenes were being enacted in the camps that sprang up in Nevada, Montana, Idaho, and Colorado.[4] At the same time the larger mining-towns which grew up around the more important gold and silver deposits offered entertainment even more typical of this violent era.

The most fantastically extravagant of them all during the entire period from 1860 through 1880 was Virginia City, Nevada. The Comstock Lode yielded in these two decades treasure estimated at $300,000,000, and some twenty-five thousand people, almost entirely men, worked and played on that barren mountainside with an intensity hardly paralleled in any other community of the West.[5] The narrow streets were always crowded with quartz wagons taking the mines' daily output to the reducing mills, and freight teams laden with supplies which had been brought over the long mountain road from California. Stage-coaches were setting off or arriving almost hourly in front of the hotels; riders of the Pony Express dashed madly through the tangled traffic; and sometimes a string of camels might be seen laboriously packing salt up the steep trails.

Mark Twain was in Virginia City during the height of its boom as a reporter on the *Territorial Enterprise*. He found it "the livest town, for its age and population, that America had ever produced." He was fascinated by its carefree, gambling spirit, by all its color and movement. "There were military companies," he wrote, "fire companies, brass bands, hotels, theatres, 'hurdy-gurdy houses,' wide-open gambling palaces, political pow-wows, civic processions, street fights, murders, inquests, riots, a whisky mill every fifteen steps ... and some talk of building a church!" [6]

The miners who thronged every thoroughfare had only one objective when their long, back-breaking shift was over—entertainment. Over a hundred saloons were ready to aid them. The more pretentious "two-bit" houses (every kind of drink cost a quarter) were the most sumptuous establishments in town—long mahogany bars, glistening chandeliers, a bright façade of mirrors, showy pictures in heavy gilded frames. No expense was spared to enable the miners to drink and gamble in as garish an atmosphere as the easy money of Virginia City could provide.

Faro, roulette, monte, and poker had their devotees. Another game was keno. "Fline glame," was the Chinaman's reputed comment. "Velly slimple. Dlealer slay 'Kleno,' and ellybolly ellse slay 'O Hlell!'" [7] After one house had experimented by having on hand "a real living, pretty, modest-looking young girl, in a close-fitting black silk dress," the custom spread of having female croupiers and dealers, through whom thousands of dollars changed hands nightly without causing comment. [8] Gambling was so much a part of the life of the mining-town that everything about it was taken for granted.

The hurdy-gurdy houses were a favorite resort. In a community where women were so scarce, their popularity may well be imagined. An eastern visitor reports that they were not all given over entirely to the usual personnel of such establishments. Such respectable women as the town might boast frequented some of the dance-halls, and they were invariably treated with deep respect. But more generally standards were not maintained on such a high level. "Four girls, about fifty men, an Irish fiddler, a bar-keeper and a bar, constituted the outfit," reads the description of one cheap house. "The gents were charged fifty cents each for a dance with the fair damsels, and after the dance were required to pay a like sum at the bar for drinks for themselves and their partners. . . . Gambling, prostitution, dancing and drinking were sometimes combined." [9] As in the case of saloons, the more expensive hurdy-gurdies had the most luxurious fittings. The dance-floors were highly polished, the music was provided by a full orchestra of skilled musicians, and the assorted collection of available ladies rivaled that of any eastern dance-hall.

Amusement of another kind was provided in Virginia City by prize-fights. The keen interest they aroused among the miners, supplemented by the betting and drinking, sometimes led to critical situations. But though a disputed decision often found the patrons hauling out their guns, the *Territorial Enterprise* (was it Mark Twain's phrase?) could usually report that the referee "failed to be killed." [10]

"A rush was made into the ring to break up the fight in a general row so that the bets might be declared off," an alarmed easterner wrote of one disputed prize-fight, "and instantly fifty pistols clicked and were drawn. . . . Colonel Beidler at once sprang into the ring, drew his revolvers, and declared that he would kill the first man who attempted to interfere with the fight. All well understood that when Beidler's pistol was drawn it meant business; and the ring was almost instantly cleared, leaving him standing alone in the center. 'Boys,' said he, 'this must be a fair fight. Go on with the show!' and time was promptly called again." [11]

There were occasionally other sports. Many of the miners were Cornishmen (it was a mixed population of all nationalities), and their canvas-jacketed wrestling matches were a popular spectacle. Sunday horse-races were held on the one level spot on the mountainside; rifle- and pistol-shooting contests sometimes took place; and members of the Virginia Alkali and Sagebrush Sporting Club chased coyotes with greyhounds on Forty-Mile Desert. But sooner or later every one came back to gamble at the Eldorado, dance at the Melodeon, and drink at the Sazerac, the Delta, or the Howling Wilderness.[12]

"The Comstock is an improving place to live on," declared the *Gold Hill News* of December 7, 1876. "Both Gold Hill and Virginia are well supplied with schools, and there is no lack of churches. We have more saloons than any place in the country. Every Sunday when there is a show in town we have a matinee and an evening performance. On the Sabbath, also, we are entertained with a horse-race or a fight between a bulldog and a wildcat. Every month or so the prize-fighters favor us with a mill, which we all go to see and then indict the fighters, as a sort of concession to the Puritanical element. . . . Every Saturday night small boys parade up and down the principal street of Virginia, carrying transparencies which inform our sport-loving people where cockfighting may be enjoyed. Faro, keno, chuck-a-luck and roulette may be found in every second saloon, and a special policeman, wearing his star, frequently conducts the game. Taking everything into consideration, there are few pleasanter places to live than on the Comstock." [13]

->>)<<-

THEATRICAL entertainment had had an unusual popularity in the mining-camps, indeed throughout the West, since the California gold-rush. It brought the miners glimpses of a world from which they were otherwise completely cut off. Nowhere did strolling players, minstrel bands, variety shows, and straight dramatic companies win a more enthusiastic reception. In no other part of the country had the theatre come "into such unchastened, free and abundant life." [14] The miners showered gold-dust with equal abandon upon the quavering soprano who touched their sentimental hearts with her rendering of "When the Swallows Homeward Fly," and upon Edwin Booth (he was listed in the San Francisco directory of the 1850's as "comedian and ranchero" [15]) in his early performances of *Hamlet*. They cheered themselves hoarse when the beautiful heroine was finally rescued in a Broadway melodrama, and brushed away the tears as they watched a juvenile troupe of Fairy Minstrels.

San Francisco had its first real theatre when the Jenny Lind was opened in 1850, some two thousand miners packing pit and gallery for a performance of *Macbeth*. Many stars of the eastern stage trod its boards: Junius Brutus Booth as well as the young Edwin Booth, Laura Keene, Catherine Sinclair (the divorced wife of Edwin Forrest), Lola Montez, the glamorous Countess of Landsfeldt who had been mistress of the King of Bavaria.... A favorite of the western stage was California's own star, Lotta Crabtree. She first played as a child actress in mining-camp bar-rooms, wandering through the mountains with her mother in a wagon drawn by tasseled mules. "La Petite Lotta," singing "Young Ladies, Won't You Marry?" and dancing her famed Spider Dance, early won her way into the miners' hearts.[16]

In Virginia City's flush days there were five legitimate theatres and six variety houses running at the same time. At Maguire's, and later at Piper's Opera House, the plays were representative of everything being staged in the East. Here were seen Shakespearean revivals and other serious dramas; Irish farces, Italian light operas, and sentimental comedies; Victoria Loftus' British Blondes; Haverly's Mastodon Minstrels; Tom shows with double quartettes of educated hounds; and French dancers in the wicked can-can. Also lectures—Horace Greeley talking on the state of the nation, Artemus Ward on "Babes in the Wood." [17]

The sensational Adah Isaacs Menken won a triumph in 1863 which is reserved for few actresses. The miners went mad over her beauty, her incomparable voice, her daring. When she appeared in *Mazeppa, or The Wild Horse,* an excited audience cheered and applauded to the echo. The climax of this stirring melodrama is reached when the heroine is strapped to the side of the wild horse to be driven off into the mountains. The Menken, wearing only a slight gauze chiton, played the part with an abandon which had the miners standing on their chairs. When the horse dashed up the rocky mountain trail with her beautiful, almost naked body lashed to its flank, pandemonium broke loose.

Virginia City had never been so thrilled. It christened a new mining district The Menken and organized a Menken Shaft and Tunnel Company. When their dazzling heroine finally left, she was laden down with the bars of bullion, silver ingots, certificates of mining stock, with which the admiring miners had expressed their homage.[18]

>>><<<

IN THE COW COUNTRY of the 1870's and 1880's the men who rode the range often got to town only once or twice a year. Their periodic binges were far less frequent than those of the miners who worked and lived at Virginia City, or those of the gold prospectors in the Sierras. They had a great deal of time on their hands. But as one of them phrased it, they were "merely folks, just plain, every-day, bow-legged humans," [19] and they sought every possible means of whiling away the tedium of long days in the saddle and empty evenings at camp or ranch-house.

The pride they developed in their horses made them eager to meet any challenge as to their speed, and the impromptu horse-race was as popular a sport on the range as in any other phase of frontier life. The cowboy was ready to bet anything he owned (except perhaps his saddle) on such races. He seldom had money, but he would put up his bridle, his rope, his quirt, sometimes the horse itself. Rival outfits would stake everything they could collectively raise on a match between two favorite horses. When a cowboy met a friendly Indian, there was invariably a race, sometimes leaving one or the other to go his way on foot.

The range-rider always had his six-shooter with him, and he amused himself by taking pot-shots at the jack-rabbits, prairie-dogs, or occasional coyotes that crossed his trail. Sometimes he gave chase to game with a swinging lariat. Cowboys would attempt to rope anything that came their way. They tried their skill on buffalo calves, went after antelopes, and sometimes even roped bears. There is the tale of one cowpuncher who made the

The Hurdy-Gurdy House at Virginia City, Montana
Albert D. Richardson, *Beyond the Mississippi*, 1867.

Cow-Town Vaudeville
Cheyenne, Wyoming. *Frank Leslie's Illustrated Newspaper*, 1877.

Bucking the Tiger

Faro in a Cheyenne gambling saloon. *Frank Leslie's Illustrated Newspaper*, 1877.

Cowboys in Town for Christmas

Drawing by Frederic Remington. *Harper's Weekly*, 1889.

experiment of throwing his rope over the smokestack of a locomotive—and was almost jerked to eternity. When wolves were
discovered attacking the cattle, a hunt would be organized with
the pack of greyhounds that many ranches kept on hand for
just such occasions. All hands would turn out for what was
exciting sport, as well as a necessary measure for protection of
the stock.[20]

The cowboy played no competitive games. He never wrestled
or boxed. They appeared futile sports when any physical encounter was generally settled by the sharp crack of a revolver.
But foot-races were sometimes held. Although the object of the
race was to reach a certain spot in the shortest possible time,
this did not mean following a straight line when run on the
western prairie. To offset the handicap of the bow-leggedness
which revealed the real horseman, the course would be plotted
over the most difficult terrain. Cunning in avoiding the hazards
of sage-brush and gopher-holes, rather than mere speed, was
the real test.

The cowboy sang a great deal to mitigate his loneliness while
riding the range or to soothe and quiet the cattle on the drive.
In his collection of cowboy songs, John A. Lomax has told of
their part in the social life of the ranch. Whenever a puncher
from another outfit drifted into camp, he was expected to sing
any new song he knew or additional stanzas for an old one.[21]
Plaintive love songs, sentimental ditties, and sorrowful dirges
grew into a balladry of the plains which has taken its place as
one of the most distinctive forms of American folk-song. With
incredible pathos the cowboy sang "The Home I Ne'er Will Live
to See," "Oh, Bury Me Not on the Lone Prai-rie," and "I'm a
Poor, Lonesome Cowboy."

Sometimes the tune was livelier:

> Whoopee ti yi yo, git along, little dogies;
>   It's your misfortune and none of my own.
> Whoopee ti yi yo, git along, little dogies;
>   For you know Wyoming will be your new home.

At night about the camp-fire there was always some one in the outfit with a banjo, mouth-organ, or jew's-harp. They would sing "The Old Chisholm Trail," "Ten Thousand God-Damn Cattle," "The Gal I Left Behind Me," or "The Little Black Bull":

> The little black bull came down from the mount-tain
>   (Hoorah Johnny and a hoo-rah Johnny)
> The little black bull came down from the mount-tain
>   Long time ago, a long time ago, a long time ago
> And he run his horn in a white oak sap-ling
>   Long time ago. . . .[22]

Apart from singing, evenings afforded little entertainment. Night after night, for weeks and months on end, the same little group of men sat about trying to kill time. They knew each other far too well—every idea, every trick of language, every irritating peculiarity—to get much pleasure from their own company. Men without women became touchy and quarrelsome. Long hard hours in the saddle, a monotonous diet of miserably cooked canned goods, made for frayed nerves and a readiness to take offense which often left the atmosphere electric.

The scene was seldom the gay, roistering one of fiction. Drinking was very rare, for the simple reason that the cowboys had no liquor. When some one did bring whisky into camp, it would not last long. Nor was there much gambling. The ranch hands generally spent all their money on their periodic trips to town and had nothing with which to bet. Dreary and apparently endless games of poker or seven-up nevertheless went on, with packs of cards so greasy from use that only those who knew them personally could guess what they were. More exciting were the occasional fights in which tarantulas were matched against each other much as favorite cocks had been on the earlier frontier. A champion spider was a much-prized possession, carefully tended.

How far monotony ruled the ranch-house is illustrated by the popularity of those contests in which the cowboys recited the manufacturers' labels on their tins of canned goods. They read very little (a few magazines, seldom books) but would carefully memorize the advertisements for condensed milk or baked beans. The eastern tenderfoot was sometimes amazed to hear the ranch-house suddenly break into a rapid singsong recital whose mysterious significance it often took him some time to discover.

A visitor could always be sure of a warm welcome among men so starved for society. The cowboys would dig up whatever cash or mobile possessions they could find in a happy attempt to take in the newcomer at whatever game he chose. Should punchers ride in from some rival outfit, the visit would be celebrated as freely as all available resources in the matter of liquor would permit. When an innocent easterner happened upon that restless company, he was greeted with a cordiality which lost nothing from the fact that the cowboys were hoping to have as much fun as possible at his expense. They hazed not because of any inherent cruelty in their nature, but because they were bored.[23]

The wild excitement of a day in town can be understood only against this background and in comparison with the almost unrelieved monotony of ranch-house leisure. It was little wonder that when the end of the round-up or drive gave the outfit a holiday, everything but the desire to have a good time was completely forgotten. The cowboy was out to enjoy himself, to make up for those long weeks whose amusements were so rare and unsatisfying. What if all his pay did disappear in a single night? He might not get to town for another six months. To gamble and drink away his money the one time he had the chance to spend it freely was unquestioned logic.

The cow-town was created by the extension of the railroad across the western plains, becoming a central point for the shipment of cattle to eastern markets. It was often no more than a string of frame houses which had little excuse for existence except as an entertainment center for all those varied elements which went into the floating population of the plains—cowboys, ranchers, freighters, teamsters, hunters, storekeepers, government officials, half-breeds, gamblers, and professional bad men. Every one went armed. Brawls and shooting affrays were common. "The town was simply an eddy in the troubled stream of Western immigration," wrote Emerson Hough, "and it caught the odd bits of driftwood and wreck—the flotsam and jetsam of a chaotic flood." [24]

To cowpunchers and ranchmen who had seen nothing but the prairie and the members of their own outfit for seemingly endless months, it was nevertheless full of high promise. They rode in booted and spurred, sometimes without fanfare but often with the wild yipping of the western thriller, and headed straight for the nearest saloon. "Buying the town" was in order if the outfit was really in money. A stack of silver dollars was planked down on the bar—"Gents, it's on us. She's opened up. The town is yours." Until it was gone, drinks were free for anybody whatsoever. There were instances of as much as $1,000 being spent on opening up a town, the saloon-keepers prorating the money until it had all been consumed in hard liquor. [25]

Many stories are told. One cowman walked into a restaurant and with a lordly gesture ordered a hundred dollars' worth of ham and eggs. Another had a champagne bath in the town's rickety little hotel. It drained the entire supply of every saloon, at five dollars a bottle, but the rancher's theory was a simple one. He wanted a bath, nothing was too good for him, and champagne was the most costly liquid of which he knew. [26]

Gambling drew the cowboy as surely as it did the miner. Any game, any time, but poker was the great sport of the cow country. Professional gamblers were always on hand, but there was not much cheating. The bad man caught with an ace up his sleeve got short shrift, as western thrillers have shown an admiring world, in a society where trigger fingers were so well exercised. "The click of a six-shooter is music to my ears, and a bowie-knife is my looking glass," was a favorite boast of the frontier. There came a time when the punchers were required to check their guns when they came into town, and the sheriff promptly took the bad man into custody, but in the early days little differences of opinion were decided in favor of whoever was quickest on the draw.

If the possible favors of the fancy ladies were largely responsible for the popularity of the dance-hall, the cowboy often made a straight course for it just for sociability and a good time. "Three of us was in the parlor of Maggie Burn's house giving a song number called 'The Texas Ranger,'" Teddy Blue wrote in *We Pointed Them North*, "John Bowen was playing the piano and he couldn't play the piano, and Johnny Stringfellow was there sawing on a fiddle and he couldn't play the fiddle, and I was singing, and between the three of us we was raising the roof. And Maggie—the redheaded, fighting son of a gun—got hopping mad and says: 'If you leather-legged sons of bitches want to give a concert, why don't you hire a hall? You're ruining my piano.'"[27] It is also Teddy Blue who tells of Connie the Cowboy Queen and her $250 dress: "They said there wasn't an outfit from the Yellowstone down to the Platte, and over in the Dakotas too, that couldn't find its brand on that dress."[28]

For the few respectable women who found their way to the Far West the cowboy had an idolatrous respect. Their rarity set them so far apart that one old-timer declared fervently that there were only two things a cowpuncher was afraid of, a decent woman and being set afoot.[29] When an occasional ball was held, young and old, beautiful and plain, were treated with awed chivalry. Such functions were popular, and the cowboys gathered in full war-paint—silk handkerchief and fancy vest, chaps and spurs—from a neighborhood of two hundred miles. Owen Wister has described such a dance in his story of how the Virginian mixed up the sleeping babies which had been parked for the evening in the woodshed. If there were not enough women to go around, which was usually the case, some of the cowboys would let themselves be "heifer-branded" with a handkerchief tied about the arm.[30]

At the end of the trail along which the cattle were driven

north from Texas was Dodge City—the Beautiful, Bibulous Baby-
lon of the Frontier. There were other cow-towns—Abilene, New-
town, Ogalalla, Julesburg, Cheyenne—where it took several
generations of orderly living to blot out the unsavory reputation of the early days, but Dodge City was reputedly the most
wicked of them all. "Her incorporated limits," a local historian
wrote, "are the rendezvous of all the unemployed scallawagism
in seven states." [31] There might be seventy-five thousand head of
cattle grazing in the surrounding meadows as they waited shipment east, and the Texas buckaroos who had driven them north
packed the saloons and dance-halls which alternated with every
business house on the town's crowded streets:

> It was hot July when we got to Dodge,
> That wickedest little town;
> And we started in to have some fun
> Just as the sun went down.
>
> We killed a few of the worst bad men
> For the pleasure of seeing them kick;
> We rode right into a billiard hall,
> And I guessed we raised Old Nick.
> The bartender left in a wonderful haste
> On that hot and sultry day;
> He never came back to get his hat
> Until we were miles away.
>
> We went from Dodge to the town Caldwell,
> As we wished to prolong the fun;
> When the marshal there caught sight of us,
> You ought to have seen him run.
> We rode right into a big dance hall
> That opened upon the street;
> The music and dancing both were fine,
> And the girlies sure looked sweet.
>
> We drank all the Caldwell whisky,
> We ate everything in sight;
> We took in all the dances,
> And they say we had a fight.[32]

-->>)<<-

THE LIBERTY and license of cow-towns and mining-camps did not last for very long. Once the civilization of the East had caught up with it, the colorful excitement of the Far West quickly faded. More orderly government led to the regulation of its wide-open entertainment palaces, and the refining influence of women toned down the freedom of a man's world. But the West's exuberant spirit of fun, its refusal to allow itself to be cramped by traditional tabus, the spirit typified by the comment that while the church might be tolerated, the saloon and the dance-hall were regarded as necessities, had its influence on the attitude of the country as a whole toward work and play. It served to undermine still further the Puritan tradition and gave a new impetus to the expansion of recreation.

chapter 11

The Rise of Sports

WHILE THE WEST WAS GOING THROUGH ITS GORGEOUS EPOCH OF gambling, drinking, and gun-play, a series of athletic crazes were sweeping through the states of the East. Baseball developed from its humble beginnings in the days before the Civil War to its recognized status as America's national game. The rapid spread of croquet caused the startled editors of *The Nation* to describe it as the swiftest and most infectious epidemic the country had ever experienced.[1] Lawn tennis was introduced to polite society by enthusiasts who had seen it played in England, and the old sport of archery was revived as still another fashionable lawn game. Roller-skating attained a popularity which extended to all parts of the country. What the sewing-machine is to our industrial wants and the telegraph to our commercial pursuits, one devotee wrote rapturously, this new system of exercise had become to society's physical and social wants.[2]

Track and field events were also promoted with the widespread organization of amateur athletic clubs; gymnastic games were sponsored both by the German Turnverein and the Y.M.C.A.; and in the colleges a spectacular sports phenomenon loomed over the horizon with the development of intercollegiate football. Society welcomed polo as an importation from abroad, took up the English sport of coaching. And finally a craze for bicycling arose to supersede all other outdoor activities as city streets and country roads became crowded with nattily dressed cyclists out on their club runs.

All this took place in the late 1860's and the 1870's. Previously the country had had virtually no organized sports as we know them to-day. Neither men nor women played outdoor games. Alarmed observers in mid-century had found the national health deteriorating because of a general lack of exercise more widespread than among the people of any other nation. Ralph Waldo Emerson had written despairingly of "the invalid habits of this country," [3] and from abroad the London *Times* had issued grave warnings of possibly dire consequences for our national well-being.[4] No transformation in the recreational scene has been more startling than this sudden burgeoning of an interest in sports which almost overnight introduced millions of Americans to a phase of life shortly destined to become a major preoccupation among all classes.

It was a phenomenon somewhat difficult to explain, but the first faint stirrings of popular interest may be traced to the decade before the Civil War. The decline of the informal sports associated with country festivals and frontier frolics, a consequence of the breaking-up of old forms of village association as the nation became more urbanized and of changes in farm economy which brought about the disappearance of such work-play occasions as the barn-raising and the husking-bee, had drawn attention to a parlous state of affairs. Many observers suddenly realized that the spectator sports of the period were a sorry substitute for what was being lost. This was not so important for the rural population, but it affected the townsman very seriously. "Who in this community really takes exercise?" Thomas Wentworth Higginson asked in the first issue of the *Atlantic Monthly*, in 1858. "Even the mechanic confines himself to one set of muscles; the blacksmith acquires strength in his right arm, and the dancing teacher in his left leg. But the professional or business man, what muscles has he at all?" [5]

A campaign was started to break down the prejudice against sports as an idle diversion and to encourage more active participation in outdoor games. "The Americans as a people—at least the professional and mercantile classes," Edward Everett declared, "have too little considered the importance of healthful, generous recreation. . . . Noble, athletic sports, manly outdoor exercises . . . which strengthen the mind by strengthening the body, and bring man into a generous and exhilarating communion with nature . . . are too little cultivated in town or country." [6] With far greater emphasis but on very much the same grounds the editor of *Harper's Monthly Magazine* and Dr. Oliver Wendell Holmes lent the weight of their authority to the new cause. The former held the want of sports responsible for turning young America into "a pale, pasty-faced, narrow chested, spindled-shanked, dwarfed race—a mere walking mannikin to advertise the latest cut of the fashionable tailor." [7] The Autocrat of the Breakfast-Table declared himself satisfied "that such a set of black-coated, stiff-jointed, soft-muscled, paste-complexioned youth as we can boast in our Atlantic cities never before sprang from the loins of Anglo-Saxon lineage." [8]

These diatribes bore some fruit in the 1850's. Skating was taken up so widely that the vogue for it became known as Higginson's Revival. Rowing grew so popular (Charles W. Eliot was on the Harvard crew) that the *New York Herald* declared that if the boating era should continue another five years, "the coming generation will relieve America from the odium of physical decline." [9] Nevertheless the flowering of sports awaited the post-war period, when they were given a primary impetus through being adopted by the world of fashion. The early rowing clubs had been composed of "young men of the highest respectability," but as the new games of the 1870's were introduced from England, for the rise of sports in the United States owed a very considerable debt to the sports revival in the mother country, it was more than ever society's leaders who first played them. [10] The attempt was even made to monopolize them. Again and again the complacent statement may be found in contemporary articles in the better magazines that such and such a sport— whether tennis, polo, or bicycling—does not "offer any attractions to the more vulgar elements of society." [11] But the real significance of fashionable approval of sports lay in the fact that it awoke the interest of democracy. The common man eagerly followed where the aristocrat led. He could not be kept from any diversion within his means. "We may turn up our noses generally at those who in this country profess to lead fashions," Caspar Whitney, an early sports writer, declared some years later, "but in the matter of showing the way to healthy, vigorous outdoor play they have set a fine example and one that has taken a firm hold upon the people." [12]

A basic need for outdoor exercise to conserve national health and the sponsorship of social leaders thus served in large measure to break down the barriers that had formerly stood in the way of the development of organized sports. Games which could appeal to every one had at last been invented or developed. And a post-war atmosphere, in which the instinct for pleasure is naturally intensified, provided fertile ground for the growth of these new forms of recreation. It is perhaps not so surprising after all that within a short quarter-century of the day when one English visitor declared that "to roll balls in a ten pin alley by gas-light or to drive a fast trotting horse in a light wagon along a very bad and dusty road, seems the Alpha and Omega of sport in the United States," [13] almost every one of our modern games was being played by a rapidly growing army of enthusiasts.

-»>)«<-

THE PIONEER of them all, baseball, had evolved from the various bat-and-ball games that the early settlers had brought with them from England. A children's game actually known as base-ball had been played in the eighteenth century. It is noted in *A Pretty Little Pocket Book, Intended for the Amusement of Little Master Tommy and Pretty Miss Polly,* which was first published in England in 1744 and soon after reprinted in this country. Jane Austen refers to it in *Northanger Abbey.*[14] Four-old-cat, rounders, and town-ball, each of which contributed something to baseball, were also being played in the early nineteenth century by young men and boys throughout the country. Samuel Woodruff, writing on amusements in 1833, speaks of New Englanders as being experts in such games of ball as "cricket, base, cat, football, trap-ball." [15]

But there was no formality about these early games—no regular teams, no accepted rules of play, no scheduled contests. Cricket was the only one at all organized. New arrivals from England almost invariably formed cricket teams. It was an occasional diversion in all parts of the country, played north and south and on the western prairies. It was most general in and about Philadelphia, where groups of English factory-workers played weekly games.[16] But cricket never really took hold in America. Its leisurely pace could not be reconciled with a frontier-nourished love for speed, excitement, action. It was steadily driven to the wall as the far more lively game of baseball, slowly taking its modern form and shape, made a more universal bid for popularity.

The date of baseball's emergence as a game definitely different from rounders or town-ball has been patriotically determined by a national commission which set out in 1907 to establish its American origins. But there is no recorded evidence to justify its conclusion that modern baseball stems from Abner Doubleday's supposed adoption of the diamond at Cooperstown, New York, in 1839.[17] Although town-ball as it was generally played at that time had four bases at the corners of a square and there were no foul balls (one hit the ball in any direction and ran), the diamond and other attributes of the modern game had already been adopted in both rounders and children's base-ball. The beginnings of the organized sport may perhaps be more accurately traced to a group of New York business and professional men who about 1842 began playing it at the Elysian Fields in Hoboken. They formally organized the Knickerbocker Club and under the lead of Alexander J. Cartwright adopted a code of rules which was printed in 1845. There were to be nine players

A Great Game for the Baseball Championship

Return match between the Athletic Base Ball Club of Philadelphia and the Atlantics of Brooklyn, Philadelphia, October 22, 1866, won by the Athletics, 31 to 12. Lithograph drawn and published by J. L. Magee. Courtesy of Harry T. Peters.

The Game of Croquet

Drawing by C. G. Bush. *Harper's Weekly*, 1866.

A Spring Meeting of the New York Archery Club

Drawing by T. de Thulstrup. *Frank Leslie's Illustrated Newspaper*, 1880.

on each side, three men out constituted an inning, and the game was won by the first team to make twenty-one runs, or "aces" as they were then called.[18] The first match game on record was played a year later with a picked team which called itself the New York Baseball Club, the "all-stars" winning 23 to 4 in four innings.

In keeping with their social status, the members of the Knickerbocker Club played in neat uniforms of blue trousers, white shirts, and straw hats. As important as the game was the formal dinner which followed it. For some time, indeed, every effort was made to keep baseball an exclusive sport, and not until the 1850's were more democratic clubs organized and the Knickerbockers compelled to recognize that workers as well as gentlemen could play the game. For there was no need in baseball to undergo the expense of maintaining a boat club or keeping up a stable of riding-horses. It wanted only an open field, a bat, and a ball. "The great mass, who are in a subordinate capacity," a contemporary pointed out succinctly, "can participate in this health giving and noble pastime."[19]

One of the first clubs that brought a more democratic spirit into the baseball world was the Eckford Club of Brooklyn, formed in 1855. By this year the Knickerbockers had many rivals in and about New York. Games were being placed regularly among such teams as the Gothams, the Putnams, the Harlems, the Excelsiors, and the Eagles. But the Eckford Club had this distinction: its members were shipwrights and mechanics. They suffered the disadvantage in comparison with other clubs of not having very much time to practise, but they soon proved their worth by defeating the Excelsior Club, made up of merchants and clerks.[20] The Newark Mechanics Club was among other organizations composed of workingmen, while one of the best teams playing on the Boston Common, where games were often scheduled at five in the morning so as not to interfere with the players' work, was made up of truckmen.[21] And then in 1856 a young man named Henry Wright, employed in a jewelry manufactory and also a professional bowler with the St. George Cricket Club, joined the Knickerbockers. Social barriers were breaking down completely. The ball clubs wanted to win their games. Here also was a hint of the professionalism toward which they were headed. Another decade and Wright will have gone to Cincinnati to organize the Red Stockings as the country's first admittedly professional team.[22]

Baseball slowly spread north, south, east, and west. It drove out town-ball in New England and cricket in Philadelphia, made its way to the Mississippi Valley (Chicago had four clubs in 1858), crossed the trans-Mississippi frontier, reached out to the Pacific Coast. Everywhere it was bringing men and boys into active outdoor play. It was also becoming highly organized. The National Association of Base Ball Players was formed in 1858, with twenty-five clubs applying for charter membership, and two years later delegates from fifty organizations attended its annual meeting. New York and New Jersey led in the number of clubs (New England had a separate association for teams still playing town-ball), but Philadelphia, Washington, Detroit, Chicago, and New Orleans were but a few among the cities where baseball was now established.[23]

The game was attracting spectators as well as players, and a wider public interest was growing out of the reports carried in the newspaper of the interclub matches. It still had features strange to modern times. A man was out on a ball caught on the first bounce; pitching was an underhand throw. Even though there were players who "sent the ball with exceeding velocity," the scales were more heavily weighted in favor of the batter than they are to-day. No gloves were worn. We find *The Spirit of the Times* praising Mr. Wadsworth of the Knickerbockers for his fearlessness "in the dangerous position of catcher." Contemporary prints portray the umpire sitting out in the field somewhere near first base under an umbrella, in frock-coat and stove-pipe hat.[24]

But baseball was exciting. In 1858 some two thousand persons

actually paid fifty cents admission for a match at the Fashion
Race Course, the first recorded game with gate receipts.[25] Two
years later the champion Excelsiors, of Brooklyn, went on tour
and defeated challenging clubs in cities throughout New York,
Pennsylvania, Delaware, and Maryland. Returning for a match
with another Brooklyn team, the Atlantics, they played a game
which drew fifteen thousand spectators.[26] Baseball was on its
way.

The Civil War interrupted this forward march, but it brought
an even larger popular following. The game was everywhere
played behind the lines and in base camps, almost on the battle-
field. Country boys and factory-workers were introduced to the
new sport, and with the end of the war they took it back to their
home communities. One result of wartime playing is seen in the
attendance of clubs at the first post-war meetings of the National Association. The total jumped to ninety-one in 1865. A
year later the membership, representing seventeen states and the
District of Columbia, totaled 202. "Since the war, it has run like
wildfire," the *Galaxy* declared editorially. Charles A. Peverelly
believed it to be beyond question "the leading feature in the
outdoor sports of the United States." And by 1872 the magazine
Sports and Games categorically stated that it had become "the
national game of the United States." [27]

The American genius for organization was outdoing itself in
the growth of the National Association, however, and the keen
rivalry among member clubs was promoting professionalism. The
practice developed of engaging expert players for a local club
through offering them better-paid jobs in the community than
they could normally expect to obtain. On occasion players were
directly paid for their services in important games. A confusing
quasi-professionalism invaded the ranks of what had formerly
been a wholly amateur sport. The next step was inevitable. In
1869 the Cincinnati Red Stockings were definitely hired as a
professional team for a country-wide tour. They did not lose
a game that summer, and the practical advantage of salaried

players was recognized by all those sports followers primarily interested in championship teams.

These moves toward professional baseball were both cause and consequence of the heavy betting that began to be made on interclub games. For the gambling fraternity quickly became interested in the new sport. It was taken up as professional foot-races and prize-fighting had been. Charges also began to be made that the gamblers were not only beginning to control the ball players, but were operating pools and arranging for games to be won or lost on a strictly business basis.[28] Amateur members of the National Association bitterly contested the increasing influence of these new elements in the game, but their organization was losing its control. In 1871 its place was taken by a new association frankly composed of professional players.

For a time this association did not function very effectively. It was either unwilling or unable to suppress gambling, and base-ball fell under a cloud of popular disapproval. Efforts at reform were finally crowned when five years later William A. Hulbert undertook the organization of the National League of Professional Baseball Clubs. Rules and regulations were now adopted which set up strict standards for inter-club competition.[29] With an original membership made up of teams from New York, Philadelphia, Hartford, Boston, Chicago, Louisville, Cincinnati, and St. Louis, baseball had a controlling body. Through its ministrations there grew up the immensely complicated system of franchises, major and minor leagues, player contracts, and other business controls that now characterize the professional game. The National League gave baseball a new stability, restored public confidence in the contests among league teams, and put the sport really on its feet.

Amateur playing had naturally suffered from the conflict with professionalism and the disrepute into which the game had been brought by gambling. But it quickly responded to these new developments. Completely divorced from the professional game so far as organization was concerned but following its lead on all playing rules, it flourished as it never had before. Baseball became the favorite game in the colleges. It was played by every high school and was encouraged by Y.M.C.A.'s. Ball clubs became a feature of every American community.

The game had many qualities that appealed to the average young American. It met his newly felt need for healthful outdoor exercise. It offered him competitive team play. But perhaps Mark Twain had an even more suggestive explanation of its popularity. "Baseball is the very symbol," he wrote, "the outward and visible expression of the drive and push and rush and struggle of the raging, tearing, booming nineteenth century." [30]

->>)<<-

CROQUET had in the meantime performed the miracle of getting both men and women out-of-doors for an activity they could enjoy together. The first of the post-war games to be introduced from England, it reached an even broader public than baseball. Croquet was more than a game; it was a social function. Contemporary writers were soon pointing out what an unmixed blessing it was for the American damsel, and warning bachelors to beware.[31]

" 'Charming' is the universal exclamation of all who play or who watch the playing of Croquet...," an early rules book stated. "Hitherto, while men and boys have had their healthy means of recreation in the open air, the women and girls have been restricted to the less exhilarating sports of indoor life.... Grace in holding and using the mallet, easy and pleasing attitudes in playing, promptness in taking your turn, and gentlemanly and ladylike manners generally throughout the game, are points which it is unnecessary for us to enlarge on.... Young ladies are proverbially fond of cheating at this game; but they only do so because they think that men like it." [32]

George Makepeace Towle has an idyllic picture of people playing croquet: "The sunshine glimmering through the branches —the soft velvety grass—the cool, pure country air—the quiet broken only by the twittering of the birds, and now and then a passing footstep." [33] Only occasionally did some controversial issue arise to mar the sweet felicity of the croquet court. There was the problem of "spooning." This was not a mode of behavior, but the practice of hitting the croquet-ball by what is now called the pendulum stroke. Obviously women in hooped-skirts were at a disadvantage. *The Nation* gave its considered opinion: "We agree that spooning is perfectly fair in a match of gentlemen, but it is decidedly ungenerous when played with ladies, unless those ladies are bloomers." [34]

Croquet was by no means confined to the fashionable lawns of the effete East, however. It went west with the homesteaders. Many accounts tell of its popularity in the small towns of the prairie states. So great was the vogue in the 1870's that manufacturers put out playing sets with candle-sockets on the wickets for night playing.

Archery and lawn tennis, the former the revival of an old sport and the latter newly introduced from England about 1874, had also been taken up widely by this time. They too were sports, gentle and genteel, which could be played by both sexes. "The contestants were ladies and gentlemen from the cultured circles of society," *Harper's Weekly* reported of an archery tournament in the White Stocking Park at Chicago in 1879, "and while the rivalry among the shooters was keen to the last degree, an air of such refinement and courteous dignity as is not often witnessed by observers of public games characterized every one connected with the contest." [35] Writing on tennis in 1881, the magazine *Outing*, whose establishment reflected the rising interest in sports, assured its feminine readers that this was far too refined a game to offer any attractions for the lower orders of society. A lady who took part in a tennis match would find herself "in the company of persons in whose society she is accustomed to move." [36]

At this stage of its development, lawn tennis as played in the United States did not involve hard, overhand serves, back-court drives, or smashes at the net. Women players suffered only the slightest handicap in having to hold up the trains of their long, dragging skirts; they were not expected actually to run for the ball. It was patted gently back and forth over a high net stretched across any level space of lawn. Competition gradually led to changed methods of play, and with the organization of the United States National Lawn Tennis Association (there were forty member clubs in 1883) and the institution of annual tournaments at Newport, men began to take the game more seriously. The active features of play that now characterize it were developed. A group of players whose names are still remembered emerged from the ranks—R. D. Sears, James Dwight, Robert D. Wrenn, William A. Larned, Dwight F. Davis. . . . Finally in 1900 the establishment of the International Davis Cup matches definitely marked the transformation of tennis from a pastime to a sport.[37]

-»»)«(«-

ROLLER-SKATING had been introduced by James L. Plimpton in 1863, and New York's social leaders, hoping it could be restricted to "the educated and refined classes," quickly made it fashionable. Their Roller Skating Association leased the Atlantic House in Newport and made over its dining-hall and piazza into a skating-rink. It held weekly assemblies where such distinguished guests as General Sherman and Chief Justice Bigelow watched "tastefully dressed young men and girls, sailing, swimming, floating through the mazes of the march, as if impelled by magic power." [38]

But Newport soon had to surrender to the democracy. Rinks were built in every town and immense ones established in the cities, with a general admission of fifty or twenty-five cents, which welcomed all comers. In Chicago the Casino accommodated four thousand persons—three thousand spectators and one thousand skaters. There were not only dancing and racing. Professor A. E. Smith introduced special fancy skating—the Richmond Roll, the Picket Fence, the Philadelphia Twist ("rolling his limbs far apart and laying his head sideways on one of them"), and the Dude on Wheels. Night after night the band played, the new Siemens lights shone down on the hard-maple floor, and a vast attendance crowded the Casino's spacious and elegant rink.[39]

Going further west, skating was even more popular. The Olympian Club Roller Skating Rink in San Francisco advertised five thousand pairs of skates and 69,000 square feet of hard-maple floor. It was holding races, roller-skating polo, and "tall hat and high collar" parties.[40]

Young and old skated—men, women, and children. For a time no other sport seemed able to match its popularity. A writer in *Harper's Weekly* cited a gravestone inscription:

> Our Jane has climbed the golden stair
> And passed the jasper gates;
> Henceforth she will have wings to wear,
> Instead of roller skates.[41]

—»)(«—

BUT IT REMAINED for bicycling to become the most spectacular craze of all. While it had had a brief vogue in the 1860's (the first velocipedes—the French "dandy horses"—were known as early as the opening of the century), it was the introduction about 1876 of the high-wheeled bicycles, supplanting the old wooden bone-shakers, that first made it a popular sport. Within half a dozen years of the first manufacture of the new wheels, there were some twenty thousand confirmed cyclists in the country; in 1886 the total had swelled to some fifty thousand, and a year later it was over a hundred thousand. Clubs were organized in almost every town and city throughout the land, and to bring together organizations of like interest and promote cycling as a sport, they banded together, in 1881, to form the League of American Wheelmen.[42]

"There has been heretofore in our American life, crowded to excess as it has been with the harassing cares and anxieties of business," a writer in *Harper's Monthly Magazine* stated in July, 1881, "so little attention paid to the organized practice of health-giving outdoor exercise, to which bicycling is peculiarly adopted, that the organization of this League of American Wheelmen can not fail to be recognized as an important subject for public congratulation." [43]

The safety bicycle and the drop frame for women were still almost a decade away. This was the first enthusiasm of the high-wheeled pioneers, those daring riders who went forth perched on a postage-stamp saddle athwart a sixty-inch wheel. A header from that dizzy eminence meant broken bones, if not a broken head. But forth the wheelmen rode—high-necked jackets, close-fitting knee-pants, and little round hats (later, ventilated duck helmets and imported English hose)—prepared to defy all the hazards of the road. They generally went in company. Club runs were the fashion. The cyclists mounted to the bugle call of "Boots and Saddles," and sober pedestrians watched in awe as they wheeled past in military formation.

It was also the era of impressive bicycle parades, competitive club drills, hill-climbing contests, and race meetings. On July 4, 1884, news of the bicycle world included a meet on the Boston Common drawing thousands of spectators; a parade of seventy cyclists at Portsmouth, New Hampshire; the first club run of the Kishwaukee Bicycle Club at Syracuse, Illinois; races for the Georgia championship at Columbus; and medal runs at Salt Lake City. Thomas Stevens was off on his famous bicycle trip around the world, and in New York a bicycle school with thirty uniformed instructors was teaching Wall Street bankers to wheel to band music.[44]

The rôle of women in this bright dawn of the bicycle age was limited but none the less well recognized. The high-wheeled machine was too much for them, but they were given the tricycle. Here was recreation on "a higher plane than the ball-field or the walking rink," an outdoor activity which marked "a step towards the emancipation of woman from her usually too

inactive indoor life." [45] In this vigorous propaganda to promote
female cycling, *The Wheelman* also called upon the support of
ministers and physicians. Bicycling was both godly and healthy.
One word of warning, from A Family Physician: "Do not think
of sitting down to table until you have changed your under-
clothing, and, after a delightful wash and rub-down, quietly and
leisurely dressed again." [46]

Tricycles were not scorned by men. They were sometimes
as fast as the bicycle (the mile record was 2:33 minutes for the
tricycle, 2:29 minutes for the bicycle in 1890),[47] and a day's run
in the country could be managed with a good deal more ease.
Professor Hoffman's *Tips to Tricyclists* was written for both the
sexes. It was an all-inclusive guide, with advice on the wearing
of celluloid collars and on management of breath, on cleaning
the machine and on the desirability of lady cyclists' carrying
menthol cones for emergencies.[48]

There were all types of tricycles—the Surprise Tricycle, the
Quadrant Tricycle, the Coventry Rotary Tricycle. Another vehicle was the Sociable. It was in effect a small self-wheeled carriage, the cyclists happily sitting beside each other. It was widely
advertised for honeymoons. Other machines completely defy
description—the Coventry Convertible Four in Hand and the
Rudge Triplet Quadricycle.[49]

The social consequences of bicycling, to be so much more
apparent in the next decade, were already becoming evident in
the 1880's. Although the price of machines ($100 to $125 for an
ordinary and $180 for a tricycle) still made them an expensive
luxury, the number of cyclists was increasing year by year. The
rediscovery of the outdoors had received its greatest encouragement, and the League of American Wheelmen was performing
heroic services in demanding improved roads. "Bicycling is a
fraternity of more permanent organization," *Outing* declared in
1882, "than ever characterized any sport since the world began." [50]

->>><<<-

The First National Tennis Tournament at New Brighton
Drawing by H. A. Ogden. *Frank Leslie's Illustrated Newspaper*, 1880.

Washington Meet of the League of American Wheelmen
Frank Leslie's Illustrated Newspaper, 1884.

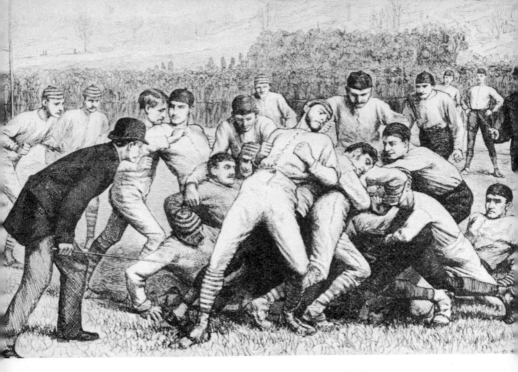

Yale Meets Princeton in Football

Their fifth match, at St. George's Cricket Club, Hoboken, Thanksgiving Day, November 27, 1879, a scoreless tie. Drawing by A. B. Frost. *Harper's Weekly,* 1879.

THE RÔLE of the colleges in the rise of sports was not one of leadership. It was not their example that first set people playing games, bicycling, or generally getting outdoors for recreation. The epidemics sweeping the country did not pass them by,[51] but undergraduates neither introduced nor popularized any one of the games that have so far been described. The only sport they developed was intercollegiate football.

It descended from a game played in England at least as early as the days of Edward II. "For as much as there is great noise in the city," reads a decree of 1314, "caused by hustling over large balls from which many evils arise which God forbid; we forbid such game to be used in the city in the future."[52] And again and again in later years England's sovereigns fruitlessly legislated against a sport which the common people insisted on playing. The early colonists brought it to this country, and throughout the eighteenth and the first half of the nineteenth centuries it was popular in the colleges. The game generally played in this period was something like association football, or soccer, but it was completely unorganized, and any number of players was usually allowed on each side. The first recorded intercollegiate contests (there is notice of an earlier game between two groups of Boston schoolboys),[53] took place in 1869 between Princeton and Rutgers. They played three games with twenty-five men on each team.[54]

A revival of football at Harvard and Yale about 1872 (it had been prohibited for some years because of increasing roughness)[55] was the first real step in its emergence as an organized sport. The English variant known as Rugby, rather than association football, was played, and at a conference among representatives of Harvard, Yale, Princeton, and Columbia a set of rules derived from those of the English Rugby Union was formally adopted. If the game was still far removed from the intercollegiate football we know to-day, its development from that date, 1876, followed a steady and persistent course.

Among the early changes which transformed Rugby into our

modern game were the reduction of the number of players from fifteen to eleven; their assignment to specific positions in line and backfield; new provisions for running with the ball, kicking, and passing; and the substitution of the modern "scrimmage" for the old "scrummage"—that confused huddle of the original game in which, instead of being passed back, the ball was indiscriminately kicked out after being put in play. When the new Intercollegiate Football Association gave its sanction to these new rules in 1881, there was little left of English Rugby in American colleges.[56]

Football aroused spectator interest from the start, and the Big Three of the eastern colleges—Harvard, Yale and Princeton —at first completely overshadowed all other teams. It was long before comparable elevens were in the field. The Thanksgiving Day games of these universities were consequently the great events of the fall season. Some four thousand spectators turned out for the first Princeton-Yale game in 1878; little more than a decade later, attendance was almost forty thousand.[57]

Few adults found themselves able or willing to play football. Although teams made up of former college players were for a time quite active, the game was primarily for boys. But many were glad to watch so exciting a sport. Its dependence upon brute force satisfied atavistic instincts as could no other modern spectacle except the prize-fight. Baseball had become the national game because so many people played it as well as watched it. Football was destined from the first to be primarily a spectator sport.

→»«←

THIS phenomenal expansion in the field of sports was the most significant development in the nation's recreational life that had yet taken place. Apart from all the considerations already mentioned, athletics provided an outlet for surplus energy and suppressed emotions which the American people greatly needed. The traditions of pioneer life had influenced them along very definite lines, and the restrictions of urban living warred against a feeling for the outdoors which was in their blood. With the gradual passing of so much of what the frontier had always stood for, sports provided a new outlet for an inherently restless people.[58]

In subsequent years they were to become far more general. Outdoor recreation was to develop into a much more marked feature of American life as new opportunities opened up for ever larger numbers of people to play games. The democracy was to take over sport to an extent which its limited leisure and lack of resources still made impossible in these decades after the Civil War. But the path had been cleared. America had discovered a new world.

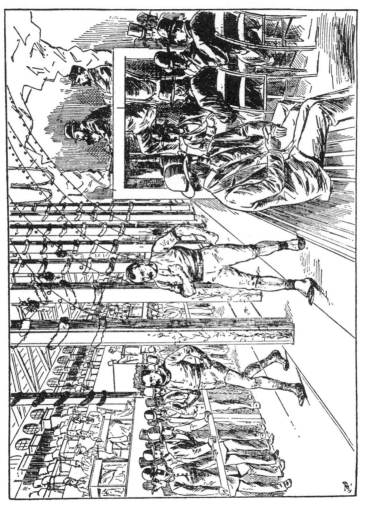

A Six-day Walk for the Pedestrian Championship
The O'Leary-Hughes match at Gilmore's Garden, New York.
New York Graphic, Oct. 5, 1878.

chapter **12**

The New Order

WITH THE RISE OF SPORTS SUPPLEMENTING THE CONTINUED growth of commercial amusements, there was a steadily broadening interest in recreation in the 1880's and 1890's. The doldrums of half a century earlier had been left far behind. The gospel of work still held good, but it was tempered by a new realization of the need for play. The decline of puritan influence resulted in wider popular sanction for many diversions which had once been generally disapproved. And the new sports themselves, as a writer in *Outing* declared, had made a breach in the walls "which that awful personage Mrs. Grundy had raised up to separate the sexes in outdoor games." [1] The era of Victorian repression was drawing to a close.

Newspapers and magazines all reflected this. During the summer of 1886 the *New York Tribune* devoted no less than five hundred columns to sports, also issuing its *Book of Open-Air Sports,* and a decade later William Randolph Hearst started a custom which the entire press quickly adopted. He began publishing daily in the *New York Journal* a page headed "In the World of Professional and Amateur Sports." [2] Magazines devoted to these new activities were also started. *Outing* had shown the way. It was followed by a wide choice of weeklies and monthlies ranging from the *American Canoeist* to the *Bicycling World,* from the *Ball Players' Chronicle* to *Archery and Tennis News.*

It could still be said that many more people watched sports than took part in them. James F. Muirhead, a sympathetic but critical English observer of the new movement, reported that games were widely played in the East but in the Middle West "baseball and other sports, like dancing in China, are almost wholly in the hands of paid performers." [3] Nevertheless, hundreds of thousands were being recruited annually to fill the ranks of a growing army of sportsmen and sportswomen. The outdoor movement was gathering increasing momentum. There was a vogue for walking and mountain-climbing, fishing and hunting, camping in the woods. A craze for canoeing is attested by notices of railroad excursions into the country with freight-cars equipped with special canoe racks and also with accommodations for folding boats. Steamship lines advertised outings for amateur photographers—"Up the river the artists sailed, popping away with their cameras." [4]

There were summer resorts. It was no longer only Saratoga, Newport, Long Branch, and a relatively small number of fashionable watering-places that represented this phase of recreation. The number of resorts, especially in what was becoming the vacationland of New England mountain and seashore, was legion. In May, 1890, the *New York Tribune* was running some eight columns of summer-hotel advertisements, appealing directly to the middle class rather than to the more exclusive ranks of society. The popular *Summer Tourist and Excursion Guide,* listing moderate-priced hotels and cheap railroad excursions, represented a far departure from "The Fashionable Tour" of half a century earlier.

The attractions the resorts offered also mirrored the changing scene. One hotel, inordinately proud of its gas-lights and electric bells, glowingly advertised extensive grounds for lawn tennis, croquet, and archery. Another singled out as its most popular feature its facilities for fishing, boating, driving, tennis, and croquet.[5] Every seashore resort stressed the bathing. There were no longer any reservations as to its propriety. The prudent female still went into the water fully clothed. *Godey's Lady's Book* advertised a costume of Turkey red "consisting of a yoke polonaise and full drawers," to be worn with a sash around the waist, long black stockings, and a straw hat.[6] But the old prejudices

Camping Out

Lithograph by N. Currier after a painting by Louis Maurer, 1856. Courtesy of Harry T. Peters.

The Great International Caledonian Games

Jones Woods, New York City, July 1, 1867. Lithograph by Kelly and Whitehill, designed and lithographed by J. L. Giles.

against men and women going into the surf together had completely disappeared.

Visitors from abroad in the 1890's were as much struck by the way Americans were now seeking out opportunities for play as those who had come to this country in the 1840's had been impressed by our apparent lack of interest in amusements. The United States was still the Land of the Dollar. We were a nation absorbed in money-making. But there was a new appreciation of the rôle of recreation "as a leaven to the toilsome year of the world." [7] Among others, James Bryce, as keen an interpreter of the American scene as any European who has ever visited the United States, found a remarkable faculty for enjoyment among Americans, a power to draw happiness from simple and innocent pleasures which was seldom found in overburdened Europe. "The sadness of Puritanism," he wrote, "seems to have been shed off." [8] Two French travelers made reports which contrasted even more sharply with those of their mid-century predecessors. Paul de Rousiers was specially impressed with what he considered the general air of honesty and decency about our recreation; [9] Paul Blouet by the freedom and gaiety with which American men and women took part in so many activities together. "They have not the English tendency," the latter told his countrymen, "to convert their pleasures into funeral services." [10]

→»)«←

THESE GAINS had been made gradually. Americans generally had not suddenly thrown off that psychological restraint which one writer termed "the doom of work." [11] Many of the generation of the 1890's had had much too deeply imprinted on their minds the moral lessons taught by the little homilies they had read as children in the famous McGuffey readers. In one of them, "The Idle Boy Reformed," a little lad who unaccountably disliked work asked several animal friends to play with him. The invariable answer was, "No, I must not be idle." The story concludes: " 'What? is nobody idle? Then little boys must not be idle.' So he made haste and went to school and learned his lesson very well, and the master said he was a good boy." [12]

Even when decreasing hours of labor (the twelve-hour day had now largely given way to the ten-hour day) and such revolutionary changes as Saturday half-holidays and two-week summer vacations afforded a new measure of justified leisure, there was still the old prejudice against any frivolous "mispense" of time. It was particularly strong in rural sections and primarily directed against commercial entertainment. The pleasures of the city stood condemned, as partaking of the Devil, by those who did not have the opportunity to enjoy them. It was the cry of the Lollards against the pernicious amusements of the fourteenth century; of the early middle-class Puritans against the diversions of the English aristocracy; of the humble followers of the New England way against the fashionable pleasures of the rich merchants; of the frontier converts to Methodism against urban dancing, card-playing, and theatre-going.

The metropolis stood for vice and wickedness. Religious journals painted its traps and pitfalls in lurid colors, vividly revealed its pleasures as sinister invitations to evil. New York was the outstanding symbol of "all the abominations which curse humanity," but readers of the more exciting exposures were warned that "the giddy voluptuaries who find pleasure in guilty abandon and corrupt morals are not indigenous to New York, but flourish to a lesser degree in all great cities." In *Metropolitan Life Unveiled, or Mysteries and Miseries of America's Great Cities,* the author was careful to point out that he was not prompted by "pessimistical reflections," but unmasked the sins of the cities solely that the beauties of refinement and purity might appear nobler by contrast.[13] Yet naturally enough the warnings of the godly only heightened the discontent of country youths with a life which so signally lacked these dangers and excitements. Bright lights were made all the more alluring.

Vitriolic attacks which would have had the admiring approval of Cotton Mather were still being launched against the theatre.

As a leader of the die-hards, the Reverend Josiah W. Leeds was profoundly shocked that playhouses should be looked upon with more tolerance than during the early days of the Republic, although they were probably "as low in character and proportionally as great in number as they were in Paris when that city was under the sway of the God-denying, blood-seeking, and depraved leaders of the French Revolution." He would tolerate nothing that had to do with the theatre. "If avowed Christians of 're-spectability' would have the vile variety theatres of the poorer classes removed from our cities," he warned, "such persons cannot consistently give countenance to the playhouses of the so-styled 'better sort'; and if they would have the low music-halls, with their tawdry and lewd accessories abolished, they, on their part, should have naught to do with the elegant opera, its alluring ballet and unsavory plot." [14]

But while the heirs of the Puritan tradition might still rail again all urban entertainments, clinging tenaciously to outmoded ideals of conduct, they could not possibly prevent developments which were an inevitable consequence of changing social and economic conditions. The church as a whole adopted a more realistic attitude. It listened to the people, realizing it had lost the power to impose arbitrary prohibitions. When it disapproved of certain types of commercial amusements, it sought to substitute its own entertainments. "The church must not attempt to take away the theatre, the dance, the card party," stated William D. Hyde, "unless it can give in its place not merely a religious or intellectual substitute, like a prayer meeting or a literary society, but a genuine social equivalent." [15] "If amusing young people aids to save them," the *Northwestern Christian Advocate*, an organ of the Methodist Episcopal Church unequivocally stated in one issue, "then the work is fully and gloriously worthy of the church." [16]

Provision was made in the new institutional or socialized churches of the 1880's and 1890's for libraries, gymnasiums, and assemblies; for games, concerts, and amusements. One of them built a $400,000 People's Palace to meet the community's needs for "sanctified amusement and recreation." [17] The Y.M.C.A. had already become a leader in the promotion of sports (it had some 261 gymnasiums in cities throughout the country [18]), and other religious organizations vied with the churches themselves in providing social activities of all kinds. It was the era of sociables, fairs, suppers, and strawberry festivals. In mild and innocent form, these affairs could reproduce through raffles, grab-bags, charades, games, and refreshments the sophisticated pleasures of more worldly society. [19]

But again it would be misleading to imply that this revolutionary change in the attitude of the church was accomplished without strong opposition from within the ranks. Religion was combating the rivalry of entertainment over its hold upon the public, but not all churchmen realized what was happening. "We are not informed," Dr. William Bayard Hale caustically wrote in *The Forum*, "...that the Church at Ephesus or Philippi ever advertised a bazaar, a clam-bake, or a strawberry social. We have no information that St. Paul was accustomed to give stereopticon lectures, Barnabas operating the lantern. It is not clearly established that St. Athanasius ever arranged a kirmess, a broom-drill, or a pink tea." [20] He cited flagrant examples of churches seeking at one and the same time to raise money and entertain their members. It was his forthright conclusion that "the world does not need the church as a purveyor of vaudeville."

The crusading Mr. Leeds sprang joyfully into the fray. He was as strongly opposed to church socials as to the lowest music-hall performances. He had no tolerance whatsoever for the idea that the church should in any way recognize the popular craving for amusement—"It used to be held that Jesus and His work furnished ample resources to meet the loftiest aspirations of a saved soul." He condemned with equal vigor dramas, comedies, farces, suppers, fairs, and entertainments of any conceivable sort. A strawberry festival was a step which led straight to the variety show or public dance-hall:

And fairs and shows in the halls were held,
And the world and her children were there,
And laughter and music and feasts prevailed
In the Place that was meant for prayer.[21]

Observance of the Lord's Day also brought about another clash with conservative religion. Its dedication to rest and meditation had broken down somewhat in the late eighteenth century, and then, as we have seen, been vigorously revived early in the nineteenth. Now the doctrine was again being undermined. The great influx of foreign immigrants, bringing with them wholly different ideas of how Sunday should be spent, had a great influence in the cities. The Germans particularly followed the customs of the Continental Sabbath, so completely at variance with those of the Puritan Sabbath, and their picnics and beer-garden entertainments became a Sunday feature wherever they had settled in large numbers. Industrious, sober, hard-working, they set an example which was widely followed. The popularity of Sunday excursions and the practice of making the day primarily an occasion for recreation spread rapidly after mid-century among working people.[22]

In the running fight against this trend, rural America stubbornly maintained its old-fashioned ways. South Carolina continued to make church attendance compulsory as late as 1885, and the rock-ribbed state of Vermont attempted to enforce the old-time bans on its statute-books that forbade all Sunday diversions. Wherever the evangelical religions had a popular following, there the Sabbath was rigidly observed. Even in the cities the more conservative ministers preached innumerable sermons against profaning the Lord's Day, promising dire punishment for whoever dared to depart from the straight and narrow path. Excursions to the country, picnics and ball games, Sunday concerts, came under as severe a ban as theatre-going, dancing, or card-playing. "You cannot serve God and skylark on a bicycle," one minister told his abashed congregation. Such militant organizations as the American Sabbath Union, the Sunday League of

America, the Lord's Day Alliance, were startling proof of the vitality of the strong forces still arrayed in support of this phase of Puritan doctrine.[23]

In one part of their campaign these religious forces had powerful allies. When they urged legislation to maintain the Sabbath that forbade all work on that day, they could count upon the support of the Knights of Labor and the American Federation of Labor. But on the issue of recreation on the Lord's Day there was a definite parting of the ways. Labor was as much in favor of complete Sunday freedom in this respect as the religious reformers were opposed to it. Times had greatly changed, but the forces of labor could ask their religious friends, as King James had asked the leaders of Puritan reform, "For when shall the common people have leave to exercise if not upon the Sundayes and Holydays, seeing they must apply their labour, and winne their living in all working dayes?"

The fight to maintain the sanctity of the Lord's Day was inevitably foredoomed in the light of changing social conditions. "Where is the city in which the Sabbath is not losing ground?" one discouraged reformer asked in 1887. "To the mass of the workingmen Sunday is no more than a holiday . . . it is a day for labor meetings, for excursions, for saloons, beer-gardens, baseball games and carousels." [24]

In the West, if not in the East, even the theatres were opening on the Sabbath. Sunday notices in such a paper as the *Chicago Tribune* advertised special attractions for the day—a spectacular melodrama at one theatre and a comic-opera company at another. All the variety houses and music-halls were open.[25] There was no question that the city had broken the shackles imposed upon Sunday amusements by religious dogma. And the freedom once won would not be surrendered. Judged by modern standards, great numbers of Americans still observed the Sabbath religiously, but for many others the day had become by the 1890's one for play and enjoyment which presented a striking contrast to conditions in mid-century. It was the most important single development of the late nineteenth century increasing the opportunities of the common man for recreation.

-->>><<<-

ON A VISIT to this country during these years, the English soci-ologist Herbert Spencer recognized the changes that had come over the recreational scene. He also drew attention to another aspect of the popular attitude toward amusement. "Old Froissart, who said of the English of his day 'that they take their pleasures sadly after their fashion,'" Spencer wrote, "would doubtless, if he lived now, say of the Americans that they take their pleasures hurriedly after their fashion. In large measure with us, and still more with you, there is not that abandonment to the moment which is requisite for full enjoyment, and this abandonment is prevented by the ever-present sense of multitudinous responsi-bilities." [26]

It was natural that Americans should not entirely escape the shadow of work in their play, should carry into it something of the competitive spirit which characterized their other activities. In the best of circumstances there was likely to be that residue from old traditions. Horace Greeley had noted the tendency to make play a business rather than a diversion from business as early as 1876. He complained that with teachers for every art, science, and "ology," there should be no room for professors of play. "Who will teach us incessant workers," he asked plaintively, "how to achieve leisure and enjoy it?" [27]

And in 1880 James A. Garfield, in an address at Lake Chau-tauqua, had made a striking characterization of the age on whose threshold America now stood which both emphasized and carried one step further the ideas expressed by Horace Greeley. "We may divide the whole struggle of the human race into two chapters," Garfield declared; "first, the fight to get leisure; and then the second fight of civilization—what shall we do with our leisure when we get it." [28]

In going on to discover what Americans were now doing with

their increasing leisure, it must be realized that the pattern of recreation had become inconceivably complex. Every year new strands were being woven into it. At no point is it possible to draw a complete picture of America at play. The scene in the 1880's and 1890's can only be traced in broadest outline through a general account of the principal diversions of the various groups that made up contemporary society.

chapter **13**

Metropolis

W HAT WAS TYPICAL OF URBAN AMUSEMENTS AT THE CLOSE OF
the past century? Everything, and nothing. But the great
mass of city dwellers sought out as they had throughout the century
the most lively and exciting popular entertainment. In the 1840's
spokesmen of labor had declared that the intolerable burden of
working conditions in the city demanded "excitement fully proportioned to the depression." It was even truer half a century
later. Imperial Rome had sought to appease the restlessness of its
laboring masses by providing the free spectacles of the circus and
gladiatorial combat. Imperial America had its amusement palaces, its prize-fights, its concert-saloons, for which the modern
workingman had to pay.

These phases of recreation now bulked larger than ever on the
national horizon. The tremendous growth of cities made them of
great importance. In 1850 there had been but eighty-five urban
communities with a population of more than 8,000; there were
almost seven times as many by the end of the century. Between
1880 and 1900 alone the urban population had more than
doubled, rising from fourteen to thirty million. New York and
Brooklyn accounted for over two million in 1890; Chicago and
Philadelphia for over a million each; Boston, Baltimore, and
Washington for about half a million apiece. There were in all
twenty-eight cities with more than 100,000 inhabitants.[1]

These great masses of people were made up of all types and
all nationalities. In Chicago the foreign-born numbered nearly as
many in 1890 as the entire population ten years earlier. Germans,
Swedes, Norwegians, Bohemians, Irish, Italians, Poles, thronged

its busy streets. New York presented an even more polyglot population. It had as many Italians as Naples, as many Germans as Hamburg, twice as many Irish as Dublin, and two and a half times as many Jews as Warsaw. It had thickly settled districts taken over in their entirety by Hungarians, Greeks, Syrians, Chinese.[2] In large part the foreign elements carried on the humbler tasks of society, but they also began to crowd and push the native Americans in this bustling, thriving urban world. Competition was intense. Yet every year more people were irresistibly drawn to metropolis from rural America. In some parts of the country there was actual depopulation. New England villages were abandoned as their inhabitants fled to the great eastern manufacturing centers; even in Missouri, eastern Iowa, southeastern Indiana, and western Illinois the countryside was depleted in favor of the young and vigorous cities of the Middle West.[3]

These swarms of newcomers from the country and from abroad went into all trades and occupations. They became day laborers, street-car conductors, mechanics, factory-hands, teamsters, hod-carriers, clerks, grocers, haberdashers, restaurant keepers, carpenters, policemen . . . and also domestic servants, garment-workers, salesgirls, typists, telephone operators. . . . New occupations were opening up every day as the city and the machine more and more dominated the changing economy.

Despite long hours of work and the economic precariousness of their lives, or all the more because of such conditions, these wage-earners were eager for amusement of any kind. Little attention was paid to their social welfare. The cities had not yet developed their present park systems; there were no municipal recreation programs. It was difficult if not impossible to escape crowded streets and noisome tenements. The sports and outdoor activities being so widely taken up by the country at large were not yet within the realm of practical possibility for the majority of urban workers. Their entertainment was necessarily passive, commercialized, and cheap.

Sunday "Social Freedom" in the Bowery

A religious paper's view. *Illustrated Christian Weekly*, 1874. Courtesy of
the New York Historical Society.

A Chicago Pool-Room on Sunday

Drawing by T. de Thulstrup. *Harper's Weekly,* 1892.

Barnum had pioneered in meeting such limitations of taste and pocket-book. He had had innumerable imitators. Public amusements—tawdry though they might often be, sometimes vicious—had expanded with the growth of cities at a rate never before known. The American metropolis far surpassed that of Europe in the wealth and variety of entertainment it offered to its surging population.

→»)«(←

THE MID-CENTURY THEATRE had played a leading rôle in satisfying urban needs. We have seen the great playhouses of the period packed with "all classes of fraternized humanity." But now the separation of different types of theatrical entertainment just starting in the 1850's had been carried through to its logical conclusion. The circus, the variety show, and burlesque were completely divorced from the legitimate stage. There was a new popular theatre of farce and melodrama quite distinct from the serious drama and polite comedy produced for the world of culture and education.

The old stock companies had also largely given way to a further variant of the star system. Managers staged what they hoped would be a successful play, in the main built up about a single actor or actress, and kept it on the boards as long as they possibly could. Its welcome exhausted in the city, it was then sent to the provinces. The "traveling combination" typified the theatre of the 1890's, and there was a phenomenal growth in the quantity, if not the quality, of companies on the road. They brought to many smaller cities whatever had first pleased metropolitan audiences, both popular entertainment and the more sophisticated plays. Throughout the country "temples of amusement" with the people's own prices (ten, twenty, and thirty cents) blatantly defied the "temples of art" given over to classic revivals and contemporary problem plays.

The new Bowery in New York, opening on the eve of the Civil War, had been one of the first of the truly popular theatres. A reporter of the *Herald* found the house on its first night "jammed with the democracy, unwashed and unterrified, to the number of a couple of thousand." In a smoke-laden atmosphere redolent of beer and sweat, this boisterous audience watched the play with an enthusiasm untempered by any polite conventions. A sergeant-at-arms with a rattan cane did what he could to keep the Bowery "bhoys" in order, but woe betide the player who did not please that shirt-sleeved gallery. Catcalls and hisses might still be emphasized, as they had been in an earlier day, by a barrage of eggs and rotten fruit.[4]

Many of this theatre's old customs survived at the Bowery of the 1890's. It was a house which combined melodrama and variety for the delectation of as rough-and-ready an audience as ever crowded its predecessor. Admission to a box was seventy-five cents, but the gallery cost only a dime. House policemen endeavored to maintain order. The officer assigned to the parquet was accustomed to stand throughout the performance with his back to the orchestra leader, a formidable figure with long black mustaches, wearing a derby. Any one who became too noisy would feel the sharp rap of his cane and the hissed warning, "Cheese it!" The theatre had a convenient bar. Throughout the show waiters hurried about, and glasses of foaming beer were continually being passed back and forth.[5]

The People's, the Windsor, the Third Avenue, the National, the London, were other popular New York houses largely given over to melodrama at ten to thirty cents.[6] Chicago had a bloc of what were called provincial theatres, presenting "entertainment of the more democratic type." The Alhambra and the Madison Street Opera House had a wide fame. At the Park the actresses were glad to join members of the audience for a casual drink, and boys sold rotten cabbages—even an occasional dead cat—to the gallery gods.[7] An air of somewhat greater respectability hovered over Boston's Grand Opera House and the People's Theatre in Philadelphia (it was advertised as "the largest and handsomest popular price theatre in America"), but standards of decorum were not unduly high. The playhouses of San Francisco and other western cities granted nothing to those of the East in their air of democratic informality.

The dime-novel influence dominated this popular theatre. Melodrama was all the rage, staged with extravagant elaboration. Four acts with twenty-odd scenes were the rule for a good sizzling play of death and destruction. Harbor-fronts with lapping waves of real water were ingeniously constructed, and rugged papier-maché mountains erected with rock faces and fearsome precipices. Horses raced on treadmills, railroad trains were wrecked, and violent explosions sent the property houses crashing. Through these exciting scenes strode scowling, heavy-mustached villains who treacherously bound lovely girls on the railroad tracks before approaching locomotives, or locked them in gloomy subterranean dungeons while the river slowly rose to the only window. But the handsome hero was always in time for a dramatic last-minute rescue. Murder, arson, burglary were vividly depicted—everything but rape and seduction. The theme often involved the pitfalls that beset the innocent country girl lured to the big city, but she was invariably saved from that fate worse than death.

There were five main characters in this popular drama, and the audience came to know exactly what to expect of each of them—the hero and heroine, the light-comedy boy, the soubrette, and the heavy man. Owen Davis, accustomed at this period to turn out ten to twenty melodramas a year reaching an audience of seven million (he had a good plot, he explained), once tried to have the comedy boy fall in love with some one other than the soubrette. He had to revise his play: the audience was too bewildered.[8]

The melodramas were written by the ream—*Under the Gaslight* (one of the earliest and most popular), *Only a Working Girl, The Limited Mail, Dangers of a Great City, The Turf Digger's Doom, The Power of Gold, Wilful Murder,* and *Nellie, the Beautiful Cloak Model.* In *On the Bowery* Steve Brodie himself jumped off a shaky Brooklyn Bridge and plunged through the trap amid a shower of rock salt thrown up by stage-hands. *The Naval Cadet* found James J. Corbett heroically saving the heroine from a foul cellar dive: "So you've come for the gal," sneered the villain, gliding stealthily forward, an ugly knife clenched between his gleaming teeth. Gentleman Jim would calmly take off his white gloves, lay them carefully beside his silk hat, and step forward.[9] How the audience stamped and shouted as evil was vanquished by honor in the person of the new champion prize-fighter!

Virtue always won in the last round of melodrama. Poverty was honorable and innocence unassailable. Currency was given to the most noble sentiments. "An honest shop girl is as far above a fashionable idler as heaven is above earth," the honest shop girl sententiously declaimed. Sympathetic audiences at *The White Slave* learned for all time that "rags are royal raiment when worn for virtue's sake."

Most popular of all the melodramas were the westerns, reflecting the romantic glamour that clung to the passing frontier. Its wild and woolly heroes appeared in person—"Texas Jack" Omohundro, "Wild Bill" Hickok, and "Buffalo Bill" Cody. They reënacted for cheering audiences saloon brawls, stage-coach hold-ups, and blood-curdling Indian attacks. Trusty rifles and murderous six-shooters barked continuously in *The Gambler of the West,* and at every bark another redskin bit the dust. Between the acts Jack Dalton threw bowie-knives at Baby Bess, the Pet of the Gulch, and Rattle Snake Oil was sold at a dime a bottle in the lobby.[10]

After his success in such plays as *The Scouts of the Plains* and *The Red Right Hand; or The First Scalp for Custer*—their thrilling scenes sometimes interpolated (shades of Mr. Barnum!) with a temperance lecture—Buffalo Bill launched his Wild West, Rocky Mountain and Prairie Exhibition. It went from triumph to triumph, playing to over a million people in one five-months season: Indians, cowboys, Mexicans; wild Texas steers and buf-

faloes; the Deadwood Coach and Sitting Bull; Annie Oakley and
Buffalo Bill himself in his broad white sombrero.[11]

Almost as popular as the melodrama, greatly favored by the
lone male in the big city, were the burlesque shows. They had
come in shortly after the Civil War, in those wicked days when
the cancan was all the rage and English burlesque queens first
offered up their "fatted calves at the shrine of a prodigal New
York audience." [12] There had been outraged protests against this
type of show. Critics almost wept at the public's "porcine taste
for indelicate buffoonery," but the managers of the popular
theatres knew a good thing, from a strictly commercial point of
view, when they saw it. If reformers chose to describe a production as a "disgraceful spectacle of padded legs jigging and
wriggling in the insensate follies and indecencies of the hour," it
seldom hurt box-office receipts.[13]

The modern version of burlesque soon omitted entirely the
gaily extravagant satire which had distinguished the early performances of the Black Crook Company, the British Blondes, the
Red Stocking Blondes. The advertisements of the 1890's told the
whole story: "50—Pairs of Rounded Limbs, Ruby Lips, Tanta-
lizing Torsos—50." Many theatres in the large cities were given
over entirely to this entertainment; traveling companies took it
on the road. In 1895 Sam T. Jack, "King of Burlesque," was proprietor of Lily Clay's Colossal Gaiety Company, the Ada Richmond Folly Company, the Creole Burlesque Company.... The
rounded limbs and dazzling torsos of these merry maidens were
clothed in "close-fitting, flesh colored silk tights," but the Madison
Street Opera House in Chicago happily advertised that this was
really far more attractive than no costume at all.[14]

Variety also had come into its own in this popular theatre; it
was taking form and shape as modern vaudeville. The transition
was an important one. While the acts did not differ greatly from
those at Niblo's, the American Museum, or the mid-century
Theatre of Mirth and Variety, they marked a distinct improvement over the music-hall show that had flourished in the 1860's

and 1870's. Recognizing that there was a far larger audience for this type of entertainment if it were reasonably decent, a new generation of producers was determined to rescue variety from the ill repute into which it had fallen and elevate it to "a high plane of respectability and moral cleanliness." [15]

Tony Pastor had initiated refined vaudeville, entertainment for the whole family, in New York, and his famous theatre was soon rivaled by the Globe, the Olympic, and the Theatre Comique. Other cities gave it a no less enthusiastic welcome. By the 1880's there were six vaudeville houses in Philadelphia, two in Baltimore, two in Chicago, three in St. Louis, and three in San Francisco.[16] As in the case of melodrama and burlesque, traveling companies took it on the road. Among the more popular troupes listed by M. N. Leavitt, who controlled six companies himself, were Tony Pastor's Combination, Harry Minor's Comedy Four, Tillotson's Varieties, The All Star Specialty Company, and Charlie Shay's Quincuplexals. Here was a new departure in entertainment —"natural offspring of the old-time minstrel, circus and variety sketch stage." [17]

There were acrobats and trained animals, sentimental ballads and comic songs, bicycle-riders and fancy roller-skaters, jugglers and magicians, innumerable dancing acts—all the tricks and stunts that have always been a lowly adjunct of the legitimate stage. Often one-act farces or comedies were given—*Lost in New York* or *The Mud Town Rubes*. Sometimes there were prudent borrowings from burlesque.

Among the head-liners in the 1890's were Weber and Fields, Montgomery and Stone, Maggie Cline singing "Throw Him Down, McCloskey," and Lillian Russell "Kiss Me Mother, Ere I Die"; Carmencita in her Spanish dances; Sandow, the Strong Man; the Russell Brothers in short skirts ("Maggie, have you put fresh water in the goldfish bowl?" "No, they ain't drunk up what I give 'em yesterday."); Pat Rooney dancing his famous jig; and the Cohan family with Master George in *The Lively Boot-black* and *Peck's Bad Boy*.[18]

The entry into this profitable field of entertainment of B. F. Keith and F. F. Proctor brought about still further expansion of vaudeville. The former introduced the continuous performance at his Boston theatre in 1883 (Barnum had offered it for holidays half a century earlier at his American Museum), and a decade later Proctor adopted it at his New York Pleasure Palace. At the Ladies' Club Theatre still another forward step was taken—the show began at 11 A.M. and ran for twelve hours.[19]

As vaudeville spread to the provinces, theatres were organized in chains, and a nation-wide system for booking individual acts was developed. The two-a-day circuit came into being. One group of theatres alone was estimated to provide entertainment for five million every year. Refined vaudeville, observed one commentator at the close of the century, belonged to the era of the short story and the department store: "It may be a kind of lunch counter art, but then art is so vague and lunch is so real." [20]

There were performances at the popular theatres other than melodrama, burlesque, and vaudeville. Farces, musical shows, comedies, and serious drama were sometimes produced. The better houses warmly welcomed the stars of the legitimate stage; there was still a taste for good theatre. Even the People's and the Windsor, on New York's notorious Bowery, interrupted their usual programs to stage *Macbeth, King Lear,* and *Hamlet.*[21] But in comparison with an earlier day, the general public was far more interested in shows which pretended to be nothing more than entertainment. It unreservedly approved "the cheap and coarse sensationalism" decried by the critics. It thoroughly enjoyed "the silly buffoonery and vulgar nonsense" which offended the purists. When Keith and Proctor joined forces early in the twentieth century to establish their well-known circuit, the number of houses under their control alone soon grew to four hundred.[22] Vaudeville, spiced with melodrama and burlesque, had become the principal commercial amusement of America's urban democracy.

->>)<<-

DIME MUSEUMS, dance-halls, shooting-galleries, beer-gardens, bowling-alleys, billiard-parlors, saloons, and other more questionable resorts made up another whole world of entertainment whose glaring gas-lights symbolized the lure of the wicked city. And in the 1890's it often was wicked. It was an age of notoriously corrupt municipal governments. The line between virtue and vice was hard to distinguish; perfectly respectable places of entertainment shaded off imperceptibly into notorious dives. There were plenty of dance-halls that found "the young mechanics and dressmakers in their glory," but as many where the floor was crowded with prostitutes. Every large city had its red-light district given over to saloons and sporting-houses. Drinking, gambling, and prostitution had become tremendous social problems as the size of the constantly growing cities made control more and more difficult, particularly when politics formed its profitable alliance with vice.

The dime museums, which preyed upon the gullibility of their patrons rather than upon any less innocent tastes, had taken over the curiosities and freaks which had always had a peculiar attraction for the populace. Again Mr. Barnum had pointed the way. Here could be seen the fat woman and the sword-swallower, the bearded lady and the ossified girl, the tattooed man and the iron-jawed lady. There were always a stuffed mermaid, a wild man from Borneo, and a snake-charmer. What passer-by could resist the feverish ballyhoo of the museum barker when he offered them—frankly—such a show as the world had never seen? "The greatest, the most astounding aggregation of marvels and monstrosities ever gathered together in one edifice! From the ends of the earth, the wilds of darkest Africa, the miasmic jungles of Brazil, the mystic waters of the Yang-tse-Kiang, the cannibal isles of the Antipodes, the frosty slopes of the Himalayas and barren steppes of the Caucasus; sparing no expense, every town, every village, every hamlet, every nook and cranny of the globe has been searched with a fine-tooth comb to provide a feast for the eye and mind.... No waiting, no delays. Step up, ladies and gentlemen, and avoid the rush. Tickets now selling in the doorway."[23]

Sometimes a special performance would be given in the basement with such celebrities as Jo-Jo, the Dog-faced Boy, or Peerless Corinne, the Circassian Princess and Sword Swallower. And an extra dime was often drawn from the unwary by the promise of a chance to see "the unclad female form in all its loveliness"—generally a dim view of a show-window dummy.

Music-halls, free-and-easies, concert-saloons, provided an opportunity to drink in the garish atmosphere created by music, scantily dressed girl waitresses, and beautiful entertainers. Chicago, which liked to call itself the Paris of America, had scores of these places,[24] but New York really held unchallenged leadership. In 1898 the police of Gotham listed ninety-nine amusement resorts, including saloons with music and entertainment, on the Bowery alone. They classed only fourteen of them as respectable.[25] It was at one of these places that a singing waiter named Izzy Baline, crooning to delighted audiences such songs as "Just Break the News to Mother" and "You Made Me What I Am Today," started on a career which led to fame and fortune on Tin Pan Alley under the name of Irving Berlin.

At dance-halls and other establishments, local social clubs held balls and assemblies as they had since mid-century, generously inviting the public at the usual admission charge (lady included) of one dollar. The Zig Zag Club social was an event in San Francisco; Chicago went in for masquerade balls; and a fixture of the New York social calendar was the annual ball at Tammany Hall of the Chuck Connors Association. The latter was a democratic assemblage. Members of the Racquet Club and the New York Athletic Club came down town to mingle with representatives of the Knickerbocker Icemen, the East Side Democratic and Pleasure Association, the Lee Hung Fat Club, and the Lady Truck Drivers.

Toward the close of the century the electric trolley began to provide a Sunday or holiday substitute for these amusements.

Steamboat and even railroad excursions had long been possible, but here was a far easier and cheaper means of getting away from the city. The trolley ride was an outstanding feature of week-end recreation: the amusement parks to which the pleasure-seekers were carried became the holiday Mecca of thousands upon thousands of workers.[26] A writer in *Harper's Weekly*, impressed by the immense crowds that throughout the summer took advantage of these excursions, described the parks as "the great breathing-places for the millions of people in the city who get little fresh air at home." [27] And another observer declared that their pastimes yielded more enjoyment "than all the courtly balls and fashionable dissipation indulged in by fortune's favorites." [28]

The new rapid-transit companies not only offered reduced rates for daytime trips into the country, but advertised special trolley carnivals in the evening—the cars gaily illuminated with multicolored lights and boasting even a number of musicians to provide popular band music. They established their own amusement resorts in the outskirts of cities from Claremont, New Hampshire, to San Antonio, Texas. Some of these parks had little more than a pavilion or dance-hall; others had all possible attractions—roller coasters, merry-go-rounds, circle swings, bump-the-bumps, and shoot-the-chutes. In 1893 the Ferris Wheel crowned the attractions of the Midway at Chicago's World Fair, and soon thereafter it was the star feature of hundreds of trolley parks throughout the country.

Chicago had its Cheltenham Beach, popular for barbecues and clam-bakes, and later its famous White City. There were Paragon Park near Boston, the Chutes at San Francisco, and Forest Park Highlands at St. Louis. Crowds listened to band concerts, watched balloon ascensions and parachute jumps, cheered at professional bicycle races. At Manhattan Beach near Denver there was an ostrich farm and two open-air theatres. Willow Grove at Philadelphia had an auditorium seating ten thousand people.[29]

Winter Amateur Athletic Meet at the Boston Athletic Club
Drawing by Henry Sandham. *Harper's Weekly*, 1890.

The Bathing Hour on the Beach at Atlantic City
Drawing by Frank H. Schell. *Harper's Weekly,* 1890.

A Double Play to Open the League Season
Boston at New York. Drawing by W. P. Snyder. *Harper's Weekly,* 1886.

Coney Island also had by this time those varied entertainments which continue to draw throngs of New Yorkers every summer day. Bathing-houses lined the beach, minstrel bands played on the boardwalk, and everywhere the shrill cry of barkers advertised carrousels, freak shows, shooting-galleries, and dance-halls. In 1897 George C. Tilyou opened his famed Steeplechase Park with a fantastic array of his own inventions—the Bounding Billows, Blow Hole, Barrel of Love, Human Roulette Wheel, Electric Seat, and Razzle Dazzle.[30] There was "a spurious toboggan slide of mammoth proportions," one observer noted, and on the boardwalk was being sold something new and strange which proved a more practical mobile form of nourishment than the clam chowder which had formerly ruled supreme. This new concoction was "a weird-looking sausage muffled up in two halves of a roll."

->>><<<-

ONE of the most popular acts on the vaudeville stage in these days was De Wolf Hopper's rendering of a famous poem:

Oh! somewhere in this favored land the sun is shining bright;
The band is playing somewhere, and somewhere hearts are light.
And somewhere men are laughing, and somewhere children shout;
But there is no joy in Mudville—mighty Casey has struck out.[31]

It was sign and symbol of the immense interest and enthusiasm baseball everywhere aroused. The fans crowded the grand stands and packed the bleachers almost every summer afternoon to watch the professional teams. "The fascination of the game," *Harper's Weekly* commented, "has seized upon the American people, irrespective of age, sex or other condition." [32] It was estimated that daily attendance at the games of clubs organized under the National Agreement was some sixty thousand, with the annual total amounting to almost eight million.[33] When the matches of small-town clubs and semiprofessional leagues were included, it was many times this figure. Baseball had come a long way from those early beginnings traced in mid-century. It was far and away the leading spectator sport, a boon to bank clerk and factory-worker, shopkeeper and mechanic, the business executive and his office-boy.

Together with the growth in popular interest, there had been a number of changes in the game itself since the National League was organized in 1876. The umpire had been empowered to call four balls and three strikes; a ball had to be caught on the fly for the batsman to be out—in his hands and not in his cap, as the practice had been; restrictions on pitching had been removed to make possible new refinements in curves and fade-aways; gloves were being worn; and the risks of the catcher's position had been reduced by arming him with mask, breastpad, and mitt. There had been difficulty over the best type of ball. It was at first too fast. Among the immense scores rolled up in this period was one of 201 to 11 at a game in Buffalo. Then the substitute ball had proved too dead. A twenty-four inning game between Harvard and Manchester ended in a scoreless tie. Finally a better balanced ball made more reasonable scores the rule. The game became generally faster, and with much improved playing, it was more exciting than ever.[34]

The National League had a friendly rival in the American Association, with which it held an annual championship series, but in 1889-90 a serious threat developed to its dominance over the professional game. The players themselves, in protest over what they considered unfair practices, attempted to win control through organization of the National Brotherhood of Baseball Players. Big-league ball was thrown into chaos; attendance dwindled away alarmingly. But the revolt was short-lived. The Brotherhood collapsed after a single season, dragging the American Association down in its fall, and the National League emerged from the conflict stronger than ever. It was left alone in the field with twelve member clubs, six in the East and six in the West, and it did not again have a major rival (although there were many minor associations) until the formation of the American League in 1899.[35] After a brief struggle for supremacy, these two associations amicably divided the field represented by the larger cities, and their establishment of an official World Series in 1903 added still more to popular interest.

Professional baseball had become at once big business, entertainment for the masses, and the guide and mentor of the thousands of amateur players throughout the country. Every city followed closely the fortunes of its own team, with the newspapers giving tremendous publicity to all league games. The genius of the sporting page had already arrived half a century ago, and he was enriching the American language with the expressive, pungent vocabulary of sport. On May 4, 1891, Chicago won a notable victory over Pittsburgh under the inspired leadership of "Pop" Anson. On the following morning Leonard Dana Washburn started his account of the affray in the Chicago *Inter-Ocean* in a new style of reporting:

> You can write home that Grandpa won yesterday.
> And say in the postscript that Willie Hutchinson did it. The sweet child stood out in the middle of the big diamond of pompadour grass and slammed balls down the path that looked like the biscuits of a bride. The day was dark, and when Mr. Hutchinson shook out the coils of his right arm, rubbed his left toe meditatively in the soil he loves so well, and let go, there was a blinding streak through the air like the tail of a skyrocket against a black sky. There would follow the ball a hopeless shriek, the shrill, whistling noise of a bat grippling with the wind, and a dull, stifled squash like a portly gentleman sitting down on a ripe tomato. . . .
> There were ten of the visiting delegation who walked jauntily to the plate and argued with the cold, moist air. Mr. Field lacerated the ethereal microbes three times out of four opportunities to get solid with the ball, and Brer Lewis Robinson Browning walked away from the plate with a pained expression twice in succession. The Gastown folks found the ball six times. Two of their runs were earned.
> Mr. Staley, who pitches for the strangers, did not have enough speed to pass a street car going in an opposite direction. His balls wandered down toward the plate like a boy on his way to school. If our zealous and public-spirited townsmen did not baste them all over that voting precinct it was because they grew weary and faint waiting for them to arrive. . . .[36]

The entire country was proud of the Chicago White Sox and the All-American team that A. G. Spalding took on a world tour in 1888-89, playing in Ceylon, in the shadow of the pyramids, and before the Prince of Wales in England.[37] Baseball had its national heroes, worshiped by small boys from Maine to California. There was not an American who did not recognize the fame of "Pop" Anson, "Iron Man" Joe McGinnity, and Honus Wagner, or know the significance of "Slide, Kelly, Slide." It was the national game beyond possible dispute.

"Let me say," declared Cardinal Gibbons in a speech made in 1896, "that I favor Base Ball as an amusement for the greatest pleasure-loving people in the world. . . . It is a healthy sport, and since the people of the country generally demand some sporting event for their amusement, I should single this out as the one best to be patronized and heartily approve of it as a popular pastime." [38]

-»>«<-

THERE WERE other spectator sports, though none really compared with baseball in popular appeal, during this period at the close of the past century. Racing and trotting matches were flourishing, drawing large crowds to the rapidly multiplying city tracks. Chicago had three, and four clustered about New York. It was the day of Salvator's reign as the horse of the century. His sensational victory over Tenny at Sheepshead Bay was cheered by an excited mob of many thousands.[39] Professional rowing matches —from single sculls to six-oared lap-streak gigs—created more excitement than they ever have since. In the days of the memorable duel between Edward Hanlan, Canada's Boy in Blue, and Charles E. Courtney, later coach at Cornell, they were a major sport.[40] Intercollegiate football, of course, had its followers, but we shall trace its further development in a later chapter—it was still more a sport of society than of the masses.

If there was a rival to the national game in sustained popular interest, it was prize-fighting, not wholly out from under the cloud of disapproval but nevertheless arousing a nation-wide excitement which official bans on championship bouts in no way diminished. The fortunes of favorite bruisers were followed avidly, and although it was still true that comparatively few people actually saw the fights, the reports of them were read by millions. An English visitor was somewhat shocked that his newspaper one morning in 1892 gave twelve prominent columns to a championship bout while the death of John Greenleaf Whittier rated only a single inside column.[41] But it was a correct appraisal of public interest.

The great event of the prize-fight world was the emergence of a champion of champions who dominated the ring from 1882 to 1892. America has perhaps never had a sports hero comparable to John L. Sullivan, the Strong Boy of Boston. He climbed to eminence over the prone body of Paddy Ryan, but it was when he knocked out Jake Kilrain in a fierce, grueling, seventy-five-round battle at New Orleans, the last of the bare-knuckle championship fights, that the great John L. was acknowledged lord of all he surveyed. His fame resounded throughout the world after this epic encounter, from which he won a purse of $20,000 and a diamond-studded championship belt presented by *The Police Gazette*.[42]

Boston's hero—the city once turned out *en masse* to honor him at a ceremony which found the Boston Theatre packed: the aldermen and mayor in the boxes, Beacon Street in the orchestra, and the gallery overflowing with the Irish [43]—owed his tremendous popularity to an aggressive pugnacity which made him always eager for a fight. He toured the country, first offering $50, and then raising the ante to $1,000, to any one who would stay with him four rounds. Mobs fought their way to see him whenever he appeared. On one occasion New York's new Madison Square Garden was crowded to the doors with a motley throng which embraced every element in the city's diverse population from Fifth Avenue to the Bowery. His only losing fight was with that insistent enemy John Barleycorn. Once when the great

John L. was scheduled to fight Charlie Mitchell, the English boxer, liquor won the preliminary round. When the gong rang, the Strong Boy staggered into the ring, not in his usual green trunks encircled by an American flag, but in full evening dress with a shirt-front flashing with diamonds. He was ready to fight —he was always ready, drunk or sober—but to the bitter disappointment of an excited audience the referee called off the bout.[44]

When Sullivan finally went down to defeat at the Olympic Club in New Orleans before Gentleman Jim Corbett, fighting under the Marquis of Queensberry rules, with five-ounce gloves, the world appeared to totter. An incredulous public refused to believe the dire news which appeared in bold-face headlines from coast to coast. The Strong Boy of Boston knocked out? It was not believed possible. A sorrowing poet sang of his downfall. To the tune of "Throw Him Down, McCloskey" the entire country joined in the chorus:

> John L. has been knocked out! the people all did cry
> Corbett is the champion! how the news did fly.
> And future generations, with wonder and delight,
> Will read in hist'ry's pages of the Sullivan-Corbett fight.[45]

Corbett reigned for five years, another popular champion, and then on St. Patrick's Day, 1897, was knocked out by the flying fists of Robert Prometheus Fitzsimmons, inventor of the solar-plexus punch. The bout was held in Carson City, went to fourteen rounds, and was fought for a $15,000 purse.

->>>⟨⟨⟨-

"THE SOCIAL CIVILIZATION of a people," Lord Lytton has written, "is always and infallibly indicated by the intellectual character of its amusements." [46] On the basis of those most widely enjoyed by the urban democracy of the nineteenth century, American civilization would not appear to have attained a very high level. Living and working conditions in the large city were primarily responsible for this. "When there is a lack of nourishing food and of the tonic of pure air," a thoughtful contemporary observed, "debilitated nerves crave excitement; hence the large number of saloons, gambling hells, dance halls, and theatres in the most crowded portions of the city." [47]

It is easy to overemphasize these more lurid aspects of urban recreation. Any account of public amusements forces far into the background the simpler pleasures of home and family life. Nevertheless it does remain true that the concentration of such large numbers of people in very small areas, working with the intensity enforced by the new industrialism, made them demand in their leisure hours stimulation that could relieve the strain of their long day in factory, store, or office. The simplicity and spontaneity of community life in the country or small town could not be preserved in the city. Mass entertainment was an inevitable development. Excursions into the country, the opportunity to enjoy sports for themselves, other active types of amusement were developing, but at a discouragingly slow rate. The democracy had asserted in ever-stronger terms its right to play. America had become a pleasure-loving nation, but the character of its amusements, in so far as the urban population was concerned, could not but cause serious misgivings.

The new century was to witness many changes. Living and working conditions were to be improved, stricter and more honest supervision was adopted for places of amusement that were definitely undesirable, and the growth of city park systems soon held out the promise of greater opportunities for outdoor activities. Recreation became a primary concern of the twentieth-century social movement to reform the evils of urban life, and there was already impending a revolution in the field of commercial amusements which was to have incalculable effects. Although it could hardly be recognized at the time, the 1890's represented the culminating stage in the development of many of those popular forms of entertainment which were the past century's answer to the needs of metropolis.

chapter 14

World of Fashion

THE WAYS IN WHICH SOCIETY MAY AMUSE ITSELF AFFORD, IN
any country and at any time, an exceptional opportunity
for the display of wealth and the assertion of social importance.
Thorstein Veblen has graphically demonstrated this conscious
or unconscious motivation in many forms of recreation. It is
clearly evident throughout American social history. The worthy
citizens of eighteenth-century Philadelphia vied with each other
in the magnificence of their banquets, loading their tables with
massive silver plate and serving such a choice selection of imported wines that the visiting John Adams stood amazed at the
"sinful feasts." The planters of Virginia rode to hounds in close
imitation of the English country squires whose social status they
sought to emulate in every possible way. Merchants of New York
and Boston were already aspiring to yachts in the 1850's, their
sons to membership in the exclusive boating clubs, while all the
fashionable world sought out Saratoga or Newport as a step
upward on the social ladder.

It was in the latter half of the past century, however, the
Gilded Age of American civilization, that society most flagrantly
bent its pleasures to display. The newly rich born of industry's
great advance since the Civil War—owners of railways, copper-
mines, textile-mills, steel-plants, packing-houses, and cattle
ranches—sought to establish social leadership through their extravagance in entertainments and amusements. A little band of
idle rich held the final redoubt in the fashionable world of the
1880's and 1890's, and the families of the new plutocracy felt it
essential to prove beyond shadow of doubt that they too were

idle and rich. It was not in the American tradition, which esteemed riches and abhorred idleness, but urban society was running after strange gods. And, in any event, the new plutocrats generally supplied the riches and left it to willing wives and a younger generation to demonstrate the idleness.

With the first post-war boom in the 1860's, observers began to note that New York society was becoming entirely based upon wealth, social prestige being won by those who had the most splendid carriages, drawing-rooms, and opera boxes. George Makepeace Towle has described the balls and assemblies—ladies in sparkling tiaras, suppers of oysters and champagne, fountains gushing wine or sprays of perfume. He was somewhat horrified by "so unceasing a round of glittering gaiety and dissipation." [1] The advance of the new millionaires was picturesquely described as "the Gold Rush" by representatives of older social traditions. "From an unofficial oligarchy of aristocrats," Mrs. John King Van Rensselaer sadly wrote, "society was transformed into an extravagant body that set increasing store by fashion and display." [2]

Nor was New York alone in this competitive rage for showy display. A sycophant press might boast that its ornate fancy-dress balls and ten-thousand-dollar dinner parties were the most expensive ever known, but the world of fashion throughout the land was closely following its lead. There was an epidemic of gaudy magnificence in the amusements of what went for society. One Chicago magnate brought an entire theatrical company from New York to entertain a group of his friends, and a wealthy woman in another city engaged a large orchestra to serenade her new-born child. [3] San Francisco was notorious for its "terribly fast so-called society set, engrossed by the emptiest and most trivial pleasures." [4] A fortunate miner who had struck it rich in Virginia City drove a coach and four with silver harness; another had champagne running from the taps at his wedding party. [5]

The famous ball with which Mrs. William K. Vanderbilt crashed the gates of society in 1883 was admitted by the press to have been more magnificent than the entertainments of Alexander, Cleopatra, or Louis XIV.[6] It was soon outshown by other affairs of New York's Four Hundred. In his *Society as I Have Found It,* Ward McAllister describes dinner parties with squadrons of butlers and footmen in light plush livery, silk stockings, and powdered hair; orchestras concealed behind flowered screens; and every out-of-season fruit and vegetable served on golden plates. At society's fancy-dress balls, men weighed down in suits of medieval armor tripped over their swords as they attempted to dance quadrilles; the women wore wreaths of electric lights in their hair to add a new luster to their diamonds.[7]

"Everything that skill and art could suggest," McAllister notes at one point, "was added to make the dinners not a vulgar display, but a great gastronomic effort, evidencing the possession by the host of both money and taste."[8] But always taste was secondary, and Crœsus was crowned society's Lord of Misrule. A marveling correspondent of the London *Spectator* found America's newly rich pouring out money on festal occasions as from a purse of Fortunatus, making feasts as of the Great King Belshazzar.[9]

For one ball the host built a special addition to his house providing a magnificent Louis XIV ball-room which would accommodate twelve hundred. Another time a restaurant was entirely made over with a plum-shaded conservatory, a Japanese room, and a medieval hall hung with Gobelin tapestries especially imported from Paris. At a reception given at the Metropolitan Opera House, twelve hundred guests danced the Sir Roger de Coverley on a floor built over stage and auditorium, and were then served supper at small tables by three hundred liveried servants. It was a world of jewels and satins, of terrapin and canvasbacks, of Château Lafite and imported champagne—"luxurious in adornment . . . epicurean in its feasting."[10]

In the cities of the West, where the golden stream flowed so freely in these thriving days and those who would scale society's heights often had so much to forget, even greater extravagances were sometimes recorded. It took many diamonds and much

Baltimore Society Dances for Charity

Grand ball at the Academy of Music for the benefit of the Nursery and Child's Hospital. *Frank Leslie's Illustrated Newspaper*, 1880.

Trotting Cracks of Philadelphia Returning from the Races

Having a brush past Turner's Hotel, Rope Ferry Road. Lithograph by
H. Pharazyn, 1870. Courtesy of the New York Historical Society.

*Fashionable
Turnouts in
Central Park*

Lithograph by Currier and Ives after sketches from life by Thomas Worth, 1870. J. Clarence Davies Collection, Museum of the City of New York.

wine for some of the new dowagers to erase entirely the mark of the laundry tub or kitchen sink. Only money could do it, and the sensational inspired most newspaper copy. The new plutocracy gave dinners at which cigarettes were wrapped in hundred-dollar bills or the guests found fine black pearls in their oysters. For one gala occasion the room was filled with cages of rare song-birds and dwarf fruit-trees, while half a dozen graceful swans swam in a miniature lake. There was a famous horseback dinner. "The guests were attired in riding habits," wrote Frederick Townsend Martin; "the handsomely groomed horses pranced and clattered about the magnificent dining-room, each bearing, besides its rider, a miniature table. The hoofs of the animals were covered with soft rubber pads to save the waxed floor from destruction." [11]

The Bradley Martin ball in 1897 created the greatest sensation of the Gilded Age. The ball-room of the Waldorf-Astoria Hotel was converted into a replica of Versailles and sumptuously decorated with rare tapestries and beautiful flowers. Mrs. Bradley Martin, as Mary Queen of Scots, wore a necklace of Marie Antoinette's and a cluster of diamond grapes once owned by Louis XIV. The suit of gold-inlaid armor worn by Mr. Belmont was valued at ten thousand dollars. The publicity given this affair was incredible. The *New York Times* and the *Herald* virtually gave over their front pages to descriptions of it, and the London papers all carried cabled dispatches. On the morning after the affair, the London *Daily Mail,* with allowance for the difference in time, reported: "Mrs. Bradley Martin, we have every reason to believe, is dressed at this very moment in a train of black velvet lined with cerise satin, and a petticoat, if it is not indiscreet to say so, of white satin, embroidered with flowers and arabesques of silver." The London *Chronicle* congratulated New York society on its triumph—"It has cut out Belshazzar's feast and Wardour Street and Mme. Tussaud's and the Bank of England. There is no doubt about that."

But there were limits to which even the American public

would go in condoning such heartless extravagance in a year when there was widespread distress among the poor. The storm of disapproval that followed in the train of this ball drove the Bradley Martins out of the country. Depressed by their unexpected notoriety, they settled permanently in England.[12]

-»>«<-

FOR ALL the lavish prodigality of these affairs, and despite the widespread publicity they obtained, they were not important. They directly touched the lives of only a very small coterie in the upper brackets of the fashionable world. Society in a broader sense, members of the community in which wealth was allied with culture, had many other forms of recreation where their patronage had some real significance. One of these was the legitimate stage, as contrasted with the more popular theatrical entertainment of the urban democracy.

The small, luxuriously appointed theatres where reserved seats ranged in price from one to three dollars had become the home of a relatively exclusive amusement. Every city had its fashionable playhouses. Writing of New York, Henry Collins Brown speaks of the friendly social atmosphere of Wallack's, Daly's Fifth Avenue Theatre, the Madison Square ("most exquisite theatre in all the world"), and the Union Square. In Chicago there were McVicker's and Hooley's; Boston offered the Museum and the old Boston Theatre. These houses appealed to the carriage trade. Here, in a new elegance of surroundings—the pit had become the parquet with sloping floor; upholstered plush seats were furnished throughout; steam heat (the Lyceum also had "medicated air, charged with ozone") had replaced the foyer stove; and the new electric lights were being installed— the world of fashion could enjoy the play in a quiet and comfortable atmosphere far removed from the democratic hurly-burly of mid-century.[13]

The productions at these theatres generally centered about some starred actor or actress, although a few able stock companies still survived, and they often achieved long-sustained runs comparable to those of to-day's popular plays. With the great expansion of popular entertainment for the masses, it had become not only possible but also necessary for managers of the better theatres to pay more attention to the cultural standards of their comparatively limited and sophisticated audience. There were revivals of Shakespeare and other classic writers; well-staged productions of serious contemporary drama, both American and foreign; and comedies and light operas which bore little resemblance to the blood-and-thunder melodrama and questionable burlesque that ruled at the people's theatres.

Contemporary critics often failed to realize that the divorcing of popular entertainment from the legitimate stage rivaled development of the star system as the outstanding feature of theatrical history in the second half of the century. Forgetting the slapstick and circus stunts with which it had been so heavily cluttered, they looked back nostalgically to the theatre of an earlier day and remembered only Shakespeare. They could not understand how a public which had once seemed to enjoy the drama so much had shifted its allegiance to vaudeville and burlesque. Deciding it had degenerated into "vulgarians," they damned the producers for their "practical, shopkeeping cultivation of this popular appetite." They often seemed totally unaware that vaudeville's assumption of the task of entertaining the million, which the theatre itself had once borne, was actually affording the legitimate stage far greater opportunity for the development of the drama than it had ever had before in the democratic society of America.[14]

In time they looked back upon this period, as dramatic critics are so wont to do, with entirely different eyes. In retrospect the actors and actresses who supported the legitimate stage, even the plays produced at the more fashionable playhouses, took on Olympian stature. The years between 1870 and 1890 were said in many critical memoirs to stand out as the theatre's golden age.[15] The last decade of the century fell under something of a cloud. The rise of a theatrical trust, dominated by a group of managers who appeared to be deserting the ways of Wallack and Daly, threatened to impose a monopolistic control which considered only the box-office.[16] But even in those days there could be no real question that dramatic standards were far higher than in mid-century.

If one chose one's theatre, it was not necessary to see an equestrian exhibition or sensational melodrama, as had so often been the case in the first half of the century. There was no need, as there once had been, to sit through cheap variety acts to enjoy *Romeo and Juliet,* or listen to a series of comic songs as entr'actes in a performance of *Hamlet.* And in response to a more intelligent audience, contemporary playwrights were beginning to write with a little more perception and sense of reality than had inspired *Putnam, the Iron Son of '76, The Lady of Lyons,* or *The Drunkard.*

Bronson Howard had written *Young Mrs. Winthrop* and *Shenandoah,* William Gillette his *Held by the Enemy* and *Secret Service.* There were *The County Fair* by Charles Barnard and Neil Burgess, and Steele Mackaye's phenomenally successful *Hazel Kirk.* A serious attempt to introduce realism to the stage was made by James A. Herne with *Shore Acres* and *Margaret Fleming.* Still more important, perhaps, were the plays of European dramatists. Ibsen, Pinero, Oscar Wilde, and Shaw all had a wide and friendly reception on the American stage.

In this golden age of the theatre, Mrs. Fiske was adding to her laurels in *Becky Sharp* and *A Doll's House;* Clara Morris played in *Camille* and Fanny Davenport in *Tosca;* Richard Mansfield introduced *Cyrano de Bergerac;* E. H. Sothern was starring in *The Prisoner of Zenda,* James O'Neill, the father of Eugene O'Neill, in *The Count of Monte Cristo* (in which he acted almost five thousand times), and William Gillette in *Sherlock Holmes.* Until he left the stage, Edwin Booth was the greatest of Shakespearean stars; his tour of the country with Lawrence Barrett in 1890 was a continuous triumph. There was none really to take his place. But Mansfield, Barrett, McCullough, and Mantell carried on the Shakespearean tradition among the actors, while Julia Marlowe was a lovely Rosalind in *As You Like It,* and Mary Anderson made an incomparable Juliet. Many other names —producers, dramatists, and actors—might be mentioned: Charles Frohman and David Belasco; Augustus Thomas and Clyde Fitch; the Barrymores, John Drew, Otis Skinner, Mrs. Leslie Carter, Margaret Anglin. . . . There were also such foreign stars as Henry Irving and Tommaso Salvini, Helena Modjeska, Sarah Bernhardt, and Eleanora Duse.

Among the light operas, *Pinafore,* first of the delightful concoctions of Gilbert and Sullivan to cross the Atlantic, was a sensation. It was first played at the Boston Museum, on November 25, 1878, then in San Francisco and Philadelphia, and finally in New York. There it was produced simultaneously in half a dozen theatres. There were children's companies, church-choir companies, and colored opera companies playing *Pinafore.* The fish exhibition had to be removed from the Aquarium for an engagement in what had been Castle Garden.[17] All New York, all America, sang and whistled "Little Buttercup."

Still another triumph was won by English operetta in the 1880's when *Erminie* had a phenomenal run of 1,256 performances at the New York Casino. Soon thereafter the Boston Ideals presented in Chicago the most popular of all American light operas, Reginald De Koven's *Robin Hood.* It was followed by other De Koven scores, and at the close of the century John Philip Sousa and Victor Herbert were further embellishing this type of polite musical entertainment with *El Capitan* and *The Wizard of the Nile.*

Concert singing, visits by foreign musicians, and orchestral playing also revealed a growing taste among the sophisticated for more serious music. Jenny Lind had paved the way for the tours of European artists in the middle of the century, and Ole Bull had made two memorable visits. In the 1890's Ysaye, Paderewski, Fritz Kreisler, Adelina Patti, Melba, Calvé, and Madame

Schumann-Heink were all on tour. Symphonic music had had its start with the organization of the New York Philharmonic as early as 1842, but it was not until 1878 that this orchestra had any real rival. In that year the New York Symphony Orchestra was established, to be followed in another three years by the Boston Symphony, and in 1891 by the Chicago Orchestra. Walter Damrosch and Theodore Thomas were adding a new interest to the musical scene.

Grand opera also had become firmly established. It had long been a distinctive feature of the social life of New Orleans, and there had been various attempts to introduce it in New York and other cities. Troupes of Italian singers had come and gone; elaborate opera houses had been opened—usually to fail after one or two seasons. "Will this splendid and refined amusement be supported in New York?" we find Philip Hone asking in 1833. "I am doubtful." And for almost half a century his doubts were largely justified. It was in 1883 that the Metropolitan Opera House, costing nearly $2,000,000, provided grand opera with its first really permanent home in America.[18]

The opening of the Metropolitan, for all its importance in the world of music and drama, illustrated even more vividly than any formal dinner or fancy-dress ball society's irresistible impulse to make its amusements an occasion to flaunt its wealth. For true music-lovers of the 1880's the operas currently being given at the Academy of Music fully met all artistic standards. The sole difficulty was that while there was plenty of available room at these performances in orchestra and galleries, every box at the Academy was taken for the season. And society had made an opera box one of the hall-marks of social success. The Metropolitan was built not in response to a demand for music, but to meet this need for fashionable display.[19]

It was financed by a group of social aspirants stung into action by the refusal of an offer of $30,000 for one of the boxes at the Academy of Music.[20] They would have their own opera house. Naturally enough its predominant feature became its two ornate

When Wallack's Theatre Was New

Harper's Weekly, 1882.

Defense of the "America's" Cup

Winner *Magic* leading. Painting by James E. Buttersworth, 1870. Courtesy of the Metropolitan Museum of Art.

New York's First Coach

Colonel De Lancey Kane's "The Tally-Ho" on its first run, May 1, 1876. Lithograph after a painting by H. C. Bispham. Courtesy of Harry T. Peters.

tiers of boxes. At the formal opening it was toward the Golden
Horseshoe rather than the stage that all eyes turned. "The
Goulds and the Vanderbilts and people of that ilk," the *New
York Dramatic Mirror* reported with forthright candor on that
memorable occasion, "perfumed the air with the odor of crisp
greenbacks. The tiers of boxes looked like cages in a menagerie
of monopolists." [21]

This did not mean that the Metropolitan did not uphold the
highest standards of operatic art. It did. Italian operas were
staged during its first season, and musical history was made when
German music and the Wagnerian operas were given the Metropolitan's formal approval in 1884.[22] The company made an annual post-season tour, visiting Boston, Chicago, Cincinnati, St.
Louis, Baltimore, Washington. . . . The world of society in these
cities had its opportunity to emulate that of New York. Grand
opera took its place, despite a sprinkling of more humble music-
lovers in the upper galleries, as one of the most exclusive and
fashionable of all diversions.

➤➤〈〈〈

SOCIETY had been the pioneer in the promotion of sports. We
have seen that in the middle of the century the more wealthy
had been almost the only people with the leisure and means
to enjoy them. As the opportunity to play games became available for a wider public in the 1890's, the world of fashion tended
more and more to favor those activities of which the expense
definitely excluded the common man. The same impulse that
motivated the rivalry over elaborate entertainment and opera
boxes was responsible for an attitude toward sport in which
conspicuous waste rather than simple enjoyment became the
general rule. James Gordon Bennett, Jr., determined to win the
position in society denied his father, made sport his means of
entrée into that exclusive world. He sailed yachts and fought
his way to the proud post of commodore of the New York Yacht
Club; he took up coaching and drove his four-in-hand in the

Newport parade; he introduced polo and founded the Westchester Polo Club.[23]

The days were indeed far distant when society, in the person of members of the old Knickerbocker Club, had taken up baseball and endeavored to keep it an exclusive pastime. "Naturally," wrote a correspondent of *Outing* in 1894, describing the sporting life of fashionable Philadelphia, "since baseball is so much of a professional game, it can hardly come under the head of what we recognize as out-of-door recreation." [24] But society could still approve archery and tennis. Tournaments in these lawn games remained social functions. When the clubs of archers, merry bowmen, or toxophilites that made up the National Archery Association had their annual meeting in 1897 on the grounds of the Chicago White Sox, band music and refreshments still contributed to the enjoyment of a select gathering.[25] The tennis matches at Newport, despite increasing interest in a sport which had become so much more active and competitive, were also a festival of the fashionable world. As late as 1886 the *Tribune Book of Open-Air Sports* complacently stated that lawn tennis remained "the game of polite society, essentially one for ladies and gentlemen.[26]

Yachts and horses were expensive enough to be proof against any alarming tendency toward democratization, and society was enthusiastic over these artistocratic pastimes. There was a great revival of yachting, marked by renewal of the America's Cup races. The wealthy engaged in lively competition both in the regattas for smaller boats (the one-design classes had been introduced) sponsored by such organizations as the New York Yacht Club, and in the purchase of expensive and elaborate ocean-going yachts. In the same way, ownership of a stable of thoroughbreds became highly fashionable, and the very rich extended their patronage as never before to the turf. The exclusive American Jockey Club was founded, an ultrafashionable course laid out at Jerome Park, and the Kentucky Derby became an annual feature of an invigorated racing calendar.[27] The common man could watch the races, and the gambling fraternity made a profitable living from betting on them, but only the very wealthy could support a stable.

The horse was glorified in other ways. Fox-hunting in the English manner was taken up by clubs on Long Island, in the suburbs of Philadelphia, and in Virginia and Maryland. In 1885 the National Horse Show was instituted, to become one of the outstanding social events of the year. There was a beginning of polo, introduced in 1876, at Westchester and Newport. Coaching was imported from England, a further refinement of the fashionable driving that already crowded the roads of such resorts as Tuxedo and Lenox with expensively turned out dog-carts, buckboards, landaus, and phaetons.[28]

The annual coaching parade in New York was one of the city's most colorful shows. Four-in-hand drags and tally-hos bowled down Fifth Avenue in the crisp autumn air, the guards gaily winding their horns, while crowds lined the street to watch their triumphant progress. The coaches were painted pink, blue, or dark-green with under-carriages of some sharply contrasting shade, and the beautifully matched and carefully groomed horses wore artificial flowers on their throat-latches. Society rode proudly atop these splendid equipages, the men in striped waistcoats and silk toppers, the ladies holding gay parasols over their immense picture hats.[29]

For the fullest enjoyment of these varied sports, a new institution sprang into being in the 1880's—the country club. The first of the genus is believed to have been the Brookline Country Club, near Boston, but it was soon followed by the Westchester Country Club, the Essex Country Club, the Tuxedo Club, the Philadelphia Country Club, the Meadowbrook Hunt Club, and the Country Club of Chicago. Those near the shore promoted yachting and sailing; others were a center for hunting, pony-races, and polo. Coaching parties drove out from the city for sports events, dances, teas, and the annual hunt ball.[30]

Together with such pastimes as lawn tennis, archery, and trap-shooting, some of these clubs began also to provide facilities for a game new to America. It was far more important than yachting, coaching, or polo. It was not for very long to remain, as *Harper's Weekly* termed it in 1895, "pre-eminently a game of good society." It was soon to give rise to a tremendous growth in country clubs which were to become the special prerogative of the great middle class in cities and towns throughout the country. This sport, of course, was golf.

It did not really take hold in this country, despite its hoary antiquity in Scotland and occasional attempts to introduce it on this side of the Atlantic ever since colonial days, until after 1888. The organization in that year of the St. Andrews Club, near New York, may well be taken as the first important date in golf's history in the United States.[31] Other courses were built—whatever number of holes was most convenient—after St. Andrews had showed the way. Soon a great number of the country clubs about Boston, New York, and Philadelphia had their links. By 1892 golf was spreading westward. It took Chicago by storm and moved on to St. Louis, Milwaukee, Denver, and the Pacific Coast. In 1894 the United States Golf Association was formed.[32]

No other game has evoked such scorn among the uninitiated. The democracy still considered tennis a rather feminine game, a chance to sport white flannels and gay-colored blazers rather than exercise. It simply did not know what to make of the absurd spectacle of enthusiastic gentlemen in scarlet coats furiously digging up the turf in frenzied—and wholly serious—efforts to drive a little white ball into a little round hole some hundreds of yards away. Nor were the red coats of these pioneer golfers the only article of costume that seemed singularly inappropriate on the rolling fairways of the new courses. They wore elaborate leg-wrappings to protect themselves from the gorse indigenous to Scottish hills but quite foreign to this country, and they pulled down over their foreheads visored caps in the best Sherlock Holmes tradition. Women had not yet taken up the game, although it was already being urged upon them as an admirable compromise between "the tediousness of croquet and the hurly-burly of lawn tennis," but together with wondering little boys who had been pressed into service as caddies, they often accompanied their lords and masters about the links. The public guffawed, little dreaming of golf's popularity in another two decades or of the public courses of to-day.[33]

->>><<<-

IN THE FIELD of spectator sports, which we have seen becoming more and more important toward the close of the century, the world of fashion also showed a lively interest. If it paid little attention to baseball, it rubbed shoulders with the roughest elements of the sporting world at horse-races and prize-fights. But above all else it turned out *en masse* for intercollegiate football. The games of the Big Three, which still provided the grand climax of the football season, were fully as much social as sporting events in the 1890's. In New York a parade of coaches would make its stately way to the playing-field. No small part of the crowd, after lunching on chicken sandwiches and champagne, watched the game from atop tally-hos.

"The air was tinged with the blue and the orange and the black as the great throngs poured through the city over the bridges, invaded Brooklyn and swept like a rising tide into Eastern Park," the *New York Tribune* reported after one Yale-Princeton game. "They came by the railroads, horsecars, drags and coaches and afoot. Coaches, drags and tally-hos decorated with the blue or the orange and black wound through the thoroughfares and quiet side streets in a glittering procession, freighted with jubilant college boys and pretty girls, who woke the echoes of the church bells with the cheers and tooting of horns. In an almost endless procession they inundated the big enclosure, and when it was 2 p.m. the sight was that of a coliseum of the nineteenth century, reflecting the changes and tints of a panoramic spectacle." [34]

The great crowds attracted by football—totaling thirty and

forty thousand [35]—were naturally not entirely made up of those in the higher social brackets. The game had a wider appeal, as the tremendous publicity given it clearly proves. At the time of the Yale-Princeton game in 1895, the *New York Journal* published a full two and a half pages of news and sketches—running accounts of the game, a full page of technical descriptive comment by James J. Corbett, signed stories by the captains of the teams, and a feature article entitled "The Journal's Woman Reporter Trains with the Little Boys in Blue." [36] But despite this furor of publicity, football was a sport for the classes rather than the masses. It largely reflected the interests of the college world.

It was dominated by the eastern universities. In one season Yale had a championship team—with such great players as Heffelfinger and Hinkey—which won thirteen games and piled up a season's score of 488 while its own goal-line was uncrossed. But colleges throughout the country were now taking it up and playing increasingly better football. By the late 1890's the Army-Navy game had become an established annual feature; among southern colleges, Virginia, Vanderbilt, Washington and Lee, had well-known teams; in the Middle West there was already fierce competition among such colleges as Michigan, Minnesota, Wisconsin, Ohio State, and the new University of Chicago; Leland Stanford stood out among Pacific Coast teams. [37] Even though Walter Camp might not have to look much beyond the Big Three for his famous All-American teams, there were signs that the East's supremacy would soon be challenged. Intercollegiate football had become a nation-wide sport.

Bitter criticism had marked its progress. The attacks made upon football overemphasis in the 1890's make comparable comments in the 1920's and 1930's appear mild and innocuous. The preference accorded football-players in their college work, undue absorption in the game through long training-seasons, the prevalent spirit of winning at any cost, and the open hiring of star players awoke a resentment which echoed throughout the country. *The Nation* was foremost in these early onslaughts: it saw

Polo at Jerome Park

James Gordon Bennett on the white pony, center. Painting by H. C. Bispham, 1877. Courtesy of the Piping Rock Club.

Discussing "pitchers" in the Princeton Inn Grill

A Corner of the Grand Stand

"My big brother"

Going to the Game

The Social Side of Intercollegiate Baseball

Drawing by A. I. Keller. *Harper's Weekly*, 1896.

all the worst elements of American character reflected in the game. "The spirit of the American youth, as of the American man, is to win, to 'get there,' by fair means or foul," it declared caustically, "and the lack of moral scruple which pervades the business world meets with temptations equally irresistible in the miniature contests of the football field." [38] Although far more sympathetic, the special sports writer of *Harper's Weekly* was fully as outspoken against the rising tide of professionalism. It was prevalent among the eastern colleges, but even worse in other parts of the country. No one could have any conception, Caspar Whitney wrote in 1895, "of the rottenness of the whole structure through the middle and far West. Men are bought and sold like cattle to play this autumn on 'strictly amateur' elevens." [39]

The brutality of the game awoke even fiercer attacks. It was the day of flying wedges, tackle-back tandems, and other mass plays. And the injuries these tactics inevitably caused were supplemented by casualties arising from the frequent slugging and free-for-all fights which the referees were powerless to control. A fair-minded English observer was horrified at the roughness of the games. And his impressions of it were amply confirmed in a report he quoted from *The Nation* on the Harvard-Yale game of 1894. It declared that one-third of the original combatants had had to be carried off the field. "Brewer was so badly injured that he had to be taken off crying with mortification. Wright, captain of the Yale men, jumped on him with both knees, breaking his collar bone. Beard was next turned over to the doctors. Hallowell had his nose broken. Murphy was soon badly injured and taken off the field in a stretcher unconscious, with concussion of the brain. Butterworth, who is said merely to have lost an eye, soon followed. . . ." [40]

The New York *World* expressed a growing conviction that reform was absolutely imperative "if ruffianism and brutality and sneaking cowardice are not to be bred into our youth as a part of their training." [41] Writing in *Harper's Weekly*, Theodore Roosevelt (apostle of the strenuous life) defended the game as best he could, but he also declared in forthright terms that roughness and professionalism must cease if football was to be preserved.[42]

This chorus of disapproval compelled action. Under the leadership of Walter Camp, efforts were made to bring about reforms. The block game was done away with through the adoption of the rule requiring surrender of the ball after the fourth down unless a gain of ten yards had been made; massed rushes were discouraged by providing for more open play; and referees were empowered to deal drastically with slugging or any unnecessary roughness. The attempt was made to prevent professionalism and enforce stricter rules of eligibility.[43] Nothing could be done to suppress the instinct to win by almost any means (that had become a part of football, and spectator interest already demanded a fierce and bitter struggle), but the game was saved from this threat of suppression for the further triumphs which awaited it in the twentieth century.

→»)«←

THE SOCIAL WORLD as represented by the little coterie of the very wealthy who gave elaborate fancy-dress balls, had their boxes at the opera, and hunted or played polo at the new country clubs was insignificant in numbers. That larger group of the privileged who less ostentatiously supported the legitimate stage, had the leisure to enjoy such sports as tennis and golf, and made up the college-bred crowd at football games was considerably larger, but still it did not bulk very large in a total population which had grown by the 1890's to more than sixty-three millions. Nevertheless this world of society in the broader sense had a tremendous influence in the development of recreation, for it set the standards that the democracy tried to follow as best it could.

Social activities received immense publicity in the Gilded Age. The extravagant balls of New York and Chicago millionaires, the yacht-races and the polo matches, the coaching parade at

Newport, were written up with great gusto and vivid detail in the nation's press. All the world knew what was happening in these circles, and very often it wanted to go out and do like-wise. The middle class was ambitious to take up every activity on which society had set the stamp of fashionable approval.

While this too often meant that a premium was placed on ostentation, it also encouraged the healthy growth of many forms of amusement. It can at least be said that society's sponsorship of the theatre and opera, of sports and outdoor activities, partly counteracted in its social effects the example it set in luxury and extravagance.

chapter 15

Main Street

THE SMALL TOWN WAS THE BACKBONE OF THE NATION IN THE closing decades of the past century. It was more typically American than the city. The people who lived and worked and played in its familiar environment largely made up the middle class which carried forward the traditions and ideals of democracy. The quarterly town dances of the Middle West were attended by banker and mill-hand, lawyer and grocery boy, their wives and their sweethearts. Every one gathered at the ball park of a Saturday afternoon to watch the local team in action and listened that evening to the amateur band concert in the public square. The town might have its "old whist crowd" and "young dancing crowd," as William Allen White wrote of Kansas in the 1890's, its "lodge crowd," its "church social crowd," and its "surprise party crowd," [1] but they primarily represented people of common interests getting together. There was already a right and a wrong side of the railroad tracks, but social distinctions were not as rigid as they were to become in a later day.

This neighborliness made for a pleasant informality, but it also imposed its restraints. The Victorian era was passing, but the town clung to old ways. The fact that every one knew what every one else was doing enforced a certain conventionality which often made for dullness. There had been no expansion in recreation comparable to that in the city. Conservatism was implicit in the social order, and any departure—the introduction of the two-step at the Pastime Club's annual assembly, a production of *Sappho* at the opera house—led to a storm of criticism.

John Quincy Adams would have known just what to expect at

a small-town party in this period. It would not have differed
greatly from an evening at Newburyport a century earlier. He
would have known how to play most of the games, including
I Love My Love with an A. He would often have found that forfeits still involved that "profanation of one of the most endearing
expressions of love" which had once so disturbed him, and thoroughly approved a contemporary game book that suggested
substitute forfeits to enable the players to avoid the "childish
and absurd kissing of the one you love best." And the performance of the young lady of the house, with guitar accompaniment
should there be no piano, might well have been as trying as he
had found it in the 1780's.

The church still played a dominant rôle in setting the tone of
social life. Its ban on drinking, for example, had the support of
all the better elements in the town. Lodge night or the firemen's
ball was sometimes a lively occasion, but even where the community was not thoroughly dry through local option, alcoholic
drinks were seldom served at the parties of either the surprise-
party crowd or the young dancing crowd. Nor did the old whist
crowd play cards for money. Church-going folk in the 1890's—
and that meant almost every one—did not countenance gambling
in even its mildest forms. The Sabbath was generally observed.
Whatever might be true of the city, it was not yet a day of
recreation for the town.

→»《←

To MAKE UP for the restraints it imposed upon more worldly
amusements, the church provided its own entertainments. Ladies'
Aids, Christian Endeavors, and missionary societies engaged in
lively competition over their sociables, fairs, and festivals. The
Congregational ladies, the Methodist ladies, the Baptist ladies,
were rivals in both good works and good times. The Sunday
School picnic was a great occasion. The church had always been
a center of social life since those distant colonial days when New
England's farmers drove in to Sunday sermons and midweek

lectures, gossiping at the horse-sheds after service, but it now recognized a social obligation in sponsoring community recreation.

At the church supper, which became so universal a feature on the small-town social calendar, the entertainment was mild and innocuous by urban standards. Lectures and talks, readings and poetic recitations by the more gifted members of the congregation, instrumental music and singing, occasionally tableaux or charades, made up the usual program. Sometimes lecture courses were definitely arranged to meet the competition of commercial entertainment. The First Church of Chelsea, Massachusetts, at one time advertised in the local paper "a people's course" of ten lectures for fifty cents, with popular speakers, readings, music, and stereopticon views.[2]

At the fairs, bazaars, and strawberry festivals, which had the further goal of raising money, there were usually grab-bags or fish-ponds, fortune-telling, and guessing games. Young men were invited to spend ten cents to see something they would hate, and then were shown a mitten. A cake would be sold piece by piece until some lucky purchaser found the ring that had been cooked with it. At five cents a cup one could draw lemonade out of a miniature well. The popularity of beauty contests (which had come down from colonial fairs) found expression in a vote for the prettiest girl at the festival, the blushing winner then being called upon to sell kisses. A daring innovation was a game in which young men bid for partners hidden behind a curtain raised just high enough to reveal their ankles.

In the attack that Dr. William Bayard Hale made upon the extent to which churches were entering the amusement field, he listed an exhibition of waxworks, a living-picture show, a performance of *The Mikado,* and a song recital in which the Peak sisters sang the ballad, "Do You Know the Mouth of Man?" One church staged the Blackbird Ballet, Sacred Female Minstrels, the performers appearing in burnt cork and bloomers.[3]

These more exciting ventures into the realm of vaudeville were admittedly exceptional. The typical church entertainment mirrored the spirit of an age in which the small town faithfully observed Victorian concepts of propriety. In the *Eighty Pleasant Evenings* issued by the United Society of Christian Endeavor, there was no suggestion of such sprightly entertainment. Take the popular Patriotic Social: " 'Uncle Sam' or 'Columbia' in appropriate costume may receive the guests. Flags and bunting should decorate the walls, together with portraits of famous Americans, which may be made an occasion for a guessing contest. Have a 'post-office,' the letters consisting of extracts from patriotic speeches. . . . The following program has been rendered on one occasion:

> CHORUS. 'Star Spangled Banner.'
> RECITATION. 'Independence Bell.'
> SOLO. 'The Dying Soldier,' or 'The Soldier's Farewell.'
> RECITATION. 'Old Ironsides.'
> CHORUS. 'Red, White and Blue.'

A list of historic battles, with the generals commanding them should be prepared in advance. . . . These may be passed and matched to arrange partners for refreshments, which may consist of saltines, cheese, and phosphate of wild cherry." [4]

→»)«←

THERE WERE other "jolly affairs" besides church suppers and Ladies' Aid sociables. Trolley parties, progressive tiddly-winks, taffy-pulls, and surprise parties were popular. "A pleasant surprise was held last night at the elegant residence of Oliver J. . . . in honor of the fortieth anniversary of the birth of Mrs. Ella . . . ." reads the account of one such party in the 1890's as recorded in *Middletown*. "Every face was beaming with delight, and happiness flowed from heart to heart. . . . After dinner a season of song and prayer was had, after which the house was made to ring with music. . . . Mr. McC. . . . favored us with a song, 'A Thousand Years My Own Columbia!' " [5]

When cards were introduced, this generation usually played, in addition to whist, such games as euchre, five hundred, seven-up, progressive fifty-eight, or Sancho Pedro. And there were always parlor games and conundrums: Dumb Crambo, Fiz Buzz, Wall Street Brokers, the Feejee Islanders at Home, Princess Hugger Mugger, and Hot Cockles. These were in many instances simply new variations of old games, and such favorites as Authors, Twenty Questions, and Going to Jerusalem were still popular.[6] For over a century successive American editions of Hoyle had been setting the established rules of play.

Music not only played an important part in these evening entertainments but entered into the whole life of the town. In addition to local bands, there were many choral societies. Young people often went out of an evening to serenade one another, or gathered at the home of one of their number for "a sing." Every family that prided itself on respectability had a piano. "There is no country," a French writer reported, "where there are so many pianos and players on them."[7] In a few homes an odd contraption known as a talking-machine might be found (Edison had put it on the market about 1878), but with its tin-foil cylinder record, turned by a hand crank, it was still a rather disappointing instrument. Generally people who wanted music had to produce it themselves. Throaty tenors and quavering sopranos lustily sang the songs given popular currency by the minstrel show, the musical-comedy road company, and the circus. The barber-shop quartette was in its heyday; the young lady with a passable voice needed no other charms to be the success of the party.

The songs were sentimental, and old songs were the best songs. The Southern melodies introduced by the minstrels—"Old Black Joe," "Carry Me Back to Ole Virginny," "The Old Folks at Home" —were always favorites. At every party there was some one to sing such Scotch or Irish ballads as "John Anderson, My Jo," "Comin' Through the Rye," and "Annie Laurie." Then there were "Juanita," "Oh, My Darling Clementine," "Wait Till the

Clouds Roll By, Jennie," "In the Gloaming," and "Kiss But Never Tell"—

> A starry night for a ramble,
> In the flowery dell,
> Through the bush and bramble,
> Kiss, but never tell!
> Kiss, but never tell to any—
> Telling breaks the spell.

Sometimes the theme was the dangers of the wicked urban world:

> I've come to the great city
> To find a brother dear,
> And you wouldn't dare insult me, Sir,
> If Jack were only here.

"The Sidewalks of New York," "On the Banks of the Wabash," "Just Tell Them That You Saw Me," "O Promise Me," "The Bowery," "My Gal Is a High-Born Lady," were all of the 1890's. It was in this prolific decade that Charles K. Harris wrote "After the Ball":

> Many a heart is aching
> If you could read them all;
> Many the hopes that have vanished
> After the ball.

Reflecting prevailing standards of decorum was the pretty lament, "What Could the Poor Girl Do," which described the dilemma of the young lady endeavoring to keep her dress off the pavement on a rainy day:

> But what could the poor girl do?
> Boys, what could the poor girl do?
> She'd a pretty little shoe, and she liked to show it too,
> So I couldn't blame the girl, could you?

They were sung, these songs and many others, as they never had been before or have been since. Young and old joined in the chorus. Many were the parties that broke up to "Auld Lang Syne" or "Good Night, Ladies." [8]

Dancing was probably not as general as it had been in the late eighteenth century or as it was to become in the early decades of the twentieth. But various clubs and associations gave annual balls; businessmen and their wives attended dancing-classes which usually terminated in an assembly or German. The program of one dance held in Marion, New York, during this period included the following numbers: lancers (5), waltz (4), polka (3), military march (3), quadrille (2), York (2), Portland Fancy, Caledonia, and Virginia Reel. It opened with a grand march and closed with "Home Sweet Home." [9] In more worldly circles the two-step was coming into vogue. The music of John Philip Sousa, touring the country with his famous band, had introduced a more lively rhythm into dancing. "The Washington Post," so popular that in other countries it gave its name to the two-step, was everywhere played at the more fashionable dances.[10]

->->)(<<-

LODGE NIGHT had become a nation-wide institution. Fraternal orders were nothing new. Freemasonry had crossed the Atlantic in colonial days and in the 1820's had been for a time a disturbing political issue. The Independent Order of Odd Fellows also dated from the middle of the eighteenth century, and among other organizations that were either offshoots of the Masons and Odd Fellows or had been newly formed somewhat in imitation of them were the Elks, the Knights of Pythias, and the Ancient Order of United Workmen. But after 1880 there was a phenomenal increase in the number and membership of these orders. No less than five hundred were founded before the close of the century, and the nation-wide enrolment suddenly leaped to over six millions, something like forty per cent of the male population over twenty-one.[11]

The country fairly bristled with temples, camps, clans, castles, conclaves, rulings, hives, and tents. Some of them were limited to workers in certain trades and occupations, others made up their membership from immigrant groups, and there were many Negro orders. To the older organizations were added the Ancient Arabic Order of Nobles of the Mystic Shrine, the Independent Order of Good Templars, the United Order of Druids, the Tribes of Ben Hur, the Independent Order of Gophers, the Prudent Patricians of Pompeii, the Mystic Workers of the World, the Modern Woodmen of America, the Concatenated Order of Hoo-Hoo. . . . Every town had one or more lodges, their membership embracing every element in its society. Initiation ceremonies, the induction of new members, carnivals, and other fraternal social functions became more and more important.[12]

Many men joined the orders for the sake of the sickness and death benefits they provided, which were the nominal purpose of their being formed; others took out membership because they felt it advisable for business or to make useful social contacts. But such prosaic reasons could not possibly explain the amazing stampede to become a Mason or an Odd Fellow, an Elk or a Gopher, in the last quarter of the nineteenth century. It was the urge to be accepted as one of the crowd—half a century earlier Alexis de Tocqueville had diagnosed America as a nation of joiners—and to be able to slip away for a time from one's humdrum daily routine into a mysterious world of pageantry and make-believe.

The elaborate ceremony and ritual of the lodge, with its secret grips and passwords; the colorful regalia of the officers; the grandiloquent titles and forms of address, provided such a striking contrast to workshop or factory, to the dull level of so much home life, that their appeal could hardly be withstood. There were so few other ways to forget the cares of trade or business— no movies or radio to create an even more fantastic land of never-never. Any one might find himself a Most Illustrious Grand Potentate, Supreme Kahalijah, or Most Worthy and Illustrious Imperial Prince on lodge night. In gorgeous robes of state, jeweled collars, imposing helmets or high-crowned fezzes; carrying the swords, lances, and axes that constituted the impressive symbols of their office, butchers and bakers and candlestick makers strutted for a brief hour before a worshiping audience of Knights and Nobles, Nomads and Rams—sometimes Daughters of Isis or Pythian Sisters—in all the magnificence of the borrowed plumes of mystic imagery. The lodges had become a national vice, a contemporary critic wrote in the *Atlantic Monthly;* a contributor to the *Century* found them the great American safety-valve.[13]

Many other organizations were witness to the national love for joining something. One foreign visitor, touring the country in 1892, was amazed at the number and variety of associations "founded simply to make it easier to procure some pleasure." [14] But most of them had at least originally a practical purpose. Militia companies still held annual musters, and though they may not have been as exciting occasions as the old colonial training days, the whole town would turn out to watch the drills and parades, listen to the band music, and help the militiamen celebrate. More colorful were the musters and carnivals staged by the local volunteer firemen. Sometimes companies from the neighboring towns of half a state would gather, resplendent in red shirts and shiny helmets, for fierce contests with the old hand-pumping engines. The company that sent a stream of water farthest won a championship as important as that of the local baseball league. There were also local posts of the G.A.R., workingmen's clubs, sports clubs, and businessmen's associations pointing the way to Rotary and Kiwanis. The town was honeycombed with such organizations, and everywhere the general pattern of their activities was much the same.

Women were not left out of this movement to organize. They had auxiliaries formed on the lines of the men's fraternal orders— Daughters of Rebekah, Pythian Sisters, Daughters of Isis; associations such as the Women's Relief Corp and Ladies' Aid; and a wide array of social clubs which multiplied in this period as

Knights Templar in Conclave at Chicago

Ball tendered the Grand Encampment by the local commanderies. *Frank Leslie's Illustrated Newspaper*, 1880.

A Chautauqua Tent
Courtesy of H. J. Thornton.

The Lighter Side of Chautauqua

Feichtl's troupe
Tyrolese yodeler
Courtesy of H.
Thornton.

never before. There were Shakespeare and Beethoven Circles, Noon-Day Rest Clubs, Old Maids' Socials, and Ladies' High Jinks, to a total, before the century closed, which is only partially indicated by the twelve hundred associations formally banded together in the General Federation of Women's Clubs.[15]

"We have art clubs, book clubs, dramatic clubs, pottery clubs," a contemporary wrote. "We have sewing circles, philanthropic associations, scientific, literary, religious, athletic, musical and decorative art societies." [16] A visiting Frenchwoman declared that the absence of men would make her compatriots feel "as if they were eating bread without butter." [17] The American women appeared to get along very well under these distressing circumstances.

These clubs represented a conscious effort to fill the increasing leisure that the machine age was making available to the middle-class housewife. Her ordinary work was greatly cut down by factory manufacture of things formerly made in the home and by the introduction of innumerable labor-saving devices. "House-keeping is getting to be ready-made, as well as clothing," one magazine writer stated in 1887.[18] While the men generally had as long hours of work as they had had before, their wives found themselves with free afternoons which they could devote to outside activities. A zealous pursuit of culture, rather than pleasure, was the primary goal of the woman's club, but the lectures, reading of members' papers, and discussions over the tea-table fell within that vague territory where the boundaries between instruction and recreation can hardly be defined.

->>)<<-

AN ENTIRELY different phase of recreational life centered about the local opera house. Here traveling lecturers, road companies, and variety shows periodically appeared to give the townspeople their one taste of urban entertainment. In quick sucession they might welcome Russell H. Conwell giving his famed talk on "Acres of Diamonds" (this popular version of the idea that there are riches in your own back yard was given over five thousand times); a Merry Maidens burlesque show; Robert Mantell in a repertoire of Shakespearean plays; an Uncle Tom's Cabin company; and a traveling combination presenting the latest Broadway hit.[19] Although the opera house might attempt to book "first class attractions only," it was in much the same position as the mid-century theatre. Its productions had to reach all members of the community. If serious drama and vaudeville acts were not combined in one performance, as they so often had been in the 1850's, popular demand caused them to alternate almost weekly.

The annual session of Chautauqua was for many a small town the grand climax of this entertainment. It was sometimes the sole occasion when outside talent mounted the platform to offer a glimpse of what was happening in the larger world. This institution—for "the Chautauquay" had a nation-wide scope—had developed out of a camp-meeting course for Sunday-School teachers started in 1874. As it grew to embrace the whole field of adult education, other Chautauquas were established throughout the country, the summer courses were supplemented by winter lecture series, and reading groups enrolled in the Literary and Scientific Circle. In the 1890's there were some seventy Chautauquas. When the twentieth century developed its far-flung system of chain organizations, totaling some ten thousand in 1919, the nation-wide audience slowly grew to an estimated forty million.[20]

Chautauqua was cultural and educational. Its lectures, however, were always supplemented by an entertainment program. When a meeting was held, especially in the small towns of the Middle West, it would be attended by hundreds of neighboring farmers as well as townspeople. They would camp on grounds made available near the auditorium or lecture tents, and for a solid week enjoy an astounding succession of learned and inspirational talks interlarded with the performances of xylophone orchestras, Swiss yodelers, jugglers and magicians, college-girl

Who's Who in Chautauqua 1920

First Day

AFTERNOON AND EVENING

The New York Glee Club

Great male quartet direct from remarkable record in eastern cities. Andres Merkel, 1st tenor, George D. Dewey, 2nd tenor, D. Ward Steady, baritone, and Wm. J. Williams, basso. Four soloists with a most unusual ensemble. Song harmony by music's most popular voice combination.

EVENING

Lou J. Beauchamp "Taking the Sunny Side"

Known as "The Laughing Philosopher." Said to cause more laughter in one evening than any man on the platform. Traveled more than million miles in old world and the new. Nineteen ocean trips. Investigated the lives of the underworld in America's large cities, writing for the press. His books selling through two and three editions, and translated into foreign tongues. Poems on child-life part of the folk lore of the land.

Second Day

AFTERNOON AND EVENING

Germanie Mallebay Company

Headed by Mlle. Mallebay, noted opera singer from Paris, and favorite pupil of M. Hettich of the National Conservatory. Three other artists, Miss Helen Carney, violinist, Clyde Matson, tenor, and Miss Margaret Everett, pianist and accompanist. One of the strongest musical companies on the American concert stage.

EVENING

Frank Dixon

"The Indispensable Tools of Democracy"

A keen, constructive satirist. One of America's foremost economists, who for 17 years has used platform to discuss country's vital problems. One of the "platform giants" of this day. Masterful, scholarly, brilliant, eloquent. Loaded with burning facts about democracy, which the people want to know.

Third Day

AFTERNOON

Elwood T. Bailey

"The Call of the Hour"

An intensely human speaker, painter of graphic word pictures, inspirer to action. Close student of men and situations. Was with the "Devil Dog" Marines at Chateau Thierry, wounded and gassed. Fired with the spirit of Americanism, brotherhood and loyalty.

EVENING

"The Elixir of Youth"

The great American farce comedy with New York cast. Concerning the discovery of a substance supposed to transform old age into youth. Funnier than "It Pays to Advertise." Concocted along the lines of the greatest number of laughs. The best joy-tonic, world-brightener, delicious, sparkling cure for the blues on the market. Runs over with witty lines, ludicrous situations, funny characters.

Fourth Day

AFTERNOON AND EVENING

Dixie Girls

Five talented, winsome girls from below the Mason-Dixon line. Dispensing the sunshine and charm of the Southland, telling stories of their own native southern folk, and singing and playing the rich, southern melodies.

EVENING

Robert Bowman

Through years of study, observation, and experience, achieved the front rank among character impersonators. By the aid of stage "make-up" brings the world's most interesting characters to the chautauqua platform. "The Immortal Lincoln," "Shylock," "Our Imported Americans," and "Characters From Life and Literature," some of the high spots in his humor and pathos

Fifth Day

AFTERNOON

"County Fair"
"Hey, Skinnay! C'm On Over!"

Lots, 'n lots, 'n lots of fun! Big County Fair n'everything! Balloon Man, Nigger Baby Rack, Prize Animals, Powerful Katrinka, Sword Swallower, Fire Eater and Fortune Teller,—'n whole shootin' match! Big parade and stunt program at chautauqua.

Prof. Abel Cantu *"Mexico Today"*

Of a fine, Mexican family, educated in the colleges of his own land, followed by graduate work in American universities. Professor at University of Wisconsin, and Crane Technical High School of Chicago. Authoritative information on Mexico at a time when the subject of intervention is momentous.

EVENING

Landis Singing Orchestra

Form a six-piece orchestra, rendering gems from the symphony classics and syncopated rag-time melodies, a male quartet harmonizing on the tunes the people love to hear, and a vocal, mixed sextet, presenting songologues and "pep" stunts new and novel.

Junior Chautauqua 9:00 a. m.   Afternoon Program 2:30 p. m.   Evening Program 8:00 p. m.

Program of a Typical Chautauqua Week

The Redpath-Vawter System offerings at Milford, Iowa, June 2-6, 1920.

octettes, boy whistlers, dramatic monologists, and jubilee singers. Sports also were encouraged in the afternoon, with croquet for the ladies and baseball for the men. "The Chautauqua," declared one of its early speakers, "is a cross between a camp meeting and a country fair." [21]

The atmosphere was highly moral. There could be no drinking or smoking; the Sabbath was rigidly observed. A Methodist Dining Tent or Christian Endeavor Ice Cream Tent supplied all refreshments. Since Chautauqua derived its chief support from the churches and ladies'-aid societies, the emphasis was always placed on the importance of "the Work." As entertainment inevitably proved the more potent drawing-card, it had to be given all possible protective coloring. The prominent singer "lectured" on "The Road to Mandalay"; the monologist "gave a reading" rather than a dramatic performance. When in Chautauqua's later days a musical company staged *Carmen*, it was considered necessary to have the heroine work in a dairy rather than in a cigarette factory.[22]

To meet the town's insistent demand for lectures, the Redpath Lyceum Bureau had for long been sending out the most prominent speakers—P. T. Barnum and Horace Greeley, Wendell Phillips and Henry Ward Beecher, Mark Twain, Bill Nye and James Whitcomb Riley, Presidents Grant, Hayes, Garfield, and McKinley, William Jennings Bryan, Viscount Bryce....[23] Here was a strong force, one of the most powerful in operation in the 1890's, to broaden the lives of the middle class. Chautauqua was a typically American institution whose cultural and recreational aspects were subtly merged in an age which did not yet know the radio.

The more openly avowed entertainment presented at the opera house by the traveling road companies, which between 1880 and 1900 (as listed by the *New York Dramatic Mirror*) increased from some forty-odd to over five hundred,[24] included almost everything that was being staged at city theatres. Among the performances scheduled for the small towns of Indiana dur-

ing a week in December, 1898, were a repertoire of Shakespearean plays, several comedies from Broadway, a minstrel
show, a musical comedy, and several melodramas and variety
shows. The Boston Lyric Opera Company was playing at the
Grand Opera House in Marion, and the John L. Sullivan Company was booked at Kokomo. Logansport was enjoying Black
Patti's Troubadours, and Elkhart a concert series by Sousa's
Band. Eldon's Comedians (Pearl White was once a member of
this troupe) staged at Dunkirk three plays representing the most
distinctive phases of American life—*The Slums of Greater New
York, A Country Sweetheart,* and *The Pride of the West.* At the
Grand Opera House in Anderson there was a revival of an old
favorite by Jerome's Black Crook Extravaganza Company.[25]

At any time during the 1890's at least one opera house somewhere in the land was producing *East Lynne;* Denman Thompson was always on the road in *The Old Homestead* (it earned
over $3,000,000); *The Two Orphans* had already had more
than twenty-five hundred performances; and Joseph Jefferson,
beloved from coast to coast, had become a part of American
folklore in the familiar rôle of Rip Van Winkle.

The smaller towns seldom had very much choice as to what
they might see. "Doubtless there are worse theatrical companies
than those which visit Kansas," William Allen White wrote in
the *Atlantic Monthly* in 1897, "but no one has ever described
them." [26] In many cases they were poorer than the old stock
companies they had so completely displaced. There were not
enough actors to meet the growing demand of the local opera
houses, and performances were staged that would have em-
barrassed the hardy troupers who barn-stormed through the
Mississippi Valley in pioneer days. Their quality would hardly
have been known from the advance notices. Every variety or
minstrel show promised something bigger and better than the
town had ever seen. The poorest of the little comedy troupes,
rushing through the countryside playing one-night stands at
villages which were hardly on the map, were billed as star at-

tractions straight from Broadway. One may follow their blazing path—the Bootle's Baby Company, the Hands Across the Sea Company, the She, Him, Her Comedy Company—as they arrived in town of a late afternoon, hopefully staged their show, and either that very night or early the next morning were again on their way. During a single fortnight in December, 1889, one such company played fourteen stands from Creston, Iowa, to Adrian, Michigan; another put on an equal number of performances in a string of eastern towns from Herkimer, New York, to Keene, New Hampshire.[27]

Marie Dressler has recalled in her reminiscences many of the trials and tribulations these second-rate companies experienced on the road. She played in cheap dramatic stock for a weekly wage of $6.00, and, as in an earlier day, the cast often did not know their lines and ad-libbing was a necessary art. At some of their brief stands the excitement of their arrival brought out welcoming crowds, and after the performance the stage door would be blocked with local admirers. In other places their reception would be so frigid that they were forced to play to almost empty houses and perhaps would be left completely stranded. A lingering prejudice against everything connected with the theatre led many a New England boarding-house to refuse to take in actors or actresses. They were ostracized in a world of railroad trains, second-rate rooming-houses, and cheap restaurants.[28]

The musical shows had the most difficult time. For all their glowing advertisements—"breezy dialogue, gorgeous stage settings, dazzling dancing, spirited repartee, superb music, opulent costumes"—their settings were often woefully inadequate, their costumes old and dingy, and their performances uninspired and shabby. It was a practice to recruit new members of the cast while on the road. Marie Dressler tells of the surprising church attendance of the producers, watching the choir for possible additions to their show's chorus.

The Tommers were still playing America's favorite drama in

village and hamlet. Their performances, heralded by street parades, might be staged at either the local opera house or under canvas. To make up for possible deficiencies in the cast, and also for the lack of novelty in the old play, some announced two Uncle Toms, two Simon Legrees, two Little Evas. One company added prize-fighters to its cast, having the colored pugilist Peter Jackson spar a few rounds with Joe Choynski.[29] These expedients were not always successful. After one performance a Minnesota newspaper reported laconically: "Thompson's Uncle Tom's Cabin Company appeared at the opera house last night. The dogs were poorly supported." [30]

Despite the large number of traveling combinations, there was another basic disparity in the theatrical entertainments of town and city entirely apart from the general standards of acting. This was the relative infrequency of performances at the opera house in contrast to the wide choice of nightly entertainment offered by the dozen or more theatres and vaudeville houses in the larger cities.[31] The small town had more in the way of commercial amusements than ever before, but this was often not more than a single show in the week. And sometimes the opera house would be darkened for months on end.

->>>)<<(<-

OUTDOOR ACTIVITIES represented a more important phase of recreation. Lawns, back yards, and playing-fields, so totally lacking in the cities, opened the way to active participation in the new sports and games that had been introduced by society. In every part of the United States, on Saturday afternoons and holidays, even in some localities on Sundays, there were in progress baseball matches among teams representing the town, the factory, the athletic club, the high school, or the Y.M.C.A. This sport was a distinctive feature of New England town life; it had invaded the rural areas of the South. In the newspaper of any western town one may read of local games. Under such names as the Striped Stockings or Blue Belts, teams in Kansas and Nebraska carried on a lively feud, the Wichita *Eagle* stating as early as 1873 that baseball (closely pressed by croquet, mumble peg, and keno) was the community's favorite game.[32]

A more interesting development was the rapidly growing popularity of the new indoor winter sport of basketball. It has a unique status. It is the only popular American game that is not derived from some sport whose origins may be clearly traced to England. Baseball and football have been thoroughly Americanized by a slow process of evolution, but basketball sprang fully developed on a world which little realized that in time it was to be played by more persons (including boys and girls) and draw larger numbers of spectators than any other sport—not excepting either professional baseball or intercollegiate football.

Working at the Y.M.C.A. training school in Springfield, Massachusetts, in 1891, James A. Naismith became impressed with the very real need for an indoor game that might serve during the winter as a practical substitute for baseball and football. It had to be active and highly competitive, but he hoped to avoid the roughness which in these years was bringing football into such disrepute. Basketball, the result of his thinking along these lines, caught on immediately. Its sponsorship by the Y.M.C.A. provided the means to carry it throughout the country—and also to other parts of the world. It was taken up almost at once by colleges, high schools, and athletic clubs.[33]

So popular did it become that, as in the case of both baseball and football, the problem of professionalism soon arose. Basketball was threatened by all the evils of gambling and fixed games.[34] Strict enforcement of amateur rules, however, was more feasible in the case of basketball than in that of either baseball or football because it was so widely played by Y.M.C.A. and school teams. It was for many years kept on a non-professional basis, and so popular did it prove among boys that a modified form of it was devised for girls.

Among other games, the craze for croquet, which at one time had been so universal that manufacturers could not keep up with the demand for sets, had somewhat subsided. It remained a popular pastime, but it no longer aroused the nation-wide excitement of the days when for the first time it allowed boys and girls, men and women, to enjoy an outdoor game together. They were now doing too many things in company for croquet to have its original novelty. Interest in tennis was increasing, but at a relatively slow rate. It was still largely a sport for society. The young college graduates of the 1890's were bringing it back with them to the home town, but it had to overcome the prejudice that it was rather a sissy game which no good baseball player would be seen playing.

In *The Gentleman from Indiana* Booth Tarkington describes the sensation caused by his hero when he appeared in tennis flannels. Dim memories were stirred in the minds of the store-keeping postmaster and his sister over "that there long-tennis box we bought and put in the window, and the country people thought it was a seining outfit."

" 'It was a game, the catalogue said,' observed Miss Selina. 'Wasn't it?' "

" 'It was a mighty pore investment,' the postman answered." [35]

The popularity of roller-skating had also waned. Boys and girls still skated happily on the period's wooden sidewalks, but adult skating no longer aroused the enthusiasm of the 1880's. The cities had their rinks, but in many a provincial town they had been converted to other uses. A. G. Spalding did not find it necessary to issue another guide, and the sale of skates fell off heavily.

The most universal sport of city, town, and country was bicycling. We have seen how it first won popular favor, but the golden age of the wheel was the 1890's. The invention of the safety bicycle, equipped with pneumatic tires, and of the drop-frame for women riders had made it available for every one. There were something like a million bicycles in the country in 1893, and soon production was running each year as high as this nation-wide total.[36] Every sizable community had its club, associated with the League of American Wheelmen, and rising armies of riders sallied forth every week-end. One commentator found cycling rapidly becoming "more popular than all other out-of-door recreations combined";[37] another declared it to be a final answer to those captious critics who "used to call us money-grubbers, and talk about our excessive lust for the almighty dollar." [38]

It met opposition in some quarters. Its effect on other activities and occupations was occasionally viewed with alarm. A writer in *The Forum* declared that the piano trade had been cut in half, and that of the livery-stable reduced to little more than a third, because of the competition of the bicycle. Even the barbers suffered because the young man took his girl out bicycling instead of to the theatre, and therefore did not need to get a shave! Bicycling led to wholesale violation of the Sabbath. The churches were empty while long lines of Sunday cyclists could be seen rolling down hill "to a place where there is no mud on the streets because of its high temperature." [39] And while bicycling for women was generally encouraged, the Women's Rescue League, in Washington, issued a fierce blast against it on both physical and moral grounds. It declared that within ten years all female cyclists would be invalids, and in the meantime the temptations of the road were daily swelling the army of outcast women.[40]

Nevertheless, cycling remained so popular that no question of the day agitated the monthly journals more seriously than bicycle fashions for women. What could be done about the amply-skirted? "Her windage is multiplied, and so is the exertion she needs to bring to bear on her riding," sadly lamented one handbook. "Added to that, her mind is continually on the strain that her skirt may be preserved in a position of seemliness." [41] *Godey's Lady's Book* as usual came to the rescue. It advocated a kilted skirt trimmed with fancy brandenburgs, jacket bodice and vest, cloth cap and leggings. Other arbiters of fashion favored divided skirts and top-boots; there were suggestions that even bloomers ("bifurcated garments extending from the waist to knee") might be worn without offense to female dignity and modesty. Victorian scruples were giving way before the demand for greater freedom in costume. Folded screens to protect the feet and ankles from view when mounting or riding were advertised in the *Scientific American,* but the lady cyclist seldom bothered with them.[42] "A few years ago," one writer commented, "no woman would dare venture on the street with a skirt that stopped above her ankles, and leggings that reached obviously to her knees.... [The bicycle] has given to all American womankind the liberty of dress for which the reformers have been sighing for generations."[43] It was a development, this recognition that women too had legs, of very real significance.

Bicycling was exercise and sport. It was the rediscovery of the outdoors. It was romance. What popular song of the 1890's is better remembered than "Daisy Bell":

> ...you'll look sweet,
> Upon the seat
> Of a bicycle built for two.

Businessmen, housewives, working people, youths and maidens, all took to the wheel.

The League of American Wheelmen had its consuls everywhere to further the interests of cyclists. It gave the stamp of official approval to League hotels and promoted the good-roads movement. With mass production came lower prices and still further popularity. The bicycle had more than fulfilled its early promise. The countryside was transformed under its influence. The editor of *Scribner's* asked in 1896 whether anything had happened since the building of the first locomotive to affect so materially the human race. Four years later an expert of the Census Bureau declared that few articles ever used by man had created so great a revolution in social conditions.[44]

Other outdoor activities of the town might be cited. Among those who owned a carriage, or could afford to patronize the

Puck's Suggestion to His Religious Friends

Frederick B. Opper in *Pickings from Puck*, 1895.

local livery-stable, there was always a great deal of driving and
informal trotting matches. Young men still found the buggy ride
the most pleasant way of courting. Winter sleighing had lost
none of its popularity, and skating always had its enthusiasts.
There were many rod and gun clubs, which promoted competitive shoots with neighboring towns as well as hunting and
fishing. Athletic clubs, drawing upon both business and working-class membership, occasionally held track and field events.
But the outstanding form of outdoor recreation in the American
town of the 1890's, for old and young, men and women, was
bicycling.

-》》《《-

SMALL-TOWN STUFF! Skim through the pages of the local paper,
in New England, the South or the Middle West, at any time
during the 1890's, and there is the record of those amusements
and entertainments which so largely served to give the American
town its distinctive character. Simple and homely, far removed
from the glittering gaiety of the urban world, they provided the
recreation half a century ago of a people still living in what
we nostalgically call the horse-and-buggy era.

In one town during a single week at the close of the century,
new officers were formally installed at the Golden Cross Com-
mandery, a Baptist ladies' social was attended by over one
hundred ("supper was served and all sorts of games and music
helped to make the time pass quickly away"), and the dramatic
club staged a performance for the benefit of the Grange. The
Fessenden Helping Hand Society gave a supper and social, and
a traveling company presented *My Friend from India* at the
Opera House. Twelve pairs took part in the Tuesday-night whist
tournament, forty couples attended the adult dancing-class, and
a number of informal sleighing parties were held. There were
announced, among other coming events, a banquet of the Wheel
Club, at which the governor of the state and other prominent
guests were to be treated to a number of "entertaining musical

features"; an old-fashioned dance sponsored by the Oasis Encampment, I.O.O.F.; a lecture under the auspices of the Daughters of the American Revolution; a basketball game with a neighboring town; and a fair and festival of the Universalist Society, dancing from 8:30 to 1 with Leitsinger's orchestra.[45]

Here it all is—a life which had not greatly changed in the course of years and was to continue almost uninterrupted in some parts of the country for another half-century. But the inventions of a new age were soon to alter greatly the underlying pattern, not as much as in the city or in the more completely rural areas, but enough to broaden the town's horizons and to introduce into its simple life a growing sophistication.

chapter 16

Farm and Countryside

CONTEMPORARY OBSERVERS WERE GENERALLY WELL AGREED UPON the lack of amusements in the rural America of the late nineteenth century. Life on the farm varied greatly in different parts of the country, but it could not anywhere offer social or recreational opportunities comparable to those of town or city. A majority of all Americans—two out of every three people still lived in the country despite the increasing exodus to the cities—found themselves largely cut off from both the commercial amusements and the organized sports which had so transformed urban recreation.

In the Middle West, more typical of the agrarian scene than any other part of the country, the isolation which the telephone, the automobile, and the radio have now broken down was especially marked. The farmer was often miles from his nearest neighbor, and even farther away from the town. The incessant labor, the almost unbroken daily routine, and the dreary loneliness of the great farms being opened up on the prairies have been described again and again in sectional novel and autobiography. The lack of amusements played no small part in stirring up the discontent that led to agricultural revolt and to the Populist movement of the 1890's.

An even gloomier picture is sometimes drawn of rural life in the East with its equally back-breaking work and often less favorable rewards. "As for amusements and recreation," Nathaniel Egleston wrote in 1878, "there is next to none, at least that is worthy of the name. It has been said of the New England villagers particularly that their only recreations are their funeral

271

occasions. . . . Life drags on with an almost unvarying round of toil. There is little to break up its monotony." [1]

There were several factors in the latter half of the century that tended to make the country scene duller than it had ever been before. "In town one can find the swimming school, the gymnasium, the dancing master, the shooting gallery, opera, theatre, and panorama," Emerson had written in mid-century. "In the country he can find solitude and reading, manly labor, cheap living, and his old shoes; moors for game, hills for geology, and groves for devotion." [2] But not all the world was a philosopher, and in the busy life of the 1890's the greater opportunities of the city were increasingly responsible for that drift to metropolis which had its obverse side in rural stagnation.

"Sloven farms alternate with vast areas of territory half forest, half pasturage," wrote one observant traveler in the New England of 1892; "farm buildings, partly in ruins, testify at once to the former prosperity of agricultural industry and to its present collapse." Another traveler was struck by the number of abandoned churches, dismantled academies, and moribund lodges in sections where the greater number of inhabitants had fled "to the manufacturing villages, to the great cities, to the West." [3] The mute evidence of this depopulation still remains in stone fences running through land now completely overgrown, in the crumbling foundations of houses long since deserted. Every present-day resident of New England encounters them in cross-country rambles.

Under such circumstances the young people were oppressed by the growing contrast between their drab lives and the freedom of the city. With the loss of the more active and enterprising members of the community, the stay-at-homes often lacked the initiative to make the most of such opportunities as still remained to them. They resigned themselves to the limited and circumscribed life that the depleted countryside represented. Moreover, where conditions were more favorable, as has already been pointed out, there was no longer the diversity of occupations on the farm which had given so much variety to rural life in earlier days. Without any shortening of the long hours of labor from sunrise to sunset, the farmer had to work on day after day at the same routine jobs—planting and reaping, the endless weeding of crops, and a multitude of daily chores. Nor could he count, as he had in the past, upon many interruptions to this steady grind. There were still hunting and fishing. The latter remained in some parts of the country a favorite diversion, but the good old days were passing for hunting. The farmer had his rifle or shotgun, possibly a pack of dogs, but the growing scarcity of game, and restrictions on such shooting as still remained, greatly limited the scope of what had once been such universal sport.

Something was lost—and for settlers in the Middle West it was within their own experience—as the years rolled on and agriculture became more a demanding business and less a way of life. Fencing the land and driving out the game marked progress. So did improved farm machinery—reapers, self-binding harvesters, engines for threshing grain. They also spelled the end of an era.

Hamlin Garland has described how the West was affected by these changes. "Buoyant, vital, confident," he wrote of his family and their neighbors in their early years of pioneering, "these sons of the border bent to their work of breaking sod and building fences quite in the spirit of sportsmen. . . . With them reaping was a game, husking corn a test of endurance and skill, threshing a 'bee'. . . . My father's laughing descriptions of the barn-raisings, harvestings and rail-splittings of the valley filled my mind with vivid pictures of manly deeds." But as time went on there were fewer and fewer of "the changing works" which had served to bring people together. "We held no more quilting bees or barn raisings," he wrote of conditions a decade later. "Women visited less often. . . . The work on the farms was never ending, and all teams were in constant use during week days. The young people got together on one excuse or another, but their elders met only at public meetings." [4]

For all this evidence of the dreariness of rural life, a picture of the country painted in such somber colors would nevertheless not be wholly true. There were compensations for the passing of old sports and pastimes. The farmer still had an independence and freedom which the clerk and factory worker lacked; he still had the active outdoor life from which the city dweller was cut off. He was never wholly deprived of normal recreation. His opportunities were rare, spaced at long intervals, but for that very reason they meant a great deal to him. He enjoyed them with an intensity which his city cousin, often surfeited with a wealth of easy entertainment, seldom experienced. Frequency alone is no test for the value of amusements. The isolated farm family may well have got a greater sum of enjoyment from its occasional social gathering or informal entertainment than urbanites could possibly derive from all their passive commercialized amusements. The Grange meeting, a social at the local school-house, a country dance, the Fourth of July picnic, the annual county fair, the coming of the circus—here were events looked forward to for months with eager anticipation, and remembered for months afterwards with continuing pleasure.

->>><<<-

THE GRANGE had been founded, as the Patrons of Husbandry, in 1867. A secret fraternal order, somewhat along the lines of the Odd Fellows, its organizers hoped it could do something to aid the farmers through various coöperative activities. Its growth was amazing—as might be expected in a period which was to witness such a rapid multiplication of fraternal orders, women's clubs, and other comparable organizations. Within six years there were fifteen thousand local granges scattered throughout the country, most numerous in the Middle West and South, with a total membership of a million and a half. The Patrons of Husbandry were fully embarked on a broad program of agricultural education, coöperative buying and selling, and political activity.[5]

The Grange meeting, whatever the business under discussion,

A New England Straw Ride

Frank Leslie's Illustrated Newspaper, 1869.

A Grange Meeting in an Illinois School-House

Frank Leslie's Illustrated Newspaper, 1874.

The Day We Celebrate

Engraving by John C. McRae after a painting by F. A. Chapman, 1875.
Courtesy of the New York Historical Society.

soon became the principal social gathering of the farm community. And this aspect of it was emphasized by the presence
of women, admitted from the first into full membership. They
gave the Grange a vitality it could not otherwise have had.
There were sometimes other farm organizations that promoted
rural recreation. In Iowa an Anti-Horse Thief Association, having
largely succeeded in its goal of affording protection for its members' live stock, concerned itself with the lighter side of life.[6]
But the Grange was the social leader. It undertook to organize
lectures and concerts, held young people's debates and spelling-
bees, promoted singing-schools, and arranged evenings of general entertainment.

The latter were usually held at the school-house; it was the
community center. The bleak little building might be bare and
unadorned, but swinging oil lamps and the cheerful warmth
of its large wood stove quickly transformed it into an attractive
meeting-place. The wooden benches or desk seats, initialed by
the jack-knives of countless school-boys, were rearranged for the
audience, and the chairman or speaker took the proud eminence
of the teacher's platform. The farm families would drive in from
miles around, often bringing box suppers, and spend a long evening over the simplest amusements. The program would be very
much like that of the social in a small town. Recitations were
popular, and the singing of old songs. There were sometimes
charades or tableaux. If there were refreshments, they were
usually coffee and doughnuts.

Sometimes at these entertainments at the school-house, and
once in a while at some farmer's house, there would be a country dance. They were family affairs, young and old taking part.
Chairs and tables would be pushed back, the fiddler get out
his precious instrument, and the company wait expectantly for
the shouted signal "Ba-al-ance all" or "A-al-all dance."

"It was a joy to watch him 'start the set,'" reads a description
of one country fiddler (also the butcher and horse-doctor) called
upon for a farm-house dance. "With a fiddle under his chin he

took his seat in a big chair on the kitchen table in order to command the floor. 'Farm on, farm on!' he called disgustedly. 'Lively now!' and then, when all the couples were in position, with one mighty No. 14 boot uplifted, with one bow laid to the strings he snarled, 'Already—*Gelang!*' and with a thundering crash his foot came down. 'Honors *tew* your pardners—right and left Four!' And the dance was on!" [7]

The tunes were "Money Musk," "Fisher's Hornpipe," "The Irish Washerwoman," "Cut the Pigeon Wing," "Turkey in the Straw"—all the old favorites. One very popular was the minstrel song "Old Dan Tucker." It gave rise to a dance, sometimes known as the "tag dance," which foreshadowed a modern custom. At one point the fiddler, or whoever was calling the numbers, shouted out, "Go in Tucker!" and any odd man was allowed to cut in on a temporarily unattached girl. [8]

In the New England village, a barn or shed was sometimes made over into a dance-hall where the young people from near-by farms met on Saturday nights. A description of one such hall relates that it was an unpainted one-story building with open sides—a kerosene lamp swinging from the ceiling, a few American flags as decorations, and a large sign, "Please do not spit on the floor." Buckboards and buggies were hitched to the horse-rails while the dance was on. [9]

There was a prejudice against playing the fiddle or other instrumental music in some rural communities that still did not go so far as to disapprove dancing. This did not greatly matter: the young people sang the dance tunes, and the party went on no less gaily. "Weevily Wheat" was one of the favorite singing tunes:

> Oh, Charley, he's a fine young man,
> Oh, Charley, he's a dandy;
> Charley is a fine young man,
> For he buys the girls some candy.

Another even more gay and lilting air was "Buffalo Gals," sung with many local variations:

Oh, Buffalo gals, ain't you comin' out tonight,
Ain't you comin' out to-night, ain't you comin' out to-night;
Oh, Buffalo gals, ain't you comin' out to-night,
To dance by the light of the moon?

Reminiscing of life in rural Indiana about 1880, Chase S. Osborn described such dances in a letter incorporated by Mark Sullivan in *Our Times*. "The violin (fiddle) was taboo, but we sang songs and danced to them and hugged the girls until they would often grunt as we swung them clean off the floor or ground, in the barn or house or on the green:

Higher up the cherry trees the sweeter grows the cherry,
The more ye hug and kiss the gals the sooner they will marry.

And 'Billy Boy'—'She's a young thing and cannot leave her mother!' It was the time of Captain Jinks of the Horse Marines, and 'Down in a Coal Mine'. . . . And ' 'Round and 'Round the Mulberry Bush.' " [10]

In the more thickly settled and prosperous areas the simplicity of these evening entertainments and country dances was already a thing of the past by the end of the century. Here recreation on the farm followed more nearly that of the town, and might be closely associated with it. But for a great part of the Middle West those twin phenomena, lack of opportunity and narrow religious views, had the restraining influence so often observed in earlier days. They upheld a prejudice against any departures from old customs which was intensified for the older generation by what they heard of urban amusements.

More exciting and colorful than the school-house socials was the annual Grange picnic. It did not bring together only friends and neighbors. From a radius of perhaps a hundred miles, as in earlier pioneer days, the farmers and their families gathered at the grove that had been selected for the meeting. A few of the more prosperous might drive in spring-board buggies, but farm wagons were far more common. Two families would double up, making a "bowery wagon" out of their wagon-box by means of a few planks, and hitch up four-horse or six-horse teams. Members of the different lodges formed in line as they drew near the grove, carrying gay banners on which the women had emblazoned the lodge mottoes. "Some of the columns had bands," reads a contemporary description, "and came preceded by far faint streams of music, with marshals in red sashes galloping to and fro in fine assumption of military command." [11]

There were invariably speeches. If the picnic was held on the Fourth of July, the fervid political oratory that the West loved so much might hold the audience of farmers and their wives for hours. Basket lunches of cold fried chicken—a Grange picnic involved wholesale slaughter in the hen-roosts of the community —were next on the program. The band played, the men talked politics, and the women gossiped. There were often sports in the afternoon, and this was the nearest approach to the old rural pastimes of colonial days: races of all kinds, wrestling matches, and that most popular of rural diversions, pitching horseshoes. There was usually a baseball game. "Nothing more picturesque, more delightful, more helpful," Hamlin Garland has recalled, "has ever arisen out of American rural life. Each of these assemblies was a most grateful relief from the sordid loneliness of the farm." [12]

Sometimes the Fourth of July was celebrated by a gathering in the nearest town—however distant it might be. On July 1, 1890, the local paper of one small Illinois town printed its entire issue in red ink to draw the farmers' attention to the attractions it was planning for the Fourth. In response to such a glowing appeal, they came into town in greater numbers than on any previous holiday. A parade headed by a military band started the festivities, and this was followed by the usual patriotic address and an afternoon of sports. The townspeople had set up refreshment stands where the farmers supplemented their basket lunches. In the evening the firemen gave a ball at the city hall. [13]

The Fourth was always a tremendous day for men and women who day after day, week after week, seldom saw even their nearest neighbors. If they went to town, its life and movement, however small the place might actually be, held them enthralled. The games and sports were incidental. The crowd, the incessant activity of a large number of people, provided the real fun of the day at every Grange picnic or holiday celebration.

-»>«<-

THE ANNUAL state or county fair had its reason for being in the familiar exhibits of cows and pigs and chickens; pumpkins, corn, and tomatoes; jellies, pies, and fancywork. Farmers and their wives competed eagerly for the prized blue ribbons. But as time went on, the side-shows gradually overshadowed the main tent. "The people," sighed Josh Billings, "hanker fur pure agrikultural hosstrots." [14]

From colonial days America had enjoyed market fairs, and whether in New England or in the South, horse-races, prize contests, and the exhibitions of traveling showmen had been one of their distinctive features. When Elkanah Watson introduced the modern country fair early in the nineteenth century, he intended something quite different. The Berkshire Agricultural Society was concerned with crop rotation, use of fertilizer, careful seed selection, and intelligent animal-breeding. Its annual meetings were to teach a lesson the farmers could understand. The experiment was successful and quickly copied. In the period immediately following the Civil War there were over twelve hundred state, district, county, and township agricultural societies, and the greater number of them held annual fairs with an attendance from a few hundred to as many as ten thousand farmers.[15]

From the very first, plowing contests and speed trials had been necessary to show the advantages of careful breeding, and it was not long before the horse-race and the trotting match assumed an importance not entirely warranted on scientific grounds. Heavy milk-producers, mammoth sows, and prize pumpkins drew their crowds, but special stands had to be built at the track to hold the throngs that flocked to the harness races. We have seen what was happening in mid-century when even onetime Puritan New England produced crowds of thirty thousand for the trotting matches of the Boston Agricultural Club. After the Civil War the thousand-odd agricultural societies all had their races. A very reasonable economic motive furthered this development: the trotting matches drew so many people that they virtually supported the whole fair. Large purses consequently were put up to draw horses from all over the country and thereby attract still greater crowds. The fastest trotters, and a new professional class of drivers, made the rounds every fall. In the 1870's Goldsmith and American Maid were the bright stars of the Grand Trotting Circuit, and a few years later the famous Maud S lowered the mile record to 2:08¾ minutes. Adoption of the bicycle sulky and improvements in the tracks soon afterwards made the two-minute mile an almost everyday occurrence.[16]

Other commercial amusements now appeared. At first they were not officially permitted, but traveling showmen naturally took advantage of the crowds attracted by the fair. "On the outside of the grounds," stated the report of an Ohio fair in 1858, "there were any number *of outside shows;* learned pigs, fat women, snakes, monkeys, all jumbling together in Biblical confusion, while lager beer saloons and melon stands supplied those in quest of such delicacies." [17] It became obvious that if these amusements were to become associated with the fair, they might as well be within the grounds as without them, making their contribution to the running expenses of the often hard-pressed management.

"The same horse trots, ball-games, bicycle races, livestock exhibits, and trials of draught horses," a contemporary wrote of a New England fair in the 1890's, "the same side-shows, fakirs, freaks and uproarious fun that always go on such occasions." [18] Prizes were given for female equestrianism as well as for hooked rugs and samplers, for velocipedestrianism as well as for superior Guernseys. In 1888 a Rhode Island fair advertised "a grand tournament of bicyclers, a balloon ascension ... polo games, steeple chasing, football match, and racing by wheelbarrows, greased poles, sacks and horses." [19]

On the day of the fair the town would be crowded, the grounds densely packed with medicine shows and itinerant peddlers adding to the confusion and excitement. Hamlin Garland has described the tremendous impression made upon him as a small boy by one of these fakirs. He was a tall, lean man with long black hair, wearing a large white hat, and had as his assistants a little fat man and a sad-eyed girl with a guitar. Dr. Lightner's spiel on his magic oil entranced the boy, but the girl was romance incarnate. As they sang

> O Mary had a little lamb,
> Its fleece was black as jet,

"her voice, a childish soprano, mingled with the robust baritone of the doctor and the shouting tenor of the fat man, like a thread of silver in a skein of brass." [20]

After the Chicago World's Fair one exhibition could be counted upon as certainly as a prize sow or a trotting race. "The lady on my right, who I now interduce," the barker might be heard announcing at every fair throughout the country, "is the world-famed Little Egypt." At other tents on hundreds of midways were dancing-girls, lady boxers, baby shows, and graphic reproductions of the Streets of Cairo—a camel, a donkey, and a few ragged Chicago Arabs. [21] There were always freak exhibitions —the three-legged calf and two-headed chicken; candy booths and soft-drink stalls; shooting-galleries and merry-go-rounds. Where the fair was not big enough to support professional trotting races, farmers drove or rode their own horses. A popular feature was the boys' race—a mad, helter-skelter run on ponies or plow-horses.

Again the farmers would bring their basket lunches of cold chicken and stay the entire day, not spending very much but seeing everything. And again what they enjoyed most were the crowds which gave them a fleeting taste of town life.

->>)((<-

WE LEFT the circus in the 1850's with Barnum touring the country with his Grand Colossal Museum and Menagerie. It had greatly expanded since those days; it reached its highest peak in the last quarter of the century. At least forty large shows were on tour, and many more smaller ones. They played cities, towns, and hamlets, pitching the big top wherever they could hope to draw a crowd. Popular everywhere, the circus meant for the farmer the one taste of theatrical entertainment that he might ever have a chance to enjoy. The circus had a glamour about it which nothing else in rural life could equal.

Barnum's name was still one to conjure with in the circus world. Historians point out that it was really William C. Coup who was the prime mover in establishing the Greatest Show on Earth and that James A. Bailey was the real circus king of the 1890's.[22] But it was Barnum's reputation that packed the main tent. Joining forces with Coup in 1871, he had brought together, with an immense fanfare of ballyhoo, the largest collection of wild animals, curiosities, acrobats, equestrian performers, and clowns ever assembled. There were giraffes from Africa and cannibals from the Fiji Islands; Admiral Dot (successor to General Tom Thumb) and Esau the Bearded Boy; more elephants than ever before; and, wonder of wonders, a hippopotamus—"blood-sweating Behemoth of Holy Writ." The big top was the largest tent area the world had ever known; it covered two rings, and then three rings. The entire company, animals and all, toured by rail in sixty-one special cars.[23]

With its accommodations for ten thousand and then twenty thousand people, this circus naturally played only the larger towns. But the farmers somehow got there. The railroads ran special half-rate excursion trains, and they camped out on the circus grounds. It was more than the event of a year; it seemed

The Country Fair

Proof before letters of a lithograph by Currier and Ives after a drawing by
Louis Maurer, 1866. Courtesy of Harry T. Peters.

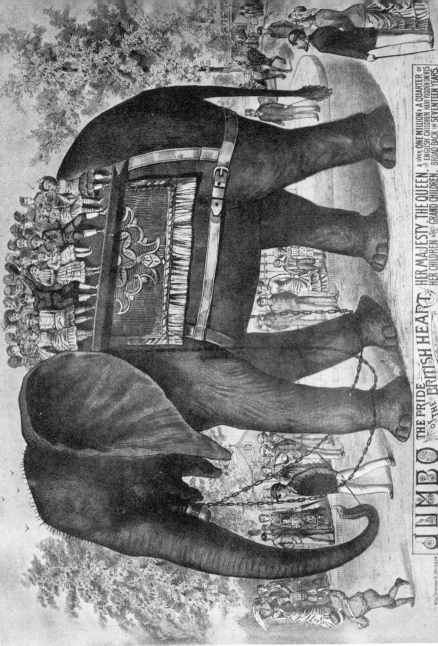

Jumbo

Lithographed one-sheet poster, about 1882. Courtesy of Strobridge Lithographing Company.

the event of a lifetime. Each season this popular show (it was already firing a man from the mouth of a cannon as one of its great attractions) took in anywhere from one to two million dollars in gross receipts.[24]

When his circus was almost totally destroyed by fire in 1880, Barnum made another merger. Barnum and Bailey's was born— a still bigger and better Greatest Show on Earth. The fire from whose ashes he had, Phœnix-like, arisen in still greater splendor, the irrepressible showman announced, had only served to illuminate his path of duty as the American people's champion amusement provider. Nor had he forgotten his earlier technique. Barnum still lectured on temperance; he still took care to enlist church support. He was not in this circus business merely to make money, he told the country. It was his mission to "provide clean, moral and healthful recreation for the public." [25]

A sensation almost comparable to those he had achieved in mid-century with his famous mermaid, General Tom Thumb, and Jenny Lind awaited him. His purchase of Jumbo, the world's largest elephant, from the Royal Zoölogical Gardens in London created an international furor in 1882 which brought the Greatest Show on Earth an avalanche of publicity. Englishmen were incensed. They were afraid that the loss of Jumbo would be followed by that of Shakespeare's grave or the Tower of London. All possible means were exhausted to prevent the famous pachyderm's departure. Barnum was adamant. Whatever the difficulty or expense, Jumbo was to be brought to America.

On the fateful day set for his removal, the elephant lay down in the middle of a London street. All England cheered. Barnum's agent cabled frantically for instructions. "Let him lie there a week if he wants to," came the quick answer. "It's the best advertisement in the world." When he finally reached this country, Jumbo led a torch-light parade for the opening of the circus at Madison Square Garden, cheered by half a million people.[26] Little wonder that villagers and farmers would travel miles to see him whenever they had an opportunity.

Barnum and Bailey's had many rivals. The Ringling brothers had developed their Classic and Comic Concert Company into one of the world's great circuses; and the Sells Brothers Circus and Menagerie, merging with Hadj Tahara's Wild Moorish Caravan, boasted four rings and fifty-one animal cages. Then there were Forepaugh's Circus and Menagerie, Van Amburgh's, the Irwin Brothers, Whitney's, Williams'....[27]

The smaller road shows copied these larger circuses in every particular, their grandiloquent advertisements making equally fantastic claims. Miles Orton's New York and New Orleans Circus, Menagerie and Wild West Show toured through Illinois making one-night stands, admission twenty-five cents. With fifty star performers and the marvelous racing elephant Lizzie, its posters shouted from a hundred barns that it was the greatest circus of all time.[28] In Nevada, Montgomery Queen's Caravan, Circus and Menagerie advertised its "grand centralization of genius, concentration of merit, monopoly of equestrian stars, avalanche of attractions." [29]

In rural areas and small towns the program for circus day followed time-honored custom.[30] While the small boys were out at dawn to herald its arrival, watching the elephants cautiously test the bridges wherever the approaching road crossed a stream, the farmers gathered from all directions. Every kind of vehicle would be drafted into use. There were great farm wagons, drawn perhaps by a pair of powerful Clydesdales, the grown-up members of the family sitting stiffly in their best Sunday clothes and the excited children sprawled in the straw behind them; buckboards and carry-alls; phaetons and mule teams. Occasionally the son of some rich farmer might whirl by in a side-bar buggy, his best girl beside him, scattering clouds of dust over the plodding wagons. Even before the morning parade officially opened the day's festivities, the town's quiet streets would be a whirl of excitement. Strolling mountebanks, candy and popcorn sellers, vendors of palm-leaf fans and toy balloons, three-card monte men and sly practitioners of the shell game. Everywhere rang out the shrill cry of the vendors of pink lemonade—"Lemo! Lemo! Ice-cole lemo! Five cents, a nickel, a half-a-dime, the twentieth-potofadollah! Lemo! Ice-cole lemo!"

The parade would burst upon these excited crowds with a blast of trumpets which rattled all the windows on Main Street. The band sweated and puffed at their instruments as they rode proudly by in the great circus wagon, with its twenty- or even forty-horse hitch; chariots driven by helmeted Romans rumbled along behind wagon cages between whose bars could be seen chattering monkeys, restless tigers; the equestrienne performers, dazzling visions of grace and loveliness, haughtily sat their plumed and prancing steeds; the elephants swung ponderously by with swaying howdahs; and the clown made his uproarious progress through the crowd in a flashing donkey cart. Above the crack of whips and rumble of wheels floated the steam calliope's shrill rendition of the popular circus songs: [31]

> My love has joined the circus,
> And I don't know what to do,
> She feeds the elephants crackers and cheese,
> And she plays with the kangaroo.

or the rollicking tune of Van Amburg:

> He sticks his head in the lion's mouth,
> And holds it there awhile,
> And when he takes it out again
> He greets you with a smile.

Even more familiar to later generations was another popular song to which the circus gave a nation-wide currency:

> He flew through the air with the greatest of ease,
> The daring young man on the flying trapeze;
> His movements so graceful, all girls he could please
> And my love he purloined away.

A midsummer sun might beat down relentlessly on all this tinseled display. The dust might swirl in great clouds about the ponderous elephants and rumbling chariots. But none could resist the excited cry, *The circus is coming!*

After basket lunches, the crowd flowed to the flagged and tented circus lot, and soon the familiar call, "Right this way to the big show!" was packing them in close rows on the wooden benches which rose around the sides of the tent. The bands blared forth the signal for the grand opening march. Here it all was—the ring-master cracking his whip, the cry of the popcorn vendors, the white-faced clowns, the dizzying swings on the flying trapeze, the living statues, the pervasive smell of sawdust. . . .

Even after the equestrians had given their last exhibition of trick riding, the tumblers and tight-rope dancers performed their final stunts, the day was not quite over for those whose endurance could stand further excitement. There were still the freaks and wild animals, and the raucous voice of the announcer declared that the minstrel show, all the songs and dances of the big city, was just about to start. As the tired holiday-makers finally jogged homewards in the gathering dusk, the children asleep on the straw-covered floor, it is not surprising that they often felt they had had entertainment enough to last them for many months.

"Each year one came along from the east," Hamlin Garland has written in vivid portrayal of what the circus meant not only for the small boy but for the entire family on the western prairie, "trailing clouds of glorified dust and filling our minds with the color of romance. . . . It brought to our ears the latest band pieces and taught us the popular songs. It furnished us with jokes. It relieved our dullness. It gave us something to talk about." [32]

chapter 17

The Role
of Moving Pictures

THE TWENTIETH CENTURY WAS TO BE MARKED BY CHANGES
quite as revolutionary and far-reaching in the patterns of
popular recreation as in any other phase of American life. The
growth of industry and further scientific and technological advance, new trends in urban and suburban living, the remarkable
increase in leisure time for the great masses of the people—all
had their pervasive effect on the popular pursuit of pleasure.
The amusement scene of the new century soon came to bear
little resemblance to that of the 1890's, whether in the realm of
fashion or in the countryside, in metropolis or on Main Street.

Three inconspicuous events in 1895 foreshadowed what were
to become the major innovations in a still unperceived future.
Two young men who had been closely following an invention
of Thomas Edison called the kinetoscope, succeeded in producing a jerky, flickering moving picture on a small screen at a
public performance at the Cotton States Exposition in Atlanta.
A pioneer race for the new horseless carriages was held at
Chicago on Thanksgiving Day, two of the six entries (gasoline-
driven) actually completing the fifty-two-mile course in a little
over ten and one-half hours. And, on the other side of the
Atlantic, Guglielmo Marconi publicly demonstrated (although
the continuing skepticism of the Italian Government sent him
the next year to England) the practicality of the wireless teleg-
raphy that was to lead first to radio broadcasting and then
in time to television.[1]

There were to be many other developments in the field of
recreation, most notably a great expansion in both spectator

and participant sports, but these products of the new technology were ultimately to provide the predominant ways in which Americans sought out entertainment. An industrial age that crowded people into great cities and deprived them of so many of their traditional diversions, that was constantly increasing the leisure time of the country's great mass of workers, had finally brought into being new and compensating forms of amusement.

Moreover for all the remaining vestiges of the old puritan attitude toward play, the twentieth century was to see general acceptance of the principle that it was the natural right of the American people, whatever their social status, to use their new-found leisure for recreation as they saw fit. The movies were to become the equivalent of the popular theatre for everyone, no matter how poor; the automobile was in time to be made available for all elements in society; and radio-television would bring entertainment directly into the homes of virtually every family the length and breadth of the land. The concept of democracy coalesced with the profitable economy of mass production to make the movies, automobiles, radio and television so widely available. It was not by accident that in no other country of the world did any comparable diffusion of these new means of amusement take place among the masses of the people.

-»)«‹-

Moving pictures were the first of these inventions in point of time and also the first to reach any great number of people. They were originally displayed as a curious novelty in phonograph parlors, billiard-rooms, and penny arcades in the early 1890's. One put a nickel in the slot of one of the new-fangled kineto-scopes, looked eagerly through a peep-hole, and saw the magic of tiny figures actually moving against a dim and blurred background. It might be a man sneezing, a girl dancing, or a baby being given its bath. It was a very brief entertainment, but the wonder of moving figures brought a steady flow of nickels to the pockets of enterprising showmen.[2]

When the experiments of several other inventors (Mr. Edison soon lost interest in what he regarded as a rather childish toy) succeeded in transferring these moving pictures to a screen where a large number of people could see them at the same time, they were taken up by the variety houses. The year following the showing at the Cotton States Exposition, a first New York performance took place at Koster and Bial's Music Hall on Broadway and "living pictures" soon thereafter became one of the popular features on vaudeville programs everywhere.[3] They still had little more than their novelty to commend them. The flickering figures on the screen could hardly compete with live acrobatic dances and popular song hits. Gradually losing their appeal for patrons at the better variety shows, the movies consequently retreated again to the penny arcades. Their proprietors set up their machines in darkened rooms ("pickpockets could go through you as easy as an eel through water") and drew in masses of the city's workers, often immigrants, who could not afford any better entertainment.[4]

In 1905 an important forward step was taken in the presentation of these pictures. A few years earlier an Electric Theatre had been established in Los Angeles solely for their exhibition, but it was the Nickelodeon that John P. Harris opened in McKeesport, Pennsylvania, just a decade after the movies had first been shown, that started the real boom.[5] The nickelodeons were soon numbered in the thousands. A writer on the "Nickel Madness" in *Harper's Weekly* stated in 1907 that nearly a quarter million people—men, women, and children—were flocking daily "through the gaudy, blatant entrances." [6]

"In almost every case," reads a contemporary description of these theatres, "a long, narrow room, formerly used for more legitimate purposes, has been made over into what is popularly known as a 'nickelodeon.' At the rear a stage is raised. Across it is swung a white curtain. Before the curtain is placed a piano, which does service for an orchestra. Packed into the room as closely as they can be are chairs for the spectators, who number from one hundred to four hundred and fifty. Directly above the entrance is placed the moving picture, which flashes its lights and shadows upon the white curtain dropped in front of the stage. Many of the machines are operated by means of a tank filled with gasoline or some similarly inflammable material." [7]

The same story was being repeated not only in every city in the country but in every town and hamlet. A vast public that had never attended the theatre, even the popular "ten, twent, thirt" melodrama, found in these brief twenty-minute shows entertainment which had never before been within its reach.[8]

The moving picture inevitably had caustic critics. The nickelodeons were called silly and time-wasting, if not actually pernicious. Anthony Comstock found in the darkened theatres intimations of immorality which sent anticipatory shivers up his puritanic spine. Censorship was threatened from the day when social reformers in Atlantic City protested the "hypogastric rhythm" of a peep-show depiction of Dolorita's Passion Dance. "The authorities request us not to show the Houchi Kouchi," the exhibitioner sadly wrote the producer, "so please cancel order for new Dolorita. . . ." [9] The kinetoscope's first kiss created a sensation and it was perhaps the editor of a small Chicago magazine, *The Chap Book,* who most forthrightly expressed a widespread disapproval. "In a recent play called The Widow Jones," he wrote, "you may remember a famous kiss, which Miss May Irwin bestowed on a certain John C. Rice, and *vice versa.* Neither participant is physically attractive, and the spectacle of their prolonged pasturing on each other's lips was hard to bear. When only life size it was pronounced beastly. Magnified to Gargantuan proportions and repeated three times over it is absolutely disgusting. . . . Such things call for police interference." [10]

A decade later the Chicago *Tribune* attacked the nickelodeons, declaring that in a majority of cases no voice was raised to defend them "because they cannot be defended. They are hopelessly bad." [11] On Christmas Eve of 1908 Mayor McClellan of New York revoked five hundred and fifty licenses because of objections by the city's pastors. He announced that future permits would be granted only on agreement not to operate on Sundays and not to show pictures tending "to degrade the morals of the community." [12] More generally, however, these show-places were treated with casual condescension, being dismissed as "a harmless diversion of the poor" and "an innocent amusement and a rather wholesome delirium." [13]

In the past popular amusements had generally evolved from diversions that were originally available only to the wealthy. In America this had been true to a great extent of the theatre itself, for the audiences in colonial days were the rich and the fashionable. It was a long time before the popular theatre developed. The first appeal of the movies, however, was to the masses rather than the classes. They were cheap and popular from the very beginning. The support which in time enabled them to raise their standards came entirely from their nickel-paying customers.

This had not happened by chance. The early promoters in the moving picture industry were often New York garment-workers or fur-traders who had bought up the penny arcades, and then the nickelodeons, to merchandise films as they would try to sell any other commodity. And their dependence on a mass market led to their continuing to place emphasis on quantity rather than quality. They were not troubled by an artistic conscience or concerned with culture in promoting this profitable new business. They wanted only to please the greatest possible number of nickel-paying customers. Combined with the democratic idea that popular entertainment should be made available for everyone, this brought about a development of the moving picture in the United States which was not paralleled in any other country.

In Europeans nations, notably France, where pioneer work in moving pictures was actually more advanced than in the United States, the evolution of the new amusement followed a quite different course. Instead of appealing to a mass market, the movies essayed the role of sophisticated entertainment. Foreign producers made far better films in these days (which is sometimes said to be the case a half century later), but in seeking to uphold high artistic standards they did not gain the broad, popular market that American producers won with everyday subjects that had a more universal appeal.[14] Moving pictures became a leading feature of American recreation because they were geared to popular taste and because they represented the culmination of the democratizing influences in the field of urban entertainment that had been at work for over a century.

->>)<<-

THE FILMS shown in the nickelodeon era represented a striking advance over the flickering glimpses of dancing-girls first seen in the penny arcade kinetoscopes. With the production of longer pictures in the late 1890's, incidents (man sneezing) had first been elaborated into brief scenes (employer flirting with stenographer). As the films then stretched out to perhaps a thousand feet, endless variations were developed on the chase motive. The cowboy hero began to track down the western bad man, the city sleuth to pursue bank-robbers and hold-up men. In the simplest form of the latter, the thief was chased through streets crowded with city traffic until the inevitable collision with a fat woman, who felled him with her umbrella and sat on him until the police arrived. Other pictures exploited even more blatantly the opportunities for comic relief. The subtle uses of a banana peel, of a small boy with a hose, and of a precariously balanced can of paint were developed with highly successful consequences. The custard pie was discovered.

Prize-fights and religious pictures also made their debut, two

In the Days of the Kinetoscope

A kinetoscope, phonograph, and graphophone arcade in San Francisco. Courtesy of the Museum of Modern Art Film Library.

The Last Word in Picture Theatres

Radio City Music Hall, New York, capacity 6,200, offering elaborate ballet and other stage presentations with feature films. Courtesy of Radio City Music Hall.

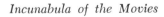

Incunabula of the Movies

Left, top to bottom: scene from *Cripple Creek Barroom,* an Edison film of 1898 (Museum of Modern Art Film Library); a daring scene for the nickelodeons about 1910 (Culver Service); William S. Hart in an early Western (Culver Service); Mary Pickford and Owen Moore in *Caprice,* 1913 (Museum of Modern Art Film Library).

Right, top to bottom: scene from a nickelodeon gangster film (Culver Service); Mabel Normand and Mack Sennett in *Barney Oldfield's Race for a Life,* 1913 (Museum of Modern Art Film Library); Charlie Chaplin in *Between Showers,* 1915 (Culver Service); Pearl White in *The Perils of Pauline,* 1914 (Museum of Modern Art Film Library).

outstanding events in motion-picture progress being the filming of the Corbett-Fitzsimmons fight and the Oberammergau Passion Play. News and travel had a wide appeal. For presentations of Hale's Tours of the World, the theatre was darkened, a whistle blew to announce the start of the trip, the seats began to sway through an ingenious system of rockers and brakes, and on the screen were flashed scenes of some distant part of the world taken from the window or rear platform of a speeding train.[15]

In 1903 an entirely new departure was *The Great Train Robbery*. Here for the first time the moving picture attempted to tell a story, and the success of the experiment was so immediate that every producer turned to one-reel thrillers.[16] The old melodramas, especially those of the West, were taken over from the popular theatres. By 1908 one magazine writer reported that the magnates of the nickelodeon world were paying from $15 to $30 for a good plot—"or even more"—and that the actors performing in these pictures received "all the way from $15 to $40 a week."[17]

In most of these films the modern movie-goer would still have felt something strangely lacking. There was no romance, no sex interest. It took time to adapt the formula of boy-meets-girl to the screen, but when the motion pictures had once discovered love, they clung to it. All its various aspects were promptly developed with unflagging zeal—love as sentiment and love as biological instinct. If the latter interpretation was to await fuller exploitation in later periods, romance had won a place for itself well before the nickelodeon days were over. Among the pictures being shown in Chicago in 1907 were *Cupid's Barometer*, *A Seaside Flirtation*, *The Course of True Love*, and *The Gaieties of Divorce*.[18]

Culture was not entirely ignored in the popularity of humor, thrills, and love. Shakespeare duly appeared on the silver screen. The patrons of one theatre were advised that, without any change in the five-cent admission charge, they could see "the superb, soul stirring, heart rendering tragedy, Romeo and Juliet . . . accompanied with an intensely tragic lecture by Dr. Lamberger." [19]

For some time there were no stars. The best known of the early screen actresses, Florence Lawrence, was known only as "The Biograph Girl." [20] Not until the closing years of the nickelodeon era did feature films and feature players emblazon their starry path across the cinematic skies. "Little Mary" films, first shown in 1909, pointed the way. They enshrined Miss Pickford as America's Sweetheart and fastened the star system upon moving pictures even more firmly than it had been fastened upon the theatre. Every audience, Keokuk or New York, was convulsed by the antics of John Bunny; held its breath in fear and trembling as Bronco Billy or Tom Mix thundered across the western plains, and became easy prey (at least its male components) to the charms of Norma Talmadge and Lilian Gish.[21] The nickelodeons had become something far more than "flimsy amusement for the mob." With ten thousand theatres playing to a nationwide audience of ten million weekly, they were doing a greater volume of business by 1910 than all the legitimate theatres, variety halls, dime museums, lecture bureaus, concert-halls, circuses and street carnivals combined.[22]

->>> <<<-

BEFORE the outbreak of the First World War, the movies had graduated from the nickelodeon era. Improvements in the techniques of photography, transforming the flickering films of the early days to increasingly clear-cut, distinct pictures; the introduction of multireel films; the appearance of a host of new movie stars, and more comfortable, higher-priced theatres were together responsible for a new day. One of the films pointing the way was a comedy Mack Sennett produced in 1914 in which Marie Dressler had the star role—*Tillie's Punctured Romance*.

With Miss Dressler played a newcomer to the movies—an odd little man with a postage stamp mustache who wore baggy pants, carried a cane, and walked with a queer waddling gait.[23] Charlie Chaplin was an immediate success. Within two years, so rapidly were the movies now forging ahead, in no small part owing to his own inimitable, universal appeal, he received a fabulous offer of $670,000 for a year's work.[24]

Incidental to a circulation war among Chicago newspapers, the year 1914 also saw an epidemic of moving-picture serials which proved to be a greater drawing-card than almost anything so far produced. A nationwide public breathlessly followed weekly installments, released both in the newspapers and on the screen, portraying the thrilling adventures of Dolly of the Dailies, Lucile Love, or the mysterious Florence Gray. The most famous of all the serials was *The Perils of Pauline*, with Pearl White:

> Poor Pauline, I pity poor Pauline
> First they tie her to a tree
> Then they send her out to sea. . . .[25]

Still more important, marking as definite an advance in moving-picture production as had *The Great Train Robbery*, was D. W. Griffith's filming of *The Birth of a Nation*. This famous picture (it was to earn in all more than $18,000,000) had harsh overtones of racism that unhappily reflected the prevailing attitudes of that day, but from a technical point of view, it proved once and for all that American movies could provide entertainment which neither the fashionable nor the sophisticated could scorn. It broke away from the limitations of the stage and utilized the improved motion-picture techniques as had no previous film. Its distant scenes, switchbacks, fade-outs, and close-ups revealed what imagination and intelligent direction could really do with this new medium. The producers were able to give a first-run showing of the picture at a legitimate theatre, with legitimate-theatre prices. Here was a far departure from nickelodeon days. While the moving picture remained primarily entertainment for the masses, it now began to reach as well a more discerning and exacting public.[26]

The growth of more luxurious and higher-priced theatres, slowly driving out the nickelodeons, both reflected and furthered this new development. It was again in 1914 that Samuel L. Rothafel, who six years earlier had been exhibiting films in the unused dance hall above the saloon where he worked as a barkeep in Forest City, Pennsylvania, opened the Strand on New York's Broadway. It was the prototype of the new-styled moving picture palaces—large, elaborate, and expensive, with pipe-organs and full scale orchestras replacing the jangling pianos of an earlier day. A decade later this famous showman opened another theatre—Roxy's—which awed even New York with its gaudy magnificence. This Cathedral of Motion Pictures could seat six thousand people in its auditorium, and its squads of uniformed ushers were often required to maintain order among another two thousand waiting in the lobbies for admission.[27] With its musical numbers and ballet-dancing, the show built about the feature moving picture almost rivaled grand opera. As other cities struggled to keep up with New York through bigger and better theatres, the movies had come of age.

->>><<<-

The 1920's found this most popular entertainment scaling new heights with a reckless abandon which reflected the pervasive extravagance of that exciting decade. Production costs skyrocketed. A million, two million, three million, four million (*The Birth of a Nation* had cost $100,000) were spent on a single spectacle.[28] The ballyhoo about the stars, drawing their ten and twenty thousand dollars a week, would have filled even P. T. Barnum with envy. And the public loved these stars all the more because they were such expensive luxuries. A society in which money played such an important role basked in reflected glory.[29]

Hollywood had now become the great center of the movie industry. Jesse Lasky pointed the way when in 1911 he rented a barn, for $200 a week, to film *The Squaw Man* against a western background.[30] The advantages of California sunshine soon became apparent, and the rising film magnates flocked to the Coast. Here the movie world worked and played, and a host of inspired press agents described with intoxicating detail the fabulous life that centered about Hollywood's burgeoning studios. Movie magazines carried to every fan the fascinating, and sometimes lurid, details of the community's loves, marriages and divorces. The stars became the arbiters of fashion and the molders of form. Shopgirls, stenographers, and high school students were dutiful worshippers at the Hollywood shrine. When Rudolph Valentino, the passionate sheik of millions of love-lorn maidens' dreams, died in 1926, the crowd that waited to see him lying in state in a New York funeral parlor stretched for eleven blocks.[31]

There were good performers and good films in these years. Charlie Chaplin remained the screen's greatest actor bar none, and Mary Pickford was still America's sweetheart. Constance Talmadge and Lilian Gish continued to be favorites; Gloria Swanson worked havoc with her glamorous charm; Harold Lloyd won tremendous popularity with his comedy roles; the muscular Douglas Fairbanks was a certain drawing card. . . . And among the pictures were *Ben Hur, The Covered Wagon, The Thief of Bagdad, Gold Rush, Beau Geste,* and *The Three Musketeers.* But for every such film there were also scores of second-rate movies that exploited the more blatant features of the postwar letdown in manners and morals. Their titles were revealing. As reported in the sociological survey *Middletown,* the citizens of one small city could in a single week choose among four such alluring pictures as *The Daring Years, Sinners in Silk, Women Who Give,* and *The Price She Paid,* and when

the programs then changed, the offerings for another week
were *Rouged Lips, The Queen of Sin,* and *Name the Man—A
Story of Betrayed Womanhood.*

"Brilliant men, beautiful jazz babies, champagne baths, midnight revels, petting parties in the purple dawn," advertised the
producer of *Alimony,* "all ending in one terrific, smashing climax
that makes you gasp." The features of *Flaming Youth* were
graphically described: "neckers, petters, white kisses, red kisses,
pleasure-mad daughters, sensation-craving mothers, by an author
who didn't dare sign his name; the truth, bold, naked, sensational." [32] Even though continued progress was being made in
turning out pictures of far higher standards, the sex dramas and
ultrasophisticated comedies, with their exaggerated emphasis on
the supposed fast life of high society, often appeared to dominate
the scene.

There was no question that the public liked these pictures.
As ever greater crowds nightly packed what had now become
the country's twenty thousand theatres, people from every walk
of life found in them the vicarious excitement, the thrills, and
the heart interest that for a time enabled them to escape the
troubles and disappointments of their own lives. The man
working all day on the assembly line in an automobile factory,
the tired housewife leaving the children with a neighbor for
her weekly night at the pictures, did not want entertainment on
any higher plane:

> Please don't uplift me when I go
> To see a moving picture show.

"The movie," an English observer wrote in the *Adelphi,* "is
the art of millions of American citizens, who are picturesquely
called Hicks—the mighty stream of standardized humanity that
flows through Main Street. . . . The cinema is, through and
through, a democratic art; the only one." [33]

->>)<<-

So THE MOVIES in the 1920's. But even greater triumphs awaited this popular entertainment which had so marvelously evolved from the kinetoscope of only three short decades earlier. In 1928 Warner Brothers released a new film—Al Jolson in *The Jazz Singer*.[34] Science had brought together sight and sound: here was the talkie. There had been a few earlier talking pictures, but it was the great success of *The Jazz Singer* that marked the real turning point in the movies' evolution. Within a year the conquest of the silent film was complete. Sound effects were hurriedly inserted in such films as could not be entirely made over, vocal numbers were added whenever possible, and all-dialogue pictures were produced as quickly as the necessary equipment could be obtained. As theatres throughout the nation were wired for sound, the movies boomed as never before. The industry's annual receipts rose by 1929 to the tremendous total of $1 billion and weekly attendance jumped to an estimated 110,000,000—the equivalent of four-fifths of the entire population going to a show once a week throughout the entire year.[35]

The depression brought about a drastic decline in these figures as forced economies curtailed all private spending. The theatre managers had to watch dwindling audiences and declining receipts. Moreover the industry was almost overwhelmed by an immense superstructure of wildly extravagant production costs and fabulous salaries for the stars. In a frantic attempt to attract greater patronage, everything possible was done to make the movies more enticing. The practice of offering double features was inaugurated, and many houses also resorted to bank nights and money games—screeno, lucky numbers, and bingo. These novel lures eventually combined with improving economic conditions to reverse the downward trend in admissions, and before the end of the 1930's, the industry was once again back on its feet.[36]

The revolution wrought by sound had in the meantime given rise to a new galaxy of stars and introduced new types of pictures. Many of the familiar figures of the movie world continued in the talkies after their success in silent films; a few staged remarkable comebacks after a period of eclipse while they adapted themselves to an unfamiliar technique. Actors and actresses of the legitimate stage, who had often scorned the pantomine of the silent film, made their hopeful way to California in droves, and a good many remained. Singers and dancers, for whom the talkies represented an entirely new opportunity, were suddenly in great demand. In a whirl of expanding energy, Hollywood was willing to give almost anyone a chance to demonstrate what could be done in this new form of entertainment.

The diversity of the pictures was perhaps the most characteristic feature of the movies in the 1930's. In filling the democratic role that the popular theatre itself had once played, their nightly programs often showed a marked resemblance to those of the nineteenth-century playhouses. The movies not only offered straight theatre, but modern equivalents for the old equestrian melodramas, burlesque performances, variety shows. At first-run houses there might be seen in quick succession a classical play filmed with all the artistry the producers could now command, an extravagant girl-and-music show, a blood-and-thunder western melodrama, a detective thriller, a sophisticated comedy, and a slap-stick farce. A single performance, again like the theatre a century earlier, invariably included one of these feature films as a major attraction; a specialty act which might be dancing or singing; a news reel (an innovation for which the popular theatre had had no parallel), and a comedy short which took the place of the nineteenth-century afterpiece.

The feature films derived from the plays of the legitimate stage ranged from *Camille* to *Petticoat Fever,* from *Pygmalion* to *Idiot's Delight*. Historical romances were elaborately produced: *Disraeli* was a favorite picture one year, and in another *Cimarron,* a story of Oklahoma pioneering. *Gone With the Wind* was a sensation in 1939. Well known classics were adapted to the screen, with such notable successes in these years as *Cap-*

tains Courageous and *David Copperfield.* With the use of sound tracks new possibilities opened up with animated cartoons. The "Silly Symphonies" had a great success, but far more important —then and for the future—was Walt Disney's inauguration of cartoon fairy-tales with *Snow White and the Seven Dwarfs.*

The reigning stars during the 1930's also revealed how diverse moving-picture entertainment had become. Mickey Mouse rivaled Greta Garbo, and the Dionne quintuplets competed with Clark Gable. Lawrence Tibbett and Zazu Pitts, Will Rogers and Jean Harlow, Adolph Menjou and Shirley Temple, Bette Davis and James Cagney, Mickey Rooney and Vivien Leigh, each had an enthusiastic following.[37]

→》《←

THROUGHOUT these years in which the movies were reaching an ever broader segment of the public, with children constituting something like a third of the nationwide audience, the inevitable question again arose of their effect on manners and morals. The reformers who had protested the "hypogastric rhythm" of Dolorita's Passion Dance in nickelodeon days became more than ever aroused with the lurid tone of so many of the movies of the 1920's. They could not close their eyes to advertisements that invited the youth of the land to learn through the movies "what love really means, its exquisite torture, its overwhelming raptures. . . ." Surveys which showed that the love theme led all others, followed closely by crime and sex; that the heroes of the films, if not "great lovers" were usually gangsters and criminals, led to widespread agitation for official censorship.[38]

When these threats from reform quarters were reenforced by a storm of popular disapproval aroused by the revelation of a number of scandals in Hollywood, the motion-picture industry decided it would have to take action. In some trepidation it summoned to the rescue Will H. Hays, a politician high in the councils of the Republican party, and appointed him czar of the Motion Picture Producers and Exhibitors of America. Taking over his responsibilities in 1923, Hays issued an ultimatum. "We must have toward the mind of a child, toward that clean and virgin unmarked slate," he announced, ". . . the same sense of responsibility, the same care about the impressions made upon it, that the best teacher or the best clergyman, the most inspired teacher of youth would have." Having thus sternly admonished the movie producers, he sought also to reassure the public that in spite of some temporary overemphasis on jazz babies and red-hot kisses, the industry still held Service as its Supreme Purpose.[39]

Some progress was made in the exercise of a reasonable restraint over the content of films under the auspices of the Hays organization and except in six states (Pennsylvania, Ohio, Kansas, Maryland, New York and Virginia), the movie industry succeeded in averting the threat of censorship. There continued to be a profusion of movies playing up the supposed fast life of society and the exploits of gangsterism, but the clean-up campaign did at least something to restore the movies' prestige.

A decade later, however, the old problem arose even more seriously. Producers and exhibitors had let down their self-imposed bans in desperate efforts to combat the effects of the depression. Everything went. A worried public became deeply concerned, and the mounting protests of the Legion of Decency and other citizens' groups finally convinced the moguls of Hollywood that unless they moved more strenuously to put their house in order, it would this time be done for them. Galvanized into action, the Hays organization undertook to co-operate with the reform agencies and established a Production Code which it was prepared to enforce throughout the industry.

This code set up certain standards governing the portrayal of crime, love-making, exposure of the human body, and profanity. There were to be no more scenes of seduction—"the treatment of bedrooms must be governed by good taste." More specifically, as revealed in the correspondence of the code's administrator, film characters were not to kiss savagely, get too drunk, lie around in their underwear, or use such words as "louse" and "floozy." One producer was advised to delete the business of "spraying perfume behind the ears," and another was told to cut out a character's stepping on a cockroach since "such action is always offensive to motion picture patrons." Robin Hood was not allowed, in the film of that name, to kick the Sheriff of Nottingham in the stomach; in *Dead End* there was a ban on "the action of Spit [one of the Dead End kids] actually expectorating." [40]

The code led to marked improvement after its adoption in 1934 but many critics now turned about to agree that the controls being exercised were much too strict. They found the movies at the mercy of every pressure group in the country and unable to deal realistically with any serious theme or important social problem. One commentator caustically declared that he "would rather take a chance on sullying the great American public rather than stultifying it." [41] While censorship whether from within the industry or without remained a constant and insoluble problem, the changing mores of another generation were soon to leave the moralities of the Hays code far behind.

The movies in any event continued to maintain and build up their tremendous popularity as the theatres that had successfully weathered the storm of the depression drew ever increasing crowds. It was estimated in 1935 that weekly attendance had dropped to some 77,000,000, but two years later it had risen by some fifteen per cent. Before the decade ended, it was passing the 100,000,000 mark and approaching the record figures of 1929. [42]

->>><<<-

NEVER AGAIN would the movies play quite such a prominent role in the recreational life of the American people as they were playing on the eve of America's entry into World War II. Attendance naturally fell off sharply during the period of hostilities and then enjoyed a brief spurt of popularity comparable to pre-war days in 1946-47. But apart from other problems in a new age, there was a shadow over the future of the moving picture industry in the form of the countless television aerials that now began to pierce the sky over all the land. Americans by no means gave up going to the movies, but a good many of them were to prefer to stay at home and watch television—often seeing re-runs of the old movies that the booming new entertainment industry was bringing to the more convenient screen in the corner of the living room. An increasing number of motion picture theatres found themselves forced to close as patronage fell off, and in the mid-1950's attendance was averaging little more than half what it had been in the golden days of the movies' greatest popularity.[43]

Hollywood—although it had lost its position as the almost monopolistic center of the moving picture industry—fought valiantly against this trend. Its slogan was that "Movies Are Better Than Ever" and it did everything possible to justify such a claim. Whether or not there was any improvement remained, as in the case of everything about the movies, subject to continuing controversy. Some critics nostalgically asked what had happened to the pictures of the good old days; others found the movies more realistically attempting to depict the modern scene, and, going beyond mere entertainment, dealing honestly with the problems of the human condition.

The general run of films nevertheless conformed very much to pre-war patterns with a shifting emphasis from year to year on musical extravaganzas, science fiction, war stories, horror films, and the time-proved westerns. There was nothing quite like *Gone With the Wind* (which was re-issued and by 1962 had grossed in its nearly quarter century $75 million), but a number of spectaculars were both immensely expensive and highly successful. *Ben Hur* and *Quo Vadis* fell into such a category and also *Cleopatra,* which was to be quite as renowned for the tangled affairs of Richard Burton and Elizabeth Taylor as for its great crowd-filled scenes. Among other much less ambitious but notable pictures were *The Best Years of Our Lives, High Noon, Marty, A Street Car Named Desire, The Diary of Anne Frank*, and *Hud*. Once again novels were often adapted to the screen. A new *David Copperfield* was one very successful film, and even more critically acclaimed as well as popularly received was *Tom Jones*. A number of documentaries won high favor, the *March of Time* continued, and there was always Walt Disney.

Some of the stars survived the war; many new ones glittered brightly in the movie firmament. Spencer Tracy, Humphrey Bogart, Gary Cooper and Cary Grant were among the more popular, and also Ava Gardner, Marilyn Monroe, Susan Hayward and Audrey Hepburn. Occasionally the immense vogue for some teen-agers' idol—James Dean or Elvis Presley—recalled the hysteria of the days of Rudolph Valentino. In the early 1960's a new generation of young stars—sometimes teen-agers playing for teen-agers—made their appearance.

As for new technical developments, there was nothing quite so dramatic as the introduction of talking pictures had been. However, there was increasing use of Technicolor (especially in the spectaculars), and the advent of the wide screen and three-dimensional pictures marked an exciting new advance in photography. Cinescope was a pioneer, *This is Cinerama* was first shown in 1952, and four years later *Around the World in 80 Days* was produced by the Todd-AO process.[44]

A more general development of particular importance was the changeover, which proceeded very rapidly during the 1950's, from the large moving picture palaces of the years between wars to small neighborhood houses in the cities, "twin movies" in suburban shopping-centers, and drive-ins everywhere else.

Among the small urban movie houses, the rising number of art theatres was a postwar phenomenon which did not necessarily encourage the American movie industry. They generally imported foreign pictures: Italian films, which first won recognition with *Open City* and *Shoeshine;* Swedish films, as conspicuously represented by Ingmar Bergmann's *Wild Strawberries;* French films, which introduced Brigitte Bardot; and even Japanese films, beginning with *Rashomon.* Going back to the earliest traditions of foreign film-making, these pictures often had a beauty and sensitivity that still seemed to elude Hollywood, and in many cases their directors handled sex with an even greater disregard for convention than the most uninhibited of American producers.

The drive-ins were not greatly concerned with the artistic excellence of the movies they exhibited. Found on the outskirts of towns and cities, and sometimes along highways seemingly far from any population center, they were family entertainment ("Remember the Kar and Kiddies are Free") and a haven for teen-agers. They invariably presented double features—such combinations perhaps as *The Gun Hawk* and *Bikini Beach,* or *Red Lips* and *The Horror of It All*—but given a balmy, moonlight night in July or August, the quality of the film hardly mattered for a good part of the audience. The drive-ins were also long on refreshments: popcorn, candy bars and hot dogs were very much a part of the evening's entertainment.[45]

By the 1960's these drive-ins accounted for more than a third of the country's moving picture theatres. Their popularity was further attested by the telling statistic that in comparison with an annual weekly movie attendance of 50,000,000, they brought the average summer attendance up to 80,000,000 weekly.[46]

->>>·<<<-

WHAT HAD BEEN the effect of the movies on other forms of popular entertainment during these years of their rapid growth and later comparative decline? They had begun, even in nickelodeon days, to draw away the patrons of popular melodrama and the devotees of variety and burlesque. In the 1920's, the onetime people's theatres were either closed or made over into movie palaces; the variety shows were so completely eclipsed that the old two-a-day vaudeville circuit disappeared altogether, and the doors of the local opera houses (unless they were wired for sound) were everywhere boarded up. So, too, the movies overshadowed the circus and the country fair; the traveling carnival and the amusement park. Such simple small-town diversions as lodge night, the Grange meeting, and the church social could hardly match their strident appeal. None of these traditional forms of recreation disappeared. But farm families no longer looked forward to circus or fair with the eager anticipation of the day when they provided the only semblance of urban entertainment, and people in small towns lost some of their taste for older, simpler diversions with the movies' easy accessibility.

As time went on, the changes the movies had brought about in the recreational scene were still further emphasized as other factors also served to turn people away from the popular amusements of the nineteenth century. The role of the automobile in breaking down the isolation of rural life and the advent of the radio and then television were indeed even more important than the movies. The latter only initiated that process of change, bound up with scores of other new developments—technological, economic and social—that has in this century created new patterns of recreation throughout the country.

The movies also had a significant effect on the legitimate theatre which was to prove somewhat paradoxical in its long-term consequences. They brought about the rapid decline of the traveling companies which had once carried Broadway shows to small towns, and led to the consequent concentration in a few cities, primarily New York, of almost all major theatrical productions—classical drama, the modern comedy, the problem play, and musical revues. At the same time, by so substantially limiting the legitimate theatre to the more sophisticated audiences of metropolitan centers, the movies indirectly encouraged theatrical producers to present more serious plays and to foster the drama as a cultural force as well as entertainment. Without attempting to intrude into the field of dramatic criticism, it may at least be said that beginning with the 1920's, the legitimate theatre increasingly offered plays which were of a different caliber than those designed to appeal to the largest possible nationwide audience. It was able to give more scope to such dramatists as Eugene O'Neill, Tennessee Williams, and Arthur Miller.

If the legitimate theatre was unable to recover the universally popular position it had held while hundreds of traveling companies were constantly on the road, it nonetheless continued to play a highly important role in the entertainment world. There was something of a revival of stock companies, especially summer stock, in the 1930's; other cities were to follow the lead of New York with its Theatre Guild and Group Theatre, and during the depression years, the Federal Theatre Project became for a time an active force in promoting new plays. Under such stimulating influences there was also a mushroom growth of community theatres with some 500,000 amateurs playing before an estimated annual audience of fifteen million.[47]

There were impressive indications in these developments of a new growth of popular interest in the legitimate theatre. But it was still true that the audience it reached, even when stock companies and community theatres were taken into account, remained a relatively limited one. In numbers it could in no way compare with the many millions who were still streaming into moving-picture houses in every city, town and hamlet throughout the land.

A very restricted role but also a fresh vitality characterized the theatre in the years following World War II. Broadway annually produced—with varying success and sometimes complete failure—from fifty to a hundred plays attended not only by New Yorkers but by visitors from all over the country. Also, a new departure in the 1950's which greatly stimulated all kinds of

theatrical experimentation was the increasing production of
"off-Broadway" shows. However, from the point of view of
popular interest, which is the major concern of this narrative,
New York's greatest contribution to the entertainment of the
country as a whole was the musical. Beginning with *Show Boat*
and *Oklahoma,* and then continuing (among many others) with
South Pacific, The King and I, and *My Fair Lady,* a series
of such plays had record runs on Broadway itself, toured all
major cities, and were then made into equally successful moving pictures.

Away from New York, summer stock—"the straw-hat circuit"
—expanded far beyond its prewar scope with hundreds of resident companies, often strengthened by visiting stars, playing in
tents and made-over barns. This phase of theatrical activity,
reaching far more people than the ten million or so who annually bought tickets for New York shows, soon led to the
formation of professional summer stock companies (there were
about 150 as early as 1952) and to what were called "package
companies," in which a star with a complete supporting cast
made the summer theatre circuit. They staged both old and
new plays, participated in the Shakespearian revivals, and especially in New England became a permanent fixture of the
summer scene. Still another innovation was the growth of
"musical tents" which put the Broadway shows under canvas.
It was reported in 1964 that thirty-two such theatres were in
operation and staged their performances (including most notably
My Fair Lady) for several hundred thousand people.[48]

Again nothing could bring back the good old days of the
1890's when as many as 500 traveling companies might be on
the road throughout the entire year, but neither the movies nor
any other kind of entertainment could wholly kill off the age-old
appeal of the live theatre.

THE PLACE of moving-picture theatres in American life at the opening of the 1960's may not have been as impressive as it had been between the wars. Wholly apart from any revival on the legitimate stage, they had been forced into a very secondary role by the universal appeal of television. Nevertheless, admissions at moving picture theatres which at the opening of the 1960's averaged 2.5 billion a year (accounting for receipts of $1.2 billion) could hardly be ignored.[49] The movies still held a very important position in the entertainment world.

They remained for the most part adapted to that level of popular taste which would bring in the largest number of cash-paying customers. With some notable exceptions, the great majority of the several hundred films produced annually (about half the number produced in the 1930's), made no pretence of aspiring to any higher goals.

Critics were as always in a state of constant alarm, and many of them felt that the postwar movies were exerting an unhappy influence not only—as in the 1920's—by exaggerating the violence in American life, but by producing "sick" films in which the heroes or heroines might be alcoholics, homosexuals or other neurotic characters. A great deal too much attention, it was said, was being given to "symbolism, sadism and sex." But while most of these pictures were obviously designed to titillate the taste of a mass public, some were honestly seeking to explore the basic social and personal issues of the day. There was less sentimentality and more realism than ever before in the best of these pictures, and in their treatment of modern life they were portraying on the screen something of the troubles, uncertainties and psychological frustrations of an age of anxiety. Their very strength sometimes carried them beyond what many people considered the bounds of good taste, but they could hardly have expressed the message they were seeking to convey if their preoccupation was always good taste rather than reality.

"So long as true filmmakers continue to probe the many complexities of man, to analyze his strange behavior under all stresses and strains," wrote Bosley Crowther, the film critic of the *New York Times*, "there is reason to respect the medium. It is when they fail to do so that it's time to scream."

It was still true, however, that both the movies which dealt with sex and violence for their own sake, and those in which such themes were seriously treated as inescapable aspects of the condition of man, were generally overshadowed by films that were wholly innocuous—"formula films"—in their handling of romance, adventure and high comedy. The producers were constrained by the very nature of their business, as it had developed in this country from the days of the penny arcade and the nickelodeon, to try to give the great masses of the American people what it was believed they wanted. The movies were originally projected as a democratic amusement, and they were as much so in the 1960's as in the early 1900's.

chapter 18

A Nation on Wheels

THE EARLY HISTORY OF THE AUTOMOBILE, INSOFAR AS RECREATION is concerned, could hardly have afforded a more striking contrast to that of the movies. There were in all in this country some three hundred horseless carriages—gasoline buggies, electrics, steam cars—when moving pictures were first thrown on a screen in 1895. When John P. Harris opened his pioneer moving-picture theatre a decade later, there were about eighty thousand.[1] But though the early period of automobiling coincided so exactly with the years of the nickelodeon madness, the automobile and the movies in those years reached entirely different groups of people.

The movies were for the masses, the automobile for the classes. The distinction could not have been more pronounced. The generalization may be hazarded that none of that vast nickelodeon audience ever hoped to own or even drive a car, while very few of the little band of wealthy automobile owners would have condescended to go to the movies. The first decade of the century witnessed a remarkable expansion in both areas, but it was then impossible to foresee that different standards of entertainment would soon draw all classes of society into the moving-picture theatres, and that the reduced costs of operating an automobile would in time enable all the world to motor. It was not until after 1920 that the movies and motoring could be grouped together as popular forms of recreation in which class barriers were not recognized.

The restriction of motoring to the wealthy in the early period of the automobile was not primarily due to the cost of the cars.

Although current prices ran as high as $7,000, runabouts could be bought for under $500 and Ford touring-cars for $780 as early as 1911.[2] This was not cheap from the workingman's point of view, but what really made touring such an exclusive prerogative of the rich was the expense of upkeep and operation. The lowest figure given in a magazine article appearing in 1907, was $358 for a six-months' season in which the car-owner drove 3,370 miles. New tires cost $100, minor parts $96, repairs and work on the engine $70, and gasoline $45. Another estimate for an expensive car set the total for a year's operating expenses at $3,528. A number of extras were included in this figure: a cape top and glass front, a speedometer, an exhaust-blown horn, and an allowance ($264) for motoring clothes.[3] Nevertheless it graphically reflected the continual drain for repairs and new tires which featured all motoring. The year's upkeep of a car appears generally to have come very close in those days to its original cost.

The new "automobility" came in for its full share of jokes and jibes, and also bitter denunciation, as the common man watched the newly rich ride proudly through the gates of society in their Cadillacs, Locomobiles, Packards, and Pierce-Arrows. *Life* parodied "The Charge of the Light Brigade" in 1904:

> Half a block, half a block,
> Half a block onward,
> All in their automobiles,
> Rode the Four Hundred.
> 'Forward!' the owners shout,
> 'Racing car!' 'Runabout!'
> Into Fifth Avenue
> Rode the Four Hundred.[4]

Some three years later, Woodrow Wilson, then president of Princeton University, gravely warned that "nothing has spread socialistic feeling in this country more than the use of the automobile." He declared that to the worker and the farmer the motorist was "a picture of the arrogance of wealth, with all its independence and carelessness." [5]

An expensive amusement not only summed up the general opinion of the automobile in these pioneer years, but appeared to be all that could be expected of it. It was a plaything for the rich. Motoring and automobile racing took a place in the lives of wealthy sportsmen which had formerly been held by coaching; it was regarded as a sport comparable to yachting or riding to hounds. Operating expenses and the inevitability of breakdowns for long shut out any idea of the automobile's more general usefulness, either as a means of transportation in the business and commercial world or as a popular recreation for the people as a whole. As late as 1911 Charles J. Glidden could single out as the primary effect of the advent of the automobile that it had "completely revolutionized the life of well-to-do people." [6]

The sport of motoring was hazardous and exciting as well as costly in the first decade of the century. A long course of instruction was necessary to learn how to drive, the schools providing preliminary practice in gear-shifting and steering behind dummy wheels before the pupil was allowed to venture on the road. He was also taught something about the engine, how to make the necessary repairs and replace parts. Many car-owners became adept at tinkering with the engine, but this phase of motoring was not always considered fun. "The nerve strain of working over those jarring parts, if you have no mechanical instinct," wrote one harassed motorist, "would take away all the pleasure of ownership." [7] One of the most popular automobile jokes was that of the car-owners' ward in the insane asylum. A visitor one day was surprised to find it apparently empty. The physician in charge explained that the patients were all under the cots fixing the slats.

Vast preparations had to be made for a day's run, let alone for the vacation tours which were becoming popular as the automobile very gradually became a more reliable vehicle.

New Toys for the Wealthy

An advertisement in *Collier's Weekly,* 1909.

The Thomas 6 Cyl., 70 H. P. Flyer—Equipped with "Flyabout" Body—$600
The most Powerful, Complete and Luxurious Stock Car Made
—complete with glass front, top and speedometer.

Thomas 4-60 Flyer $4500
Thomas 6-40 Flyer $3000
Thomas Town Car $3000

E. R. THOMAS MOTOR CO., Buffalo, N. Y.
Members of Association Licensed Automobile Manufacturers

Send 25c in stamps
complete illustrated st
of New York-Paris R

Cars and Costumes of Pre-War Days

Culver Service.

Vacationing on Wheels

A modern 28 foot aluminum trailer provides most of the comforts of home. Wide World Photos.

Among the items of extra equipment necessary were a full set of tools, elaborate tire-changing apparatus, a pail of water for overheated brakes, extra spark-plugs, tire chains for muddy roads, and a "rear basket with concealed extra gasoline supply." Clothes also were important. In this period the cars were all open, many of them without tops or even wind-shields, and the roads were incredibly dusty. The motorist had to be prepared for all contingencies, laden down with dusters, raincoats, umbrellas, and goggles. A single-breasted duster with Eton collar and three patch pockets was recommended for mild weather, but men were further advised to have wind cuffs to be attached to their coat sleeves, caps with visors and adjustable goggles, and leggings for repair work.[8]

For women the problem of the proper motoring clothes was even more important. One had to be fashionable, but everyday styles were hardly adapted to exposure to sun, wind, and dust. In the early 1900's bell-shaped ruffled skirts trailed the ground, and large picture hats were fastened upon imposing pompadours with a multitude of gleaming hat-pins. When motoring, all this fine array had to be carefully protected. Long linen dusters were worn, lap-robes tucked securely about the legs, and hats tied down with long veils knotted tightly under the chin.[9]

A hundred miles was considered an excellent day's run and even then there had to be a lot of "sprinting at thirty miles an hour" to get over such a long distance. The average speed was a good deal lower than this, but fast driving had already become a problem. Its effect, commented one automobilist, "is that of drinking several cups of strong coffee," [10] and this generation appears to have had a strong urge to experience this intoxicating sensation. To control these maddened motorists, who frightened horses, upset carriages, and more and more frequently maimed and killed other users of the roads while they escaped uninjured, strict speeding regulations were adopted in a number of states. The law in New York provided a maximum of ten miles an hour in congested areas, fifteen miles an hour in the outlying sections of cities and towns, and twenty miles and hour in the open country.[11]

Driving at night was not a usual practice, but one enthusiast contributed a special article on midnight motoring to the October, 1907 issue of *Country Life*. He painted a glowing picture— the darkness pierced by the flaming arrow of the acetylene headlight, the road opening up like a titanic ribbon spun solely for the motorist's pleasure, the muffled roar of the motor in the deep silence of the night. It was a wonderful sensation as, with hands gripping the seats, hair blown back by the rushing wind, the car's passengers plunged "into that big mysterious dark always just ahead, always just beyond reach." One word of warning was given about night running. Should a carriage be encountered, the driver should be ready to stop at once and attempt to calm the frightened horses by throwing his lap-robe (an essential article of equipment) over the headlights.[12]

Suggestions for driving advised care not only for the safety of the highway, but to combat the prejudice that the automobile still aroused among non-motorists. The horn should be used gingerly because a sudden squeeze was frightening to both horses and pedestrians; headlights should be blown out on city streets; persons having trouble with their horses should be treated courteously, "especially ladies who are apt to be rather helpless in such cases." A final injunction urged special consideration for pedestrians. If they were forced to dodge a speeding car, they were very apt to describe it later, to the ill repute of all motoring, as "one of those (adjective) automobiles." [13]

->>><<<-

By 1914 the motor car had passed well beyond this pioneer stage. There were some two million in the country, and mass production was enabling the manufacturer to turn out cars that could be purchased for as little as $400. More important, the automobile had been so greatly improved that constant breakdowns were no longer the invariable rule of the road, and it was possible to operate a car without the prohibitive expenses of earlier days. Highways also were becoming immeasurably better. Although an advertisement for one second-hand car gave as the reason for sale that its owner had motored from Illinois and could not return because of bad roads, the constant pressure of motorists was beginning to take effect in the construction of macadam and even concrete highways throughout the country.

Henry Ford played a leading part in making the automobile more easily available to a broader public. His Model T was the most familiar of all makes, with half a million of them on the road. Hundreds of "tin Lizzie" jokes showed the place they had won in the country's life. Do you know what Ford is doing now? was a question the wary learned to ignore. But the answers were legion: enclosing a can-opener with every car so the purchaser could cut out his own doors; painting his cars yellow so that dealers could hang them in bunches and retail them like bananas; providing squirrels to retrieve any nuts that might rattle off. . . . Another story was that of the Illinois farmer who stripped the tin roof off his barn, sent it to the Ford factory, and received a letter saying that "while your car was an exceptionally bad wreck, we shall be able to complete repairs and return it by the first of the week." [14]

The ubiquity of the Ford, as well as of the Ford joke, clearly indicated that the automobile had completely passed through that state when it could be considered a plaything for the rich or an instigator of socialism. It was reaching the American public —the workingman and the farmer. And throughout the period of the First World War and its immediate aftermath, this general process of diffusion went on at an increasingly rapid rate. The two million cars of 1914 had become nine million by 1921. In another five years this number had doubled.[15] So great was public interest in the automobile that when Ford completely reorganized his assembly lines and brought out a new car in

1927, the formal unveiling of the Model A attracted almost as much attention as a presidential inauguration. Thousands flocked to the Ford showrooms in Detroit, the mounted police had to be called out in Cleveland, a mob stormed the exhibition at Kansas City, and a million people fought to get a glimpse of the new car at the Ford headquarters in New York.[16]

Succeeding years saw a still further increase in the number of passenger cars on the road, and by the 1930's the total had risen to over twenty-five million. There was already an automobile for more than two-thirds of the families throughout the country.[17] Moreover such far-reaching improvements had been made that these new cars bore little resemblance to the horseless carriage of forty years earlier.

The automobile of the 1930's was long and low, showing a definite trend toward streamlining, and the touring car had almost entirely given way to the closed sedan. It was equipped with such an array of new conveniences—from self-starters to heaters—that one could motor with a degree of comfort the pioneer automobilists could not possibly have imagined. Winter motoring—certainly for short trips—had become almost as feasible as summer outings. Should anything go wrong, the uniformity of popular models made repairs comparatively easy, but motorists could count so much more definitely on their cars' dependability that they were no longer greatly concerned with what might lie under the hood. It was seldom necessary even to change tires, so greatly had their durability and potential mileage been increased. Everyone could drive a car, and everyone did. In the 1890's the tremendous vogue for the bicycle had given the impression that America was a nation on wheels. Half a century later this appeared to be even more true—but on automobile wheels.

->>⟩⟨⟨<-

THE AUTOMOBILE through these years progressively opened up broader and broader horizons in the field of recreation. It provided the easiest possible means of transportation from the country to the amusements of town or city, and from town or city to the sports and outdoor activities of the country. For countless millions the automobile was for the first time bringing the golf course, tennis court, or bathing beach within practical reach. It made holiday picnics in the country and weekend excursions to hunt or fish vastly easier. It greatly stimulated the whole outdoor movement, making camping possible for many people for whom woods, mountains and streams had formerly been inaccessible. It provided a means of holiday travel for a people always wanting to be on the move.[18]

The manufacturers of the popular automobile models glowingly recounted the joys of a Sunday or holiday motor trip in the advertisements they spread through the weekly magazines. In one, the car owner was invited to make the most of the next sunny Sunday—"tell the family to hurry the packing and get aboard—and be off with smiles down the nearest road—free, loose and happy—bound for green wonderlands." Another quoted a midwestern bank president in a two-page spread in the *Saturday Evening Post* as declaring that "a man who works six days a week and spends the seventh on his own doorstep certainly will not pick up the extra dimes in the great thoroughfare of life." [19] The drive into the country was to provide health and fun for all the family—and inspiration for more effective work in factory, shop or office.

What the automobile ("the enricher of life") meant in the lives of countless working-class families as ownership became more and more widely diffused in the years between the two world wars, was graphically revealed in the comments made by wives interviewed by the authors of *Middletown* in 1929. "The car is the only pleasure we have," one of them stated; another declared, "I'll go without food before I'll see us give up the car." An automobile was ranked in value ahead of ownership of one's home; far above a telephone, electric lighting, or a bathtub.[20]

The experience of the depression years fully confirmed this

general willingness to sacrifice almost anything else in order to keep an automobile. Generally being paid for on the instalment plan, it was the last thing to go among those families which experienced all the bitter hardship of unemployment and poverty. One of the steadiest selling products in the declining market of these years was gasoline, bought by countless impoverished families heroically economizing on food and clothes to pay for their Sunday and holiday outings.

In no other country in the world had motoring for pleasure at this time developed on any such grandiose scale. Everywhere else the use of the automobile for recreation was largely limited, as it had been in this country in the early days of the century, to the more wealthy classes. Only in the United States had a higher standard of living and mass production made possible such general automobile ownership. A car for his family, to be used primarily for pleasure, was accepted as a valid ambition for every member of the American democracy.

Apart from its daily and weekend use, more and more people had also begun by the 1930's to rely upon the automobile for their vacations. Contemporary articles depicted the joys of touring with an enthusiasm which quite matched that with which the Sunday afternoon spin was extolled. Every section of the country vied in seeking to persuade the prospective motorist to visit it. Chambers of commerce, resort proprietors, and oil companies joined in the appeal, glowingly advertising the attractions of seashore and mountain, and the exhilaration of the great open spaces. New England was a summer vacation land, and Florida a popular winter resort. The national parks and forests, especially those of the West, drew increasing hordes of eager motorists in an overwhelming response to the popular slogan, See America First.[21]

The face of the country became crisscrossed with the new macadamized highways and soon every route was lined with filling stations, lunch-rooms, hot-dog stands, curio shops, antique stores, and places to spend the night. Apart from the established hotels and inns catering to the wealthy and fashionable, the overnight accommodations that first sprang up along the nation's highways were very simple. Motels got a start in the West by the late 1930's, but what the motoring tourist more generally found was an overnight cabin—one of a row of little frame houses (sometimes with a carport), and adjacent but rarely private washroom and toilet facilities.[22]

About this time the automobile trailer made its appearance as a further boon for those vacationists with the migratory impulse so instinctive among Americans. A people whose forebears had crossed the prairies in a journey of several months could now make their way west in a fraction of the time with this twentieth-century equivalent of a covered wagon coupled to their car. In its bright dawn enthusiasts saw the trailer as facing a future comparable to that of the automobile itself. They predicted that a million of them would be on the road in a matter of a year or two, and that another decade would see half the population living and traveling on wheels!

Some seven hundred manufacturers rushed into the trailer business in the 1930's. Small machine shops, bicycle makers and out-of-work carpenters hoped they had discovered the boot strap to pull them out of the depression. This over-confident boom soon faded away in the face of a more realistic appraisal of the trailer's future. On the eve of the Second World War the trade journal *Trailer Travel* estimated that perhaps one hundred thousand trailers rather than the millions expected were in operation.[23] Nevertheless they made steady if less spectacular gains, and trailer parks were established in many parts of the country—in the national parks, at Florida resorts, and on the gounds of New York's World Fair. For a growing though still relatively small number of people, the trailer offered not only a means of travel but a way of life.

An important consequence of touring was the growth of a travel industry of immense proportions. In 1935, the American people were reported to have spent almost five per cent of their total income on vacation expenses. More than half this amount, or about $1,330,000,000, represented automobile operating expenses that could be reasonably allocated to the pleasure use of cars.[24] Here was a sum greater than the total of all moving picture admissions, greater than the cost of any other form of recreation whatsoever. Add to it all the other expenses of motoring—hotels, tourist camps, restaurants—and some idea may be gained of the importance of the industry catering to the motorists' needs. Half a century earlier there had been nothing comparable to automobile touring; it had, before the Second World War, become an economic as well as social phenomenon of the utmost significance.

The automobile as recreation awoke in some quarters the concern and dire forebodings that have marked the advent of almost every new popular amusement. It was said to encourage extravagance and irresponsibility; and weekend motoring was decried as still further undermining the oldtime sanctity of the Sabbath. There was already the grave moral problem of what might be taking place in the parked sedan, or at the roadside tourist camp. And on a somewhat different level, critics found the automobile encouraging a passive, inactive way of spending leisure time that might better be employed in sports or other more energetic outdoor pursuits.

One worried sociologist of the 1930's devastatingly described the futility of the popular Sunday afternoon spin—the crowded highways, traffic jams, and accidents; the car windows tightly closed against spring breezes; and whatever beauties the landscape might offer hidden behind forbidding lines of advertising billboards. "One arrives after a motor journey," he wrote, "all liver and no legs; one's mind asleep, one's body tired; one is bored, irritable, and listless." [25]

The countryside was in these days far more obscured by advertisements than it has since become as a result of anti-billboard campaigns: there were certainly horrendous traffic jams on the limited highway network of the pre-war era. What the

critics of motoring forgot, however, was that without the automobile the great majority of Sunday and holiday motorists, as
well as tourists traveling farther afield on their vacations, would
have remained cooped up in crowded cities and towns. The
alternative to the country drive would have been the movie,
the dance-hall or the beer parlor. The steamboat and the railroad had begun a century earlier to open up the world of travel
and provide a means of escape for city dwellers to field and
stream, seashore and mountain, but these means of travel were
by their expense limited to the very few. The automobile was
opening new horizons for millions of persons who could not
otherwise afford to travel at all.

→≫)(≪←

THE PATTERNS of holiday motoring and vacation touring so well
established by the close of the 1930's were almost immeasurably
broadened in mid-century. More and more people took to the
open road, and it goes without saying they traveled farther and
faster. A vast postwar program of highway construction knit
the entire country closely together, tourist facilities multiplied
enormously, the national parks expanded their camping grounds,
and the whole travel industry enjoyed a spectacular boom.
There were 65,000,000 passenger cars registered in 1962—nearly
three times as many as a quarter of a century earlier—and it was
again estimated that some two-thirds of their use was for recreational purposes. A report of the American Automobile Association in 1964 stated that over 100,000,000 Americans had taken
vacation trips that year and spent some $25 billion in the
process.[26]

The Sunday afternoon spin more often became a weekend
trip; the vacation tour could easily span the continent. Apart
from the new freeways, turnpikes, thruways and interstate highways (to say nothing of the new cars themselves), there was a
spectacular development in tourist accommodations. The primi-

tive overnight cabins gave way to the luxurious motels demanded by an increasingly affluent society. With their wall-to-wall carpeting, tiled bathrooms, television sets, swimming pools, and very often attached restaurants, they marked a new stage in the evolution of automobile travel. The motels catered to many people other than vacationists, but summer long they were crowded with tourists driving back and forth across the country, and in some states were almost as well filled during the winter. Skiers headed north to mountain slopes; sun-worshippers drove to Florida, Arizona or California.

At the same time the automobile continued—in what was called "Operation Outdoors"—greatly to encourage camping in national parks and forests. Hundreds of thousands of vacationing families in heavily laden sedans, specially outfitted station wagons, and occasionally trailers, courageously set out every summer to explore the wilds. Available guide-books listed more than 9,000 campsites in both national and state parks which generally provided central washing and toilet facilities as well as fireplaces, tables, benches, and trash receptacles.[27] Here the midtwentieth-century pioneers of the open road unpacked their voluminous equipment, set up their tents, built their fires, and became for a time self-reliant frontiersmen. They came from every part of the country and every walk of life: college professors and mechanics, lawyers and factory workers, Wall Street clerks and midwestern storekeepers. The automobile tourist encampments at the state parks in the East, at the national parks in the West, were a microcosm of American society.

It was sometimes suggested that camping had lost something of the rugged character of the day when the outdoor movement first attracted hikers, mountain climbers, and canoeists. "Roughing it," Robert H. Boyle wrote in his *Sport—Mirror of American Life*, "now means toting collapsible tables and chairs, gasoline stoves, Polaroid sun glasses and electric blankets to the seas, streams and lakes." [28] Still and all, even quite comfortable camping in the national parks was far removed from always staying on interstate highways and spending every night in a luxury motel. For all its limitations, it was a return to the woods and had its sense of personal adventure for all the family.

As a result of this popular movement, automobile visitations in national parks and forests, including both campers and more casual tourists, increased in midcentury years at a rate of some ten per cent annually. It was reported in 1962 that the number of visitors was 80,000,000, more than doubling any prewar figure, and that since records had first been kept in 1904, the over-all total exceeded a billion.[29]

This overwhelming number of visitors awoke widespread concern over the urgent need further to protect national parks and forests as places of uncommercialized popular recreation, and an Outdoors Recreation Resources Review Commission, under the chairmanship of Laurence S. Rockefeller, was appointed to report to the President and Congress on possible conservation measures. After a thorough study, which projected far into the future the possible demand for additional camping areas, it made a comprehensive report which in 1964 stimulated congressional action. Plans were laid for a twenty-five year federal program, in cooperation with the states, to preserve scenic, water and land recreational facilities on a pay-as-you-go basis throughout the entire country.[30] In opening up the parks to such constantly swelling crowds of tourist-campers, vacation motoring had created a problem that only such a far-reaching program could possibly resolve.

With a naturally far more restricted appeal than general pleasure motoring, two conspicuous fads flourished in postwar years. The one was sports cars and the other hot rodding. The importation of fast and expensive foreign models provided the wealthy with the means for a new form of sport, and also of conspicuous display, which recalled the earlier days when all motoring was a privilege of what had been called the new "automobility." On the other hand, the hot rod cult was developed as a lower middle class fad by young men and teen-agers whose passion was drag-strip racing in second-hand cars with "souped up" engines. It was estimated at the opening of the 1960's that there were as many as a million and a half hot rodders. Many of them were organized into such clubs as the Road Runners, the Untouchables, the Black Widows or the Cannibals, and in some parts of the country their reckless driving and irresponsible behavior had created a serious social problem.[31]

—>>)<(<—

THE AUTOMOBILE has had in scores of ways a social and economic impact on this nation that can hardly be exaggerated. It has revolutionized transportation and effected every phase of business and trade activity; it has linked the country with the city and the city with the country as they have never before been linked in all history; it has completely transformed the patterns of suburban life, and it has reached out into the broad field of education by making possible consolidated schools. Fully as important as its role in these and other areas, the automobile has given an entirely new dimension to recreational life which could hardly be more universal in reaching all strata of the nation's population.

chapter 19

On the Air

I N 1920 THERE WERE SOME FIVE THOUSAND AMATEUR RADIO FANS in the United States. Their chief amusement was picking up on crude, home-made receiving sets the wireless-telephony messages, principally from ships at sea, which marked the quarter-century advance in communications since Marconi's experiments in the 1890's.[1] Broadcasting grew out of this amateur activity. When experiments were made in putting news and music on the air, the realization grew that this new medium had startling potentialities for entertainment. They had been foreseen some four years earlier by David Sarnoff, ambitiously planning a "Radio Music Box" for every home, but apart from a few limited demonstrations it was not until 1920 that broadcasting in its modern sense became an actuality.

Among the experiments with music in that year, those of Lester Spangenberg, a former navy radio operator, have been credited with constituting the first regular broadcasting. Volunteer pianists and banjo-players began to meet nightly at the Spangenberg home in Lakeview, New Jersey, and a program was sent out on which hundreds of other amateurs tuned in.[2]

A few months later, enthusiasts who lived near Pittsburgh were also surprised to hear music which was being broadcast—though the word was hardly known—from a plant of the Westinghouse Electric and Manufacturing Company. They liked it; a number of them wrote in suggesting a regular program. One was consequently put on the air—baseball scores and popular music every Wednesday and Saturday night—and soon afterwards a Pittsburgh department store began advertising "ap-

proved radio receiving sets for listening to Dr. Conrad's concerts." The Westinghouse officials suddenly realized that they
had inadvertently stumbled on something. Here was a way to
increase sales of equipment to radio fans by providing entertainment, news reports, and educational features for those who
enjoyed listening in.[3]

Arrangements were promptly made to establish the famous
KDKA, the first permanent, commercial broadcasting station.
It was formally opened on November 2, 1920, to broadcast to
a few listeners (some of whom were provided with free receiving sets) the results of the Harding-Cox election. The success
of the experiment led to further expansion of KDKA's activities
and within a year to establishment of other pioneer stations.
From that date the rapid expansion of broadcasting and growth
of the great invisible audience constituted one of the most amazing phenomena of the decade. When another presidential contest came around in 1924, the news of the election of Coolidge
was sent out over a nation-wide hook-up which reached five
million homes. Twelve years later the number of household receiving sets had more than quadrupled, and the great majority
of people throughout the country first learned of Roosevelt's
second election over the air.[4]

-»»«-

WITH THE rapid multiplication of broadcasting stations in those
first years after 1920, the ether was soon crowded with music,
stock-market reports, accounts of sporting events, and bedtime
stories. In January, 1921, the rector of the Calvary Episcopal
Church in Pittsburgh allowed the first broadcasting of a church
service; a few months later Herbert Hoover made the first public address over the air in an appeal for funds to support European relief work.[5] The Dempsey-Carpentier fight was broadcast.
The New York Times printed an inconspicuous news item re-
ferring to it as an interesting experiment in wireless telephony,

The First Broadcasting Station

Station 2ZM, owned and operated by Lester Spangenberg at Lakeview, New Jersey, 1920.

A Modern Television Control Room

The master control room of NBC-TV at Rockefeller Center, New York. Courtesy of NBC-TV.

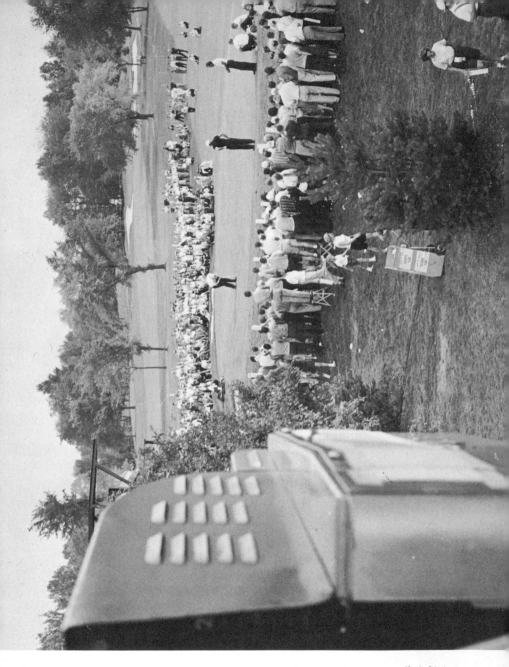

*Television
Goes to the
Golf Course*

Television cameras record a tense moment during *Big Three Golf.* Courtesy of NBC-TV.

but a growing army of radio enthusiasts realized that something epochal was taking place.

Before the end of 1922 there were hundreds of broadcasting stations, and a new entertainment industry (WJZ in Newark, New Jersey, was an imaginative pioneer in developing popular programs) was fully launched.[6] "There is radio music in the air, every night, everywhere," wrote a startled newspaper editor in San Francisco. "Anybody can hear it at home on a receiving set, which any boy can put up in an hour." [7] Hundreds of thousands were making the same discovery and rushed to buy radios. President Harding had one installed in his study at the White House. All the world wanted this new device annihilating space and bringing entertainment into the home with the twist of a dial. "The rapidity with which the thing has spread," one astounded observer commented, "has possibly not been equalled in all the centuries of human progress." [8]

There was a great deal more on the air than what might normally fall under the head of entertainment, but radio made its spectacular advance because it was the most novel amusement the American people had ever known. Following the example of the electrical manufacturers who had first supported broadcasting as a means to increase radio sales, other manufacturers, department stores, and newspapers soon seized the opportunity to operate stations which would enable them to get their names before the public in a favorable light. They were not always sure what to do, but at first it did not really matter. The novelty of any broadcast made it a success. Pioneer radio enthusiasts, listening far into the night with head-phones clamped securely to their expectant ears ("ear-muffs" were considered far superior to loud-speakers), were more interested in picking up distant stations than in the quality of near-by music. Involving intricate experiments with new devices, a constant struggle against static, and all-night vigils, radio listening was originally an exciting sport rather than a passive amusement. It was highly competitive and sometimes quite exhausting.[9]

Programs covering the entire day—from setting up exercises at 6:45 A.M. to jazz at midnight—were inaugurated as early as 1923 by such stations as WJZ. Music predominated, soprano solos proving most popular, but there were also informing talks on every conceivable subject and ingenious radio dramas. A trial was made of what were called "omni-oral" productions at which the entire evening's program revolved around a single subject. "A Night Out of the Past" or "A Night in India" was presented with related music and talks.[10]

It was radio's awkward age. Critics concerned about its influence in the transmission of ideas became gravely worried over what was happening. In October, 1924, a writer in the *New Republic* declared that jazz was the principal entertainment on the air, and ninety per cent of everything else was "sheer rubbish." "The development of motion pictures in the United States," he stated, "was held back half a decade because at first it was in the control of fly-by-nights, adventurers and reformed pushcart peddlers, not one in a hundred of whom had reached the social level where one takes off one's hat indoors. Radio broadcasting seems threatened by the same fate." [11] As in the case of the movies, however, radio was destined for popular entertainment even if it meant jazz and rubbish. In attempting to satisfy public taste, the new industry was filling its primary function in providing amusement for the American people as a whole.

Improvements in technique and organization certainly went ahead faster in these years than the quality of entertainment. Nation-wide hook-ups were inaugurated in 1924 for the national political conventions. A few years later, chain broadcasting, linking stations over the entire country, enabled listeners everywhere to hear the same run-of-the-mill nightly programs. Sensing the potentialities of a medium reaching an audience which now numbered many millions, national advertisers ushered in a new era in broadcasting with sponsored programs over these networks. Leading manufacturers sought to associate in the mass mind the excellence of the entertainment they provided with the excellent qualities of their tooth pastes, automobiles, cigarettes, mattresses, ginger ales, deodorants, watches, or cough drops. Performances became more elaborate, radio headliners were developed, and still further impetus given to the contagious craze so rapidly engulfing a great majority of American homes.[12]

Throughout the land orchestras hammered away day and night at "Mister Gallagher and Mister Shean," and then at "Yes, We Have No Bananas," "Barney Google," or "Valencia." "Ol' Man River" kept rolling along, the crooning voice of Rudy Vallee ("I'm just a Vagabond Lover") stirred millions of feminine hearts; husky-toned torch singers soothed masculine breasts with "Moanin' Low" and "Am I Blue?" Then there were Roxy and his Gang, the Happiness Boys, the A. and P. Gypsies, the Cliquot Club Eskimos, the Ipana Troubadours. . . .

Saxophones, trombones, ukuleles supplied an orgy of sound such as the world had never known. Writing in 1928, Charles Merz declared that twenty to thirty million Americans were "listening in on the greatest single sweep of synchronized and syncopated rhythm that human ingenuity has yet conceived. This is our counterpart of the drum the black man beats when the night is dark and the jungle lonely. Tom-tom." [13] Tin Pan Alley was rejuvenated. It was no longer the minstrel show, the vaudeville team, or the circus that spread the new songs throughout the country. It was the radio. It gave them an immediate and universal vogue—an almost instantaneous nation-wide popularity.

This music was not the whole show. Classical music—piano recitals, concert singing, symphonies, opera broadcasts—appealed to a small but nevertheless growing public. After 1927 there was general agreement among musicians that radio was definitely serving to improve the popular taste.[14] Women particularly favored symphonic music, and national advertisers discovered that concerts as well as dance music might serve the cause of expanding sales. Soon many millions were listening to the Metropolitan Opera on Saturday afternoons and to the New York Philharmonic-Symphony orchestra every Sunday.

An interesting influence was exerted on the phonograph. Record playing had become one of the most popular of all home diversions. The American people were in 1919 spending more on phonographs and records than they were on all musical instruments, on all books and periodicals, or on all sporting goods. The radio caused an almost immediate collapse in these sales, the total dropping in twelve years from $339,000,000 to $17,000,000.[15] As a general medium of entertainment, the phonograph nearly disappeared. But what now happened was that greatly improved and more expensive phonographs, combined with radios, slowly began to make up some of this lost ground, and there was a boom in the sale of recordings of classical music.

The phonograph industry, that is, went through a transformation somewhat comparable to that experienced in theatrical enterprise. The radio supplied the popular product, as had vaudeville and then the movies, and phonographs were largely produced for the more cultured audience which wanted its Beethoven or Bach always on hand. In the 1930's this trend was very marked, and the parallel between the radio and movies, on the one hand, and phonographs and the legitimate theatre, on the other, remained an interesting phenomenon of the contemporary amusement world. In time even the piano trade, which also had fallen into the doldrums, felt the quickening effect of a new appreciation for music which the radio inspired but did not wholly satisfy.

Music in general (popular and classical) made up some three-fourths of radio's programs in its early years. Next in popularity were the broadcasts of sporting events—football games, prize-fights, and major-league baseball games.[16] There was for long no more familiar voice in all the land than that of Graham McNamee excitedly describing the winning touchdown, the knock-out blow, or the ninth-inning home run. Radio theatre had also been developed into a new art. There were mystery plays, melodramas, and variety acts. Humorous broadcasts had a great vogue. When stock-market prices began to crash and breadlines lengthened after 1929, literally millions of people turned on their radios every night to listen to the complicated business and domestic affairs of Amos 'n' Andy. Other radio head-liners came and went as the great American people took up first one and then another with that inconstancy which has always been so characteristic of the popular mood.

At the same time religious services, public functions, political talks, were broadcast regularly. News reports—not only sports and market prices but all foreign and domestic news—were featured every hour on the hour. The radio commentator became a new figure in the world of affairs. Countless lectures falling within the educational field were zealously promoted as sustaining programs. Throughout the day, housewives, half-listening to the radio as they went about their work, were regaled with health talks, fashion hints, recipes, and general household advice. There were children's stories and spelling contests. It all came under the head of entertainment, however serious some of the talks and speeches. The process of taking it in was so completely painless. Should the listener ever become bored, a twist of the dial would change his program.[17]

-≫≫)《≪-

WITH FURTHER expansion in the 1930's, for the sale of radios did not suffer from the depression as much as many other forms of entertainment: the invisible audience grew still larger. The twelve million sets in use at the opening of the decade had in all increased to some forty millions by its close.[18] More than four-fifths of the entire population could listen in, and sometimes did, to nation-wide hook-ups on special occasions. There were not only radios in more than twenty-six million private homes; in countless clubs, taverns, hotels, schools, hospitals, and other institutions, but also five million of them in automobiles. It was hard to escape them. Traveling salesmen marooned in a small town, cruising taxicab drivers in the cities, even farmers driving their tractors, had radios. They were one of the most commonplace features of American life.

While there had been a continued advance in broadcasting classical music, growing appreciation of folk-songs, new experiments with radio drama, and possibly greater discussion of public affairs than in the 1920's, the more popular features of broadcasting still largely filled the air. Tin Pan Alley continued to turn out songs to meet every need; stars of both the stage and the movie world were drafted for radio "appearances"; dance music was always available on a dozen stations. The minstrel show had a belated revival over the air, and vaudeville a new incarnation. Countless thrillers were adapted for broadcasting, and exciting serials were followed as eagerly, and by an even larger audience, as *The Perils of Pauline* had been followed on the screen a quarter-century earlier.

The diversity of entertainment on the air made the attractions of moving-picture theatres appear stereotyped. The program changed generally at fifteen-minute intervals. The listener inadvertently tuning in on "The Woman in White" could hardly discover what was going on before another voice had begun a new chapter in "Aunt Jenny's Story." Melody and Madness succeeded Information, Please; the sketch Blondie was sandwiched between two song recitals; the major-league baseball broadcast (the moment the last man was called out) was followed by a talk on Men and Books; Little Orphan Annie gave way to Science in the News; church hymns were squeezed in after the sketch Valiant Lady; Zinn's Orchestra, Buck Rogers, and Uncle Don followed in quick succession; Mrs. Roosevelt was worked into the Hobby Lobby between two variety shows; the Goldbergs were succeeded by Life Can Be Beautiful; a Success Session paved the way for the Chicago Symphony;

Edwin C. Hill on the news led to Percy Faith's Music; Lowell Thomas followed immediately after the Ink Spot Quartet; the Lone Ranger. . . .[19] It was a mad world. Here was something for all the family, but one had to be quick to catch it.

"The lives of most of my friends," Weare Holbrook wrote in a sketch, "The Ears Have It," in the *Herald Tribune Magazine,* "seem to be governed by radio programs. In planning any social function, one must allow for the vagaries of the Charlie-McCarthophiles, the Jack-Bennyites, the Eddie-Cantorians, the Information Pleasers, and other devotees of ethereal cults; and the East Teabone Friday Evening Bridge Club has disbanded, simply because it is impossible to get a quorum any more.

"When I hear my host and hostess speaking in a preoccupied manner, and see them glancing surreptitiously at the clock, I no longer feel constrained to say, 'Well, I guess I'd better be running along.' Instead, I say, 'How about turning on the radio?' And it is gratifying to observe the eagerness with which they respond to my suggestion." [20]

From an economic as well as social point of view, radio had become immensely important. Its advertising potential far exceeded the industry's own sales of sets, as manufacturers and retail merchants increasingly geared their selling campaigns to radio programs. A flood of orders was the invariable response when announcers told a gullible public (after the heroine had been swung over the edge of a cliff, or the swing band had emitted its last squawk) that now was the time to change to winter oil—or winter underwear—or that a special liver pill would relieve that tired feeling. Never before had entertainment become not only such a big business in itself, but also an integral part of the country's basic economic system.

The radio reached more people than even the moving pictures or the automobile. Every study of how people spent their leisure time in these years before World War II placed listening-in highest on the list of popular amusements.[21] Reading was put off, card tables closed up, conversation languished, in favor of the programs broadcast day and night from the country's hundreds of radio stations.

-»»«-

It was hardly given to this nationwide radio audience in between-war years to realize ʰat an even more startling and dramatic form of entertainment would soon be on the air. But television was just over the horizon, and its development was to be even more awesome than that of radio itself. The latter had taken some twenty years to win its predominant position and reach as many as twenty-six million private homes; television was being watched in half again as many households within less than ten years of its immediate postwar beginnings. Even more than in the case of the movies, automobiles or radio, the television story can only be told in superlatives.[22]

It had been initially introduced on the eve of World War II when visitors at New York's World Fair in the threatening summer of 1939 had a first opportunity not only to hear but to see over the air. And while the new invention had not yet, in its own terms, advanced very much beyond the kinetoscope phase of the motion picture, electronic engineers were already successfully experimenting with home receiving sets and promised phenomenal new developments in broadcasting. Still, it was not until after the close of hostilities that commercial operations became feasible. A handful of pioneer stations, in New York, Schenectady, Philadelphia, Chicago and Los Angeles then began "telecasting" for what were in 1946 some 10,000 pioneer television owners.[23]

There was no equivalent for the headphones of radio's early days: the first television sets were table models, with a screen $5\frac{3}{4}$ by $4\frac{1}{2}$ inches which could "accommodate two or three viewers sitting very close together." The rather dim pictures on these small screens (repeatedly "snowed out" by static) somewhat resembled the movies of nearly half a century earlier, while programming followed very much the pattern of the first radio broadcasts. Sports and news events had a freshly exciting appeal by showing and not merely reporting what was happening. Just as the Dempsey-Carpentier prize fight had been an epochal radio broadcast, so television a quarter of a century later fostered its debut with the Louis-Conn fight.

Technical advance—the spreading networks with coaxial cables and microwave relays, bigger and better "telesets"—made rapid headway. Color television was optimistically envisaged as early as 1946. This same year it was also predicted that airplanes flying in fixed formation at 30,000 feet would soon provide a system of "stratavision" whereby a single program could be directly and simultaneously transmitted to the entire country. These forecasts were somewhat premature; nevertheless, some fifty broadcasting stations were in operation within two years and the few thousand owners of television sets had grown to an approximate million.[24]

Radio still continued to overshadow television. It was in its very heyday during the late 1940's, available in 35,000,000 out of the country's total 39,000,000 homes, and the broadcasting companies claimed that all but two per cent of the American people were listeners. Further technical developments, such as the introduction of FM and generally improved reception, had been made and programs were, if possible, even more diversified than before the war. Musical entertainment still accounted for more than half radio's time on the air, and it was followed in order by dramatic productions, news reports, comedy skits and quiz shows. The leader in the latter field was Truth and Consequences which in these days offered a $20,000 prize for identifying the voices of well known persons over the air. Many prewar features were still very popular, including the redoubtable Amos 'n' Andy, and the reigning stars were Bob Hope, Bing Crosby, Jack Benny and Fred Allen. But while radio would continue to be a great drawing card, with sets being installed in more and more automobiles as well as more and more homes, the future lay with television.

Its real boom got underway with the opening of the 1950's as the number of television sets (the screens were now sixteen inches) rose from ten to sixty million within a decade and broadcasting stations multiplied from 100 (where they had been temporarily frozen as the Federal Communications Commission wrestled with the problems of channel allotment) to 700. In response to this insatiable popular demand, the nationwide broadcasting companies—CBS, NBC and somewhat later ABC— frantically expanded their programs. The stars of radio quickly adapted themselves to being seen as well as heard (in a reverse procedure to that whereby the stars of the silent films had had to retrain for the talkies), and producers successively introduced a host of new features to the staples of pioneer days.[25]

Television, of course, followed the lead of radio in providing continuous entertainment for all the family. The housewife could see as well as hear soap operas as she went about her daily chores; children could watch the bedside story being acted on the screen, and of an evening the entire family could choose among the sports events, re-run movies, vaudeville acts, theatrical skits, or new, specially tailored television shows. The latter were headed at the opening of the 1950's by the Saturday Night Revue starring Ed Wynne, Fred Allen, Jack Benny, and Jimmy Durante.

A first appeal of television was of course its newness, but it was not long in establishing itself far more securely. As the radio editor of *The New York Times* wrote in 1957, it could be regarded "somewhat in the same light as indoor plumbing . . . indisputably a fixture of the household but no longer a novelty." [26] A sign of the inability of millions of families to tear themselves away from that intriguing screen in the living-room was the apt invention of TV dinners.

As in the case of radio, there was from the first one serious flaw in the minds of many people to television's performance.

This was the commercials. They even more abruptly—and annoyingly—interrupted seen entertainment than heard entertainment. Cigarettes and toothpaste, deodorants and cathartics, were no more appealing when subjected to view in the midst of sports events, moving pictures or theatrical performances than when they were advertised with the singing commercial, however lovely the young ladies displaying the advertisers' products might be. But this was the price the public had to pay—and was seemingly willing to pay—if this form of entertainment were to remain in private hands. For it quickly became even bigger "big business" than radio. The advertising revenue of the broadcasting companies soared to greater heights with each passing year, and by 1960 had passed the billion dollar mark.

Once television hit its full stride, it presented programs that in many ways exceeded in popular interest anything that the more limited radio broadcasting could possibly offer. It could take its viewers to a meeting of the United Nations, a political convention, or any other great public gathering. It amazingly depicted current events, almost surely reaching an all-time high when it brought to millions the assassination of President Kennedy and then the dramatic murder of his assassin. It also enabled an uncountable audience to watch directly, week in and week out, the autumn football games, the annual World Series, the Olympic Games, and any number of other sports tournaments from bowling to skiing.

Its daily news coverage was an outstanding feature, with such commentators as Walter Cronkite, Chet Huntley and David Brinkley becoming as familiar as any public figures in American life, while other programs were developed whereby a nationwide audience could itself see and hear the important leaders of the day discussing current issues. Edward R. Murrow pioneered in the 1950's with Person to Person and See It Now, and among other comparable features, Face the Nation and Meet the Press were later to become important weekend fixtures. Television also encouraged popular education (over and beyond closed circuit classes in schools and colleges) by putting on study seminars, music appreciation courses, and language classes.

Nevertheless, television's primary field—as in the case of the radio—remained entertainment for the great masses of the American people. A viewer might begin the day with the news and weather reports, or with Captain Kangaroo; continue with a wide choice throughout the day and prime evening hours, and then finally relax with the ancient re-run movies of the Late, Late Show. Changes in pace were sometimes quite as confusing as they had been with radio. A Laurel and Hardy farce might be followed by a scientific talk on "The Smog Problem"; a discussion on communism somehow run into Bob Burns and His Bazooka; the International Hour merge imperceptibly (if one looked away for a few moments) into Dennis the Menace.

The broadcasting companies, ever attuned to the weekly ratings, were constantly striving to fill the passing hours with features that would persuade the greatest possible number of people to turn the knob of the household set to their individual channels. Some adult programs proved to be hardy perennials— Gunsmoke, I Love Lucy, Dragnet—while children remained faithful year after year to Lassie and Mickey Mouse. And then there were—among so many others—As the World Turns, What's My Line, the Lawrence Welk Show, the Perry Mason Show, the Loretta Young Show, the Danny Kaye Show. Many individual entertainers, however often they changed their sponsors and their programs, sustained their popular appeal through the years. Milton Berle was the original "Mr. Television." The ranks of the already familiar radio stars were soon swelled by the Jackie Gleasons, Arthur Godfreys, and Jack Paars.

There was a short-lived craze for expensive spectaculars in the mid-1950's, one company paying $300,000 for a single ninety-minute show; and with more continuing success, live theatre was introduced at this same time with Playhouse of the Stars, Playhouse 90, and the Ford Theatre. Quiz shows, led off by The $64,000 Question which in some three years was to give away over $2 million and twenty-nine Cadillacs, proved to be immensely popular. They came to a sudden and sad end, however, with disclosures of "payola" and especially the scandal involving the Columbia professor Charles Van Doren who had won $219,000 (with a little inside help) on Twenty-One.[27] Occasional single programs made television history: Mary Martin playing in Peter Pan, the Sadler Wells Ballet, Laurence Olivier in Henry V, Mrs. Kennedy taking an estimated 30,000,000 viewers through the White House. . . .

Among the general run of television offerings, sports events could not fail; moving pictures, both old and new, good and bad, were presented around the clock; and then there were always the vaudeville shows, mystery plays, gangster melodramas, and westerns which in their varying form had been the stock-in-trade of the old popular playhouses, the movies, and so far as possible, the radio. The Federal Communications Commission kept a wary eye on television, repeatedly calling it to account for "excessive commercialization" and warning against the trend—as in the movies—toward an overemphasis on sex, violence, and crime in its dramatic offerings. Rather than strict censorship, however, the Commission offered a prize to rescue "the television wasteland from the cowboys and private eyes." The industry's answer to all such criticism was its spectacular news coverage; its discussions of important issues, domestic and foreign; its interviews with the world's great in every possible field, and its presentation of classical drama, symphonic music, and the opera.

->>)<<-

THROUGHOUT ALL these years of entertainment over the air, from the first popular radio programs of the 1920's to the elaborately organized television shows of the 1960's, the question of the influence on society of a form of recreation which absorbed so much of the time of the American people—old and young—continued to be a topic of impassioned debate and fierce controversy. It was estimated in 1960 that television was in use in the average home from five to six hours every day. Here was a social force of transcendent importance.

Was television drawing the family together, or was it dividing it because there could be no common agreement on what program to watch? Was it imposing a new regimentation on American lives, or was it encouraging a greater diversity in popular interests? Was it a dangerous medium for demagogic political appeals, or had it proved to be an admirable instrument for popular education on public issues? Was it debasing cultural standards by its vulgarity, or was it elevating them through bringing classical drama, music and literature into the average home? Was it altogether frivolous, inane and stultifying, or had it significantly broadened the intellectual horizons of the people as a whole?

The profound effect of radio and television on American society could in some instances be immediately discerned. One might cite the midcentury McCarthy-Army hearings, the Kennedy-Nixon debates in 1960—or the Beatlemania which swept the country a few years later. Yet there could be no real consensus on how television positively or negatively affected the evolution of a mass culture. Its influence could hardly be measured. In his comprehensive study *The Age of Television*, Leo Bogart maintained that for all the charges brought against it, it had not had any revolutionary effects on society or converted the nation from an active to a passive attitude toward recreation.

The world remained much the same, he concluded, but since the advent of television, "we experience it in new and different ways." [28]

Two public opinion polls sought in 1965 to survey more accurately popular attitudes. A Roper poll found the public little concerned about TV's possible harmful effects and the total audience still increasing. A Harris poll discovered what it characterized as "a growing disenchantment" among better educated adult Americans and far more TV viewing on the part of "the less affluent, less articulate, and the older age group." Discussing these polls the *Saturday Review* concluded that as between continued lower-level programming for the mass audience or efforts on the part of at least some stations to upgrade their offerings, a first "major fork" had been reached in television's further development.[29]

By and large there was only one thing that could be said without dispute: apart from all other considerations, here was a form of popular entertainment going far beyond anything the world had ever before known in simultaneously reaching day in and day out, in their own homes, so many people.

chapter **20**

Sports for All

THE IMMENSE IMPORTANCE OF THE MOVIES, AUTOMOBILE touring, radio, and television in giving entirely new dimensions to popular recreation is indisputable. At the same time, the interest in sports which had become so notable in the latter half of the nineteenth century fully kept pace with these new developments of the twentieth century. Among spectator sports, horse racing, both college and professional football, major league baseball, and during the 1920's if not later years prize fighting, attracted the largest crowds ever assembled since the gladiatorial contests of Imperial Rome. Moreover as the new century advanced, far more people than ever before were every year taking part in a bewildering array of active sports ranging from swimming to bowling, from fishing to softball, and including tennis, golf, skiing, scuba diving. . . . Even though the American people in the midtwentieth century were perhaps spending more time in motoring, going to the movies, or twirling the dials of their radio and television sets, sports often appeared to be a national obsession.

Lord Bryce felt this to be true as early as 1905. He then wrote that one of the most striking innovations in the life of the American people since his earlier visits to the United States was "the passion for looking on and reading about athletic sports." Baseball and football matches excited "an interest greater than any other public events except the Presidential election." [1] By the 1920's the upward trend that characterized everything about that legendary decade from stock prices to women's skirts had brought about a still greater fervor for such spectator sports. An annual total of several score millions of persons were estimated to make up the crowds that so eagerly crowded the country's race tracks, grandstands, ball parks and football stadia. Indeed the 1920's are still looked back upon as sports' Golden Age.

A galaxy of national heroes made newspaper history and have left undying legends of their prowess: Babe Ruth, the acknowledged Sultan of Swat with his season record of sixty home runs; the Four Horsemen of Notre Dame galloping down a score of football fields to win new laurels for Knute Rockne; Jack Dempsey and Gene Tunney with their million-dollar gates at Boyle's Forty Acres and Soldiers Field; the towering figure of Bill Tilden in tennis and Bobby Jones with his grand slam in golf. . . . Later heroes have won national laurels and many of the old records have fallen, but no athletes have risen higher in sports' Hall of Fame.

Observing the contemporary scene in the 1920's, many critics deplored what they considered the unhappy influence of "spectatoritis." They lamented that the United States had become "a nation of onlookers" with too many of its people getting outdoors and exercising only in the short walk to the entrance gate of ball park or stadium. "One day in 1926," F. Scott Fitzgerald wrote, "we looked down and found we had flabby arms and a fat pot and couldn't say boop-boop-a-doop to a Sicilian." [2] But while there was some justification for such unhappy reflections on the public's unathletic passivity, appearances were often deceptive. If the crowds watching were larger than ever, so in fact were the number of persons actively engaged in sports.

The great masses of the urban democracy, as well as the fashionable world and the middle class, were in the 1920's discovering new opportunities for play. The automobile, as we have seen, had greatly helped to open up the country—seashore and mountain, field and stream—to countless workers who had been almost wholly cut off from it with the growth of cities. There had also been a steady growth in the opportunities for sports and athletics within the cities themselves—more public parks and more playing fields, more swimming pools, softball diamonds, tennis courts and golf links. An organized recreation movement, whose origins may be traced back to the first provision of urban playgrounds for children, was vigorously promoting every kind of outdoor activity and winning a widespread response.[3]

With the depression this movement was further stimulated by the Federal Government's support through the Works Progress Administration. As of 1937, the WPA had allotted some $500,000,000, about ten per cent of its total expenditures, for new parks and new recreational facilities.[4] It was estimated that the yearly attendance at public bathing beaches and swimming pools totalled two hundred million, that a comparable count at baseball and softball diamonds was thirty million, and that public tennis courts and golf courses respectively drew eleven million and eight million.[5]

Even these figures did not of course tell the whole story of participation in sports. Nobody really knows—for this or later periods—how many people actually went swimming, played softball or tennis, took up bowling or skiing in a given year. But the available evidence for the 1920's and 1930's clearly indicates that there was a far greater increase in the number of people taking part in such athletic activities than in the number of those who were watching others play. The American people, that is, were as a whole spending many more hours (and statistics show they were spending four times as much money) on amateur sports as on professional sports.[6]

If this were true in the 1920's and 1930's, it has been far more the case since the close of World War II. Spectator sports have remained highly popular, but attendance figures in midcentury did not keep pace with the growth of population and in some cases relatively declined. This was, of course, partially due to television. Many people stayed at home to watch football and baseball, even tennis and golf, on the living room screen. But

Pioneer Sportswomen
Culver Service.

The Houston Astrodome

A fish-eye lens's view of the new home of the Houston Astros, the last word in modern sports arenas. The star-like circle over second base is a gondola containing lights and loudspeakers which can be raised or lowered for various types of events. W i d e W o r l d Photos.

what was much more important was the staggering increase—far outstripping population growth—in the number of people engaging in an ever broadening range of outdoor activities and in playing both old and new indoor games. What has been called the "revolutionary boom" in participant sports has proved to be one of the most striking social phenomena of postwar America.[7]

->>><<<-

AFTER THE TURN of the century, intercollegiate football continued to forge ahead as one of the country's outstanding spectator sports. But it had first to survive a crisis even more serious than than that of the 1890's for the reforms which had then been adopted to combat both professionalism and roughness did not entirely resolve football's problems. Injuries and even fatalities continued to mount (the death-roll reached forty-four in 1903) and the press so universally condemned the game as it was being played that many colleges and universities contemplated abolishing it altogether. With football thus becoming a national issue, President Theodore Roosevelt stepped resolutely into the fray and summoned its leaders to a White House conference to work out reforms that might save the game. The forward pass, the on-side kick, and separation of the rush lines were thereupon devised to make football less dangerous, and these innovations gradually led to a more open—and also far more interesting—game.[8]

By the 1920's football was consequently more popular than ever before and the several hundred thousand spectators crowding the college stadia every Saturday afternoon were supplemented by the many millions of fans who hovered over their radios in comfortable, heated living-rooms to follow the games play-by-play, and then spent Sunday mornings devouring long accounts in the newspapers' sports sections of how it had all happened. Football reigned supreme from the opening of early practice to the Tournament of Roses. "It is at present a religion," a contributor to *Harper's* stated in 1928—"sometimes it seems to be almost our national religion." [9]

It was not only Harvard, Yale and Princeton which now attracted the great crowds. Universities and colleges throughout the country had built great new concrete stadia (the Yale and California bowls seated eighty thousand each; Illinois, Michigan, Ohio State and several other universities could handle seventy thousand) [10] which altogether boasted a total capacity of two million. Empty almost every day of the year except for those fabulous Saturday afternoons in the autumn, the quickened interest of the public then taxed them to the utmost. It was estimated that during the season as many as twenty million spectators (attendance generally doubled between 1921 and 1930) watched a game which had been largely taken away from college undergraduate or graduate and given over to a sports-hungry public which supported football as a grandiose commercial amusement.

It was a colorful, exciting show. Every year saw a new sensation: the "praying colonels" of Centre College blazing through the sky like a meteor, and as quickly fading out; Princeton's "Team of Destiny" briefly lighting up the dimmed prestige of the one-time Big Three; and Red Grange, an Illinois team by himself, flashing past all other heroes. Even in this glamorous period the line between intercollegiate football and the newly set up professional game was sometimes hardly distinguishable. Red Grange was one of the first of college players who deftly stepped over it after his last college season. While student admirers framed his football jersey at Illinois (also circulating a petition to nominate him for Congress), he joined the Chicago Bears at a salary of $30,000, signed a $300,000 movie contract, and was presented to President Coolidge.[12] Here was fame— and also fortune.

Educators continued to be something less than enthusiastic over an emphasis on football that seemed to make the academic standing of their institutions a negligible factor in the public mind in comparison with a football championship. But the general public—and also the greater part of the nation's college alumni—only asked for more victories. An editorial in the magazine *Liberty* found the protesting faculty members jealous. "The problem is not the elimination or restriction of football," it declared, "but how long it will be before red-blooded colleges demand the elimination or restriction of those afflicted with this inferiority complex." [13] In 1929 a report of the Carnegie Foundation heavily scored the mounting overemphasis and professionalism in the sport, but the colleges now had too great a vested interest in football for it to fan the old fires of controversy into a very fierce flame.

Football suffered something of a setback during the depression. The sale of big-game tickets declined just as severely as that of any other market commodity. But it withstood these slings of outrageous fortune; it kept its strong hold on the public. And then after the interruption of war it zoomed forward to still greater heights of popularity. Television even more than radio made college football the country's most popular Saturday afternoon indoor attraction, but ever greater crowds also crammed the stadia whose capacity was enlarged, whenever possible, in some individual cases now accommodating as many as 100,000 persons.

The game had its usual vicissitudes. There were repeated outcries against excessive commercialization, an unsavory game-fixing scandal in 1947, and continued controversy over football scholarships. University faculties periodically renewed their old struggle against the exaggerated role of football in college life and the concentration on winning championships at whatever cost. But far from submitting to any such move to deemphasize football, its sponsors extended the season by setting up more regional championships—the Rose Bowl, the Sugar Bowl, the Cotton Bowl, the Orange Bowl.[14]

There were various changes in the game—the T-formation, the

two-platoon system, constantly shifting regulations on substitutions—but it remained essentially the same. Every season had its quota of "upsets, surprises, thrills, records" and a new set of popular heroes. The Saturday afternoon ritual was ever more deeply fixed in American life. Even though in some ways it did not quite recapture the glamor of the 1920's or seem to provide such exciting players as the legendary stars of that earlier decade, college football in postwar years more than held its own. It was reported in 1961 that something like twenty-five million persons had attended the countrywide games and no one could measure how many more watched them over television.[15]

In the meantime, new developments had given a tremendous impetus to the professional sport. Its beginnings could be traced back to the opening of the century and the American Professional Football Association was organized in 1920. But while the game attained a measure of popularity in the days of Jim Thorpe, the great Indian athlete, and was further boosted when Illinois' Galloping Ghost joined the ranks, professional football did not come of age until after 1945. With the veteran National League supplemented by the American League, it then became the fastest growing of all spectator sports both in actual game attendance and its nationwide television audience.

The teams adopted wonderfully expressive names—the Green Bay Packers, the Houston Oilers, the Boston Patriots, the Buffalo Bills, the Denver Broncos—and they had their own galaxy of stars. With a more open game and such special features as the sudden-death extra period, professional football thereupon built up a popular following that rivalled if it did not surpass that of the somewhat ambiguously amateur sport. While yearly attendance (in spite of packed stadia) could never attain the total drawn to the hundreds of college games, it had risen to three million in 1960, and then in another three years added over two million more.[16]

Baseball had not fared so well as a spectator sport since those days in the 1890's when it was the universally acknowledged national game. Even though its longer playing season sometimes enabled it to draw as large a total audience as football, there was at least relatively a persistent decline in the over-all number of spectators actually watching baseball being played. Small town games suffered a sharp setback from the growth of so many other sports (even though the Little Leaguers were in later years to draw their thousands of admiring parents);[17] interest in college baseball rapidly waned, and attendance at professional-league games by no means kept pace with the growth of the cities supporting the teams.[18]

If this were true even in the golden day of spectator sports in the years between wars, it became even more so after 1945. There were a number of new developments in the major leagues. Both of them extended their membership from eight to ten cities as air transportation enabled them to make their coverage more truly national. Among other shifts the New York Giants migrated to San Francisco (the Mets taking their place) and the Brooklyn Dodgers moved to Los Angeles. A galaxy of new stars became as well known as those of the 1920's—Stan (the Man) Musial, Ted Williams, Joe DiMaggio, Mickey Mantle, and Willie Mays. . . . Yet for all this, and in spite of persevering efforts to attract more paying customers with night games, ladies' day games, and other gimmicks, even major league attendance could hardly hold its own. It reached a record 20,900,000 in 1948, but in the early 1960's never quite attained this total.

A basic reason for the changing status of baseball in terms of actual attendance at the ball park—far more than in the case of football—was again television. There was little reason to watch the games of the minor leagues or, as many people apparently thought, to buck urban traffic in getting to even major league games, when a twist of the dial brought the best baseball in the country so easily into the home. And by this same token it was quite possible that television coverage and the continuing newspaper publicity was actually enlarging the nationwide baseball audience. It was in fact estimated at the opening of the 1960's that whatever actual attendance at the games might be, baseball had some sixty million devoted fans.[20] Perhaps after all it could still substantiate its ancient claims to being the national game.

Another spectator sport, one which had its brief day of glory immediately after the First World War but then rapidly declined, was prize fighting. The promotor Tex Rickard, in whom was embodied so much of the ballyhoo spirit of the 1920's, took over this once disapproved and banned sport, and with a genius for showmanship which rivaled that of P. T. Barnum, made it at once respectable and glamorous. The fashionable world fought for tickets whose high prices were in themselves proof that prize fighting had undergone some sort of social regeneration. Women forgot their traditional scruples in enjoying the ring's primitive combat. The sporting men, who were only a flashier, better-dressed counterpart (with more money to bet) of the nineteenth century "fancy," happily paid whatever the speculators demanded for ringside seats. Championship bouts came in rapid succession and the public mania for watching sports perhaps reached an all-time high in the series of heavyweight bouts that now made pugilistic history.

There had been a succession of world champions since James J. Corbett (all of eight thousand persons watching the epic encounter) had dethroned the great John L. Sullivan in 1892—Robert Prometheus Fitzsimmons, James J. Jeffries, Tommy Burns, Jack Johnson, and Jess Willard. But the new era in prize fighting began when Jack Dempsey successfully challenged Willard in 1919 and the astute Mr. Rickard added up gate receipts of $452,000. By the alchemy of clever publicity, with an assist from radio and the movies, and the cooperation of such spirited rivals for Dempsey's crown as the flashing Frenchman, Georges Carpentier, Luis Angel Firpo, the Wild Bull of the Pampas, and finally Gene Tunney, Rickard was making the entire nation fight-conscious. Million dollar gates became the rule; what was once an outlawed sport had become big-time industry legalized in fifteen states as "boxing contests." [21]

Gene Tunney, who was to walk with the novelist Thornton Wilder and talk with the literary critic William Lyon Phelps, was the nemesis of the heretofore invincible Dempsey. The crowd that watched him win the heavy-weight championship at the Philadelphia Sesqui-centennial in 1926 broke all records, but they were shattered again the next year when he success-fully defended his crown in Chicago. Twenty-four special trains rolled into town for that great event. There were 145,000 spec-tators at Soldiers Field, with two hundred millionaires in the first ten rows. Many of those in the tremendous crowd were so far away from the ring that they could not tell through the fog of cigarette smoke that Tunney had won the fight. It hardly mattered. They had paid $2,650,000 for admission and were happy. How many millions were in the audience that listened over the radio could not be counted, but it was reported that five of them dropped dead of heart-failure when Tunney tem-porarily went down in the seventh round.[22]

Prize fighting could not quite adapt itself to the high standards with which its new champion sought to endow it, and having made a fortune of $2,000,000 in two years, Tunney retired in clouds of glory. The day of million-dollar gates was over. Fisti-cuffs would never again be the same. A new champion in the late 1930's, the redoubtable Joe Louis, enabled it to recover something of its glamor, but it was a sorry list of fighters who contended for the world's championships in succeeding years. The ancient sport became enveloped in corruption and scandal. The spectators at the bout which saw Sonny Liston dispose of Floyd Patterson in 1963 paid a mere $250,000 for their meager entertainment, or less than ten per cent of the gate at the Tunney-Dempsey encounter a quarter of a century earlier.[23] Millions may have watched over television, but there was nothing about prize-fighting in these postwar years to recapture the spirit of the 1920's.

Other sports have since 1900, and especially in midcentury years, drawn large crowds. In spite of football and baseball's continuing popularity, or prize-fighting's brief day of glory, horse racing would appear to have regularly attracted more spectators than anything else. Its appeal has never faltered since colonial days. During the 1920's interest was greatly excited by the sensational victories of the famous Man o' War, a noble horse reaching a pinnacle of contemporary fame comparable to that attained by the heroes of football, baseball and prize-fighting, and soon afterwards Gallant Fox awoke new enthusiasm with successive victories in the Kentucky Derby, the Preakness, and the Belmont Stakes. In postwar years, Citation was one horse almost rivaling these champions of an earlier day. The steady increase in race track attendance, in any event, soon led to the breaking of all previous records. In 1961 it was estimated that as many as sixty million spectators watched the horses.[24]

Basketball—both amateur and professional—has risen high in popularity. It has come to almost rival football in the college world, but its most spectacular growth has been at the high school level. The local games pack in overflow crowds in such parts of the midwest as Indiana, where the basketball mania has become almost uncontrollable, and the state high school tournaments are major events.[25]

Since the last war, both golf and tennis have also become spectator as well as participant sports. As many as forty thousand men, women and children were reported at the opening of the 1960's to be in attendance at the championship golf tourneys, where such players as Sam Snead, Ben Hogan, Arnold Palmer, and Jack Nicklaus, played their remunerative rounds. Professional golf, as suggested in an article in *Sports Illustrated* entitled "The $2,000,000 Gambol Begins" had become big business.[26] Tennis tournaments, and especially Davis Cup play, have always drawn their quota of onlookers, but in 1947 this game took a further step toward becoming a spectator sport. In that year Jack Kramer established a stable of champion amateur players turned professional (a practice that has since become almost commonplace) and initiated a series of countrywide tours in which his stars played exhibition matches.[27]

The publicity attendant upon the Olympic Games (revived in the 1890's) has built up a widespread interest in athletic meets, and especially the gruelling races of champion distance runners who were finally—and sensationally—to break the four-minute mile. Professional hockey has its enthusiastic following. With varying bursts of popularity, six-day bicycle racing and greyhound racing have had their day, while automobile racing has retained a position which has drawn crowds of 200,000 to the Indianapolis Speedway.

In the 1920's when spectator sports appeared to reign supreme, the varied reports on championship events that came over the radio were deftly satirized in an article appearing in the *Literary Digest*. "This is station KDKAWXJEAZFOW," its author wrote. "The boys are in top-notch condition and as the first ball was pitched Epinard broke clean and scored two goals on a good mashie pitch that just cleared the rightfield stands and narrowly missed killing Tilden's backhand three inches from the cup when the entire Washington team was awarded to McGraw on points just as the chukker ended. Listen to the cheering!" [28] Television has somewhat clarified this confusing picture for stay-at-home spectators. Nevertheless the plethora of broadcast sports events still suggests that the voracious zeal of the American people in watching other people play can never be fully satisfied even though they may actually be combatting "spectatoritis" by themselves playing more games than ever before.

->>><<<-

So much for spectator sports. When Americans decide they want to do something themselves in the way of sports activity, they are most likely (at least in summer months) to go swimming. On the basis of all statistical estimates, this has long been and still remains the greatest outdoor recreation among the people as a whole.

The packed beaches of the 1920's and 1930's were a first demonstration of the changes that had taken place in this form of recreation since those nineteenth century days when mixed public bathing ("the parties always go into the water completely dressed") was first daringly condoned. The beaches revealed, in the numbers of bathers, their free and informal association, and their costumes, a wholly new outlook. The bathing dress of women (even before the days of the bikini and topless suit) was a symbolic sign of a revolutionary change in the status of the female in American society. Together with abbreviated skirts and bobbed hair, slacks and shorts, it ushered in a new era. It was a final and decisive assertion of woman's right to enjoy whatever recreation she chose, costumed according to the demands of the sport rather than the tabus of an outworn prudery. Nothing more clearly demonstrated that the age of Victoria had come to an unlamented end.

Swimming was an activity more fully open to all classes of people—men, women, and children—than any other sport. The recorded attendance at public bathing beaches and municipal pools in the 1930's was almost as large as the estimated annual attendance at *all* spectator sports. And such figures did not of course take into account the throngs of swimmers of whom no records could be kept. In postwar years, the number swelled even further. There was an increase in available public beaches and an amazing proliferation of swimming pools—in town and city parks, at resorts, at motels, and in suburban yards. At the opening of the 1960's there were said to be some 300,000 such pools supplementing the opportunities to swim on ocean fronts, lakes, and rivers. While it remains impossible to more than guess at the total number of swimmers, it has been placed at thirty-three million.[29]

Such traditional outdoor sports as fishing and hunting followed close upon swimming throughout the first half of the twentieth century. With rivers and lakes being more plentifully stocked and game in many instances increasing under careful conservation controls, the number of state licenses increased each year and sales of sporting equipment bounded upward. One unusual feature of hunting was a revival of the bow-and-arrow. Fishing benefited from the new spinning rods and reels, but that old-fashioned techniques were not wholly abandoned was illustrated when one enterprising store sold thirteen million worms by mail.[30]

Somewhat comparable to such unorganized outdoor recreation, and with a comparable wide appeal, was boating. In the nineteenth century it was almost wholly limited to the wealthy, but with the development of the outboard motor, it became highly popular among elements in the population whose nautical enthusiasms had formerly found no practical expression other than watching the regattas of the exclusive boating and yachting clubs. Boating grew rather slowly in the 1920's and 1930's but then experienced an almost explosive expansion in postwar years. The development of artificial lakes and reservoirs (some 263 were built by the Army Engineer Corps) and the country's general prosperity stimulated this boom. The vogue was almost universal in the East (Long Island Sound, its little harbors lined with marinas berthing every kind of pleasure craft—both sail and power—had some 200,000 boatsmen in 1964); and it flourished mightily in other areas. Even the Midwest took to the water wherever possible: in one year more motor boat licenses were issued in St. Louis than in Boston.

At the opening of the present century, there were only a few thousand pleasure craft registered throughout the country; in the 1960's they were numbered in the millions.[31]

→≫)⟨≪←

AMONG ORGANIZED outdoor sports, golf has always had a rather unique status. By the time of the First World War it had long since proved that it was more than a passing fad. A half million players (having put away their red coats and leggings, they were soon to adopt baggy plus-fours and tasselled wool stockings) were going the rounds on some 800 courses. Fourteen years later their number had grown to two million.[32] But what gave the game its special status was the sacred aura that clung to it. Every ambitious member of suburbia felt he had to take up golf in the 1920's. It was a fascinating sport, a healthful outdoor pastime, and very good fun. It was also a helpful ladder to business and social success. Membership in a country club and the ability to play a good game were considered essential requirements for any young executive who really wanted to get ahead. The golf course was an anteroom of the business office. Every weekend fiercely determined foursomes played their eighteen-hole matches in the competitive spirit of the world they had supposedly left behind them. The talk at "the nineteenth hole" centered quite as often on the stock market as on the day's miraculous drives or muffed putts.

Golf was expensive (how else could it boast social status?) and club memberships, caddy fees, clubs and balls, all the wonderful paraphernalia of the correct golfer, led to far more money being spent on it than on any other sport. With a nationwide investment of nearly $1 billion in more than 5,000 courses, it was estimated in 1929 that the country's golfers were paying $200,000,000 a year for the privilege of enjoying their favorite diversion.[32] The weekend handicap tournament became the great event to which hundreds of thousands of suburban commuters looked forward from Monday to Friday. There was little pretense of observing the Sabbath. Church was forgotten, the home neglected, and wives deserted for the irresistible lure of the links.

The depression had a profound effect on golf. It was not only that the country clubs found themselves losing members and that some of them were forced to close. The end of an era of high-pressure salesmanship, when the stock brokers and bond salesmen had found the golf course such a profitable field of operation, took some of the artificial bloom off the ancient and honorable game. At the same time, the increasing availability of public and daily-fee courses, which materially expanded during the 1930's, opened up golf to more and more every day citizens who did not belong to the country club set. As early as 1928 Grantland Rice had written of "the democracy of golf," [33] and a decade later this term had gained considerable validity. The total number of golfers was probably somewhat fewer in 1940 than in 1930, but there were a good many more players on the public links.

This trend continued in postwar years. This is not to say that country club golf did not still dominate the game and have its important role in establishing social status. At the opening of the 1960's there were some 3,300 country clubs (or, as some of them now liked to be called, "year-round family fun centers") with a membership of nearly two million.[34] What with ever higher greens fees, more expensive playing clubs, and electric golf carts, the game also continued to invite sufficient expenditures to provide the most satisfying symbols of financial success. But country club golf did not tell the whole story. The nation's crowded courses drew a heterogeneous army of seven or eight million players who represented an increasingly broad segment of the population.

Tennis has also experienced a remarkable transformation from that distant day in the 1880's when it was considered no more than a gentle diversion of polite society, essentially for ladies and gentlemen. The game itself became progressively more active, hard-hitting, and competitive after the turn of the century, and it was being played by more and more people. National tournaments and the Davis Cup matches first stimulated a wider interest, and member clubs of the United States Lawn Tennis Association, though by no means affording a complete picture of the tennis world, increased between 1910 and 1933 from 160 to almost 1,000. There were before the Second World

War three to four million tennis players, with about a quarter of this total representing players on public courts.[35]

In dress which would have horrified their Victorian forebears —short-skirted, bare-legged—women played tennis quite as much as men. Tilden's role in generally popularizing the sport was supplemented by the play of the glamorous Suzanne Lenglen and the phenomenal Helen Wills. Their game compared favorably with that of all but the very best men players. Hundreds of thousands of girls followed their lead and then remained on the courts far beyond that age at which the preservation of "female delicacy" had once decreed China-painting and embroidery as the only approved pursuits for ladies. What with tennis, swimming and other outdoor sports, together with a passion for sun-tan, the day had certainly passed when the ideal of female pulchritude was "the slender, and delicate, and fragile form—the pale, sallow, and waxen complexion."

In the years after World War II, the leadership which Americans had once asserted in the tennis world, with consequent encouragement to the game among young people, badly faltered. The onetime firm grip on the Davis Cup was forfeited for many years to Australia, and in 1960 the American team—for the first time in twenty-four years—failed to reach even the challenge round when it was defeated by the Italians. The top tennis players did not have the stature of those of the 1920's, and the tendency to turn professional did little good to a game which had always sought to maintain the highest amateur standards. If such discouraging developments seemed for a time to affect the game's popularity, it nevertheless gradually recovered and the number of players at the opening of the 1960's was double that of thirty years earlier.[36]

A remarkable story in the history of American sports is that of skiing. It originally reached the United States by way of Norwegian settlers who organized the country's pioneer ski club at Red Wing, Minnesota, in 1883. It was not until about forty years later, however, that it began to be taken up more generally, and then in the 1930's it enjoyed a sudden and enthusiastic boom. A public which had hardly heard of skiing was carried off its feet—symbolically and sometimes literally. First to sense the gold in their snow-covered hills, New England's farmers eagerly undertook to provide food and lodgings for the venturesome skiers who began to dot every available slope. The railroads ran special trains and organized weekend excursions to the skiing country. Department stores not only hurried to stock the necessary equipment, but imported Austrian instructors who gave lessons for beginners on indoor borax slides. A steadily growing band of fanatics hung on the weekend weather forecasts; argued furiously over bindings, the proper waxes, the relative merits of the telemark and the stem Christy, and then sallied forth to risk life and limb in hazardous plunges down slope or trail.

Skiing was in some measure a highly limited sport, involving both considerable expense and difficult problems of transportation. Nonetheless the handful of enthusiasts at the opening of the 1930's had swelled by its close to something like two million. Especially in such states as Vermont, New Hampshire, Michigan, Wisconsin and Idaho (where the Union Pacific Railroad established at Sun Valley one of the most elaborate ski resorts in the world), skiing had assumed truly formidable proportions.[37]

Yet this was all child's play, the faintest harbinger of things to come, in comparison with the postwar elaboration of skiing. It was not only that the sport became increasingly popular in these later years, as did all other sports, but that it left its rather simple and innocent beginnings far behind. Bigger and better slopes were being constantly carved out of the wooded mountain sides; the old rope tows gave way to T-bars and chair lifts, and ski lodges with their nuclei of Swiss chalets and A-frame houses multiplied prodigiously. The elegancies of ski attire—parkas and stretch pants—not only added a note of superior style to the sport itself, but influenced the world of fashion

far from the ski resorts themselves. Moreover these resorts became increasingly luxurious and expanded to include heated
outdoor swimming pools and indoor ice-skating rinks; cocktail
lounges, dance floors and expensive restaurants. The *après-ski*
entertainment of the stretch pant set was almost as much a
part of the weekend as a day an the slopes.

The Midwest and even the South caught the skiing fever.
Hills were made to serve for mountains, and where nature
proved recalcitrant, they were covered with artificial snow. The
entire country became ski-conscious and while it is again impossible to give precise figures, at least five million skiers were
by the 1960's happily taking to the hills during each winter
season.[38]

-»)«-

OTHER SPORTS have shared in the general postwar boom. Where
tennis, golf and skiing may be characterized as appealing largely
to the upper middle class, such games as bowling and softball,
to cite the two most popular, have particularly drawn salesmen, office employees, retail clerks, factory hands, and other
skilled workers.

Bowling has an ancient pedigree. In its modern phase, however, it is a result of the ready availability of the thousands of
alleys that have sprung up with the growth of cities to meet the
increasing need for recreation on the part of the urban masses.
Interested equipment manufacturers were claiming in the 1930's
that some eight million men and women were bowling addicts.
The invention of automatic pin setters then proved to be an
immense boon, and with this labor-saving device alleys mush-
roomed in mid-century years and team play and tournaments
became more popular than ever. Often set up in shopping centers, the new alleys provided nurseries for children, snack bars
or cocktail lounges, and sometimes restaurants. With such encouragement, more people were said to be bowling at the open-

*Factory
Softball*

Atlanta girls in action. Wide World Photos.

College Basketball

Gymnasium of the University of California. Courtesy of the Associated Students News Bureau.

Ski School in Vermont

A group of beginners learn the basic snowplow maneuver before attempting the slopes at Mount Mansfield, Stowe, Vermont. Wide World Photos.

Heat Relief at Coney Island

A crowded section of the beach with thousands seeking to escape New York's summer heat. Some of the rides and other amusements are in the background. Wide World Photos.

ing of the 1960's—perhaps as many as thirty million—than were participating in any other organized sport.[39]

Softball developed as a modified form of baseball under various names—kitten ball, mush ball, recreation ball, and indoor baseball—but officially took its present name with the organization of the Amateur Softball Association of America in 1933. Through this organization's promotional work, sponsorship of regional tournaments, and establishment of an annual world series, softball then became a craze which swept the land as had earlier crazes for croquet, roller skating, and bicycling.

Teams were formed by factory workers and suburban commuters, church leaguers and stock brokers, members of fashionable clubs and local village societies. Industrial plants encouraged the game as providing a practical approach to recreation for their employes, and softball was played at the lunch hour in addition to Saturday afternoons and holidays. Again there were women players as well as men, and they too had their regular teams. In 1938 the Softball Association claimed a membership larger than that of any other amateur sports body in the world, proudly boasting that there were as many as 8,000 softball diamonds in some eight hundred cities with up to ten million players.[40]

The game had been a sudden craze but even though some of the original excitement died down, it was a good deal more than a passing fad. It retained a strong hold on the public and continued to be widely played in postwar years. But while the number of players substantially increased, the total was probably about half that of the bowlers.

Among other sports with a wide following among adults as well as young people were volley ball, played in the gymnasiums of athletic clubs, colleges and Y.M.C.A.'s; ping pong which took on a new lease of life under its new designation as table tennis; various kinds of target shooting, and roller skating. In a list incorporated in *Sport—Mirror of American Life*, Robert H. Boyle includes these varied sports (after boating, swimming and fishing) as in each instance drawing anywhere from fourteen to twenty million participants.[41]

Many others with a more restricted following, some of them of ancient lineage and others quite new, might also be noted. Archery and croquet have again been revived; badminton is widely played, and also handball, shuffleboard and billiards. Lacrosse, soccer, curling, gymnastics, motor cycling, trap-shooting, and squash rackets, all have their devotees. In the winter there was always ice skating and hockey. Even the traditional country pastime of horseshoe pitching has felt the quickening urge of the new sports enthusiasm with the organization of a National Horseshoe Pitchers Association. Water skiing boomed in the 1950's, and also skin and scuba diving which reportedly had as many as five million zealots. A new activity for the very few and very daring was sky diving.

The description of the beginnings of a dozen or so organized sports could afford a fair idea of this phase of popular recreation in the 1890's, but seventy-odd years later there was no possibility of encompassing the entire field. Every writer on sports—and the mounting interest was attested by publication of *Sports Illustrated,* scores of other magazines on individual sports, and a veritable flood of books—stressed the significance of the expansion that gave a new relevancy to the slogan "Sports for Everybody." The annual sales of sporting goods bounded upward, and were reported in 1962 to have risen to well over $2 billion, or some eight times the sum spent that year on all admissions to spectator sports.[42] Still, no statistics could adequately portray what had taken place in postwar years.

Sociologists have delighted in trying to analyze the new role of sports in American life. They have studied them from every possible angle: from their importance in the national economy ("Big Sport") to their influence in fostering an exaggerated will to win ("nice guys finish last"); from their value as an outlet for "group aggressiveness" to the role they play in substituting a new "fun morality" for the old puritan ethos. And on one aspect of the spectator phase of sports activity there was almost universal agreement. Commercialization, as represented for example by the fantastic salaries paid managers and players in such highly competitive fields as major league baseball and pro football (as much as $400,000 for a three-year football contract), had been carried to the most extreme lengths. No other society, declared an editorial writer in the *New York Times* in assailing the consequent distortion of values, "has had its sports so thoroughly corrupted by the commercial motive." [43]

Yet whatever the justification for all such charges, the record also clearly showed that Americans had not just become the gullible victims of professional sports promotion. They were every year placing an ever greater emphasis on active, participant sports. The average citizen, including his wife and children, might still spend a good deal of his leisure in watching others play his games for him, especially with all the convenience of television, but he was more and more inclined to seize the opportunity, whenever it offered, to go swimming or boating, play a little softball, try a few games of bowling, or take up golf, tennis and even skiing.

chapter **21**

The Changing Scene

IN THE TWENTIETH CENTURY AS IN EARLIER YEARS, THE AMERICAN
people continue to enjoy many diversions in addition to commercial entertainment and sports. The spectrum of recreation
and amusements was as broad as the interests of a population
which grew from 100 to 190 million people. Such traditional
social diversions as entertaining, dancing, playing cards and
games went through many transformations as the mores and
moralities of society reacted to the winds of change. The revolution of the younger generation after the First World War had
its far-reaching consequences; Prohibition may have brought
about the demise of the old-fashioned saloon but paradoxically
enough fostered social drinking; the depression introduced for
a time a new note of simplicity into popular amusements, and
the dramatic developments of mid-century not only encouraged
the boom in sports but in many other ways affected the way
people used their new leisure.

Throughout their entire history the American people have
been periodically swept off their feet by successive crazes and
popular fads. In the 1780's European visitors had wonderingly
commented on the popularity of dancing and the Marquis de
Chastellux was amazed by Boston's "passion" for whist. The
mid-nineteenth century witnessed enthusiastic vogues for phrenology, balloon ascensions, minstrel shows, pedestrian races,
and the phenomenon of Lindomania. In the decades after the
Civil War, we have seen the fashionable frenzy with which new
outdoor pastimes were adopted by society: the epidemics of
croquet, roller-skating, and lawn tennis which spread so rapidly
over the land. And in the 1890's this same instinct to take up

366

whatever was new or different, to rush along untrodden paths, was evident in the tremendous growth of fraternal societies and women's clubs, in the avidity with which the public welcomed "refined" vaudeville, and in the popular interest excited in amateur photography, John L. Sullivan, band concerts, and bicycling.

The twentieth century found an equally susceptible public taking up with still greater vehemence new fads and fancies, and enjoying a succession of varied diversions with an intensity born of the feverish pace of modern life. In the ballyhoo years of the 1920's this zest for novelties became almost a national mania. "One of the most striking characteristics of the era of Coolidge prosperity," Frederick Lewis Allen wrote in *Only Yesterday*, "was the unparalleled rapidity and unanimity with which millions of men and women turned their attention, their talk, and their emotional interest upon a series of tremendous trifles—a heavyweight boxing match, a murder trial, a new automobile, a transatlantic flight." [1]

There has been something especially strange and wonderful about the kaleidoscopic scene ever since the close of the Golden Nineties. Ragtime burst upon the country to drive out the old-fashioned waltzes and polkas, and then gave way after its brief day to jazz. There were crazes for diabolo in 1907, for ping-pong in 1913, for mahjong in 1923, for crossword puzzles in 1924, and for miniature golf in 1930. With bewildering rapidity the country also took up (and usually ran into the ground) dance marathons, bathing-beauty contests, bunion derbies, flagpole sitters, comic strips, greyhound races, and "Yes, We Have No Bananas."

In the somewhat chastened spirit of the depression years, bingo, amateur theatricals, treasure-hunts, monopoly, Chinese checkers, The Game, and prize contests were among the popular obsessions. In some cases a fad bit deep enough to become a lasting habit. More generally it quickly gave way to something else as with unwearied enthusiasm, everybody climbed aboard what came to be called the Great American Band-Wagon.

After the interruption once again of war, the search for new amusements was renewed with a zest heightened by the opportunities created by an affluent society. The great enthusiasm for skiing and skin diving were characteristic of the world of sport; among games scrabble and canasta came and went; barbecue cook-outs were a universal craze; do-it-yourself activities were blessed by fashion with studios springing up for amateur ceramists, weavers, and jewelry-makers. There were hula-hoops, frisbees, transistor radios, skateboards, and Shakespeare festivals. From bird watching to stock-car racing, from greenhouse gardening to dancing the twist, the American people demonstrated the amazing catholicity of their taste.

Once again how could one apply Lord Lytton's classic observation that a people's social civilization is infallibly indicated by the intellectual character of its amusements?

→≫|≪←

THE CRAZE for dancing ushered in during the years before World War I by ragtime, made this traditional social diversion more popular than it had ever been before. The bright particular stars who led this revival were Mr. and Mrs. Vernon Castle. Under the inspiration of their graceful example, hundreds of thousands of men and women enthusiastically learned the new dances introduced by the stimulating music of "Alexander's Ragtime Band" and glided happily through the mazes of the foxtrot and the hesitation waltz at fashionable *thés dansants* and in public ball-rooms.[2] One of the favorite dance tunes was "Everybody's Doing It"—and it was almost literally true.

The Castles played an influential part in setting the tone of this revival of social dancing. A later commentator wrote that the pre-war craze was "an opening engagement in that revolution in manners and morals which was to excite America during the twenties," [3] but the music and dancing of these earlier days

were far more decorous than anything in that later decade. The
bunny hug, lame duck, and grizzly bear awoke derision and
some criticism, but the Castles countered with the tango and
maxixe. At the *thés dansants* fashion decreed that actual tea be
served. "Here in America we are just beginning to wake up
to the possibilities of dancing," Mr. and Mrs. Castle wrote. "We
are beginning to take our place among the nations that enjoy
life." [4]

The next step was jazz. Known immemorially among the
Negroes of the South, it was first brought north about 1914 when
various "original" Dixieland jazz bands began playing in Chicago
night clubs and then went on to New York jazzing the ragtime
blues.[5] The real jazz was played without a score, individual
players "faking" their parts as they went along. But it was
after Paul Whiteman, who called jazz "the folk music of the
machine age," [6] undertook its orchestration—with the development of symphonic jazz—that it really caught on. And then it
swept the country like wildfire. It was so universally the dance
music of the 1920's that it gave its name to the decade. "To
write fully and adequately about jazz," Mark Sullivan wrote in
Our Times, "would be to write the history of much of this
generation." [7]

The saxophone was jazz's most essential instrument—"the
heart, soul, mind, body and spirit of the jazz orchestra." Everywhere the younger generation fox-trotted to its barbaric yawp,
clinging to one another in what one editor described as a "syncopated embrace." [8] Gradually their elders succumbed to the
contagion. All the world danced to "Kitten on the Keys," "Tea
for Two," "The Japanese Sandman," "You're the Cream in My
Coffee," "I Faw Down an' Go Boom." . . .

The violent acrobatics of the Charleston became a new rage:

> We all went to the party, a real high-toned affair
> And then along came Lulu, as wild as any Zulu.
> She started in to 'Charleston,'
> And how the boys did stare. . . .[9]

Jazz set the pace for hundreds of night clubs, pretentious outgrowth of the first humble speakeasies of these days of Prohibition. At Texas Guinan's, the Embassy Club, and Helen Morgan's, the fashionable world of New York "made whoopee" in a garish atmosphere spiced with gin and apple jack.[10] Jazz was the music for the dances of country club and fraternity, and it came over the air for dances at a million homes—roll back the rugs, turn on the radio. It dominated the taxi dance halls ("Eureka Dancing Academy—Fifty Beautiful Lady Instructors") in a hundred cities where anyone could find a willing partner for a whirl at fox-trot or Charleston at a dime a dance. "There are thirty million people who dance in the United States, daily, weekly, or frequently," a magazine writer stated in 1924. "A billion dollars for dancing by rich and poor would be a modest bill." [11]

The type of dancing inspired by jazz awoke a storm of protest from the very pure in heart. "The music is sensuous, the embracing of partners—the female only half dressed—is absolutely indecent," the *Catholic Telegraph* declared, "and the motions —they are such as cannot be described, with any respect for propriety, in a family newspaper." Other religious journals united in denouncing the new dances as "impure, polluting, corrupting, debasing, destroying spirituality, increasing carnality." [12]

Jazz and the cheek-to-cheek dancing it inspired were but another manifestation of the post-war upheaval in morals which had set the country, so the reformers sincerely believed, on a downward course that would lead to chaos and destruction. The younger generation was running wild—short skirts and rolled stockings, bobbed hair, corsets parked in the ladies' dressing room, the "insidious vintage" of rouge, cigarettes and hip-flasks, petting parties. . . . It was all a part of the spiritual confusion of an age whose reflex from a war psychosis had led to a mad pursuit of pleasure in which the standards of an earlier day appeared to have gone completely by the board.

The nation survived. The younger generation grew up to be-

come the staid parents of another age and to look back wistfully
upon their spirited revolt and their good times. So too did jazz
survive its hectic manifestations in the 1920's to demonstrate a
continuing popularity in the world of dance and in the world
of music itself. But its variations and permutations often seemed
to pass all understanding. In the 1930's the saxophones were
blaring forth new interpretations of how dance music should be
played. With the introduction of swing, a new race of "jitter-
bugs" sprang up to prove that in the popularity of every musical
innovation, the Great American Band Wagon was still lumbering
along its appointed course for all the bumps and jolts of the
depression.

The new orchestras, carrying still further the free improvising
of the first jazz bands, created a tremendous stir. They swung
the compositions of the great composers; they swung the verses
of old nursery lines. When Benny Goodman first opened up in
New York, a theatre audience largely made up of high school
students became so hysterically enthusiastic that observers compared the scene to accounts of the children's crusade. A new
generation tried its hand (or its feet) at truckin', took up and
then as quickly dropped, the shag, the Lambeth Walk, and the
chestnut tree. "If there is anything to create more consternation
in the national bosom than the new style in women's hats," an
editorial writer in the Milwaukee *Journal* observed, "It is undoubtedly the new dances." [13]

Another decade introduced boogie-woogie and bebop, and
then rock-'n'-roll. Soon thereafter (with the customary anguished
outcries from the conventional-minded) young people were dancing not only the twist but the hully-gully, the mashed potato, and
the limbo. What underlay it all was still jazz, and the music
that had first been brought out of the South by the Dixieland
bands took a fresh lease on life. It now had in postwar years a
broadening appeal that reached the most sophisticated circles,
not only as dance music but as concert music, with all the fine
variations of classical jazz, progressive jazz and cool jazz. It had

a whole vocabulary of its own. An enterprising publisher brought out *A Jazz Lexicon* to provide aid and assistance for "all those desirous of 'digging' how jazzmen talk and 'wig.' "

Such band leaders and instrumentalists of an earlier day as Tommy Dorsey and Duke Ellington, Louis "Satchmo" Armstrong and Count Basie, still had a high renown in the 1950's, but they were soon hard-pressed by a new generation of performers— Dizzy Gillespie, Stan Kenton, Lennie Tristano. The pulsating jam sessions they staged on nationwide concert tours were invariably packed by rapt, starry-eyed, jazz-hungry enthusiasts. One musical festival made history when a score of bands, brought together for a mighty orgy of jazz at—of all places—that same fashionable and one time puritan Newport where two centuries earlier the colonial legislature had banned the theatre, led to a widely publicized riot. Some 16,000 "cool cats" crowded the festival park but another 12,000 without tickets (and having imbibed rather too much beer) demanded admission. Not only the police but the marines were called out to restore order.[14]

Another revival in these years was hillbilly and other folk music—the ballads and songs of the Ozarks and Appalachia. It almost rivalled jazz and reached its apogee with the hootennany that burst upon the scene at the opening of the 1960's, both on television and also on college campuses where it spilled over in a "folk frenzy" from concert halls to field houses. "Hootennany is in big," one campus paper wrote. "College students everywhere assemble on Saturday nights to play and sing and hear such favorites as *Shenandoah* and *Tom Dooley*. . . . A wholesome outlet for the boundless energy and restlessness of youth. . . . Hooray for Hootennany." [15]

Dancing and music were more than ever before a most popular form of entertainment or amusement. It was estimated that there were five times as many people taking dancing lessons as there were students in colleges and universities; forty-seven million record players (nearly the equivalent of TV sets) were to be found in private homes, and jazz and folk music were endlessly played on the juke boxes in restaurants and taverns.

The changing fashions which could at one and the same time find the studios of Arthur Murray so crowded, jazz inspiring a succession of exotic fads, and square dancing undergoing a lively revival, certainly bore out the Castles' statement in 1914 that Americans had awakened to new opportunities for amusement. For all the enthusiasms and extravagances of later years, however, the quintessence of harmless idiocy in this area of social life was perhaps reached when café society at the close of the 1930's (the world was on the brink of war), danced to "Where Is My Little Dog Gone?" or "London Bridge Is Falling Down" and as the orchestra swung these inspiring tunes, mincingly sang:

> Down in de meddy by de itty bitty poo
> Fam we itty fitty and a mama fitty, foo.
> 'Fim,' said de mama fitty, 'fim if oo tan,'
> And dey fam and dey fam all over de dam.[16]

Cards and other games have always had their role among home diversions—who could estimate how much leisure time they consume?—and in the 1920's the more traditional forms of such play were supplemented by two crazes of that era of wonderful nonsense which have proved to be of great and lasting popularity. They were crossword puzzles and contract bridge.

Newspapers had long since run crossword puzzles as an occasional feature, but when a group of the intelligentsia—among others, Heywood Broun, Ruth Hale and Franklin P. Adams—took them up in 1924 and an enterprising new publisher dreamed of a crossword puzzle book, this indoor sport really took hold.[17] "We hired halls. We drafted by-laws and rules for amateur crossword orgies," one of the publishing firm's members wrote in describing the book's promotion . . . "We visited editors, urging them to put cross-word puzzles in the papers. . . . Soon we were selling thousands of copies a day and breaking into the best seller lists." [18] Other books followed; the newspapers began to print daily puzzles, and the boom was on.

"The Baltimore and Ohio placed dictionaries in all the trains on its main line," a contemporary wrote. "A traveler between New York and Boston reported that 60 per cent of the passengers were trying to fill up squares in their puzzles, and that in the dining-car five waiters were trying to think of a five letter word which meant 'serving to inspire fear.' Anybody you met on the street could tell you the name of the Egyptian sun-god or provide you with a two-letter word which meant a printer's measure." [19]

Supplemented by the vogue they inspired for other games, crossword puzzles appeared to the writer Kathleen Norris to have opened up entirely new vistas for the American people. "Clerks and plumbers and schoolteachers and school children," she wrote, "go home elbow to elbow in the Subway, muttering five letter words that mean commonplace. . . . Amusement, once the prerogative of royalty and wealth, is everywhere, now, and with this wave of games the nation gains a great lifting of the spirit, a sort of universal heightening per capita of the country's average enjoyment." [20] George Jean Nathan was not quite so enthusiastic. "The games and diversions that man invents for the pleasure of his leisure hours," he told the readers of the *American Mercury,* "are of such unbelievable stupidity and dulness that it is impossible to imagine even the lowest of God's animals and insects indulging in relatively imbecile relaxations." [21]

Whether he felt any better about contract bridge, which was introduced in this country just two years after the start of the crossword puzzle boom, is not recorded. It had, of course, its highly respectable forebear in auction, a game designed by three British civil servants in India which had almost wholly replaced the old-fashioned whist,[22] and this form of bridge had long been popular in the social life of city, town and suburb. But contract, with its more involved play and complicated scoring system, not only drove out auction almost overnight but immensely multiplied the bridge-playing public. It was estimated in 1931 that 500,000 people were enrolled in professionally taught bridge courses and that there were altogether some twenty million players.[23] The newspapers now had bridge columns, magazines were established to explain the game's finer points, and over 100 instruction books were on the market. Tournaments attracted an attention usually reserved for heavyweight prize-fights and the entire country hung breathlessly on the outcome of a sensational Battle of the Century among the country's leading bridge experts. "If contract is not the national game," wrote one enthusiast describing this "purest of pleasures" in an article for *Harper's*, "it is second only to golf." [24]

The promotional activities of contract's high priest, Ely Culbertson, revealed a new genius in the great art of ballyhoo. He made a card game news as never before when he magisterially introduced his approach-forcing system for bidding. If the working class still clung to pedro or five hundred, the social world made contract an almost invariable after-dinner entertainment under his beneficent guidance. And it was taken seriously whatever the stakes—or no stakes at all—for which it was being played. It seemed almost heresy to many thousands torn with anxiety as to how they should return their partner's lead, or lying awake at night smarting under the chagrin of a misleading discard, when the great maestro was quoted as having said, "after all, contract is only a game." [25]

→≫ ≪←

CROSSWORD puzzles and contract permanently enriched the nation's recreational resources, but the depression witnessed in miniature golf the spectacular rise and almost equally abrupt decline of a rather more ephemeral amusement. This game involved hitting a ball across a surface of crushed cotton-seed hulls and through various tin pipes into a series of holes which represented, as the game's name implied, a replica of a golf-course. In the summer of 1930 it was hailed, and in the utmost seriousness, as a psychological and economic answer to the industrial collapse which in spite of President Hoover's exhortations that recovery was just around the corner, was relentlessly undermining the nation's economy. Miniature golf would take the minds of the multitude off the troubles in which their lives were enmeshed; it would revive both the cotton and steel industries in creating this new demand for cotton-seed hulls and tin pipes.

Thirty thousand courses, valued as high as $125,000,000, suddenly appeared.[26] They became as commonplace along motor roads as filling-stations or hot-dog stands; they took over the empty lots in every town and city. Miniature golf was played throughout the day by its devotees, and, under glaring arc-lights, well into the night. Its cheapness was in line with the chastened spirit of the amusement-seekers of 1930, and it helped to fill the leisure of many who unaccountably found themselves without jobs. It had a further appeal in its resemblance to golf itself. Players of the "midget" game could talk as glibly as the country club crowd about the difficulties of the fourth hole, or pridefully boast of their eagles and birdies. Everybody rented putters and hit little balls around the tortuous tin-pipe courses. Here was a novel and inexpensive may for the young man to entertain his girl friend.

Miniature golf flourished through that memorable summer like a green bay tree, and when winter caused the closing of the courses, it was still confidently expected that the next season would see even further expansion. But by then the public by-and-large had tired of the game. It had really been a one-year phenomenon. A few proprietors of courses hung on, and would continue to do so down through the years. Miniature golf did not wholly disappear. After 1930, however, the motorist rarely stopped for a passing game, and the young man again took his girl friend to a movie—or else they sat on a park bench.

Elmer Davis, writing in December, 1930, when the future of

both miniature golf and the national economy appeared somewhat rosier than events were to demonstrate, paid his dutiful
respects to the game. "So perhaps miniature golf did its part,"
he said in *Harper's*, "in carrying us past a crisis. Perhaps the
business revival would have come sooner if the President, and
the Cabinet, and Congress had become miniature golf addicts
too." [27]

->>)((<-

OTHER FADS in the 1930's generally reflected the forced economies
of that unhappy decade. Bingo first became really popular in
these years for it both cost little to play and inspired the further
hope of being able to win something for nothing—or at least
for the thirty-five cents that was the usual charge for thirty-five
games. All over the country men, women and children spent long
hours trying to fill up a row of numbers on a cardboard square
in the hope of taking home a ham, a box of groceries, a tin of
coffee, or one of the rare money prizes. Bingo was played at
amusement parks, movie theatres, penny arcades, firemen's carnivals, country fairs, Grange suppers, and church socials.[28]

As it spread to the churches ("Bingo Every Night in the Holy
Spirit Room" was one rather startling announcement), a storm
of controversy arose over the ethical propriety of such open
encouragement of gambling. But while some outraged ministers
of the gospel might declare that "the Kingdom of God cannot
be established by shooting craps," the more realistic-minded
found bingo a relatively innocent pastime which was very helpful in raising church funds. "I cannot grow frenzied with the
puritanic precisionists who rate the bourgeois pastime of bingo
as a major sin," one churchman wrote. "Church bingo parties
are a healthy substitute for gossip teas, lovesick movies, and
liberal minded lecturers." [29]

Somewhat analogous to bingo was the depression-born craze
for prize contests. In newspapers and magazines, and over the
radio, the public was eloquently urged by interested advertisers

to while away the hours and win substantial awards by completing a limerick extolling some breakfast food or discovering the name of a facial cream hidden in a cartoon. If reformers again suggested that prize contests came perilously close to lotteries, generally banned since their own vogue early in the nineteenth century, millions nevertheless enjoyed them. And in most cases they accepted with patient resignation their failure to win the offered prizes—an automobile, a trip to Europe, a radio, a bicycle, or a diamond pin.

Still another widespread expression of the gambling spirit (with even less dependence on skill) was the popularity of slot machines, punchboards, and jar deals. In an article called "Ten Billion Nickels," a writer in the *Saturday Evening Post* estimated that the annual take of these gambling devices in 1939 was over $500,000,000, while a Gallup poll the same year reported that one out of every three adults in the country at least occasionally took a chance on his nickel winning the jackpot. With slot machine installations in cigar stores, filling stations, lunch counters, drug-stores and bars, here was a form of petty gambling actually more important than all the betting on horse-races, policy games and cards.

These amusements were of course to continue long after the depression. Thirty years later bingo still had its place at church socials as well as country fairs; prize contests, as we have seen, had a spectacular—if temporary—revival over television; slot machines consistently pulled in their huge take over the years, and New Hampshire actually legalized a state lottery. Nonetheless it was in the 1930's that minor games of chance first became so popular and had their greatest, if not their finest, hour. It was reported in 1938 that there had been a thousand per cent increase in all kinds of prize contests since the advent of the depression, and that twenty-five million persons were taking part in them on an average of twice a year.[30]

-»» ««-

MORE SOBER and substantial recreational activities were also encouraged in the 1930's, and then continued to expand through the mid-century years. Gardening, for example, attained a popularity it had never before experienced. It was hardly a new diversion: the first colonists brought from England the slips of plants and flowers to start their New World gardens. But it appealed to people during the depression who had never before thought of it. As Robert and Helen Lynd pointed out in *Middletown Revisited*, there was a rediscovery of the backyard when amusements farther afield became less practical, and this quickly led to a "mild mania of flower gardening." [31] Neglected strips of land blossomed out in a profusion of color, or in many cases more economically presented carefully weeded rows of vegetables. In the upper reaches of society the growing popularity of this outdoor amusement found added expression in the busy organization of garden clubs, deeply concerned with annual exhibitions in which the rivalry over dephinium and dahlia was as intense as that at the bridge table. Working-class families were content to cultivate their flowers and vegetables without any such stimulus.

In post-war years increased leisure and the steady growth of the suburbs gave a still further impetus to this home gardening. It became an almost universal weekend activity and an accepted part of the nationwide pattern of life in the new real estate subdivisions. Moreover at least a few of its more devoted—and affluent—practitioners did not let even winter interrupt their gardening. They added greenhouses to their suburban homes. In the early 1960's it was estimated that there were thirty million home gardeners in the country, a total approximating that of the participants in the most popular of outdoor sports, and that they annually spent some $2 billion on their plants, seeds, fertilizer, garden tools, and power mowers.[32]

The whole do-it-yourself mania, with its confusion of what is work and what is play, flourished alongside flower gardening. It can hardly be even guessed how many men spent how many hours puttering about their yards, refurbishing their homes, trying to make furniture in their power-tooled home workshops, or tinkering over this and that. And equally incalculable were the woman-hours consumed in amateur dress-making, sewing curtains, and home decorating. That such activities were extremely widespread and had led to the creation of a special industry to supply the necessary equipment, was suggested in the mid-1950's in an article in *Time* with the title, "Do-It-Yourself—the New Billion Dollar Hobby." [33]

There were of course—as in whatever period—many other highly specialized hobbies. They too had had a first flowering during the depression years. The department stores in the 1930's felt constrained to set up hobby sections, newspapers and magazines introduced special hobby pages (the *Rotarian* called its page the Hobbyhorse Hitching Post), radio had its Hobby Lobby, and homeowners made over their cellars into hobby-rooms. Among the rush of books to promote the idea that every man —and woman—should develop some special interest for his leisure hours, the most successful was Ernest Elmo Calkin's *The Care and Feeding of Hobby Horses.*

What were these hobbies? They included photography (especially color slides and home movies); bird watching by old and young; assembling hi-fi sets; building model airplanes; refinishing antiques, and playing in amateur string quartets. Millions of people also took up wood carving or pottery, soap sculpture, painting "by the numbers." Other specialists tried their hand at puppet shows, chased butterflies, bred scotties, raised tropical fish. . . . And then there were the collectors—collectors of stamps and coins, collectors of sea-shells, collectors of old bottles, collectors of campaign buttons, collectors of match boxes. There was never any telling what the hobbyist or collector might find to be his consuming passion.[34]

→≫≪←

ONE FINAL recreational activity, as old as the Republic but immensely expanded in the mid-twentieth century, was foreign travel. It could never compare in number with the throngs of motorists who toured back and forth in this country, visiting the national parks and generally sightseeing, but year by year an ever larger segment of the public vacationed in Europe. Americans have always felt the irresistible pull of the Old World. They have wanted to see for themselves the scenes associated with the lands of their origin, and to explore the castles and cathedrals, the museums and art galleries, that constitute Europe's cultural heritage. But whereas for a hundred years and more such transatlantic journeying was restricted to the very few, the world of wealth and fashion, the twentieth century introduced new and relatively less expensive means of transportation, together with improved tourist facilities, which made such trips increasingly feasible for more and more people. What modern times witnessed in this area, as in every form of recreation, was still another process of gradual democratization.[35]

In the early 1900's—the "good years" before the world was convulsed by war—up to 200,000 Americans were already going every year to Europe. The transatlantic steamship lines had introduced such swift, new ships as the *Mauretania*, the *Lusitania*, and the giant *Vaterland*. Scores of travel agencies (although the American Express Company did not enter the business until the 1920's) were prepared to make all necessary arrangements for continental tours (the cost varying anywhere from $400 to $5,000), and they reassuringly promised the timid that they could make up "package tours," provide "experienced escorts," and guarantee "girls carefully chaperoned."

Everywhere in Europe the traveling American, guidebook in hand, camera slung over his shoulder, had become a familiar figure. He invariably visited Paris, which had long since become known as the place where all good Americans go when they die: toured happily through Italy for which he had a special sentimental attachment—Rome, Florence, Venice; visited the lake and mountain resorts of Switzerland; perhaps took a boat journey down the Rhine to the Low Countries, and then, had he not first landed there, brought his tour to a climax in England with all its timeless associations and wealth of historic antiquity.

He sought out in every city, this typical American tourist, the Baedeker-starred sights. He gazed in awe at Gothic cathedrals and Renaissance palaces, trudged weary miles through art galleries, and indefatigably "did" the museums. He also bought souvenirs (or at least his wife and children did), sent home reams of postcards ("having wonderful time, wish you were here"), and for all the help of the tourist agencies, became on occasion hopelessly snarled in the intricacies of visiting strange lands where the inhabitants unaccountably did not speak English. In other words, the patterns of European travel were firmly set in these years before the First World War; the paths laid out which hundreds of thousands of tourists would faithfully follow in succeeding years.

The hostilities that broke out in 1914 abruptly interrupted all foreign travel, but it took on an astonishing new lease on life during the booming years of prosperity in the 1920's. Many Americans seeking to escape from the restraints of Prohibition now went abroad not only in the proverbial pursuit of culture, but to enjoy vacations in a Europe that was currently characterized as a "tumultuous playground" where such things as Volstead acts were wholly unknown. Businessmen found increasing occasion for a transatlantic voyage; vacationing middle-class families as well as the wealthier members of society stayed at European resorts; retired couples, peripatetic clergymen, school teachers and university professors swelled the tourist ranks. There were also thousands of college students, sometimes working their way abroad on cattle boats and then either bicycling or walking through England, France and Italy.

The depreciated currencies of the European countries combined with the prosperity at home during these years to open up many new avenues of foreign travel. And the growing tourist industry was fully coöperative. The steamship lines introduced cabin and tourist-class accommodations, foreign railroads and motor bus companies provided special tourist rates, and the hotels vied in doing everything possible to attract overseas visitors. In these circumstances, the American "invasion" of Europe so expanded as to provide in many ways a startling phenomenon.

Some of the American tourists in the 1920's conducted themselves in a manner not very endearing to their European hosts. Ever since a rather snobbish Henry James had once summarily dismissed the whole tourist tribe as "vulgar, vulgar, vulgar," Americans abroad had been subjected to sharp criticism as being chauvinistic and boastful, scornful of many European customs, and often rude and demanding. In the between-wars period, such charges were often justified. By their boisterous merrymaking and ostentatious extravagance (plastering their baggage with depreciated paper francs, liras and marks), a noisy minority so offended the Europeans that anti-American riots were threatened in Paris. On one occasion a mob sent frightened tourists scurrying from their sightseeing busses in the Place de l' Opéra and President Coolidge felt it necessary to warn those of his countrymen who could not respect European sensibilities that they had better come home.

Whatever may be said of European travel in these days—it reached a peak in 1929 when nearly 300,000 Americans crossed the Atlantic—it was nevertheless in the 1950's that it began to experience its really dramatic growth. The key to this new era was, of course, the inauguration of transatlantic flying (it had been initiated in 1939 but then postponed on a commercial basis until after the war), and then the further dramatic development of jet planes. While the ocean liners continued to carry their full quota of travelers, the speed and ultimate economies of flying had a revolutionary effect. The number of Americans flying the Atlantic first exceeded the ocean-borne in 1955, and within five years it accounted for some three-fourths of a steadily rising annual total.

Economy and tourist flights, together with special fifteen and twenty-one day tours, progressively lowered fares until a European vacation came within the practical range—time and expense—of a whole new class of travelers from all over the country. In 1909, William Allen White had once commented on how a European trip of a resident of Emporia, Kansas was "a matter of townwide concern," but half a century later such ventures were commonplace no matter how small the community. There were 3,000 tourist agencies throughout the country offering their services to bank clerks, shopkeepers, office employes, retired farmers, tradesmen, skilled workers. . . . The Old World could now be visited on a "piggy bank budget" in comparison with the greater costs of an earlier day. But luxury—"Europe with whipped cream"—was of course still possible.

The airplane companies and tourist agencies (as well as the steamship lines) glowingly advertised in magazines and newspapers the joys and pleasures of transatlantic travel:

> "Get Lost! Lose yourself on a Sunny European Holiday."
> "Attention: scholars, socialites, secretaries, scientists, Shakespeare buffs (and businessmen)—Escape to Europe on a giant Cunard Queen."
> "To Europe with Love! What other six letters can send the imagination soaring with such vistas of romance, history and enjoyment? Where in the world can you find such enticements, such marvelous variety that a lifetime is insufficient to enjoy them all? Nobody can resist a romance with her."

The Europe that welcomed these visitors had become highly organized in all the ways of tourism. Americanized hotels, conducted tours, staged spectacles, and carefully preserved antiquities were supplemented by an army of tourist-oriented concierges and guides, headwaiters and taxi drivers, shopkeepers and curio dealers. The travel agencies were more than ever ready to make every possible reservation—airplanes, railroads, busses, hotels, sightseeing excursions—on either an individual or group basis to smooth the vacationing Americans' path. The more experienced might travel wholly on their own; and a growing number who took their cars abroad, or, more likely, rented or bought a car in Europe, usually did so. The great majority, however, gladly accepted all possible help in surmounting the difficulties of their foreign travel.

The "packaged tour," as one critic wrote, tended to make the European trip "an assembly-line, store-boughten commodity." [36] But while something of the old spirit of adventure may have been lost under such circumstances, it was far more important that through the ease of such arrangements and their relative cheapness, so many thousands of persons in all walks of life could enjoy a vacation that in earlier years would have been beyond their wildest flights of fancy.

With their insistence that any idea of the cost of an overseas trip being prohibitive was only a state of mind, and their advertising of the very practical formula—"go now—pay later," the travel agencies were giving a measure of reality to their popular slogan—"Europe is for Everybody." The transatlantic crossings of what by the 1960's had become more than a million Americans every year, provided still another illustration of the unexampled opportunities and broad diversity of American recreation.[37]

chapter 22

The New Leisure

D URING THE YEARS OF PROSPERITY THAT ENDED SO ABRUPTLY
with the stock market crash in 1929, it first began to be
realized with some concern that American social life was undergoing a marked transformation because of the new leisure being
enjoyed by the great masses of the people. Faint voices might
be heard asking where the dominance of the radio and the
movies, the ballyhoo of spectator sports, and the successive
amusement crazes were leading the nation. The depression of
the 1930's accentuated the processes of change. Still additional
free time became available for the majority of wage earners,
partly through economic circumstance and partly through governmental action, and old ideas of the relationship between work
and play were further challenged. As a new affluence was then
superimposed on even greater leisure in mid-century years, the
questions first raised in the 1920's became even more compelling.
The American people found themselves fully launched at the
opening of the 1960's on what James Garfield had in 1880 called
the second great struggle of civilization: having attained leisure,
what was going to be done with it?

For some three and a half centuries the American tradition
had condemned leisure in placing an over-all emphasis on work
as the chief purpose of existence. "Business to the American,"
an English observer could write even in the 1920's, "is life's great
adventure; it is sport, work, pleasure, beauty and patriotism
rolled into one." [1] Puritanism had long since imposed a religious
sanction on this concept. Idleness and play could have no place
in a world where labor was the greatest good. But the revolutionary changes wrought by the machine and the rapid processes

of automation could no longer be ignored. They provided increasing leisure for people in every walk of life, and whether this was a good thing or a bad thing, there was no escaping it. It was as a consequence of such developments that there had taken place in post-war years "the explosion" in recreation so clearly indicated in the dramatic growth of commercial entertainment, sports and other popular diversions.

→≫≪←

ALTHOUGH labor agitation for shorter hours had a direct and important influence, leisure was primarily a by-product of industrialism rather than anything that had been consciously designed. Little thought had been given to its ultimate value for the people as a whole through the hurrying years of economic progress. The reduction in the hours of work had taken place almost automatically as the application of mechanical power enabled society to satisfy its normal needs in progressively less working time. While this was generally true throughout the western world, the United States particularly was confronted by a condition and not a theory.

Although there were of course many exceptions, the eight-hour day had come into general effect throughout the country by the 1920's. Statistics for twenty-five forms of manufacture then showed that the average working-week for both men and women was no more than forty-eight hours. Shop and office workers fared even better with the more general adoption of both the Saturday half-holiday and a week or two weeks' summer vacation. The further reduction in such hours occasioned by the depression, with the demand for spreading out work and increasing employment, then found a forty-hour week becoming almost the general rule. The National Industrial Recovery Act in effect lopped off a full working-day, and even after its collapse, further legislation maintained this shorter working-week as a national objective.[2]

This trend was further accentuated in postwar years as a result of the increasing emphasis of the labor unions for fringe benefits which would provide better working conditions as a supplement to higher wages. While the average work-week was not generally reduced, a two-day weekend became very widespread and vacation-time greatly increased. Some eighty-five per cent of the country's wage earners, it was estimated, had paid vacations which in some instances were going even beyond the conventional two weeks. Added to paid holidays, such free time averaged twenty days a year.

The industrial worker at the opening of the 1960's consequently had the equivalent of an additional day of leisure every week over and beyond his free time in the 1920's, and also enjoyed a progressively increasing paid vacation. If the comparison is carried back to still earlier years, he had twice as many hours available for recreation as he had had in the 1890's, while over a century his free time—even apart from vacations—had increased from about ten hours a week to more than seventy. Nothing was perhaps more striking in the changed circumstances of the American people's social life.[3]

Since the beginning of the industrial revolution no people had ever commanded anything like so much time for activities other than those directly associated with earning one's living and maintaining the home. Civilizations of the past had had many non-working days, more than is generally realized. In Egypt holidays are said to have amounted to one fifth the number of days in the year; there were fifty to sixty festival days in historic Greece, and in Rome an even greater number of days were considered "unlucky" for work.[4] Throughout subsequent years religious festivals had continued to break the monotony of labor in what was the primarily agricultural civilization of medieval Europe. The factory system, however, had soon spelled the end of such frequent holidays and also entailed much longer working-days. Only with the mid-twentieth century had the balance been redressed. The machine which had at first so greatly reduced free time, finally enabled the masses to command that measure of leisure which could give life a new dimension in terms of opportunity for play.

Moreover by the opening of the 1960's, the rising standard of living generally enjoyed by most Americans had opened up an ever wider choice of how such free time might be spent. A telling statistic on this point was the sharp increase in what economists called "discretionary income"; that is, money available to the family after meeting all costs of daily living. It was reported in 1959 that some 34 million families had at their disposal for non-essential expenses a total of $84 billion, and that they were spending as much as half this great sum on various forms of recreation.[5]

The implications of these startling developments found philosophers and social scientists even in prewar days in full cry. The "challenge of the new leisure" had to be considered in a quite different light than when recreation's sole purpose was widely accepted as being only a means to restore the capacity to work—part of that endless cycle wherein one labored to gain an opportunity to play and then played to labor more effectively. What was the role of recreation in shaping American society, and what was its significance in individual development? How important was it as an instinctive form of self expression or as an emotional escape-valve? What influence might it have in counteracting ill-health, mental instability, and crime in the urban community? These were among the questions that began to be discussed.

"The value of leisure-time activities, play and recreation," George A. Lundberg wrote in 1934 with somewhat ponderous sociological emphasis, "is usually conceded to lie in the nervous release which they afford from the customary and coercive activities which the social order imposes upon us. To the extent, therefore, that the pursuits of our leisure-time tend to become organized under conventional patterns determined by competitive consumption they lose their unique and primary value as recreation and so become merely another department of activity devoted to the achievement of prestige or status." [6]

In post-war years such discussion was intensified and broadened. Among several articles in a study entitled *Mass Leisure*, published in 1958 under the auspices of the newly formed Center for the Study of Leisure at the University of Chicago, one contributor wrote that "the most dangerous threat hanging over American society is the threat of leisure"; another stressed the need for a social science of play for "without its contributions the ways in which we spend our growing leisure may never be ennobled." [7] A writer in *The Nation* even went so far as to state ominously that the burden of leisure had become "the darkest threat to the well-being of the working man and the subject of increasing concern on the part of organized labor." [8]

Margaret Mead attacked the problem and concluded that the theory that leisure must be earned and enjoyed within the context of future work would have to be modified so as to relate its purposes more clearly to the home and family life. David Riesman took a long look at recreation in "Abundance for What?" and speculated on the new trends toward fusing work and play. "The primary problem for the future," he wrote, "will be what to do with the surplus of time and resources on our hands." As head of the Outdoor Recreation Resources Review Commission, Laurence Rockefeller advocated new approaches to end "Sunday frustration" through healthful relaxation, self-improvement, enjoyment of the best in arts and literature, and community service. The Academy of Political and Social Sciences devoted an entire issue of its *Annals* to "Recreation in the Age of Automation," and the magazine *Life* published a special supplement on "The Good Life," the latter reaching the editorial conclusion that by using leisure "to pursue true happiness, Americans can raise standards of excellence higher than anything in the world's past." [9]

There was much in all this discussion that again suggested the continuing influence of the puritan tradition and the idea that leisure ("pleasure does make us Yankees kind o' wince") should only be used for ultimately productive ends. While no longer practicable to pass laws "in detestation of idleness," it was widely held that the resources and energy of the country should be martialled to make leisure as "meaningful" as possible both from the point of view of the individual and of society. There was no gainsaying that how the people spent their free time could be of great importance to the body politic and directly affect the whole tone of American society, but all this nevertheless had its ironic aspects. The onetime acceptance of a social responsibility in promoting work was being translated into a new obligation in organizing leisure.

->>)<<-

THE SOCIAL aspects of the uses of leisure time were not the only consideration that now had to be taken into account. There was also the economic factor. Since the opening of the century the production and consumption of leisure-time goods had grown to have immense importance. The operation of the country's industrial plant had become significantly dependent on the people as a whole having the time to enjoy—and the money to spend—on the commercialized amusements and elaborate sports equipment that were the machine age's primary answer to recreational needs. Millions of persons were employed in making both for themselves and for others such essentially recreational products as radio and television sets, moving pictures, sporting goods, do-it-yourself equipment and pleasure boats, together with private automobiles whose use could be attributed at least as much to recreation as to business. There had been nothing at all like this until the twentieth century.

In 1935 it was conservatively estimated (many studies giving a higher figure) that the American people were spending something like eight per cent of their entire income on recreation— a total of $4 billion. Vacation travel, so greatly expanded through automobile touring, accounted for more than half this figure, and the remainder was about equally divided between the cost of commercial amusements and what might be termed recreational products. Among the former, motion pictures were far in the lead, followed by legitimate theatres, amusement parks, billiard parlors, bowling alleys, dance halls, and spectator sports. The principal recreational products were radios, books and periodicals, musical instruments, motor boats, games, and sports equipment.[10]

Comparable statistics a quarter of a century later provide graphic evidence of the even greater role recreational expenditures had come to play in the national economy. Estimates for 1962 ranged from a Department of Commerce figure of $21.5 billion, exclusive of automobile pleasure driving, to a comprehensive total as high as $40 billion in other unofficial surveys. As to the proportion of total income spent on recreation, there was a marked variation according to what was included in the several estimates but in comparison with the figures for the 1930's, it would appear that the overall total had risen to somewhere between ten and twelve per cent of the national income.[11]

All such statistics are obviously highly conjectural. Those relating to motoring and travel cannot be accurately apportioned between business and pleasure. Entertaining (especially if alcoholic beverages are considered) is beyond any reasonable estimate. Many other costs have no real basis for sound evaluation. But whether the attempt to estimate total recreational expenditures is made on the basis of a breakdown of national production, or on the distribution of the average family's discretionary income, the results as dramatized in the title of a *Life* article—"A $40 Billion Bill Just for Fun"—are truly staggering.[12]

Further efforts to analyze this overall estimate again reflect perhaps more statistical imagination than accounting accuracy. Nevertheless as in the 1930's, travel and the pleasure use of automobiles came first in the 1962 studies, while the next general item was money spent under the broad category of do-it-yourself activities. Following these major expenditures and approximating about the same level, around $2 billion annually, were boating, fishing, gardening, moving picture admissions, television and radio, and magazines. In further descending scale came bowling, hunting, swimming, golf, photography, musical instruments, phonographs, and theatre admissions.

Whatever the accuracy of all such figures, they at least afford startling evidence of how accustomed the American people had become by the 1960's of digging deeper and deeper into their pocketbooks for the enjoyment of their free time. The consequent importance for the national economy of the expenditures that leisure so greatly stimulated had thus become even more enhanced. "The leisure market," commented *Fortune*, "may become the dynamic component of the whole economy." And the writer of *Life's* article declared that it was the growth of leisure time which "has kept the American economy strong and growing." [13]

If the impossible had happened at any time in post-war years and the country somehow reverted to puritan concepts of the evil inherent in all amusements, the economic results would have been disastrous. Millions upon millions of people would have been promptly thrown out of work. No automobile pleasure touring, no radio or television, no moving pictures, no professional sports—the country could not have survived! Even the revival of the old puritan Sabbath, with effective blue laws forbidding all Sunday amusements, would have had incalculable economic repercussions. Play had to be considered a virtue for the sake of the nation's prosperity.

→»«←

THE SHIFTS and changes in the recreational scene, as well as the general expansion in virtually every area of activity, have had widespread repercussions in postwar years. "How does the adult

American spend his leisure time?" one magazine writer had asked in 1937 without benefit of either economic statistics or public opinion polls. "The chances are eight to ten that he will drive along Route 168, watch a 'moom' picture, listen to the Itty Bitty Kiddie Hour, or else enjoy a few inches in the bleachers while some one on the field plays for him." [14] If something like this might still be said a quarter of a century later, it may again be emphasized that not only in sports but all along the line, the adult American now had a much greater interest in active as opposed to passive employment of his augmented leisure. One contributor to the study *Mass Leisure* wrote emphatically that this was "the sharpest fact" of the postwar recreational scene.

This more active use of leisure time was conspicuously related to various home-associated activities that grew out of the rush to suburbia and the new, post-war real estate developments. The actual decline in moving picture box office receipts and the failure of attendance at spectator sports to keep pace with the growth of population may well have been counteracted by the greater amount of time spent watching television.[15] Otherwise the evidence appeared to be incontrovertible that most Americans were getting out and doing things themselves more than ever before both as individuals and as families. The do-it-yourself vogue was a case in point, and the steady proliferation of both indoor and outdoor hobbies; the tremendous increase in vacation travel with its emphasis on "Operation Outdoors" appeared to have no limits, and once again there were the many ramifications of the postwar explosion in sports.[16]

Other questionnaires about this same time also revealed what had become a very distinct class differentiation in the uses of leisure. Persons in the upper income brackets spent more time in theatre and concert going, playing bridge, entertaining, going to college football games, and playing golf. Those in the lower brackets were more likely to watch television, go fishing, play cards other than bridge, attend drive-in movies, and go to baseball games.[17]

The expansion in active recreation owed a great deal to the
encouragement of government and other organized agencies.
This was marked on the national level by the creation of the
Outdoor Recreation Resources Review Commission, the extension
of the services of the national parks and forests, and the enthusiasm with which President Kennedy fostered sports in
addition to his great interest in music and the arts. State governments also zealously developed parks and other recreational
facilities, while municipal governments embarked on long-range
programs embracing the further extension and development of
playgrounds, public golf links, museums, art galleries, and concert halls.

Outside the sphere of governmental action, the National Recreation Association fostered a great deal of promotional work,
its magazine *Recreation* running articles on everything from
"How to Make Bongo Drums" to "Art Comes to Main Street,"
from "The Family Outdoors" to "Basic Yo-Yo Tricks." Every
university had by mid-century introduced courses on recreation
(a comprehensive textbook was published in 1963),[18] and
churches and trade unions developed their own programs of
leisure-time activities ranging from hop scotch for children to
shuffle board for "senior citizens." Housing projects and shopping
centers also set up recreational facilities to satisfy the needs of
the new suburbia.

The commercial amusements which in so many ways appeared
to overshadow everything else in spite of the growth of participant
sports and other forms of active recreation, themselves pulled
in many different directions. At the opening of the 1960's it was
still being said, as in the 1930's, that their primary influence was
in accentuating the uniformity of American life. Everyone was
watching the same television programs, motoring along identical
super-highways to stay at identical motels, seeing the same
moving pictures at a thousand drive-ins. It was also maintained
that commercialization in the recreational world both encouraged
this uniformity in place of the more individualized diversions

of an earlier day, and that it was constantly degrading entertainment of all kinds. But while there was always some measure of truth in such time-worn charges, the recreational scene from any overall view was one of almost infinite variety.

Television brought Shakespeare and Beethoven to the family circle as well as I Love Lucy, and the movies produced Tom Jones as well as stale westerns. The automobile meant a great deal more than billboard-lined highways and traffic jams when it opened up the national parks to so many millions of camping and picnicking families. Even spectator sports, attracting the vast television audience, had a broader scope than ever before as their sponsors added so many new games to the more traditional football and baseball.

The so-called regimentation of American life induced by television, radio and the movies could be grossly exaggerated. It sometimes appeared to be the plaint, unconscious perhaps, of those elements in society which regretted the loss of their one-time generally exclusive hold over amusements. It was disturbing for this class which was once the only one to have the leisure and money to enjoy sports and many other forms of recreation to see them being taken up so universally. What had once been largely restricted to the genteel members of society had become the property of the people as a whole, and by that very token seemed to be vulgarized.

Yet every manufactured entertainment, for all its drawbacks, represented for the common man something he had never before known, while the successive crazes for sports and games gave his life unprecedented scope. The broad pattern of mid-twentieth-century recreation looked quite different to those who had the opportunity to enjoy it for the first time than it did to the sophisticated students of mass culture. Moreover in addition to participant sports, the steadily growing range of hobbies and other individual forms of amusement once again suggested that commercial entertainment could never wholly monopolize popular recreation. Americans might at the self-same hour happily watch the Bob Hope Show, crowd the movies to see a new western, become completely absorbed in the World Series, or be swept off their feet by some passing popular fad. They also had a range of special interests that defies description. There were those countless millions who spent no small part of their leisure, in spite of the siren call of commercial entertainment, on growing dahlias, playing on softball teams, going to concerts, working over their stamp collections, playing chess, going on camping trips, having barbecue picnics, playing the flute in amateur orchestras. . . .[19]

The people of no other country and no other age had ever had anything like the leisure, the discretionary income, or the recreational choices of the American people in mid-twentieth-century. It was overwhelming. Science and the machine had reshaped traditional patterns into hundreds of new forms. Something had undoubtedly been lost, but also a great deal had been gained. Working men and working women—factory operatives, plumbers, waitresses, bank clerks, farm-hands, stenographers, storekeepers, subway guards, mill-hands, garment workers, office boys, truck-drivers—found countless pleasures and amusements readily available that had once been restricted to the privileged few. The democracy had come into its recreational heritage. It had achieved both leisure and the means to enjoy it. Even though they might not always have used this leisure to the best advantage, the American people had learned to play.

SUGGESTED READING

SINCE THE MAJOR SOURCES ON WHICH THIS BOOK IS BASED ARE INDI-
cated in the following footnotes, it has been thought to be most
useful at this point to list only a few of the more recent and important
books on leisure and recreation rather than attempt a general bibliography. For the interested reader such a survey of the literature may be
found in "A Comprehensive Bibliography on Leisure, 1900-1953" in
Eric Larrabee and Rolf Meyersohn, eds., *Mass Leisure*, which is in itself
a very valuable collection of pertinent articles published (Glencoe, Illinois, 1958) by the Center for the Study of Leisure at the University
of Chicago.

Among other important books dealing with leisure and recreation in
mid-twentieth-century America are Max Kaplan, *Leisure in America—
A Social Inquiry* (New York, 1960); Jay B. Nash, *Philosophy of
Leisure and Recreation* (St. Louis, 1953); Martin H. and Esther S.
Neumeyer, *Leisure and Recreation* (New York, 1958); and Sebastian
de Grazia, *Of Time, Work and Leisure* (New York, 1962). An unusual
approach to certain aspects of the recreational scene and the mass-
communication media is found in Reuel Denny, *The Astonished Muse*
(Chicago, 1957). David Riesman has dealt with the general subject
in many of his writings, most notably "Abundance for What?" in
Individualism Reconsidered (New York, 1963).

A very comprehensive textbook is Reynold E. Carson, Theodore E.
Deppe and Janet R. MacLean, *Recreation in American Life* (Belmont,
Cal., 1963); the American Academy of Political and Social Sciences
devoted an issue of its *Annals* (Vol. 313, Sept., 1957) to "Recreation
in the Age of Automation;" the magazine *Life* issued a special supplement (December 28, 1959) entitled "The Good Life," and special
note should be made of *Outdoor Recreation, A Report to the President and to the Congress by the Outdoor Recreation Resources Review
Commission* (Washington, 1962) with its extensive statistical tables.

In the field of sports, the most interesting books are Robert H.
Boyle, *Sport—Mirror of American Life* (Boston, 1963), John S. Tunis,
The American Way in Sport (New York, 1958), and Herbert Warren

Wind, *The Gilded Age of Sport* (New York, 1961). An unpublished dissertation, available on University Microfilms, 1951, is John R. Betts, *Organized Sport in Industrial America.* There is also a new revised edition of Frank G. Menke's well known *The Encyclopedia of Sports* (New York, 1960), and attention might also be drawn to John Durand and Otto Bettman, *Pictorial History of American Sports* (New York, 1952).

The number of recent books on individual games is legion, ranging from Allison Danzig, *The History of American Football* (Englewood Cliffs, N.J., 1956) to Hy Turkin, *Little League Baseball* (New York, 1954); from Herbert Warren Wind, *The Story of Golf* (New York, 1948) to Morris A. Bealle, *The Softball Story* (New York, 1957).

Among many books dealing with special phases of recreation are Leo Bogart, *The Age of Television* (New York, 1958); Deems Taylor, *A Pictorial History of the Movies* (rev. ed. New York, 1950); Marshall Stearns, *The Story of Jazz* (New York, 1956), Harold D. Meyer and Charles K. Brightbill, *Community Recreation* (Englewood Cliffs, N.J., 1956), Russell P. MacFall, *Family Fun Outdoors* (New York, 1965); and Charles Edward Doell, *A Brief History of Parks and Recreation in the United States* (Chicago, 1954).

Even more valuable in many cases than all such booklength studies are the wealth of articles dealing with various phases of recreation in such magazines (among others) as *Recreation, Holiday, Sports Illustrated, Outdoor Life, Hobbies, Travel, Motor Boating,* and the *National Parks Magazine.*

NOTES

CHAPTER I

"In Detestation of Idleness"

1. Ralph Hamor, *A True Discourse of the Present Estate of Virginia* (London, 1615; reprint Richmond, 1860), 26.
2. Edward Winslow (December 11, 1621), quoted in Alice Morse Earl, *Child Life in Colonial Days* (New York, 1899), 217.
3. Thomas Morton, *The New English Canaan* (London, 1637; reprint *Prince Society Publications*, XIV, Boston, 1883), 279.
4. William Bradford, *History of Plymouth Plantation*, in J. F. Jameson (editor), *Original Narratives of Early American History* (New York, 1908), 238.
5. Peter Force, *Tracts and Other Papers* (4 vols., Washington, 1836-46), III, 2, 16.
6. Bradford, *loc. cit.*, 238; *Records of the Court of Assistants of the Colony of Massachusetts Bay* (Boston, 1904), II, 37.
7. Alexander Brown, *The Genesis of the United States* (Boston, 1890), I, 70.
8. Edward Channing, *A History of the United States* (6 vols., New York, 1905-25), I, 200.
9. Quoted in George C. D. Odell, *Annals of the New York Stage* (New York, 1927–), I, 3.
10. Philip Bruce, *Institutional History of Virginia in the Seventeenth Century* (New York, 1910), I, 528.
11. *Records of the Governor and Company of Massachusetts Bay* (Boston, 1853), I, 405.
12. *Ibid.*, II, 195; *Public Records of the Colony of Connecticut* (Hartford, 1850), I, 527.
13. *Records of the Court of Assistants . . . of Massachusetts Bay*, II, 37; *Public Records of . . . Connecticut*, I, 528.
14. See *Records of the Governor . . . of Massachusetts Bay*, II, 70, 180; William B. Weeden, *Economic and Social History of New England* (Boston, 1890), I, 224-25; *Documents and Records Relating to the Province of New Hampshire* (Concord, 1867), I, 391; Walter F. Prince, "An Examination of Peter's 'Blue Laws,'" *American Historical Association Annual Report*, 1898, 97ff.
15. *Massachusetts Historical Society Collections*, Ser. 2, Vol. X, 183-84.
16. *Records of the Governor . . . of Massachusetts Bay*, III, 224.
17. Gustavus Myers, *Ye Olden Blue Laws* (New York, 1921), 211; Arthur A. Hornblow, *History of the American Theatre* (Philadelphia, 1919), I, 24.

18. John Winthrop, *History of New England*, in J. F. Jameson (editor), *Original Narratives of Early American History* (New York, 1908), I, 325-27.
19. *Records of the Court of Assistants of ... Massachusetts Bay*, II, 37; Alexander Young, *Chronicles of the First Planters of the Massachusetts Bay Colony* (Boston, 1846), 413.
20. Force, *Tracts*, III, 2, 10; Alexander Brown, *The First Republic in America* (Boston, 1898), 278; Bruce, *Institutional History of Virginia*, I, 37.
21. *Records of the Court of Assistants ... of Massachusetts Bay*, III, 316-17; *Public Records of ... Connecticut*, II, 280; *Documents ... of New Hampshire*, I, 388.
22. *Records of the Court Assistants ... of Massachusetts Bay*, III, 316-17.
23. Frances M. Caulkins, *History of New London* (New London, 1895), 250.
24. Charles Francis Adams, "Some Phases of Sexual Morality and Church Discipline in Colonial New England," *Proceedings of the Massachusetts Historical Society*, Ser. 2, Vol. VI (1891), 496.
25. See Thomas Cuming Hall, *The Religious Background of American Culture* (Boston, 1930), Chap. I.
26. Edward Eggleston, *The Beginnings of a Nation* (New York, 1897), 124-34.
27. *The King's Majesties Declaration to his subjects concerning Lawful Sports to be used* (London, 1618; reprinted Philadelphia, 1866).
28. H. D. Traill (editor), *Social England* (London, 1895), IV, 167.
29. See Cotton Mather, *Magnalia Christi Americana* (Hartford, 1820), I, 240, quoted in Thomas J. Wertenbaker, *The First Americans (A History of American Life*, II), (New York, 1929), 92.
30. Bradford, *loc. cit.*, 126-27.
31. Samuel Sewall, *Diary, Massachusetts Historical Society Collections*, Ser. 5, Vols. V-VII (1878-82), and in abridged form, Mark Van Doren, editor (New York, 1927). See also N. H. Chamberlain, *Samuel Sewall and the World He Lived in* (Boston, 1897).
32. Sewall, *Diary* (Van Doren edition), 218.
33. *Ibid.*, 24-25, 27, 46.
34. *Ibid.*, 22, 177, 209, 255-56, 263.
35. *Ibid.* (*Massachusetts Historical Society* edition), VII, 171.
36. *Ibid.* (Van Doren edition), 151, 138.
37. Alice Morse Earle, *Customs and Fashions in Old New England* (New York, 1893). 164ff.
38. *Ibid.*, 168ff.; Wertenbaker, *The First Americans*, 200ff.
39. Winthrop, *loc. cit.*, I, 120.
40. Cotton Mather, *Diary* (March 18, 1710-11), *Massachusetts Historical Society Collections*, Ser. 7, Vols. VII-VIII (1911-12), VII, 51.
41. *Records of the Governor ... of Massachusetts Bay*, V, 63, quoted in James Duncan Phillips, *Salem in the Seventeenth Century* (Boston, 1933), 244.
42. Quoted in Wertenbaker, *The First Americans*, 196.
43. *The Statutes at Large of Virginia, 1619-1792* (Philadelphia, 1823), II, 361. See also John A. Krout, *Origins of Prohibition* (New York, 1925), 6-7.

44. Quoted in Myers, *Ye Olden Blue Laws*, 147.
45. *Ibid.*, 158.
46. Earle, *Customs and Fashions*, 256; Weeden, *Economic and Social History*, I, 294.
47. Quoted in Wertenbaker, *The First Americans*, 196-97.
48. Sarah Kemble Knight, *Private Journal* (Albany, 1865), 50. For further discussion of this point see John Dunton, *Letters from New England, Prince Society Publications*, IV; Edward Ward, *A Trip to New England* (London, 1699); Charles Francis Adams, *loc. cit.*, 477-516; and Wertenbaker, *The First Americans*, 196-200.

CHAPTER II

Husking-Bees and Tavern Sports

1. Ralph Hamor, *A True Discourse of the Present Estate of Virginia* (London, 1615; reprint Richmond, 1860), 20-21.
2. Joseph Seccombe, "A discourse utter'd in Part at Ammauskeeg-Falls, in the Fishing Season, 1739" (Boston, 1743), 17.
3. John Sharp, *A Journal of My Life-Exteriour*, in *Pennsylvania Magazine of History and Biography*, XL (1916), 286, 294, 295, 296.
4. Esther Singleton, *Social New York Under the Georges* (New York, 1902), 262.
5. Quoted in Mary N. Stannard, *Colonial Virginia* (Philadelphia, 1917), 259.
6. John Bernard, *Retrospections of America 1797-1811* (New York, 1877), 206.
7. George Alsop, *A Character of the Province of Mary-land* (London, 1666; reprinted, N. D. Mereness, editor, Cleveland, 1902), 58.
8. Charles Warren, *Jacobin and Junto* (Cambridge, 1931), 29.
9. Quoted in Ray Palmer Baker, "The Poetry of Jacob Bailey, Loyalist," *New England Quarterly*, II (1929), 67-69.
10. William B. Weeden, *Economic and Social History of New England*, I, 230.
11. Quoted in Captain Frederick Marryat, *Diary in America* (Philadelphia, 1839), I, 125-26.
12. Andrew Burnaby, *Travels Through the Middle Settlements in North-America* (London, 1775), 144-45; Bernard, *Retrospections of America*, 89. See also H. R. Stiles, *Bundling, Its Origin, Progress and Decline* (Albany, 1869).
13. Quoted in James Truslow Adams, *Provincial Society* (*A History of American Life*, II) (New York, 1936), 159.
14. Sydney George Fisher, *Men, Women and Manners in Colonial Times* (Philadelphia, 1898), I, 287*ff*.
15. Knight, *Private Journal* (Albany, 1865), 52-53.
16. Samuel Sewall, *Diary* (Van Doren edition), 163.
17. Ebenezer Cook, *The Sot-Weed Factor* (B. C. Steiner, editor), *Maryland Historical Society Fund Publications*, No. 36 (1900), 22.
18. Alice Morse Earle, *Colonial Dames and Goodwives* (Boston, 1895), 207-208; Stannard, *Colonial Virginia*, 153, 258-59.

19. Philip Vickers Fithian, *Journal and Letters* (Princeton, 1900), 42-43.
20. See Samuel Eliot Morison, *Three Centuries of Harvard* (Cambridge, 1936), 121-22.
21. George Francis Dow, *Every Day Life in the Massachusetts Bay Colony* (Boston, 1935), 112-14.
22. *Ibid.*, 114 for instances of these sports; Singleton, *Social New York Under the Georges*, 267; Alice Morse Earle, *Customs and Fashions in Old New England* (New York, 1893), 237; Martha J. Lamb, *History of the City of New York* (2 vols., New York, 1877-80), II, 453; J. Thomas Scharf and Thompson Westcott, *History of Philadelphia* (Philadelphia, 1884), II, 939ff; Jennie Holliman, *American Sports 1785-1835* (Durham, North Carolina, 1931), 127.
23. William Winterbotham, *An Historical View of the United States* (New York, 1796), II, 17; Earle, *Customs and Fashions*, 19.
24. Quoted in Albert Bushnell Hart, *Commonwealth History of Massachusetts* (5 vols., New York, 1927-30), II, 280.
25. William B. Bentley, *Diary* (Salem, 1905), I, 254.
26. Edward Channing, *A History of the United States*, I (New York, 1905), 536.
27. Daniel Denton, *A Brief Description of New York* (London, 1670), in William Gowans, *Biblioteca Americana* (New York, 1845), 3-4.
28. Alice Morse Earle, *Colonial Days in Old New York* (New York, 1896), 20; Herbert Ingraham Priestley, *The Coming of the White Man* (*A History of American Life*, I) (New York, 1930), 338-39.
29. Stannard, *Colonial Virginia*, 257.
30. Thomas J. Wertenbaker, *The First Americans* (*A History of American Life*, II) (New York, 1929), 263.
31. Hugh Jones, *The Present State of Virginia* (London, 1724; reprinted New York, 1865), 48.
32. Bernard, *Retrospections of America*, 155-56.
33. Elkanah Watson, *Men and Times of the Revolution* (New York, 1856), 262.
34. Jones, *The Present State of Virginia*, 48.
35. Marquis de Chastellux, *Travels in North America* (New York, 1827), 293.
36. Ruth E. Painter, "Tavern Amusements in Eighteenth Century America," *Americana*, XI (1916), 92ff. See also Edward Field, *The Colonial Tavern* (Providence, 1897).
37. John Adams, *Diary*, in *Works* (10 vols., Boston, 1850-56), II, 125.
38. Quoted in Earle, *Customs and Fashions*, 240.
39. Quoted in Lamb, *History of the City of New York*, II, 465.
40. Earle, *Customs and Fashions*, 238.
41. *Ibid.*, 163.
42. Winterbotham, *An Historical View of the United States*, II, 17.
43. Stannard, *Colonial Virginia*, 141.
44. Burnaby, *Travels* (reprint New York, 1904), 57-58.
45. Bernard, *Retrospections of America*, 208-209.
46. Dow, *Every Day Life*, 115.
47. Samuel Sewall, *Diary*, *Massachusetts Historical Society Collections*, Ser. 5, Vol. VII, 1.

NOTES 405

48. R. W. G. Vail, "Random Notes on the History of the Early American Circus," *Proceedings of the American Antiquarian Society*, April, 1933 (reprint, Worcester, 1934), 6-7; Scharf and Westcott, *History of Philadelphia*, II, 864; Odell, *Annals of the New York Stage*, I, 10.
49. Earle, *Customs and Fashions*, 243; Odell, I, 18, 44.
50. Sewall, *Diary*, V, 196.
51. Odell, *Annals of the New York Stage*, I, 10.
52. *Ibid.*, I, 48-49; Singleton, *Social New York Under the Georges*, 317.
53. Scharf and Westcott, *History of Philadelphia*, II, 863.
54. Dow, *Every Day Life*, 117.
55. Odell, *Annals of the New York Stage*, I, 23-24, 27, 30.
56. Scharf and Westcott, *History of Philadelphia*, II, 950.
57. *The Pope's Kingdom*, Book IV, translated from the Latin of Thomas Neogeorgus by Barnaby Googe, 1570, quoted in Joseph Strutt, *The Sports and Pastimes of the People of England* (London, 1831), lv.

CHAPTER III

The Colonial Aristocracy

1. John Adams, *Works*, II, 59.
2. *Ibid.*, II, 62, 10, 289.
3. *Quaint Advertisements*, Old Times Series, No. 4.
4. John Quincy Adams, *Life in a New England Town* (Boston, 1903), 46.
5. *Ibid.*, 77, 97.
6. *Ibid.*, 88, 91, 78.
7. Joseph Bennett, *Diary*, *Proceedings of the Massachusetts Historical Society*, 1861, 125.
8. Quoted in Justin Winsor, *Memorial History of Boston* (3 vols., Boston, 1880-81), I, 458.
9. Bennett, *Diary*, 125.
10. Dr. Alexander Hamilton, *Itinerarium* (A. B. Hart, editor) (St. Louis, 1907), 178-79.
11. Captain Francis Goelet, *Journal, New England Historical and Genealogical Register*, XXIV (1870), 53.
12. Anne Hulton, *Letters of a Loyalist Lady* (Cambridge, 1927), *passim*.
13. Walter Tittle, *Colonial Holidays* (New York, 1910), 28.
14. Marquis de Chastellux, *Travels in North America* (New York, 1827), 334-35.
15. Quoted in Winsor, *Memorial History of Boston*, I, 479.
16. Charles Warren, *Jacobin and Junto* (Cambridge, 1931), 20.
17. *Ibid.*, 26.
18. O. G. Sonneck, *Early Concert-Life in America* (Leipzig, 1907), 19, 250, 253.
19. Peter Kalm, quoted in Martha J. Lamb, *History of the City of New York* (2 vols., New York, 1877-80), II, 633.
20. J. F. Watson, *Annals of New York* (Philadelphia, 1846), 264.
21. Lamb, *History of the City of New York*, II, 633*ff.*
22. Andrew Burnaby, *Travels Through the Middle Settlements in North-America* (London, 1775), 114.

23. Sarah Kemble Knight, *Private Journal* (Albany, 1865), 70-71.
24. Alexander Macraby, quoted in Alice Morse Earle, *Colonial Dames and Goodwives* (Boston, 1895), 220.
25. Alice Morse Earle, *Colonial Days in Old New York* (New York, 1896), 220-21.
26. *Ibid.*, 221.
27. Esther Singleton, *Social New York Under the Georges* (New York, 1902), 265-66.
28. John Sharp, *A Journal of My Life-Exteriour,* in *Pennsylvania Magazine of History and Biography,* XL (1916), 420, 425.
29. Quoted in Singleton, *Social New York Under the Georges,* 303. See also George C. D. Odell, *Annals of the New York Stage* (New York, 1927–) I, 27.
30. Singleton, *Social New York Under the Georges,* 307, 308.
31. Quoted in Earle, *Colonial Days in Old New York,* 216.
32. *New York Gazette,* January 6-13, 1735-36, quoted in Odell, *Annals of the New York Stage,* I, 17. See also Sonneck, *Early Concert-Life,* 159-72.
33. Foster Rhea Dulles, *Eastward Ho* (Boston, 1930), 137.
34. Odell, *Annals of the New York Stage,* I, 5-7, 10-11, 21. For further discussion see Charles L. Daly, *The First Theatre in America;* Oscar L. Wegelin, *The Beginnings of the Drama in America.*
35. Odell, *Annals of the New York Stage,* I, 32ff.
36. *Ibid.*, 114-15.
37. *New York Gazette,* quoted in Watson, *Annals of New York,* 264.
38. Quoted in Odell, *Annals of the New York Stage,* I, 111. See also William Dunlap, *History of the American Theatre* (London, 1833), 51.
39. Odell, *Annals of the New York Stage,* I, 110-45 *passim;* Dunlap, *History of the American Theatre,* 51ff; Singleton, *Social New York Under the Georges,* 272-95; O. G. Sonneck, *Early Opera in America* (Boston, 1915), 77ff.
40. Burnaby, *Travels,* 31.
41. Marquis de Chastellux, quoted in George Morgan, *Patrick Henry* (Philadelphia, 1929), 55.
42. Philip Vickers Fithian, *Journal and Letters* (Princeton, 1900), 50, 296.
43. *Ibid.*, 202.
44. *Ibid.*, 58, 143, 144, 181, 218.
45. *Ibid.*, 59.
46. *Ibid.*, 223-24.
47. *Ibid.*, 96, 97, 185, 192-93.
48. George Washington, *Diaries* (4 vols., Boston, 1925), I, 299ff.
49. *Ibid.*, I, 126.
50. Sarah N. Randolph, *The Domestic Life of Thomas Jefferson* (New York, 1871), 26ff.
51. Paul Leicester Ford, *Washington and the Theatre, Dunlap Society Publications,* New Series, No. 8 (New York, 1899), 20-22.
52. *Ibid.*, 5-9; Odell, *Annals of the New York Stage,* I, 9, 20; Lyon G. Tyler, *Williamsburg* (Richmond, 1907), 224-26; Eola Willis, *The Charleston Stage in the Eighteenth Century* (Columbia, 1924), 25-26.
53. Tyler, *Williamsburg,* 230.

54. Josiah Quincy, *Memoir of the Life of Josiah Quincy, jun.* (Boston, 1825), 96.
55. Willis, *The Charleston Stage*, 59-77.
56. Alexis de Tocqueville, *Democracy in America* (Boston, 1876), I, 243.
57. Hamilton, *Itinerarium*, 50.
58. Burnaby, *Travels*, 87.
59. James Truslow Adams, *Provincial Society* (*A History of American Life*, II) (New York, 1936), 261-62; Singleton, *Social New York Under the Georges*, 311.
60. Carl Bridenbaugh, "Colonial Newport as a Summer Resort," *Rhode Island Historical Society*, XXVI (1933), I, 4.
61. *Ibid.*, 14, 16-18.
62. Quoted in George O. Willard, *History of the Providence Stage* (Providence, 1891), 8-9.
63. *Ibid.*, 14-15.
64. Quoted in Ford, *Washington and the Theatre*, 24.

CHAPTER IV

The Frontier

1. Frances Trollope, *Domestic Manners of the Americans* (London, 1832), I, 248.
2. William Faux, *Memorable Days in America* (London, 1823), in Reuben Gold Thwaites, *Early Western Travels 1748-1846* (Cleveland, 1907), XI, 210.
3. John James Audubon, *Delineations of American Scenery and Character* (1834; reprinted New York, 1926), 59-62; John Woods, *Two Years Residence in the Illinois Country* (London, 1822), in Thwaites, *Early Western Travels*, X, 249, 318; John Bradbury, *Travels in the Interior of America* (London, 1819), in *ibid.*, V, 280; Thomas D. Clark, *The Rampaging Frontier* (Indianapolis, 1939), 31.
4. David Crockett, *An Account of Colonel Crockett's Tour Written by Himself* (Philadelphia, 1837), 176*ff*. See also Edmund Flagg, *The Far West* (New York, 1838), in Thwaites, *Early Western Travels*, XXVI, 360-61; William N. Blane, *An Excursion Through the United States* (London, 1824), 302; Baynard Rush Hall, *The New Purchase* (New York, 1855), 104-12.
5. John Bernard, *Retrospections of America 1797-1811* (New York, 1877), 181.
6. H. M. Brackenridge, *Recollections of Persons and Places in the West* (Philadelphia, 1868), 60-63.
7. Albert Beveridge, *Abraham Lincoln* (Boston, 1928), I, 111.
8. Samuel L. Clemens (Mark Twain), *Life on the Mississippi* (1874) (Hartford, 1899), 32-33.
9. Timothy Flint, *Recollections of the Last Ten Years* (Boston, 1826), 98.
10. Thomas Ashe, *Travels in America* (London, 1808), quoted in John A. Krout, *Annals of American Sport* (*Pageant of America*, XV) (New Haven, 1929), 28.

11. William H. Herndon and Jesse W. Weik, *Life of Lincoln* (New York, 1896), I, 108-9.
12. Quoted in Marquis James, *Andrew Jackson: the Border Captain* (Indianapolis, 1933), 19. See also James Parton, *Life of Andrew Jackson* (New York, 1860), I, 253.
13. Faux, *Memorable Days in America*, in Thwaites, *Early Western Travels*, XI, 196; Woods, *Two Years Residence*, in *ibid.*, X, 264, 346; Richard Flower, *Letters from Lexington and Illinois* (London, 1819), in *ibid.*, X, 125.
14. Bessie Louise Pierce, *A History of Chicago* (New York, 1937), I, 208.
15. Flower, *Letters from Lexington and Illinois*, in Thwaites, *Early Western Travels*, X, 300.
16. Crockett, *An Account of Colonel Crockett's Tour*, 34.
17. Audubon, *Delineations of American Scenery*, 244.
18. Everett Dick, *The Sod-House Frontier, 1854-1890* (New York, 1937), 75, 266, 281.
19. William H. Milburn, *The Rifle, Axe and Saddle-Bags* (New York, 1857), 46-51; Hall, *The New Purchase*, 426-28.
20. Beveridge, *Abraham Lincoln*, I, 92.
21. Bernard De Voto, *Mark Twain's America* (Boston, 1932), 104ff.
22. James Stuart, *Three Years in North America* (New York, 1833), II, 174-75.
23. James Flint, *Letters from America* (Edinburgh, 1822), in Thwaites, *Early Western Travels*, IX, 261-62.
24. Peter Cartwright, *Autobiography* (New York, 1857), 121.
25. James B. Finley, *Autobiography* (Cincinnati, 1854), 364.
26. Cartwright, *Autobiography*, 48.
27. Herndon and Weik, *Life of Lincoln*, 11-12.

CHAPTER V

A Changing Society

1. Timothy Dwight, *Travels in New England and New York* (London, 1823), IV, 343-44.
2. Bureau of the Census, as cited in *Statistical Abstract*, 1935 (Washington, 1936), 6.
3. Michael Chevalier, *Society, Manners and Politics in the United States* (Boston, 1839), 473.
4. Quoted in George B. Cutten, *The Threat of Leisure* (New Haven, 1926).
5. T. L. Nichols, *Forty Years of American Life* (London, 1874), 206.
6. Charles Lyell, *A Second Visit to United States* (New York, 1849), quoted in Allan Nevins, *American Social History as Recorded by British Travellers* (New York, 1932), 333. See also Charles Dickens, *American Notes* (Fireside Edition), 68, 99-100; Frances Trollope, *Domestic Manners of the Americans* (London, 1832), II, 82, 142, 193; Basil Hall, *Travels in North America* (London, 1829), 258; Thomas Hamilton, *Men and Manners* (Philadelphia, 1833), 70; Frances J. Grund, *The Americans* (Boston, 1837), 119.

7. Trollope, *Domestic Manners of the Americans*, II, 142, 193.
8. Dickens, *American Notes*, 170.
9. *Ibid.*, 99, 100.
10. Quoted in Arthur A. Hornblow, *History of the American Theatre* (Philadelphia, 1919), I, 24.
11. Henry Ward Beecher, *Addresses to Young Men* (1844) (Philadelphia, 1893), 242, 253, 259. See also Dickens, *American Notes*, 68; Grund, *The Americans*, 120; Alfred Bunn, *Old England and New England* (London, 1853), II, 110-11.
12. See Edward Channing, *A History of the United States* (6 vols., New York, 1905-25), V, 175*ff*; John Bach McMaster, *History of the People of the United States* (8 vols., New York, 1883-1913), IV, 531*ff*; John A. Krout, *Origins of Prohibition* (New York, 1925).
13. Anne Royall, *Sketches of History, Life and Manners of the United States* (New Haven, 1826), 299.
14. *Voice of Industry*, March 20, 1846, quoted in Norman Ware, *The Industrial Worker, 1840-60* (Boston, 1924), 127. See also John R. Commons, *A Documentary History of American Industrial Society* (Cleveland, 1910), VI, 97.
15. Henry Wansey, *An Excursion to the United States* (Salisbury, 1798), 24; McMaster, *History of the People of the United States*, V, 575.
16. Emerson Davis, *The Half Century* (Boston, 1851), 188.
17. Nichols, *Forty Years of American Life*, 43.
18. *Democratic Press*, June 14, 1827, quoted in Commons, *Documentary History*, V, 80.
19. *The American Lyceum* (Boston, 1829), reprint, *Old South Leaflets*, VI, No. 139; Cecil B. Hayes, "The American Lyceum," Bureau of U. S. Education Bulletin No. 12 (1932), 7-9, 22.
20. Philip Hone, *Diary* (edited by Allan Nevins, New York, 1927), 515, 572-73.
21. Chevalier, *Society, Manners and Politics*, 128-29.
22. Harriet H. Robinson, *Loom and Spindle* (New York, 1898), 75.
23. Dickens, *American Notes*, 78*ff*. See also Lucy Larcom, "Among Lowell Mill Girls," *Atlantic Monthly*, XLVIII (1881), 600; "Leisure for Mill Girls," *Lowell Offering*, 11, 65*ff*; Basil Hall, *Travels in North America*, 287; David Crockett, *Life of* (Philadelphia, 1860), 92; James Silk Buckingham, *The Eastern and Western States of America* (London, 1842), I, 295*ff*.
24. *Lowell Offering*, I, 5.
25. George Combe, *Notes on the United States* (Edinburgh, 1841), I, 120.
26. See Frances Wright D'Arusmont, *Views of Society and Manners in America* (New York, 1821), 120.
27. Achille Murat, *A Moral and Political Sketch of the United States* (London, 1833), 356. See also Combe, *Notes on the United States*, II, 126; Trollope, *Domestic Manners of the Americans*, I, 166, 214, 216; Alexander Mackay, *The Western World* (London, 1850), I, 228.
28. Hamilton, *Men and Manners*, 81.
29. *Spalding Skating Guide* (New York, 1862), 51; Arthur Charles Cole, *The Irrepressible Conflict* (*A History of American Life*, VII) (New York, 1934), 189.

30. *Lowell Offering*, I, 61.
31. Basil Hall, *Travels in North America*, 195, 294; Mrs. Basil Hall, *The Aristocratic Journey* (New York, 1931), 125.
32. James Stuart, *Three Years in North America* (London, 1833), I, 497.
33. Charles William Day, *Hints on Etiquette* (New York, 1843).
34. Captain Frederick Marryat, *A Diary in America* (Philadelphia, 1839), quoted in Dixon Wecter, *The Saga of American Society* (New York, 1937), 317.
35. Trollope, *Domestic Manners of the Americans*, I, 189.

CHAPTER VI

The Theatre Comes of Age

1. William Davidge, *Footlight Flashes* (New York, 1867), 202.
2. *Arcturus*, II (1841), 29, quoted in Frank Luther Mott, *A History of American Magazines* (New York and Cambridge, 1930–), I (1741-1850), 430.
3. John Bach McMaster, *History of the People of the United States* (8 vols., New York, 1883-1913), VII, 92*ff.*
4. Reese D. James, *Old Drury of Philadelphia* (Philadelphia, 1932), 24, 66; George C. D. Odell, *Annals of the New York Stage* (New York, 1927–), II, 460; Henry Austin Clapp, *Reminiscences of a Dramatic Critic* (Boston, 1902), 134.
5. George M. Edward, *Some Earlier Public Amusements of Rochester* (Rochester, 1894), 4; John Bernard, *Retrospections of America 1797-1811* (New York, 1877), 318; Joseph B. Felt, *Annals of Salem* (Salem, 1845), II, 43-45.
6. See N. M. Ludlow, *Dramatic Life as I Found It* (St. Louis, 1880); Frances C. Wemyss, *Chronology of the American Stage from 1752 to 1852* (New York, c. 1852), 11, 14; and article on Samuel Drake in *Dictionary of American Biography.*
7. Tyrone Power, *Impressions of America* (London, 1836), I, 66, 87, 123, 141, 210, 351-52; II, 172, 191.
8. Carl Russell Fish, *The Rise of the Common Man* (*A History of American Life*, VI) (New York, 1937), 145.
9. Odell, *Annals of the New York Stage*, IV, 603; James, *Old Drury of Philadelphia*, 40-41; Arthur A. Hornblow, *History of the American Theatre* (Philadelphia, 1919), II, 26, 161; William G. B. Carson, *The Theatre on the Frontier* (Chicago, 1932), 180.
10. *New York Daily Advertiser*, quoted in Odell, *Annals of the New York Stage*, II, 8. See also *ibid.*, IV, 603; Hornblow, *History of the American Theatre*, II, 77, 443; Clapp, *Reminiscences*, 366, 493; Arthur Herman Wilson, *A History of the Philadelphia Theatre, 1835 to 1855* (Philadelphia, 1935), 38; William B. Wood, *Personal Recollections of the Stage* (Philadelphia, 1855), 299; Alfred Bunn, *Old England and New England* (London, 1853), II, 105.
11. James Silk Buckingham (1838), quoted in Dixon Wecter, *The Saga of American Society* (New York, 1937), 466.
12. Hornblow, *History of the American Theatre*, II, 143.

13. T. Allston Brown, *A History of the New York Stage* (New York, 1903), I, 415-18; Philip Hone, *Diary* (edited by Allan Nevins, New York, 1927), 870; Harry Watkins, *Journal* (*One Man in His Time*, edited by Maud and Otis Skinner, Philadelphia, 1938), 73-74.
14. Wemyss, *Chronology of the American Stage*, 178.
15. Richard Grant White, quoted in Hornblow, *History of the American Theatre*, II, 167-68.
16. Frances Trollope, *Domestic Manners of the Americans* (London, 1832), I, 187; II, 162-63. See also Odell, *Annals of the New York Stage*, VII, 655.
17. *New York Herald*, November 2, 1864, quoted in Odell, *Annals of the New York Stage*, VII, 658-59.
18. Richard Grant White, quoted in Hornblow, *History of the American Theatre*, II, 167-68.
19. Quoted in Montrose J. Moses and John Mason Brown, *The American Theatre as Seen by Its Critics 1752-1934* (New York, 1934), 40ff.
20. James, *Old Drury of Philadelphia*, 31; Odell, *Annals of the New York Stage*, II, 517; V, 485; III, 183; VII, 236-37.
21. William Dunlap, *History of the American Theatre* (London, 1833), 407ff.
22. Carson, *The Theatre on the Frontier*, 309.
23. *New York Herald*, September 19, 1838. See also *Plain Dealer*, December 3, 1836, and Francis Joseph Daly, *The Life of Augustin Daly* (New York, 1917), quoted in Hornblow, *History of the American Theatre*, II, 168.
24. Joseph Jefferson, *Autobiography* (New York, 1889), 54, 30.
25. Ludlow, *Dramatic Life as I Found It*, 64-68.
26. Sol Smith, *Theatrical Management in the West and South for Thirty Years* (New York, 1868), 79.
27. Watkins, *Journal*, 67, 103, 39.
28. *Ibid.*, 141.
29. *Ibid.*, 55-56; Clapp, *Reminiscences*, 221-36, 278.
30. Watkins, *Journal*, 83.
31. Carson, *The Theatre on the Frontier*, 311, 319, 328-30; Wilson, *A History of the Philadelphia Theatre*, 18-19, 130-31; Douglas L. Hunt, "The Nashville Theatre, 1830-1840," *Birmingham-Southern College Bulletin*, XXVIII, No. 3 (1935), 54; Watkins, *Journal*, 151.
32. Watkins, *Journal*, 230.
33. Program collection, New York Public Library.
34. Watkins, *Journal*, 68; Odell, *Annals of the New York Stage*, V, 578.
35. *New York Herald*, September 3, 1852, quoted in Moses and Brown, *The American Theatre*, 73-75.
36. Quoted in Meade Minnigerode, *The Fabulous Forties* (New York, 1924), 174-77.
37. "Durang's History of the Philadelphia Stage," *Philadelphia Sunday Dispatch*, May 17, 1854, quoted in James, *Old Drury of Philadelphia*, 26-27; Odell, *Annals of the New York Stage*, III, 21, 215, IV, 163.
38. Odell, *Annals of the New York Stage*, IV, 614.
39. Achille Murat, *A Moral and Political Sketch of the United States* (London, 1833), 367. See also *Appleton's Journal*, VIII, 580.

40. *New York Herald,* May 15, 1840, in Odell, *Annals of the New York Stage,* IV, 359.
41. Hornblow, *History of the American Theatre,* II, 143.
42. Hone, *Diary,* 480.
43. Lawrence Hutton, *Curiosities of the American Stage* (London, 1891), 157-58, 165; Odell, *Annals of the New York Stage,* V, 529*ff.* See also Olive Logan, *Apropos of Women and the Theatre* (New York, 1869), 134-37; Hornblow, *History of the American Theatre,* II, 101.
44. Odell, *Annals of the New York Stage,* V, 378*ff,* 401*ff.*
45. *New York Tribune,* December 1, 1847; *New York Herald,* March 1, 1848.
46. Quoted in Minnigerode, *The Fabulous Forties,* 144.
47. Quoted in Mary C. Crawford, *The Romance of the American Theatre* (Boston, 1925), 450-51.
48. Odell, *Annals of the New York Stage,* IV, 664.
49. *Ibid.,* V, 495.
50. Moses and Brown, *The American Theatre,* 70-71.
51. Hone, *Diary,* 573.
52. Odell, *Annals of the New York Stage,* II, 466; Hornblow, *History of the American Theatre,* I, 299.
53. Mott, *A History of American Magazines,* II, 198.
54. Quoted in James E. Murdoch, *The Stage* (Philadelphia, 1880), 429.

CHAPTER VII

Mr. Barnum Shows the Way

1. M. R. Werner, *Barnum* (New York, 1927), 52.
2. Broadside advertisement, New York Public Library.
3. Werner, *Barnum,* 65.
4. "Sights and Wonders in New York" (pamphlet, New York, 1849); P. T. Barnum, *Life . . . Written by Himself* (New York, 1855), 225.
5. Philip Hone, *Diary* (edited by Allan Nevins, New York, 1927), 12-13, 795.
6. Barnum, *Life,* 148*ff,* 242*ff,* 350*ff.*
7. George C. D. Odell, *Annals of New York Stage* (New York, 1927–), IV, 669. See also Harry Watkins, *Journal (One Man in His Time,* edited by Maud and Otis Skinner, Philadelphia, 1938), 225*ff.*
8. Watkins, *Journal,* 91.
9. Barnum, *Life,* 343. See also contemporary magazine comments in Frank Luther Mott, *A History of American Magazines* (New York and Cambridge, 1930–), II, 194-95.
10. N. P. Willis, *Memoranda of the Life of Jenny Lind* (Philadelphia, 1851), 95-97.
11. *Ibid.,* 126.
12. Barnum, *Life,* 343.
13. William Davidge, *Footlight Flashes* (New York, 1867), 127.
14. Lawrence Hutton, *Curiosities of the American Stage* (London, 1891), 124-26; Carl Wittke, *Tambo and Bones* (Durham, N. C., 1930), 45; Francis Pendleton Gaines, *The Southern Plantation* (New York, 1924), 100-101.

15. Hutton, *Curiosities*, 115-19; N. M. Ludlow, *Dramatic Life as I Found It* (St. Louis, 1880), 392-93; Robert P. Nevin, "Stephen C. Foster and Negro Minstrelsy," *Atlantic Monthly*, XX (1867), 608.

16. Joseph Jefferson, *Autobiography* (New York, 1889), 7.

17. *Holden's Dollar Magazine*, I (1848), quoted in Mott, *History of American Magazines*, I, 433.

18. Wittke, *Tambo and Bones*, 57, 58-60; Davidge, *Footlight Flashes*, 127-28; Ralph Keeler, *Vagabond Adventures* (Boston, 1872), 132.

19. See Dailey Paskman and Sigmund Spaeth, *"Gentlemen, Be Seated!"* (New York, 1928), 47ff.

20. Quoted in Albert J. Beveridge, *Abraham Lincoln*, II, 536, 597. See also Wittke, *Tambo and Bones*, 209; and Nevin, *loc. cit.*, 608.

21. Earl Chapin May, *The Circus from Rome to Ringling* (New York, 1932), 25-27; W. C. Coup, *Sawdust and Spangles* (Chicago, 1901), 141; R. W. G. Vail, "Random Notes on the History of the Early American Circus," *Proceedings of the American Antiquarian Society*, April, 1933 (reprint; Worcester, 1934), 17.

22. Vail, *loc. cit.*, 29; Joseph B. Felt, *Annals of Salem* (Salem, 1845), II, 92.

23. Isaac J. Greenwood, *The Circus* (New York, 1898), 113-14.

24. *Ibid.*, 64ff; Vail, *loc. cit.*, 35; Barnum, *Life*, 177ff; Gil Robinson, *Old Wagon Show Days* (Cincinnati, 1925), 20.

25. Greenwood, *The Circus*, 64ff; Vail, *loc. cit.*, 64-68; Odell, *Annals of the New York Stage*, II, 491.

26. Vail, *loc. cit.*, 32-40; Coup, *Sawdust and Spangles*, 140-41.

27. E. E. Calkins, *They Broke the Prairie* (New York, 1937), 245; Bessie Louise Pierce, *A History of Chicago* (New York, 1937), I, 209; Greenwood, *The Circus*, 116; May, *The Circus*, 77-79; Vail, *loc. cit.*, 35.

28. Edmund Flagg, *The Far West* (New York, 1838), in Thwaites, *Early Western Travels*, XXVI, 225.

29. Hiram Fuller, *Belle Brittan on Tour* (New York, 1858), 160.

30. Barnum, *Life*, 348-49.

CHAPTER VIII

The Beginning of Spectator Sports

1. *Atlantic Monthly*, I (1858), 881.

2. Jennie Holliman, *American Sports 1785-1835* (Durham, N. C., 1931), 158. See also Philip Hone, *Diary* (edited by Allan Nevins, New York, 1927), 156.

3. James Silk Buckingham, *The Eastern and Western States of America* (London, 1842), I, 22.

4. P. T. Barnum, *Life . . . Written by Himself* (New York, 1855), 352-55.

5. *Spirit of the Times*, November 8, 1856.

6. *Frank Leslie's Illustrated Newspaper*, June 28, 1856.

7. William N. Blane, *An Excursion Through the United States* (London, 1824), 315-17; Josiah Quincy, *Figures of the Past* (Boston, 1883), 97; Charles H. Haswell, *Reminiscences of an Octogenarian of the City of New York* (New York, 1896), 140-44. See also Ralph Henry

Gabriel, *The Evolution of Long Island* (New Haven, 1921), 169; and Max Farrand, "The Great Race—Eclipse Against the World," *Scribner's*, LXX (1921), 457-64.

8. *New York Herald*, May 13, 1845. See also article on William Ransome Johnson, "Napoleon of the Turf," in *Dictionary of American Biography*, and Gabriel, *Evolution of Long Island*, 169.
9. Hone, *Diary*, 601.
10. Marquis James, *Andrew Jackson: The Border Captain* (Indianapolis, 1933), 118.
11. Quoted in Everett Dick, *The Sod-House Frontier, 1854-1890* (New York, 1937), 279.
12. *Spirit of the Times*, November 1, 1856.
13. Hiram Woodruff, *The Trotting Horse of America* (New York, 1871), 283; Dwight Akers, *Drivers Up* (New York, 1938), 73-89.
14. *Frank Leslie's Illustrated Newspaper*, May 17, 1853, 357; Charles A. Peverelly, *The Book of American Pastimes* (New York, 1866), 164, 249.
15. Peverelly, *Book of American Pastimes*, 244ff; Holliman, *American Sports*, 158; *Frank Leslie's Illustrated Newspaper*, April 28, 1860, March 17, 1860; *New York Herald*, August 9, 1838, September 11, 1838.
16. Quoted (December 9, 1829) in Holliman, *American Sports*, 158.
17. *Frank Leslie's Illustrated Newspaper*, July 13, 1857, 28.
18. *New York Clipper*, October 18, 1856, July 18, 1857.
19. *Spirit of the Times*, July 20, 1839.
20. *Ibid.*, July 13, 1837.
21. Hone, *Diary*, 156-57; Holliman, *American Sports*, 154.
22. *New York Clipper*, April 26, May 31, June 28, 1856.
23. *Niles' Weekly Register*, XIII (1817), 128, quoted in Holliman, *American Sports*, 143.
24. Hone, *Diary*, 620.
25. *Ibid.*, 620.
26. *Spirit of the Times*, April 7, March 17, 1860; Holliman, *American Sports*, 143ff; Alexander Johnston, *Ten—And Out!* (New York, 1936), 24-30.
27. *Vanity Fair*, I (1860), 45, quoted in Frank Luther Mott, *A History of American Magazines* (New York and Cambridge, 1930–), II, 202.
28. *Spirit of the Times*, April 28, 1860.
29. *Ibid.*, September 1, 1860; *Cleveland Plain Dealer*, August 1, 1860, quoted in Arthur C. Cole, *The Irrepressible Conflict* (*A History of American Life*, VII) (New York, 1934), 191.

CHAPTER IX

Mid-Century

1. Philip Hone, *Diary* (edited by Allan Nevins, New York, 1927), 588.
2. *The American Farmer* (Baltimore), VI (1824-25), 271, 349. See also Arthur C. Cole, *The Irrepressible Conflict* (*A History of American Life*, VII) (New York, 1934), 190.

3. Timothy Flint, *Recollections of the Last Ten Years* (Boston, 1826), 386.
4. Francis J. Grund, *The Americans* (Boston, 1837), 323.
5. Fred A. Wilson, *Some Annals of Nahant* (Boston, 1928), 72; *New York Herald* (1853), quoted in Jefferson Williamson, *The American Hotel* (New York, 1930), 238; "Poem on the Mineral Waters of Ballston and Saratoga" (Ballston Spa, 1819). See also G. M. Davison, *The Fashionable Tour* (Saratoga Springs, 1825).
6. William Gregg, *Essays on Domestic Industry* (1845), in D. A. Tomkins, *Cotton Mill, Commercial Feature* (Charlotteville, N. C., 1899).
7. Quoted in Dixon Wecter, *The Saga of American Society* (New York, 1937), 437.
8. Flint, *Recollections*, 393-94.
9. Hone, *Diary*, 415.
10. Eliza Ripley, *Social Life in Old New Orleans* (New York, 1912), 142.
11. Achille Murat, *A Moral and Political Sketch of the United States* (London, 1833), 358.
12. Michael Chevalier, *Society, Manners and Politics in the United States* (Boston, 1839), 315-16.
13. Murat, *A Moral and Political Sketch*, 367.
14. Quoted in Meade Minnigerode, *The Fabulous Forties* (New York, 1924), 213-14.
15. Henry Wansey, *An Excursion to the United States* (Salisbury, 1798), 211.
16. Wilson, *Some Annals of Nahant*, 77.
17. James Stuart, *Three Years in North America* (London, 1833), I, 280.
18. *Frank Leslie's Illustrated Newspaper*, August 22, 1857.
19. Amelia M. Murray, *Letters from the United States* (London, 1856), I, 37, quoted in Cole, *The Irrepressible Conflict*, 201.
20. *New York Herald*, July 19, 1853, quoted in Williamson, *The American Hotel*, 236-37.
21. Joseph Doddridge, *Notes on the Settlement and Indian Wars* (Albany, 1876), 201.
22. William Makepeace Thackeray, *Roundabout Papers* (London, 1863), 273. See also Mark Twain, *Life on the Mississippi*.
23. Herbert Asbury, *Sucker's Progress* (New York, 1938), 229.
24. *Ibid.*, 232.
25. Thomas Clark, *The Rampaging Frontier* (Indianapolis, 1939), 244.
26. George H. Devol, *Forty Years a Gambler on the Mississippi* (New York, 1926), 27, 37, 43.
27. Harry Watkins, *Journal* (*One Man in His Time*, edited by Maud and Otis Skinner), 162-63.
28. E. E. Calkins, *They Broke the Prairie* (New York, 1937), 243-45.
29. *New York Herald*, February 21, 1848; George C. D. Odell, *Annals of the New York Stage* (New York, 1927—), IV, 43, 49. See also Cole, *The Irrepressible Conflict*, 239.
30. Everett Dick, *The Sod-House Frontier, 1854-1890* (New York, 1937), 285, 286.
31. Thomas Nelson Page, *Social Life in Old Virginia* (New York, 1897), 107.

32. A. DePuy Van Buren, *Jottings of a Year's Sojourn in the South* (Battle Creek, Mich., 1859), 88.
33. Henry Barnard, "The South Atlantic States," *Maryland Historical Magazine*, XIII, 295ff, 318. See also U. B. Phillips, *Life and Labor in the Old South* (Boston, 1929), 229, 335.
34. Susan Dabney Smedes, *Memorials of a Southern Planter* (Baltimore, 1887), 180.
35. Herbert Ravenel Sass, *A Carolina Rice Plantation in the Fifties* (New York, 1936).
36. *Agriculture of the United States in 1860* (Eighth Census), 247, quoted in Cole, *The Irrepressible Conflict*, 34.
37. Van Buren, *Jottings of a Year's Sojourn in the South*, 118.
38. U. B. Phillips, *American Negro Slavery* (New York, 1918), 314-15.
39. *American Historical Review*, III, 41.
40. D. R. Hundley, *Social Relations in Our Southern States* (New York, 1860), 263.
41. Phillips, *Life and Labor in the Old South*, 339ff.
42. Guion Griffis Johnson, *Ante-Bellum North Carolina* (Chapel Hill, 1937), 91-104, 180.
43. *Ibid.*, 111.
44. Augustus Baldwin Longstreet, *Georgia Scenes* (New York, 1840), 14, 119.
45. Frederick Law Olmstead, *The Cotton Kingdom* (New York, 1862), II, 73.
46. Frances Anne Kemble, *Journal* (Philadelphia, 1835), I, 83-84n.
47. Samuel Dexter Ward, *Diary, New York Historical Society Quarterly Bulletin*, XXI (1937), 114-15.
48. Charles Lyell, *Travels in North America* (New York, 1852), I, 58. See also Grund, *The Americans*, 323.
49. *New York Daily Tribune*, May 27, 1851, quoted in Norman Ware, *The Industrial Worker, 1840-60* (Boston, 1924), 33.
50. *New York Herald*, July 4, 1838; July 6, 1845; July 12, 1845; August 27, 1838.
51. Eric Adolphus Dime, "America's First Aeronaut," *Air Travel*, January, 1918, 214ff. See also Cole, *The Irrepressible Conflict*, 195-96.
52. Gabriel Furman, "How New York City Used to Celebrate Independence Day," *New York Historical Society Quarterly Bulletin*, July, 1937, 93-94; Charles H. Haswell, *Reminiscences of an Octogenarian of the City of New York* (New York, 1896), 62.
53. *New York Herald*, March 3, 1838; January 4, 17, 28, 1845.
54. *Frank Leslie's Illustrated Newspaper*, December 15, 1855; *New York Herald*, November 3, 1857; *New York Clipper*, June 14, 1856.
55. *New York Herald*, July 6, 1838.

CHAPTER X

Cow-Towns and Mining-Camps

1. E. C. Abbott ("Teddy Blue") and Helen H. Smith, *We Pointed Them North* (New York, 1939), 257.

2. See John A. and Alan Lomax, *Cowboy Songs* (New York, 1938).
3. William Wright (Dan De Quille), *The Big Bonanza* (Hartford, 1876), 438.
4. *Ibid.*, 29-30.
5. Allan Nevins, *The Emergence of Modern America* (*A History of American Life*, VIII) (New York, 1927), 137.
6. Samuel L. Clemens (Mark Twain), *Roughing It* (New York, 1899), II, 27-28.
7. Philip Ashton Rollins, *The Cowboy* (New York, 1922), 80.
8. Herbert Asbury, *Sucker's Progress* (New York, 1938), 316.
9. A. K. McClure, *Three Thousand Miles Through the Rockies* (Philadelphia, 1869), 412, 414.
10. Wells Drury, *An Editor on the Comstock Lode* (New York, 1936), 88.
11. McClure, *Three Thousand Miles Through the Rockies*, 424-25.
12. Drury, *An Editor on the Comstock Lode*, 91.
13. Quoted *ibid.*, 299-300.
14. Constance Rourke, *Troupers of the Gold Coast* (New York, 1928), 57.
15. *Ibid.*, 43.
16. *Ibid., passim.*
17. Drury, *An Editor on the Comstock Lode*, 54-61; Bernard De Voto, *Mark Twain's America* (Boston, 1932), 123-26.
18. George D. Lyman, *The Saga of the Comstock Lode* (New York, 1934), 270ff.
19. Rollins, *The Cowboy*, 40.
20. *Ibid.*, 174ff; Hough, *The Story of the Cowboy*, 225ff.
21. Lomax, *Cowboy Songs*, xvi.
22. Rollins, *The Cowboy*, 172; Lomax, *Cowboy Songs*, 5; Abbott and Smith, *We Pointed Them North*, 260.
23. Rollins, *The Cowboy*, 174-89; Hough, *The Story of the Cowboy*, 221-36.
24. Hough, *The Story of the Cowboy*, 238.
25. Rollins, *The Cowboy*, 296-97.
26. Hough, *The Story of the Cowboy*, 261.
27. Abbott and Smith, *We Pointed Them North*, 123.
28. *Ibid.*, 126.
29. *Ibid.*, 9.
30. Hough, *The Story of the Cowboy*, 252-53.
31. Robert M. Wright, *Dodge City* (Dodge City, 1913), 149.
32. Lomax, *Cowboy Songs*, 169.

CHAPTER XI

The Rise of Sports

1. *The Nation*, III, 115.
2. Pamphlet material on James L. Plimpton, New York Public Library.
3. Arthur C. Cole, *The Irrepressible Conflict* (*A History of American Life*, VII) (New York, 1934), 187. See also *Lowell Offering*, I, 61.
4. Quoted in D. R. Hundley, *Social Relations in Our Southern States* (New York, 1860), 41.

5. Thomas Wentworth Higginson, "Saints and Their Bodies," *Atlantic Monthly,* I (1858), 587.
6. *New York Clipper,* July 5, 1856; Edward Everett, *Orations and Speeches on Various Occasions* (Boston, 1856-72), III, 407, quoted in Cole, *The Irrepressible Conflict,* 188.
7. *Harper's Monthly,* XIII (1856), 642, 646.
8. *Atlantic Monthly,* I (1858), 881.
9. *New York Herald,* July 12, 1858, quoted in Cole, *The Irrepressible Conflict,* 189.
10. Frederick L. Paxson, "The Rise of Sports," *Mississippi Valley Historical Review,* IV, 143-68.
11. *Outing,* II (1883), 468.
12. *Independent,* LII (1900), 1361.
13. W. E. Baxter, *America and the Americans* (London, 1855), 99, quoted in Cole, *The Irrepressible Conflict,* 188.
14. Robert W. Henderson, "How Baseball Began," *Bulletin of New York Public Library,* XLI (1937), 288, and "Baseball and Rounders," *ibid.,* XLIII (1939), 303-14; Jane Austen, *Northanger Abbey* (Boston, 1898), 8.
15. Horatio Smith, *Festivals, Games and Amusements* (New York, 1833), 330.
16. William R. Wister, *Some Reminiscences of Cricket in Philadelphia before 1861* (Philadelphia, 1904), 6-9; Charles A. Peverelly, *The Book of American Pastimes* (New York, 1866), 529*ff; Spirit of the Times,* January 24, 1857.
17. In addition to articles by R. W. Henderson, cited above, see Ralph E. Renaud, "Baseball's Centenary," *New York Times Magazine,* June 11, 1939, 11*ff;* A. G. Spalding, *America's National Game* (New York, 1911), 19-23, 29-41; Francis C. Richter, *History and Records of Baseball* (Philadelphia, 1914), 17-31; John M. Ward, *Baseball* (Philadelphia, 1889), 9-34; George Wright, "Sketch of the National Game of Baseball," *Records of the Columbia Historical Society,* XXIII (1920), 80*ff.*
18. "By-Laws of Knickerbocker Club," in Spalding Collection, New York Public Library.
19. Quoted in Richter, *History and Records of Baseball,* 32.
20. *Spirit of the Times,* January 10, 1857; Peverelly, *The Book of American Pastimes,* 461; article on Alfred J. Reach in *Dictionary of American Biography.*
21. *Spirit of the Times,* December 27, 1856; *New York Clipper,* July 19, 1856.
22. Article on Henry Wright in *Dictionary of American Biography.*
23. *Spirit of the Times,* March 24, 1860; Peverelly, *The Book of American Pastimes,* 353.
24. *Spirit of the Times,* December 6, 1856; *Frank Leslie's Illustrated Newspaper,* April 26, 1856.
25. Spalding, *America's National Game,* 71; A. H. Spink, *The National Game* (St. Louis, 1910), 3.
26. *Spirit of the Times,* July 28, October 6, September 8, 1860; Spalding, *America's National Game,* 80-81.

27. Peverelly, *The Book of American Pastimes*, 508, 337; *The Galaxy*, VI (1868), 563, and *Sports and Games*, III (1872), 112, quoted in Frank Luther Mott, *A History of American Magazines* (New York and Cambridge, 1930–), III, 217.

28. Richter, *History and Records of Baseball*, 37-39; Spalding, *America's National Game*, 137-39.

29. Spalding, *America's National Game*, 210-14; Richter, *History and Records of Baseball*, 40.

30. Samuel L. Clemens (Mark Twain), *Speeches* (1923), 145.

31. George Makepeace Towle, *American Society* (London, 1870), II, 40; *Frank Leslie's Illustrated Newspaper*, quoted in Lloyd Lewis and Henry Justin Smith, *Oscar Wilde Discovers America* (New York, 1936), 381.

32. *How to Play Field and Parlor Croquet* (1865).

33. Towle, *American Society*, II, 39.

34. *The Nation*, III, 115.

35. *Harper's Weekly*, September 13, 1879, quoted in John A. Krout, *Annals of American Sport* (*The Pageant of America*, XV) (New Haven, 1929), 164.

36. *Outing*, II, 468.

37. William Patten (editor), *The Book of Sport* (New York, 1901), 309*ff*.

38. Pamphlet material on James L. Plimpton in the New York Public Library.

39. *Spalding's Manual*, 1884.

40. *San Francisco Evening Bulletin*, January 10, 1891.

41. *Harper's Weekly*, XXXIII (1889), 463.

42. *Outing* (*The Wheelman*), I (1882), 22-29, 69-70, IX, 390; *Tribune Book of Open-Air Sports* (New York, 1887), 455; L. H. Porter, *Wheels and Wheeling* (New York, 1892), 36-96.

43. *Harper's Monthly*, July, 1881, 285.

44. *Outing*, IV, 471; Walter G. Kendall, *Four Score Years of Sport* (Boston, 1933), 79*ff*.

45. *Outing* (*The Wheelman*), I (1882), 22-29.

46. *Ibid.*, I, 57.

47. *World Almanac*, 1890, 182-84.

48. Professor Hoffman, *Tips to Tricyclists*.

49. Porter, *Wheels and Wheeling*, advertisements.

50. *Outing* (*The Wheelman*), I (1882), 29.

51. Andrew M. F. Davis, "College Athletics," *Atlantic Monthly*, May, 1883, 677-84.

52. Quoted in *Outing*, XLVII (1905), 247.

53. William Saltonstall Scudder, "An Historical Sketch of the Oneida Football Club of Boston 1862-65," deposited with the Massachusetts Historical Society, 1926.

54. Parke H. Davis, *Football, the Intercollegiate Game* (New York, 1911), 42.

55. *Ibid.*, 35-37.

56. *Ibid.*, 65-72; Walter Camp and Lorin F. Deland, *Football* (New York, 1896), 63-76.

57. Davis, *Football*, 72.

58. Ira N. Hollis, "Intercollegiate Athletics," *Atlantic Monthly*, XC (1902), 534-44; Frederick L. Paxson, "The Rise of Sports," *Mississippi Valley Historical Review*, IV, 143-68; John A. Krout, "Some Reflections on the Rise of Sport," *Proceedings of the Association of History Teachers of the Middle States and Maryland*, No. 26 (1928), 84n.

CHAPTER XII

The New Order

1. *Outing*, XVII, 229.
2. William H. Nugent, "The Sports Section," *American Mercury*, XVI (1929), 336-37. See also unpublished study of newspaper content 1878-1898, Arthur M. Schlesinger, *The Rise of the City* (A History of American Life, X) (New York, 1933), 199.
3. James F. Muirhead, *The Land of Contrasts* (Boston, 1898), 107-10.
4. *Outing*, IV, 470, 476; VI, 614.
5. *New York Tribune*, May, 1890.
6. *Godey's Lady's Book*, July, 1890.
7. George Makepeace Towle, *American Society* (London, 1870), II, 87. See also *ibid.*, II, 15, 22, 40, 151.
8. James Bryce, *The American Commonwealth* (New York, 1888), II, 665, 666.
9. Paul de Rousiers, *American Life* (New York, 1892), 330.
10. Paul Blouet (Max O'Rell), *Jonathan and His Continent* (New York, 1884), 51.
11. Nathaniel H. Egleston, *Villages and Village Life* (New York, 1878), 307-08.
12. Mark Sullivan, *Our Times* (New York, 1925-35), II, 24-25.
13. J. W. Buel, *Metropolitan Life Unveiled* (San Francisco, 1883), 26.
14. Josiah W. Leeds, *The Theatre* (Philadelphia, 1884), 70, 82.
15. Quoted in Wilbert L. Anderson, *The Country Town* (New York, 1914) 281-82.
16. *Literary Digest*, XII (December 21, 1895), 228.
17. Josiah Strong, *The Challenge of the City* (New York, 1907), 222-23.
18. N. S. Shaler, *The United States of America* (New York, 1894), II, 467.
19. Towle, *American Society*, II, 25; William Bayard Hale, "A Study of Church Entertainment," *Forum*, XX (1896), 570-77. See also article in *North American Review*, quoted in *Literary Digest*, XIV (January 9, 1897), 307.
20. Hale, *loc. cit.*, 571.
21. Leeds, *The Theatre*, 78, 81.
22. Bryce, *The American Commonwealth*, II, 572.
23. Schlesinger, *The Rise of the City*, 335.
24. Samuel Lane Loomis, *Modern Cities* (New York, 1887), 104.
25. Quoted in Leeds, *The Theatre*, 67-68.
26. Quoted in Allan Nevins (editor), *American Social History as Recorded by British Travellers* (New York, 1923), 498.

27. Horace Greeley, *Recollections of a Busy Life* (New York, 1873), 118.
28. Quoted in Jesse Lyman Hurlbut, *The Story of Chautauqua* (New York, 1921), 184.

CHAPTER XIII

Metropolis

1. *Fifteenth Census of the United States*, I, 8, 9, 18-19.
2. Arthur M. Schlesinger, *The Rise of the City* (*A History of American Life*, X) (New York, 1933), 65, 72-73.
3. *Ibid.*, 67-70.
4. Quoted in George C. D. Odell, *Annals of the New York Stage* (New York, 1927–), VII, 236-37.
5. Alvin F. Harlow, *Old Bowery Days* (New York, 1931), 465.
6. *Harper's Weekly*, May 10, 1890, 370-72.
7. *Chicago by Day and Night, The Pleasure Seeker's Guide to the Paris of America* (Chicago, 1892), 34-42.
8. Owen Davis, *I'd Like to Do It Again* (New York, 1931), 105.
9. Harlow, *Old Bowery Days*, 459.
10. Henry Collins Brown, *New York in the Elegant Eighties, Valentine's Manual of New York* (New York, 1927), 138-39.
11. Richard J. Walsh, *The Making of Buffalo Bill* (Indianapolis, 1928), 181, 227*ff*.
12. *Punchinello*, I (1870), 116, quoted in Frank Luther Mott, *A History of American Magazines* (New York and Cambridge, 1930–), III, 208.
13. George Makepeace Towle, *American Society* (London, 1870), II, 21; Olive Logan, *Apropos of Women and the Theatre* (New York, 1869), 136.
14. Schlesinger, *The Rise of the City*, 300n.
15. Edwin Milton Royle, "The Vaudeville Theatre," *Scribner's*, XXVI (1899).
16. M. B. Leavitt, *Fifty Years in Theatrical Management* (New York, 1912), 185.
17. *Ibid.*, 209.
18. Harlow, *Old Bowery Days*, 466.
19. Leavitt, *Fifty Years in Theatrical Management*, 194*ff*. See also articles on B. F. Keith and F. F. Proctor in *Dictionary of American Biography*.
20. Royle, *loc cit.*, 495.
21. Harlow, *Old Bowery Days*, 456-59.
22. *Variety*, December 16, 1905. See also article on B. F. Keith in *Dictionary of American Biography*.
23. Harlow, *Old Bowery Days*, 473.
24. *Chicago by Day and Night*.
25. Harlow, *Old Bowery Days*, 454.
26. *Harper's Weekly*, XL (1896), 757-58; Henry Collins Brown, *The Golden Nineties, Valentine's Manual of New York* (New York, 1928), 57.

27. *Harper's Weekly*, XXXIII (1889), 746.
28. J. A. Dacus and James W. Buel, *A Tour of St. Louis* (St. Louis, 1878), 383.
29. "The Trolley Park," *Cosmopolitan*, XXXIII (1902), 265-72; *Street Railway Review*, XVI (1906), 121-22.
30. See article on George C. Tilyou in *Dictionary of American Biography*.
31. Quoted in A. G. Spalding, *America's National Game* (New York, 1911), 451.
32. *Harper's Weekly*, XXX (1886), 202.
33. *Ibid.*, XXXIV (1890), 356.
34. Spalding, *America's National Game*, 224-25.
35. *Ibid.*, 269-81.
36. Quoted *ibid.*, 467.
37. *Ibid.*, 251-61.
38. *Ibid.*, 442.
39. Brown, *The Golden Nineties*, 331-32.
40. Robert F. Kelley, *American Rowing* (New York, 1932), 37*ff.*
41. James F. Muirhead, *The Land of Contrasts* (Boston, 1898), 158.
42. See R. F. Dibble, *John L. Sullivan* (Boston, 1925).
43. *Ibid.*, 59.
44. *Ibid.*, 42-43.
45. Quoted in Brown, *The Golden Nineties*, 382.
46. Quoted in *Literary Digest*, VIII (December 23, 1893), 152.
47. Josiah Strong, *The Challenge of the City* (New York, 1907), 115.

CHAPTER XIV

World of Fashion

1. George Makepeace Towle, *American Society* (London, 1870), I, 292*ff.*
2. Mrs. John King Van Rensselaer, *The Social Ladder* (New York, 1924), 173.
3. Frederick Townsend Martin, *The Passing of the Idle Rich* (New York, 1911), 51-52.
4. Emily Faithfull, *Three Visits to America* (Edinburgh, 1884), 216-17, quoted in Arthur M. Schlesinger, *The Rise of the City* (A History of American Life, X) (New York, 1933), 151.
5. George D. Lyman, *The Saga of the Comstock Lode* (New York, 1934), 217.
6. Dixon Wecter, *The Saga of American Society* (New York, 1937), 338-39.
7. Ward McAllister, *Society as I Have Found It* (New York, 1890) *passim*.
8. *Ibid.*, 350.
9. Quoted in *Literary Digest*, XII (November 30, 1895), 146.
10. McAllister, *Society as I Have Found It*, 369-81.
11. Martin, *The Passing of the Idle Rich*, 30-31.
12. Wecter, *The Saga of American Society*, 369-71; Henry Collins Brown, *The Golden Nineties, Valentine's Manual of New York* (New York, 1928), 71. See also Charles A. and Mary Beard, *The Rise of American Civilization* (New York, 1927), II, 392-93.

13. Brown, *The Golden Nineties,* 108-15; Paul Blouet (Max O'Rell) *Jonathan and His Continent* (New York, 1884), 165-67; Francis Joseph Daly, *The Life of Augustin Daly* (New York, 1917), 119; George C. D. Odell, *Annals of the New York Stage* (New York, 1927–   ), VIII, 429, 559, IX, 392.

14. John Rankin Towse, *Sixty Years of the Theatre* (New York, 1916), 96-88; Henry Austin Clapp, *Reminiscences of a Dramatic Critic* (Boston, 1902), 50*ff;* Arthur A. Hornblow, *History of the American Theatre* (Philadelphia, 1919), II, 318-19; Odell, *Annals of the New York Stage,* VII, 203, X, 570.

15. *Harper's Weekly,* XXXIII (1889), 463; *Atlantic Monthly,* XLIII (1879), 453-58; Hornblow, *History of the American Theatre,* II, 318-19; William Winter, *The Wallet of Time* (New York, 1916), I, 27-29; Odell, *Annals of the New York Stage,* VIII, 559.

16. See Norman Hapgood, *The Stage in America,* 1897-1900 (New York, 1901).

17. Odell, *Annals of the New York Stage,* X, 592, 614, 651, 694.

18. Henry E. Krehbiel, *Chapters of Opera* (New York, 1909), 86.

19. Irving Kolodin, *The Metropolitan Opera* (New York, 1936), 12.

20. *Ibid.,* 2-3.

21. Quoted *ibid.,* 15-16.

22. Henry C. Lahee, *Annals of Music in America* (Boston, 1922), 67.

23. See Don C. Seitz, *The James Gordon Bennetts* (New York, 1928).

24. *Outing,* III, 354.

25. Robert P. Elmer, *Archery* (Philadelphia, 1923), 135.

26. *Tribune Book of Open-Air Sports,* 106.

27. Wecter, *The Saga of American Society,* 439.

28. *Scribner's,* XVII (1895), 692*ff; Harper's Weekly,* XXXIX (1895), 63.

29. Wecter, *The Saga of American Society,* 440.

30. Caspar Whitney, "Evolution of the Country Club," *Harper's,* XC (1894), 16*ff;* Robert Dunn, "The Country Club," *Outing,* XLVII (1905), 160-73.

31. Jerome D. Travers and James R. Crowell, *The Fifth Estate* (New York, 1936), 22.

32. H. C. Chatfield-Taylor, "The Middle West Discovers Outdoors," *Outing,* XLV (1904), 441-49; *Harper's Weekly,* XL (1896), 761-62.

33. *Century,* XLIV (1892), 602; *Scribner's,* XVII (1895), 531*ff; Outing,* XXX, 249.

34. *New York Tribune,* November, 28, 1890.

35. *Harper's Weekly,* XXXVII (1893), 1184.

36. William H. Nugent, "The Sports Section," *American Mercury,* XVI (1929), 337.

37. A. M. Weyand, *American Football* (New York, 1926), 45*ff.*

38. *The Nation,* November 20, 1890, 51.

39. Quoted in *Literary Digest,* XII (November 30, 1895), 128.

40. James F. Muirhead, *The Land of Contrasts* (Boston, 1898), 114-16.

41. Quoted in *Literary Digest,* VIII (1894), 428.

42. *Harper's Weekly,* XXXVII (1893), 1236.

43. Weyand, *American Football,* 79*ff.*

CHAPTER XV

Main Street

1. William Allen White, "A Typical Kansas Community," *Atlantic Monthly*, LXXX (1897), 171-77.
2. *Chelsea Telegraph Pioneer*, September 25, 1875, March 4, 1876.
3. *North American Review*, quoted in *Literary Digest*, XIV (January 9, 1897), 307.
4. *Eighty Pleasant Evenings*, Boston, 1898.
5. Robert S. and Helen Merrell Lynd, *Middletown* (New York, 1929), 280.
6. Leger D. Mayne (William B. Dick), *What Shall We Do Tonight* (New York, 1873); Lucretia Peabody Hale, *Fagots for the Fireside* (New York, 1895).
7. S. C. de Soisson, *A Parisian in America* (Boston, 1896), 186, quoted in Arthur M. Schlesinger, *The Rise of the City* (*A History of American Life*, X) (New York, 1933), 305.
8. For interesting discussion of these popular songs, and many specimens, see Mark Sullivan, *Our Times* (New York, 1925-35), II, 154-83, and also Sigmund Spaeth, *Read 'Em and Weep* (Garden City, 1926), and *Weep Some More, My Lady* (Garden City, 1927).
9. Sullivan, *Our Times*, III, 399.
10. John Philip Sousa, *Marching Along* (Boston, 1928), Chap. iv.
11. Albert G. Stevens, *The Cyclopædia of Fraternities* (New York, 1899), v; B. H. Meyer, "Fraternal Beneficiary Societies in the United States," *American Journal of Sociology*, VI (1901), 646-61.
12. See Charles W. Ferguson, *Fifty Million Brothers* (New York, 1937).
13. H. C. Merwin, "A National Vice," *Atlantic Monthly*, LXXI (1893), 769; W. B. Hill, "The Great American Safety Valve," *Century*, XLIV (1892), 383-84.
14. Paul de Rousiers, *American Life* (New York, 1892), 356.
15. J. C. Croly, *The History of the Women's Club Movement* (New York, 1898), 15, 88; *Nineteenth Century*, XLVII, 847.
16. *Atlantic Monthly*, XLVI (1880), 724-25.
17. Therese Blanc, *The Condition of Women in the United States* (Boston, 1895), 107, quoted in Schlesinger, *The Rise of the City*, 143.
18. "Ready-made Housekeeping," *Good Housekeeping*, V (1887), 266, quoted in Schlesinger, *The Rise of the City*, 132-33.
19. *New York Dramatic Mirror*, January 11, 1890.
20. Jesse Lyman Hurlbut, *The Story of Chautauqua* (New York, 1921), 247, 384-86.
21. Quoted in Gay MacLaren, *Morally We Roll Along* (Boston, 1938), 78.
22. *Ibid.*, 151, 169.
23. Schlesinger, *The Rise of the City*, 174. See also James B. Pond, *Eccentricities of Genius* (New York, 1900), 5ff.
24. Schlesinger, *The Rise of the City*, 291ff; *New York Dramatic Mirror*, March 25, 1899.
25. *New York Dramatic Mirror*, December 10, 1898.
26. White, *loc. cit.*, 174.

27. *New York Dramatic Mirror,* January 11, 1890.
28. Marie Dressler, *My Own Story* (Boston, 1934), 40ff.
29. J. Frank Davies, "Tom Shows," *Scribner's,* LXXVII (1925), 350.
30. W. W. Stout, "Little Eva Is Seventy-Five," *Saturday Evening Post,* CC (October 8, 1927), 10ff.
31. Lynd and Lynd, *Middletown,* 266.
32. Everett Dick, *The Sod-House Frontier,* 1854-1890 (New York, 1937), 280-81.
33. James A. Naismith, "Basketball," in *Encyclopædia Britannica.*
34. *Outing,* XXXI, 224.
35. Booth Tarkington, *The Gentleman from Indiana* (New York, 1899), 92.
36. *Twelfth Census of the United States,* X, 328, cited in Schlesinger, *The Rise of the City,* 313.
37. L. H. Porter, *Wheels and Wheeling* (New York, 1892), 9.
38. "The Rule of the Bicycle," *Scribner's,* XIX (1896), 783-84.
39. Joseph R. Bishop, "Social and Economic Influence of the Bicycle," *Forum,* XXI (1896), 680-89.
40. *Literary Digest,* XIII (1896), 361.
41. Lillian Campbell Davidson, *Handbook for Lady Cyclists* (London, 1896), 27.
42. *Godey's Lady's Book,* CXX (1890), 338; Dr. Henry J. Garrigues, "Woman and the Bicycle," *Forum,* XX (1896), 583; *Outing,* XVII (1891), 305; *Harper's Weekly,* XXXVIII (1894), 710.
43. *Scribner's,* XIX (1896), 783.
44. *Twelfth Census of the United States,* X, 329, cited in Schlesinger, *The Rise of the City,* 314.
45. *Vermont Phœnix* (Brattleboro), January 21, 1898.

CHAPTER XVI

Farm and Countryside

1. Nathaniel H. Egleston, *Villages and Village Life* (New York, 1878), 35, 42.
2. Quoted *ibid.,* 25.
3. See series of articles in the *Atlantic Monthly:* "The Problems of Rural New England," LXXIX (1897), 577-98, and "The Future of Rural New England," LXXIX (1897), 74-83.
4. Hamlin Garland, *A Son of the Middle Border* (New York, 1917), 21, 123, 209.
5. Allan Nevins, *The Emergence of Modern America* (*A History of American Life,* VIII) (New York, 1927), 169-71.
6. Everett Dick, *The Sod-House Frontier, 1854-1890* (New York, 1937), 384.
7. Garland, *A Son of the Middle Border,* 94. See also Grant Showerman, *A Country Chronicle* (New York, 1916), 46-52.
8. Mark Sullivan, *Our Times* (New York, 1925-35), II, 166.
9. Philip Morgan, "The Problems of Rural New England," *Atlantic Monthly,* LXXIX (1897), 377-88.

10. Sullivan, *Our Times*, II, 210-11.
11. Garland, *A Son of the Middle Border*, 165-66.
12. *Ibid.*, 165-66.
13. *Nauvoo* (Illinois) *Rustler*, July 1, 1890.
14. Henry Wheeler Shaw, *Josh Billings on Ice and Other Things* (New York, 1868), quoted in Wayne Caldwell Neely, *The Agricultural Fair* (New York, 1935), 193.
15. Neely, *The Agricultural Fair*, 83, 89, 96. See also article on Elkanah Watson in *Dictionary of American Biography*.
16. John A. Krout, *Annals of American Sport* (*The Pageant of America*, XV) (New Haven, 1929), 51-53.
17. Quoted in Neely, *The Agricultural Fair*, 204.
18. Alvan F. Sanborn, "The Problems of Rural New England," *Atlantic Monthly*, LXXIX (1897), 595.
19. Neely, *The Agricultural Fair*, 107.
20. Garland, *A Son of the Middle Border*, 167-68.
21. Nelson Lloyd, "The County Fair," *Scribner's Magazine*, XXXIV (1903), 129-47.
22. Earl Chapin May, *The Circus from Rome to Ringling* (New York, 1932), 113-14.
23. P. T. Barnum, *Struggles and Triumphs* (Buffalo, 1889), 284; M. R. Werner, *Barnum* (New York, 1927), 306-10; May, *The Circus*, 113-17.
24. Barnum, *Struggles and Triumphs*, 284, 331, 334.
25. *Ibid.*, 356.
26. *Ibid.*, 332*ff*; Werner, *Barnum*, 333*ff*.
27. May, *The Circus*, 224*ff*; *New York Dramatic Mirror*, 1890, advertisements.
28. *Nauvoo* (Illinois) *Rustler*, June 17, 1890.
29. *Carson Appeal*, May 29, 1875, quoted in Wells Drury, *An Editor on the Comstock Lode* (New York, 1936), 303.
30. For two colorful contemporary descriptions of circus day see Booth Tarkington, *A Gentleman from Indiana* (New York, 1899), 177-43 *passim;* Hamlin Garland, *Boy Life on the Prairie* (New York, 1899), 231-51 *passim.*
31. Quoted in Sullivan, *Our Times*, II, 171.
32. Garland, *A Son of the Middle Border*, 135-37.

CHAPTER XVII

The Growth of the Movies

1. Ben J. Lubschez, *The Story of the Motion Picture* (New York, 1920), 43; *Outing*, LXIV (July, 1914), 499-505; Paul Schubert, *The Electric Word* (New York, 1928), 3*ff*.
2. Benjamin B. Hampton, *A History of the Movies* (New York, 1931), 7.
3. *Ibid.*, 11; Terry Ramsaye, *A Million and One Nights* (New York, 1926), 233; "The Motion Picture in Its Economic and Social Aspects," *Annals of the American Academy of Political and Social Science*, CXXVIII (1926), 7.

4. Hampton, *A History of the Movies*, 12.
5. *Ibid.*, 44-45; Ramsaye, *A Million and One Nights*, 429-30.
6. Barton W. Currie, "The Nickel Madness," *Harper's Weekly*, LI (1907), 1246-47; George E. Walsh, "Moving Picture Drama for the Multitude," *Independent*, LXIV (February 6, 1908).
7. Quoted in Mark Sullivan, *Our Times* (New York, 1925-35), III, 552-53.
8. Hampton, *A History of the Movies*, 57; Walsh, *loc. cit.*, 306.
9. Ramsaye, *A Million and One Nights*, 256.
10. *Ibid.*, 259.
11. *Ibid.*, 473*ff.*
12. Sullivan, *Our Times*, III, 551-52.
13. Currie, *loc. cit.*, 1247; *Review of Reviews*, XXXVIII (December, 1908), 744.
14. Hampton, *A History of the Movies*, 29-39.
15. Walsh, *loc. cit.*, 307; Lubschez, *Story of the Motion Picture*, 58; *Annals of American Academy of Political and Social Science*, CXXVIII (1926), 10; Ramsaye, *A Million and One Nights*, 281-89, 363-78, 429.
16. Hampton, *A History of the Movies*, 31; Ramsaye, *A Million and One Nights*, 416*ff.*
17. Walsh, *loc. cit.*, 307-08.
18. Ramsaye, *A Million and One Nights*, 474.
19. Sullivan, *Our Times*, III, 553.
20. *Annals of the American Academy of Political and Social Science*, CXXVIII (1926), 11.
21. Hampton, *A History of the Movies*, 86*ff*; Ramsaye, *A Million and One Nights*, 544-45, 547-49, 605.
22. Hampton, *A History of the Movies*, 57, 92.
23. Ramsaye, *A Million and One Nights*, 645*ff*; Marie Dressler, *My Own Story* (Boston, 1934), 168-69.
24. Ramsaye, *A Million and One Nights*, 734.
25. *Ibid.*, 661; Pearl White, *Just Me* (New York, 1919).
26. Hampton, *A History of the Movies*, 130; Ramsaye, *A Million and One Nights*, 635*ff.*
27. Ramsaye, *A Million and One Nights*, 675-77; Hampton, *A History of the Movies*, 333.
28. Hampton, *A History of the Movies*, 342.
29. Ramsaye, *A Million and One Nights*, 748.
30. *Ibid.*, 625.
31. Frederick Lewis Allen, *Only Yesterday* (New York, 1931), 101.
32. Robert S. and Helen Merrell Lynd, *Middletown* (New York, 1929), 266.
33. Quoted in Hampton, *A History of the Movies*, 362.
34. *Ibid.*, 387 *ff.*
35. Julius Weinberger, "Economic Aspects of Recreation," reprint from *Harvard Business Review*, Summer, 1937, 450.
36. Preston W. Slosson, *The Great Crusade and After* (New York, 1931), 394; Hampton, *A History of the Movies*, 362.
37. *Film Daily Yearbook*, 1939.

38. Edgar Dale, *The Content of Motion Pictures* (New York, 1935), 17, 227.
39. Allen, *Only Yesterday*, 102; Will H. Hays, "The Motion Picture Industry," *Review of Reviews*, LXVII (1923), 65-80.
40. "The Hay's Office," *Fortune*, XVIII (December, 1938), 3; J. P. McEvoy, "The Back of Me Hand to You," *Saturday Evening Post*, CCXI (December 24, 1938), 8 *ff*.
41. *Current History*, L (March, 1939), 47.
42. Weinberger, "Economic Aspects of Recreation," 454.
43. *Encyclopedia Americana*, "Motion Pictures"; "The Good Life," *Life*, XLVII (December 28, 1959), 73.
44. Contemporary moving picture articles and reviews.
45. "Movie Theatres Stage Comeback," *New York Times*, Section 3, July 5, 1964.
46. *Encyclopedia Americana Annual*, 1964.
47. Albert McCleery and Carl Glick, *Curtains Going Up* (New York, 1939), 332.
48. Emily Coleman, "From Red Barn to Package and Tent," *New York Times Magazine*, July 19, 1964.
49. "The Good Life," 73.

CHAPTER XVIII

A Nation on Wheels

1. Mark Sullivan, *Our Times*, I (New York, 1925-35), 497.
2. *Country Life*, XIX (January, 1911), advertisements.
3. *Ibid.*, XII (1907), 76, 552.
4. Sullivan, *Our Times*, I, 497.
5. *Ibid.*, 111, 431.
6. *Country Life*, XIX (January, 1911), 241-42.
7. *Ibid.*, XII (May, 1907), 76.
8. *Ibid.*, X (October, 1906), 702; XII (June, 1907), 198.
9. Harold Underwood Faulkner, *The Quest for Social Justice* (New York, 1931), 170.
10. *Country Life*, XII (June, 1907), 198.
11. Sullivan, *Our Times*, I, 501.
12. *Country Life*, XII (October, 1907), 683-84.
13. *Ibid.*, XII (October, 1907), 684.
14. Sullivan, *Our Times*, IV, 63, 64.
15. *Automobile Facts and Figures*, 1939.
16. Frederick Lewis Allen, *Only Yesterday* (New York, 1931), 163.
17. *Automobile Facts and Figures*, 1939.
18. Preston W. Slosson, *The Great Crusade and After* (New York, 1931), 238-39; *Recent Social Trends in the United States*, Report of the President's Research Committee (New York, 1933), II, 921, 950 *ff*.
19. Robert S. and Helen Merrell Lynd, *Middletown* (New York, 1929), 259.
20. *Ibid.*, 255-56.
21. *Recent Social Trends*, II, 920; Jesse F. Steiner, "Research Memorandum on Recreation in the Depression," *Social Science Research Council Bulletin*, No. 32, 1937, 64.

22. Slosson, *The Great Crusade and After*, 237-38.
23. "Automobile Trailers," *The Index* (New York Trust Company), XVII (1937), 63 *ff*.
24. Julius Weinberger, "Economic Aspects of Recreation," *Harvard Business Review*, Summer, 1937, 455-56.
25. C. E. M. Joad, *Diogenes; or the Future of Leisure* (London, 1928), 42, quoted in George A. Lundberg, *Leisure—A Suburban Study* (New York, 1934), 63.
26. *World Almanac*, 1964.
27. "Recreation in the Age of Automation," *The Annals of the American Academy of Political and Social Sciences*, Vol. 313 (September, 1957), 129-30; George and Iris Wells, *The Handbook of Auto Camping* (New York, 1938); James A. Bier and Henry A Raup, *Campground Atlas of the United States and Canada* (New York, 1964-65).
28. Robert H. Boyle, *Sport—Mirror of American Life* (Boston, 1963), 25.
29. "National Parks," *Encyclopedia Americana Annual*, 1962.
30. *Outdoor Recreation for America*, A Report to the President and to the Congress by the Outdoor Recreation Resources Review Commission (Washington, 1962).
31. See "The Lower Middle Class: The Hot Rod Cult," in Boyle, *Sport—Mirror of American Life*, 135-213.

CHAPTER XIX

On the Air

1. Paul Schubert, *The Electric Word: the Rise of Radio* (New York, 1928), 194-95.
2. Alfred P. Morgan, *The Pageant of Electricity* (New York, 1939), 323-27.
3. Schubert, *The Electric Word*, 197 *ff*; Preston W. Slosson, *The Great Crusade and After* (New York, 1931), 389.
4. Julius Weinberger, "Economic Aspects of Recreation," *Harvard Business Review*, Summer, 1937, 450.
5. Slosson, *The Great Crusade and After*, 389 *n*.
6. A. N. Goldsmith and A. C. Lescarboura, *This Thing Called Broadcasting* (New York, 1930), 42.
7. Quoted in Frederick Lewis Allen, *Only Yesterday* (New York, 1931), 78.
8. "'Listening In,' Our New National Pastime," *Review of Reviews*, LXVII (1923), 52.
9. Orange Edward McMeans, "The Great Audience Invisible," *Scribner's* LXXIII (1923), 410-16.
10. Goldsmith and Lescarboura, *This Thing Called Broadcasting*, 99-101; Samuel L. Rothafel and R. F. Yates, *Broadcasting—Its New Day* (New York, 1925) *passim*.
11. *New Republic*, XL (October 8, 1924), 135-36.
12. Goldsmith and Lescarboura, *This Thing Called Broadcasting*, 177 *ff*; Slosson, *The Great Crusade and After*, 390-92.
13. Charles Merz, *The Great American Bandwagon* (New York, 1925), 50.

14. Goldsmith and Lescarboura, *This Thing Called Broadcasting,* 189.
15. Weinberger, "Economic Aspects of Recreation," 452.
16. Goldsmith and Lescarboura, *This Thing Called Broadcasting,* 209 *ff.*
17. For studies of radio programs see George A. Lundberg, "The Content of Radio Programs," *Social Forces,* VII (1928), 58-60; Hadley Cantril and Gordon W. Allport, *The Psychology of Radio* (New York, 1935), 75-76.
18. Cantril and Allport, *Psychology of Radio,* 85; Weinberger, "Economic Aspects of Recreation," 450.
19. *New York Herald Tribune,* VI, July 30, 1939, 8.
20. *New York Herald Tribune Magazine,* July 30, 1939, 9.
21. *The Leisure of 5,000 People, A Report of a Study of Leisure Time Activities and Desires,* National Recreation Association (1934), 4.
22. See Leo Bogart, *The Age of Television* (New York, 1958).
23. "Radio and Television," *Encyclopedia Americana Annual,* 1946.
24. *Ibid.,* 1948.
25. *Economic Almanac,* 1964; also material from *TV Guide;* newspaper programs.
26. Quoted from "Radio and Television," *Encyclopedia Americana Annual,* 1957.
27. *Ibid.,* 1954, 1957; Bogart, *The Age of Television,* 83 *ff.*
28. *Ibid.,* 331.
29. *Saturday Review,* May 8, 1965.

CHAPTER XX

Sports for All

1. James Bryce, "America Revisited—Changes of a Quarter Century," *Outlook,* March 25, 1905, in Allan Nevins (editor), *American Social History as Recorded by British Travellers* (New York, 1923), 542.
2. Quoted in Robert H. Boyle, *Sport—Mirror of American Life* (Boston, 1963). "The Bizarre History of American Sport," *Sports Illustrated,* XVI (January 8, 1962), 62.
3. C. E. Rainwater, *The Play Movement in the United States* (Chicago, 1921), 44 *ff;* Charles M. Robinson, *The Improvement of Towns and Cities* (New York, 1901), 156 *ff; Recent Social Trends in the United States,* Report of the President's Research Committee (New York, 1933), II, 915 *ff;* "Public Recreation Facilities," *Annals of the American Academy of Political and Social Science.* XXXV (March, 1910).
4. *Report on Progress of the Works Progress Administration Program,* June 20, 1938, 20-24, 51.
5. *Recreation Yearbook* (*Recreation,* XXXIII, June, 1939), 124 *ff.*
6. For attendance figures and expenditure estimates on sports, see *Recent Social Trends,* II, 947 *ff;* Julius Weinberger, "Economic Aspects of Recreation," *Harvard Business Review,* Summer, 1937, 452 *ff;* "The Recreational Dollar," *Business Week,* July 13, 1932; "The Sports Industry," *The Index* (New York Trust Company), XVI (1936), 127 *ff;* John R. Tunis, *Sports, Heroes, and Hysterics* (New York,

1928); Frank G. Menke (editor), *All Sports Record Book* (New York, 1935) and *Encyclopedia of Sports* (1938).

7. Boyle, *Sport—Mirror of American Life,* 45 *ff.*
8. Harold Underwood Faulkner, *The Quest for Social Justice* (New York, 1931), 291.
9. John R. Tunis, "The Great God Football," *Harper's,* CLVII (1928), 743.
10. *Recent Social Trends,* II, 930.
11. *Ibid.,* II, 930; Preston W. Slosson, *The Great Crusade and After* (New York, 1931), 274.
12. Frederick Lewis Allen, *Only Yesterday* (New York, 1931), 208-09.
13. *Liberty,* III (July 17, 1926), quoted in Slosson, *The Great Crusade and After,* 276.
14. See Allison Danzig, *The History of American Football* (Englewood, N.J., 1956); Alexander M. Weyand, *The Saga of American Football* (New York, 1955).
15. Boyle, *Sport—Mirror of American Life,* 3; Reynold E. Carlson, Theodore R. Deppe, Janet R. MacLean, *Recreation in American Life* (Belmont, Cal., 1963), 77.
16. "Football," *Encyclopedia Britannica;* Stephen Mahoney, "Pro Football's Profit Explosion," *Fortune,* November, 1964, 153 *ff.*
17. Hy Turkin, *Little League Baseball* (New York, 1954), 9.
18. *Recent Social Trends,* II, 931-32.
19. *World Almanac,* 1964.
20. Boyle, *Sport—Mirror of American Life,* 45.
21. William Cunningham, "No Wonder They Want to Fight," *Colliers,* LXXIV (September 13, 1924), 14; H. W. Clune, "Palookas and Plutocrats," *North American Review,* CCXXVII.
22. Allen, *Only Yesterday,* 210-11.
23. "Sports," *Encyclopedia Americana Annual,* 1963.
24. Boyle, *Sport—Mirror of American Life,* 3; Carlson, Deppe and MacLean, *Recreation in American Life,* 77.
25. John R. Tunis, *The American Way in Sport* (New York, 1958).
26. *Sports Illustrated,* XVII (January 21, 1963).
27. *Ibid.,* February 18, 1963.
28. *Literary Digest,* LXXXIII (October 4, 1924), 77.
29. Boyle, *Sport—Mirror of American Life,* 50, 274.
30. Robert Coughlin, "A $40 Billion Bill Just for Fun," in "The Good Life," *Life,* XLVII (December 28, 1959), 73.
31. *Ibid.,* 70; "Recreation in the Age of Automation," *Annals of the American Academy of Political and Social Sciences,* Vol. 313 (September, 1957), 109.
32. *Recent Social Trends,* II, 927.
33. Grantland Rice, "The National Rash," *Collier's,* LXXXII (October 20, 1928), 10.
34. Robert H. Boyle, "The Ways of Life at the Country Club," *Sports Illustrated,* XVI (February 26, 1962 and March 5, 1962), 51-56, 69-74.
35. *Recent Social Trends,* II, 927-28.
36. Boyle, *Sport—Mirror of American Life,* 273.

37. John Kieran, "The Ski's the Limit," *American Magazine,* CXXIII (February, 1937), 28.
38. Boyle, *Sport—Mirror of American Life,* 52-53.
39. Robert Coughlin, "A $40 Billion Bill Just for Fun," 70; "Recreation in the Age of Automation," 109.
40. "Softball," *Literary Digest,* September 11, 1937, 32-33; Frank J. Taylor, "Fast and Pretty," *Collier's,* CII (August 20, 1938), 10.
41. Boyle, *Sport—Mirror of American Life,* 273-74.
42. *Ibid.,* 174-75.
43. *Ibid.,* 72-73; Eric Larrabee and Rolf Meyersohn, *Mass Leisure* (Glencoe, Ill., 1952), 73 *ff,* 265; Tunis, *The American Way in Sport,* 137; Henry Romney, "A Startling Look Into the Sporting Future," *Sports Illustrated,* XVI (February 15, 1962); *New York Times,* January 5, 1965.

CHAPTER XXI

The Changing Scene

1. Frederick Lewis Allen, *Only Yesterday* (New York, 1931), 186.
2. Mr. and Mrs. Vernon Castle, *Modern Dancing* (New York, 1914), 37 *ff,* 155 *ff.*
3. Frederick Lewis Allen, "When America Learned to Dance," *Scribner's,* CII (1937), 11-17.
4. Mr. and Mrs. Vernon Castle, *Modern Dancing,* 38.
5. Paul Whiteman, *Jazz* (New York, 1926), 17 *ff;* Wilder Hobson, *American Jazz Music* (New York, 1939), 92 *ff.*
6. Paul Whiteman, "In Defense of Jazz," *New York Times,* March 13, 1927, quoted in Preston W. Slosson, *The Great Crusade and After* (New York, 1931), 283.
7. Mark Sullivan, *Our Times,* VI (New York, 1933), 479-80.
8. Quoted in Allen, *Only Yesterday,* 90.
9. Sullivan, *Our Times,* VI, 489.
10. Stanley Walker, *The Night Club Era* (New York, 1933).
11. Walter S. Hiatt, "Billions—Just for Fun," *Collier's,* LXXIV (October 25, 1924), 31.
12. Quoted in Allen, *Only Yesterday,* 90.
13. *Current History,* L (August, 1939), 52.
14. Marshall Stearns, *The Story of Jazz* (New York, 1956); *Newsweek,* July 11, 1960, 8.
15. See *TV Guide;* newspaper television programs; the *Lantern,* Ohio State University.
16. *Life,* July 24, 1939, 50.
17. Prosper Buranelli and Margaret Petherbridge, "How the Crossword Craze Started," *Collier's,* LXXV (January 31, 1925), 12.
18. Beatrice Barmby, "What It Means to be a Book Publisher at Twenty-Nine," *McClure's,* LIX (1927), 63, quoted in Slosson, *The Great Crusade and After,* 285.
19. Allen, *Only Yesterday,* 191-92.

20. Kathleen Norris, "I Know a Game," *Ladies Home Journal*, XLV (September, 1928), 14.
21. *American Mercury*, VI (1929), 234.
22. Elmer Davis, "Purest of Pleasures: Contract," *Harper's*, CLXV (1932), 287-95.
23. Ely Culbertson, "North West East South," *American Magazine*, CXIII (1932), 30.
24. Davis, "Purest of Pleasures: Contract," 287.
25. *Literary Digest*, October 17, 1931, 31.
26. Elmer Davis, "Miniature Golf to the Rescue," *Harper's*, CLXII (December, 1930), 5.
27. *Ibid.*, 14.
28. Catherine Brody, "With Benefit of Clergy," *Collier's*, CI (May 7, 1938), 14 *ff*.
29. *Literary Digest*, CXXV (January 1, 1938), 32-33.
30. Thurlow Reed, "Our Great American Sweepstakes," *Commonweal*, XXVIII (May 13, 1938), 67.
31. Robert S. and Helen Lynd, *Middletown* (New York, 1929), 251.
32. Reynold E. Carlson, Theodore R. Deppe and Janet R. MacLean, *Recreation in American Life* (Belmont, Cal., 1963), 73.
33. "Do-It-Yourself—the New Billion Dollar Hobby," *Time*, August 2, 1954, quoted in Eric Larrabee and Rolf Meyersohn, *Mass Leisure* (Glencoe, Ill., 1958), 280.
34. "Hobbyhorse Hitching Post," *Rotarian;* Julius Weinberger, Economic Aspects of Recreation," *Harvard Business Review*, Summer, 1937, 453; Robert Coughlin, "A $40 Billion Bill Just for Fun," in "The Good Life," *Life*, XLVII (December 28, 1959), 73; "What's Happening to Hobbies?" *New York Times Magazine*, December 27, 1953, in Larrabee and Meyersohn, 268-74.
35. See Foster Rhea Dulles, *Americans Abroad* (Ann Arbor, 1964), 141 *ff*, for material in this section.
36. Daniel Boorstin, "The Lost Art of Travel," in *The Image, or What Happened to the American Dream* (New York, 1962), quoted *ibid.*, 180.
37. William D. Patterson, "The Big Picture 1961-62," reprinted from April, May and June issues of *Travel News*, 1962.

CHAPTER XXII

The New Leisure

1. C. E. M. Joad, *Diogenes; or the Future of Leisure* (London, 1928), 65.
2. Jesse F. Steiner, "Research Memorandum on Recreation in the Depression," *Social Science Research Bulletin*, No. 32 (1937), 29; see also *Recent Social Trends in the United States*, Report of the President's Research Committee (New York, 1933), II, 828-29.
3. Steiner, 29-30; Eric Larrabee and Rolf Meyersohn, *Mass Leisure* (Glencoe, Ill., 1958), 152, 167; Office Business Economics, United States Department of Commerce, *Annual Reports*.

4. C. Delisle Burns, *Leisure in the Modern World* (New York, 1932), 260.
5. Robert Coughlin, "A $40 Billion Bill Just for Fun" in "The Good Life," *Life*, XLVII (December 28, 1959), 69.
6. George A. Lundberg, *Leisure—A Suburban Study* (New York, 1934), 17.
7. Larrabee and Meyersohn, *Mass Leisure*, 359.
8. "Labor Shudders at Leisure," *The Nation*, April 20, 1963.
9. Larrabee and Meyersohn, 12, 93, 363-85; Laurence S. Rockefeller, "Leisure—the New Challenge," *Vital Speeches*, XXVII (December 1, 1960), III; "Recreation in the Age of Automation," *Annals of the American Academy of Political and Social Sciences*, Vol. 313 (September, 1957); "The Good Life," *Life*, XLVII (December 28, 1959), 62-63. See also Max Kaplan, *Leisure in America: a Social Inquiry* (New York, 1960).
10. Julius Weinberger, "Economic Aspects of Recreation," *Harvard Bulletin*, Summer, 1937, 452 *ff*. See also Edwin E. Slosson, "The Amusement Business, *Independent*, LVII (July 21, 1904), 134 *ff*; Arthur B. Reeve, "What America Spends for Sport," *Outing*, LVII (December, 1910), 300 *ff*; Walter S. Hiatt, "Billions—Just for Fun," *Collier's*, LXXIV (October 25, 1924), 31; "The Amusement Industry," *Index* (New York Trust Company), XVII (1937), 200 *ff*.
11. Reynold E. Carlson, Theodore R. Deppe and Janet MacLean, *Recreation in American Life* (Belmont, Cal., 1963), 70; "Leisure Spending," *Recreation*, LIV (October, 1961), 428-29; Office Business Economics, *Report*, 1962.
12. Coughlin, "A $40 Billion Bill Just for Fun," 69-74.
13. *Ibid.*, 69; Larrabee and Meyersohn, *Mass Leisure*, 167 *ff*.
14. John R. Tunis, "A Nation of Onlookers," *Atlantic Monthly*, CLX (1937), 147.
15. Rockefeller, "Leisure—the New Challenge," 113.
16. "Leisure Spending," *Recreation*, 428-39; Robert H. Boyle, *Sport—Mirror of American Life* (Boston, 1963), 274-75.
17. Larrabee and Meyersohn, *Mass Leisure*, 208.
18. Reynold E. Carlson, Theodore R. Deppe and Janet MacLean, *Recreation in American Life* (Belmont, Cal., 1962).
19. "The Varied Faces of Recreation," *Recreation*, LIII (May, 1960), 208-11; "Recreation the Final Product," *Recreation*, LIII (October, 1960), 349 *ff*; previously cited books as well as articles in *Life* and *Annals of American Academy of Political and Social Sciences*. Also contemporary magazines: *Holiday, Sports Illustrated, Travel*, etc.; and special sections in the daily press.

INDEX

Academy of Music (New York), 238

Adams, Abigail, 28

Adams, Charles Francis, quoted, 8

Adams, Franklin P., 373

Adams, John, 44, 61, 230

Adams, John Quincy, 45, 139, 248

Allen, Fred, 337, 338

Allen, Frederick Lewis, quoted, 367

Alsop, George, quoted, 26

Amateur photography, 202, 367

Amateur theatricals, 49, 62, 367

American Company of Comedians, The, 54, 57, 62-66 *passim*

American Jockey Club, 240

American League, 224-25

American Museum, 122-25, 135, 219

America's Cup race, 240

Ames, Nathaniel, quoted, 26, 49

Amherst, Sir Jeffrey, 53

Amusement industry (*see also* Costs of recreation), 391-93

Amusement parks, 98, 163-64, 166, 222-23, 307

Anderson, Mary, actress, 237

Anglin, Margaret, actress, 237

Angling. *See* Fishing.

Animal-baiting, 10, 43, 138

Animal exhibits (*see also* Circus), 39, 40, 131-32

Annapolis, as colonial capital, 61, 62

Anson, "Pop," baseball player, 225

Archery, 182, 192, 202, 240, 364

Argall, Governor, 8

Armstrong, Louis ("Satchmo"), 372

"Association" of 1774, 65

Aston, Anthony, actor, 54

Astor Place riot, 104

Athletic meets, 355

Audubon, John J., quoted, 71, 77

Austen, Jane, quoted, 185

Automobile, the. *See* motoring.

Automobile racing, 287, 314, 355

Backgammon, 33, 36, 150

Bacon, Nathaniel, 18

Badminton, 364

Bailey, Hackaliah, 131-32

Bailey, James A., circus owner, 282

Ballet, 100, 116-17

Balloon ascensions, 164-65

Balls, colonial (*see also* Dancing) 48, 52, 61; in Gilded Age, 231-32

Bank nights, 299

Barbecues (*see also* Picnicking), 77, 166, 368

Bardot, Brigitte, 306

Barlow, John, professional runner, 144

Barn raisings, 26, 43

Barnard, Charles, playwright, 236

Barnard, Henry, quoted, 157-58

Barnum, Phineas, 122-27, 213, 134-35, 138-39, 282-84

Barrett, Lawrence, actor, 236, 237

Barrymores, the, 237

Baseball, origins and early development, 185-91; in 1890's, 223-26, 240, 263-64; in twentieth century, 350-52

Basie, Count, 372

Basketball, 264, 354

Bat-and-ball (*see also* Baseball), 33, 185-86

Bathing, 152-53, 202, 355-56

Bathing beauty contests, 367

435

Battledore and shuttlecock (*see also* Badminton), 52
Bear-baiting, 10
Beatles, the, 342
Beecher, Henry Ward, quoted, 89
Beer-gardens, 98, 220
Belasco, David, producer, 237
Bennett, James Gordon, quoted, 123
Bennett, James Gordon, Jr., 239
Benny, Jack, 337, 338
Bentley, William, quoted, 33, 40
Bergmann, Ingmar, 306
Berle, Milton, 340
Bernard, John, quoted, 28, 72; as theatrical manager, 102
Bernhardt, Sarah, 237
Beverly, Robert, quoted, 26
Bicycling, 194-96, 265-67
Billiards, 36, 44, 150, 156, 220, 364
Billings, Josh, quoted, 279
Bingo, 367, 377-78
Blouet, Paul, quoted, 203
Blue laws, 5-6, 18-19, 20
Boating (*see also* Regattas, Rowing), 58, 75, 357
Bogart, Humphrey, 305
Bogart, Leo, quoted, 342
Book of Sports, King James I's, 10
Booth, Edwin, 109, 172, 173, 236
Booth, Junius Brutus, 100, 109, 110, 112, 120-21, 173
Boston, social life during colonial period, 46-49
Boston Museum Theatre, 112, 113, 234
Boston Symphony, 238
Boston Theatre, 234
Boucicault, Dion, playwright, 113
Bowery Theatre (New York), 103, 105, 213-14; in 1890's, 214
Bowling, as colonial sport, 6, 10, 33, 36, 58; mid-nineteenth century, 150, 156; in 1890's, 220; as modern sport, 362-63
Boxing. *See* Prize-fighting.
Boyle, Robert H., quoted, 363-64
Bradford, William, quoted, 4, 13
Bridge, card game, 374-75
Brinkley, David, 339

Brittan, Belle, quoted, 134
Broadway Theatre (New York), 103
Brodie, Steve, as actor, 215-16
Brougham's Lyceum (New York), 117
Broun, Heywood, quoted, 373
Brown, Henry Collins, quoted, 234
Bryce, Viscount James, quoted, 203, 344
Buckingham, James Silk, quoted, 102, 150
Buckingstone, John Baldwin, playwright, 113
Buffalo Bill. *See* William F. Cody.
Bull, Ole, concert artist, 237
Bull-baiting, 10
Bundling, 28-29
Bunny, John, moving-picture actor, 294
Burgess, Neil, playwright, 236
Burlesque, 100, 117, 123, 217, 306-07
Burnaby, Andrew, quoted, 28, 51, 58, 64
Burns, Tommy, prize-fighter, 352
Burton, Richard, 305

Cagney, James, 301
Calkins, Ernest Elmo, quoted, 380
Calvé, Emma, concert artist, 237
Calvinism (*see also* Puritanism), 5 *ff.*
Camp, Walter, football coach, 244, 246
Camp-meetings, 80-83
Camping, 202, 324-25
Canoeing, 202
Captains Courageous, 300-01
Card playing (*see also* Gambling), early prohibitions against, 5, 6, 8, 19; during eighteenth century, 33, 36, 44 *ff.*; later years, 70, 150, 158, 176, 252, 373
Carnegie Foundation, report on football, 349
Carnivals, 307
Carpentier, Georges, prize fighter, 352

Carter, Charles, 37
Carter, Colonel Robert, 58-59
Carter, Mrs. Leslie, actress, 237
Cartwright, Alexander J., baseball player, 186
Cartwright, Peter, quoted, 82
Castle, Irene and Vernon, dancers, 368-69, 373
Castle Garden Theatre (New York), 127, 166
Censorship, of moving pictures, 301-03, 310-11; of television, 341
Chaplin, Charlie, 297
Charades, 158
Charivari, 79
Charleston, as colonial capital, 62, 63
Chasing a greased pig, 30
Chastellux, Marquis of, quoted, 35, 48, 58, 366
Chatham Theatre (New York), 105
Chautauqua, 258-60
Chess, 84, 397
Chestnut Street Theatre (Philadelphia), 101, 105
Chevalier, Michael, quoted, 85, 92-93, 151, 167
Chicago orchestra, 238
Chinese checkers, 367
"Chivalric tournaments," in pre-war South, 158, 162
Christy's Minstrel Band, 129
Church (see also Puritanism), attitude toward amusements in colonial period, 5 ff.; in 1840's, 88-90; in 1890's, 204-09, 249
Church entertainments, 206, 249-51, 307
Church meetings, in colonial days, 7, 18
Cimarron, 300
Cinescope, 305
Circus, 131-35, 282-86, 307
Cities (see also urban amusements), influence on growth of recreation, 84-85, 136-38, 204, 211-13
Coaching, 182, 239, 241
Coasting, 34
Cock-fighting, 33, 35, 50, 52, 57, 58, 65, 75, 138, 159, 17?

Cody, William F., as theatrical producer, 216-17
Cohan, George, as actor, 218
Collecting, 380
Colonies, early bans on amusements, 4 ff.; sports of yeomanry, 26, 31-37; country dances, 30, 33, 37-39; social life of aristocracy, 44-66; theatre, 53-57, 62-63, 64-65
Combe, George, quoted, 93
Comic strips, 367
Commencement exercises, colonial, 31
Comstock, Anthony, 290
Concerts, in colonial period, 49, 50, 53; later years, 126-27, 237-38, 372
Coney Island, 164, 223
Conwell, Russell H., lecturer, 257
Cook, Ebenezer, quoted, 30
Cook, George Frederick, actor, 109, 110
Coolidge, Calvin, 383
Cooper, Gary, 305
Corbett, James J., prizefighter, 228, 244, 352
Costs of recreation, 321-22, 391-93
Cotton, John, quoted, 6
Country clubs, 241, 359
Country fairs, 26, 30, 279-82, 307
Coup, William C., circus owner, 282
Courtney, Charles E., professional sculler, 226
Cowboys, amusements of, 174-81
Crabtree, Lotta, actress, 173
Cricket, 33, 52, 75, 186, 188
Crockett, David, 72, 76-77, 80
Cronkite, Walter, 339
Croquet, 191-92, 202, 264-65, 364, 366
Crosby, Bing, 337
Cross-word puzzles, 367, 373-74
Crowninshield, Captain David, 40
Crowther, Bosley, quoted, 310-11
Culbertson, Ely, 375
Cushman, Charlotte, actress, 109, 121

Dale, Sir Thomas, 3, 4
Daly, Augustin, 236

Daly's Theatre (New York), 234
Damrosch, Walter, 238
Dance-halls, 98, 165, 170-71, 179,
    220, 221, 370
Dance marathons, 367
Dancing (*see also* Balls), in colonial
    period, 6, 8, 14, 19, 26, 30, 33,
    37-39, 44, 45, 47-48, 52-53,
    57 *ff.*; in nineteenth century,
    76-78, 151-52, 159, 161-62,
    170-71, 179, 254, 275-77; dur-
    ing jazz age, 370-72; mid-twen-
    tieth century, 372-73
Davenport, E. L., actor, 109
Davenport, Fanny, actress, 236
Davidge, William, quoted, 100
Davis, Bette, 301
Davis, Dwight F., as tennis player,
    193
Davis, Elmer, quoted, 375-76
Davis, Emerson, quoted, 91
Davis, Owen, quoted, 215
Davis cup matches, 193, 359, 360
Dean, James, 305
Dempsey, Jack, 345, 352, 353
Denton, Daniel, quoted, 34
De Quille, Dan, quoted, 169
Devol, George H., quoted, 154-55
Diabolo, 367
Dice (*see also* Gambling), 6, 36
Dickens, Charles, 87-88, 93, 148
DiMaggio, Joe, 351
Dime Museums, 220-21
Dinwiddie, Governor, 62
"Discretionary income," 389, 397
Disney, Walt, 301, 305
Dorsey, Tommy, 372
Doubleday, Abner, 186
Douglass, David, actor, 54, 64-65
Drake, Samuel, actor, 102
Dressler, Marie, actress, 262, 294-95
Drew, Daniel, 133
Drew, John, actor, 237
Drinking, as colonial diversion, 16,
    17, 26, 30, 36; in nineteenth
    century, 67, 70, 90, 151, 168,
    170, 172, 178, 249; during Pro-
    hibition era, 366
Drive-ins, 306

Driving, of horses, 148, 158, 185,
    202, 269
Dunlap, William, producer, 106
Dunton, John, quoted, 33
Durant, Charles F., aeronaut, 165
Durante, Jimmy, 338
Duse, Eleanora, 237
Dwight, James, tennis player, 193
Dwight, Timothy, quoted, 69, 84,
    89

Edison, Thomas A., 287, 288
Egleston, Nathaniel, quoted, 271
Election days, 26, 43
Ellington, Duke, 372
Eliot, Charles W., 184
Elssler, Fanny, ballet dancer, 116-
    17, 125
Emerson, Ralph Waldo, quoted,
    183, 272
Emmett, Dan, minstrel player, 128
Endicott, governor, 4
Equestrian drama, 114-16, 123
Everett, Edward, quoted, 183-84

Fairbanks, Douglas, 297
Far West, amusements in mining
    towns, 169-74; of cowboys,
    174-81
Farm festivals, 273
Faux, William, quoted, 70
Federal Theatre Project, 308
Fencing, 44
Fink, Mike, 72
Firemen's carnivals, 256
Firpo, Louis Angel, 352
Fisher, Clare, actress, 112
Fishing, 24, 25, 26, 202, 273, 356-
    57
Fisk, James, 133
Fiske, Minnie Maddern, 236
Fitch, Clyde, playwright, 237
Fithian, Philips Vickers, quoted,
    58-60
Fitzgerald, F. Scott, quoted, 345
Fitzsimmons, Robert Prometheus,
    prize-fighter, 228, 352
Flagg, Edmund, quoted, 134

Flint, Timothy, quoted, 69, 149
Football, in the colonies, 33, 186; intercollegiate, 197-98, 243-46, 347-50; professional, 350
Ford, Henry, 317
Forrest, Edwin, 104, 109-13, 120
Foster, Stephen C., 130
Fourth of July, 166-67, 278-79
Fox hunting, 58, 60, 61, 241
Fox trot, 368
Fraternal orders, 254-56, 367
Frohman, Charles, 237
Frontier, amusements of, 67-83

Gable, Clark, 301
Gambling, in colonial days, 5, 48, 58; nineteenth century, 67, 154-55, 168 *ff.;* in 1930's, 377-78
Game, The, 367
Gander-pulling, 75, 160, 161
Garbo, Greta, 301
Gardening, 379
Gardner, Ava, 305
Garfield, James A., quoted, 209, 386
Garland, Hamlin, quoted, 273, 278, 281, 286
General Federation of Women's Clubs, 257
General Tom Thumb, 122, 124-25, 135, 283
Gibbons, Cardinal, quoted, 226
Gilbert, John, actor, 109
Gilbert and Sullivan operettas, 237
Gilded Age, 230-34
Gillespie, Dizzy, 372
Gillette, William, actor, 236
Gish, Lillian, actress, 294, 297
Gleason, Jackie, 340
Glidden, Charles J., 314
Godfrey, Arthur, 340
Goelet, Francis, quoted, 47-48
Golf, in colonial period, 52; modern game, 242-43, 357-59
Goodman, Benny, 371
Gospel of Work, 86-87, 203-04, 209, 386-87
Grange, 274-78 *passim,* 307

Grange, "Red," 348
Grant, Cary, 305
Greeley, Horace, 164, 173, 209
Greyhound races, 355, 367
Griffith, D. W., 295
Gymnastics, 182, 364

Hackett, James H., actor, 109
Hale, Dr. William Bayard, quoted, 206, 250
Hale, Ruth, 373
Hall, Captain Basil, 97
Hallams, theatrical company, 54, 62, 65, 112
Hamilton, Dr. Alexander, 63-64
Handball, 364
Hanlan, Edward, sculler, 226
Harding, Warren G., 329
Harlow, Jean, 301
Harris, Charles K., 253
Harris, John P., 289, 312
Harvard College, 31, 197, 198
Hays, Will H., 301-03
Hayward, Susan, 305
Health, as factor in growth of sports, 183-85
Heenan, John C., prize-fighter, 145-46
Hepburn, Audrey, 305
Herndon, William, quoted, 75, 82-83
Herne, James A., playwright, 236
Higginson, Thomas Wentworth, quoted, 183
Hillbilly music, 372
Hobbies, 380-81, 397
Hockey, 34, 355, 364
Hogan, Ben, 354
Holbrook, Weare, quoted, 335
Holidays, 14, 162-67, 204, 388
Hollywood, 297, 304
Holmes, Oliver Wendell, quoted, 136, 184
Hone, Philip, quoted, 92, 93, 117, 120, 124-25, 143, 144, 148, 238
Hootenanny, 372
Hoover, Herbert, 328
Hope, Bob, 337

Hopper, De Wolf, actor, 223
Horse racing, in colonial period, 30 *ff.*, 50 *ff.*; in nineteenth century, 70, 72-73, 139-41, 171, 174, 226, 240-41; in twentieth century, 354
Horseshoe pitching, 73, 364
Hot-rodding, 325-26
Hundley, D. R., quoted, 160
Hunter, Richard, actor, 53
Hunting, 24-26, 43, 70-71, 148, 159, 202, 273, 356-57
Huntley, Chet, 339
Husking-bees, 18, 26-27, 30, 43, 76, 183
Hyde, William D., quoted, 205
Hyer, Tom, prize-fighter, 145

Ibsen, Henrik, 236
Idleness (*see also* Leisure), 5 *ff.*, 85-86, 203-04, 391
Industrial workers, their leisure and recreation, 90, 388-89, 390
Irving, Henry, actor, 237
Irving, Washington, quoted, 57, 106
Irwin, May, moving-picture actress, 290

Jack, Sam T., 217
Jackson, Andrew, 73, 75, 139, 141
Jackson, William, runner, 144
James I, issues *Book of Sports*, 10, 12
James, Henry, 383
Jazz, 369-72
Jefferson, Joseph, actor, 110, 128-29, 261
Jefferson, Thomas, 61-62
Jeffries, James J., prize-fighter, 352
John Street Theatre (New York), 54-56, 101
Johnson, Jack, prize-fighter, 352
Jolson, Al, 299
Jones, Bobby, 345
Jones, Hugh, quoted, 35

KDKA, broadcasting station, 328
Kean, Edmund, actor, 62, 109, 110, 120

Kean, Thomas, actor, 54
Keene, Laura, actress, 173
Keith, B. F., 219
Kemble, Charles, actor, 109
Kemble, Fanny, 109, 121; quoted, 160, 163
Kenton, Stan, 372
Kentucky Derby, 240
Kinetoscope, 287, 288
Kline, Maggie, actress, 218
Knickerbocker Club, 240
Knight, Madame Sarah, quoted, 29, 51
Knox, John, 9
Koster and Bial's Music Hall, 289
Kramer, Jack, 354-55
Kreisler, Fritz, 237

Labor unions, and leisure, 388
Lacrosse, 364
Larned, William A., tennis player, 193
Lasky, Jesse, 297
Lawn tennis. *See* Tennis.
Lawrence, Florence, moving-picture actress, 294
League of American Wheelmen, 194-96, 266, 267
Leavitt, M. N., 218
Lecture days, colonial, 7, 29
Lectures, popular, 92-95, 257-60
Leeds, Josiah W., quoted, 205
Legion of Decency, 302
Leigh, Vivien, 301
Leisure, as a modern problem, 209, 287, 288, 386-97
Lenglen, Suzanne, tennis player, 360
Lincoln, Abraham, 73, 75, 79, 107, 113, 130
Lind, Jenny, 125-27, 135, 237
Liston, Sonny, 353
Little League baseball, 351
Livingston, William, quoted, 53
Lloyd, Harold, 297
Lodge night (*see also* Fraternal orders), 254, 255-56, 307
Log rolling, 30, 76 *ff.*
Lollards, 8-9

Lomax, John A., quoted, 175
Long Branch, summer resort, 149, 152, 202
Long Island, and colonial amusements, 34-35, 52; race courses, 140
Longstreet, Augustus Baldwin, quoted, 161
Lotteries, 378
Louis, Joe, 353
Lowell, Massachusetts, recreation of mill workers, 92-93
Ludlow, Noah Miller, 106, 108
Lundberg, George A., quoted, 389
Lyceum Theatre (New York), 234
Lyceums, 92
Lyell, Sir Charles, quoted, 87, 92, 164
Lynd, Robert S. and Helen M., quoted, 379
Lytton, Lord, 228, 368

Macaulay, Thomas B., quoted, 9
Mackaye, Steele, playwright, 236
Macraby, Alexander, quoted, 36, 51-52
Macready, William Charles, actor, 104, 109
Madison Square Theatre (New York), 234
Magic-lantern shows, 42
Mah-jong, 367
Mansfield, Richard, actor, 236, 237
Mantell, Robert, actor, 237, 258
Mantle, Mickey, 351
Marconi, Guglielmo, 287, 327
Marlowe, Julia, actress, 237
Marryat, Captain, quoted, 97
Marshall, John, 73
Martin, Bradley, 233
Martin, Frederick Townsend, quoted, 233
Martin, Mary, 341
Marty, 305
Mather, Cotton, quoted, 14, 17, 20, 48; as angler, 25
Mather, Increase, quoted, 17, 18, 20
Mathews, Charles, actor, 109

Mays, Willie, 351
McAllister, Ward, quoted, 232
McClellan, Mayor, 291
McCullough, John, actor, 237
McGinty, Joe, baseball player, 226
McNamee, Graham, 332
McVicker's Theatre (Chicago), 234
Mead, Margaret, quoted, 389
Melba, Dame Nellie, 237
Melodrama (see also Theatre), 215-17
Melville, Governor Robert, quoted, 64
Menjou, Adolphe, 301
Menken, Adah, actress, 173-74
Merry Mount, festivities at, 3-4
Merz, Charles, quoted, 331
Metropolitan Opera House, 238-39, 332
Militia musters (see also Training days), 256
Miller, Arthur, 308
Milton, John, quoted, 9
Miniature golf, 367, 375-77
Minstrel shows, introduced, 98, 122, 128-29; popularity in midcentury, 129-31; revived over radio, 334
Mississippi Valley, amusements of, 153-56
Mitchell's Olympic Theatre (New York), 104, 117
Mix, Tom, 294
Modjeska, Helena, actress, 237
Monopoly, game, 367
Monroe, Marilyn, 305
Montez, Lola, actress, 173
Montgomery and Stone, vaudeville team, 218
Morris, Clara, actress, 236
Morris-dances, 7, 43
Morrissey, John, prize-fighter, 145
Morton, Thomas, 3
Motels, 321, 324
Motion pictures. See Moving pictures.
Motion Picture Producers and Exhibitors of America, 302
Motor boating. See Boating.
Motorcycling, 364

Motoring, in years before World War I, 312-18; influence on social life, 318-23; in mid-century, 324-26; expenditures on, 321-22; and camping, 324-25
Mountain climbing, 202
Moving pictures, during nickelodeon era, 288-92; early films, 292-94; expansion 1914-1928, 294-98; advent of talkies, 299-301; mid-century decline, 304-06; censorship, 301-03; social consequences, 307, 310-11; attendance figures, 303, 304, 306, 310
Mowatt, Anna Cora, actress, 113
Muirhead, James F., quoted, 201
Murat, Achille, quoted, 116, 151
Murdock, James F., actor, 109
Murray, Arthur, 373
Murray, Walter, actor, 54, 62
Murrow, Edward R., 339
Museums, popular (see also Dime museums), 122
Musial, Stan, 351
Music (see also Concerts, Opera, Radio, Singing), in colonial period, 44, 46, 59; in ante-bellum South, 158; of jazz age, 369-70; in mid-century, 371-72
Music-halls, 221

Nahant, summer resort, 149, 152
Naismith, James A., 264
Nassau Hall. See Princeton.
Nathan, George Jean, quoted, 374
National Brotherhood of Baseball Players, 224
National Horse Show, 241
National Industrial Recovery Act, 387
National League, 190, 224, 225
National parks, 320, 324-25
New Deal, 368
New England, amusements in colonial period, 4-6, 12-13, 16 ff., 25, 26 ff., 32-33, 44-50; theatre in, 101, 102; later interest in sports, 183-84; as vacation land, 320

New York, as colonial capital, 50-57; mid-century theatre, 103 ff.; and spectator sports, 138 ff.; in 1890's, 212 ff.; society during Gilded Age, 231-32
New York Philharmonic, 238
New York Philharmonic-Symphony, 332
Newport, summer resort in colonial period, 64; in mid-century, 149-53 passim; in 1890's, 202, 241; and modern jazz festival, 372
Niblo's Theatre (New York), 105, 117, 119, 166
Nicholson, Sir Francis, 34
Nickelodeons. See Moving pictures.
Nicklaus, Jack, 354
Night clubs, 370, 373
Nine-pins (see also Bowling), 6, 36
Norris, Kathleen, quoted, 374

Olivier, Lawrence, 341
Olympic Games, 355
O'Neill, Eugene, 308
O'Neill, James, actor, 236
Opera, grand, 100, 238-39
Opera houses, 257-58, 307
"Operation Outdoors," 324-25, 394
Ordination balls, 37
Osborn, Chase S., quoted, 277
Outdoor movement, 202, 324, 394, 395
Outdoor Recreation Resources Review Commission, 395

Paar, Jack, 340
Paderewski, Ignace, 237
Page, Thomas Nelson, quoted, 157
Palmer, Arnold, 354
Panoramas, 124, 155-56
Parades (see also Militia musters), 163, 166
Park Theatre (New York), first, 101, 103; second, 103, 105, 106, 120, 142
Parker, Elisha, 52
Parlor-games, 46, 249, 374

Parties. See Balls, Farm festivals, Small town parties.
Pastor, Tony, 218
Patterson, Floyd, 353
Patti, Adelina, 237
Peverelly, Charles A., 189
Philadelphia, as colonial capital, 50
Phonographs, 252, 332
Photography. See Amateur photography.
Pickford, Mary, 294, 297
Picnicking, 51, 157, 162, 277-78, 397
Pinero, Sir Arthur Wing, 236
Ping-pong, 363, 367
Pitts, Zazu, 301
Pittsburgh, 73
Placide, Henry, actor, 109
Plays. See Theatre.
Plimpton, James L., 193
Plymouth, 3, 13, 17
Poker, 154, 170, 176
Polka, 151
Polo, 240, 241
Power, Tyrone, 102
Presley, Elvis, 305
Princeton, 31, 197, 198
Prize contests, 367, 340-41, 377-78
Prize-fighting, 144-47, 171, 172, 226-28, 352-53
Proctor, F. F., 219
Professionalization of sports (see also Spectator sports), 200-01
Punch and Judy shows, 164
Puritanism, in colonial period, 4-21 passim, 64-66; in nineteenth century, 86, 101, 205; modern influence of, 386, 390-91, 393
Pynchon, William, 48

Quakers, 23
Quarter-racing, 35, 72-73
Quincy, Josiah, Jr., quoted, 63
Quoits, 6, 64, 73, 75

Racing. See Horse racing.
Radio, invention of, 287; early development, 327-33; expansion

Radio—Continued
in 1930's, 333-36; popular programs, 331-32; in 1950's, 337-38
Ragtime, 367
Recreational movement, 346, 395
Redpath Lyceum Bureau, 260
Regattas (see also Rowing, Yachting), 141-43, 147, 166, 240
Religion. See Puritanism, Church.
Rice, Dan, circus clown, 134
Rice, Grantland, quoted, 359
Rice, John C., actor, 290
Rice, Thomas D., actor, 128-29
Rickard, Tex, 352
Riesman, David, quoted, 389
Rifle shooting, 171
Ripley, Eliza, quoted, 151
Road companies (see also Theatre), 260-63
Rockefeller, Laurence, 390
Rockne, Knute, 345
Rod and gun clubs, 269
Rogers, Will, 301
Roller skating, 182, 193-94, 265, 363, 366
Rooney, Mickey, 301
Rooney, Pat, 218
Roosevelt, Theodore, 347
Rothafel, Samuel L. (Roxy), 296
Rough-and-tumble fighting, 73-75
Rounders, 185-86
Rousiers, Paul de, quoted, 203
Rowe, John, 25, 48
Rowing (see also Boating, Regattas), 141-43, 184, 226
Roxy's Theatre (New York), 296
Rugby, 197
Running (see also Track and field events), 26, 34, 73, 75, 143-44, 175, 355
Rural amusements. See Circus, Country fairs, Farm festivals, Frontier, Grange, Husking bees.
Russell, Lillian, 218
Russell brothers, 218
Rutgers, 197
Ruth, Babe, 345

Sabbath observance, in colonial period, 5, 7-8, 10-12, 19, 33; in mid-nineteenth century, 70, 90-91; decline of, 207-09, 266, 322, 358, 393
Sailing. See Boating, Regattas.
St. Andrews Club, 242
Salvini, Tommaso, actor, 237
San Francisco, 172, 173, 194, 231
Saratoga, 149-52 passim, 202
Sarnoff, David, 327
Sass, Herbert Ravenel, quoted, 158
Sayers, Tom, prize-fighter, 145
Schumann-Heink, Madame, 238
Scuba-diving, 364
Sculling. See Rowing.
Sears, R. D., tennis player, 193
Seccombe, Joseph, quoted, 25
Sennett, Mack, 294
Sewall, Samuel, quoted, 13-15, 25, 39, 40; at training day, 29
Sharp, John, quoted, 25
Shakespearean drama, in colonial period, 57, 62-63, 65; nineteenth century, 110-12, 116, 172, 173, 219, 236-37; in early movies, 293; summer stock revival, 309
Shaw, Bernard, 236
Shooting galleries, 220, 223
Shooting matches, 26, 29, 36-37, 43, 52, 71-72, 160
Show-boats, 153-54
Shuffle-board, 6, 36, 364
Simpson, Edmund, producer, 107
Singing (see also Songs), 15, 26, 30, 46, 175-76, 252-54
Six-day bicycle races, 355
Skating, 34, 96-97, 184, 269, 364
Skiing, 360-62
Skin-diving, 364
Skinner, Otis, actor, 237
Sky-diving, 364
Slaves, amusements of, 158-60
Sleighing, 33, 51, 148, 269
Slot machines, 378
Small town parties, 45-46, 251-52
Smedes, Susan Dabney, quoted, 158, 161
Smith, Sol, producer, 108
Snead, Sam, 354

Soccer, 364
Social clubs, 63-64
Society, in colonies, 44-66; nineteenth century, 148-52, 230-34; sponsors sports, 184-85, 187, 192, 239-42; and motoring, 312-14
Softball, 363
Songs, minstrel, 130; cowboy, 175-76; old favorites, 252-54, 276-77; circus, 285; popular, 324, 369
Sothern, E. H., actor, 236
Sousa, John Philip, 254
South, colonial sports, 24, 26, 30, 35; colonial society, 57-63; theatres in, 62-63, 102; amusements of ante-bellum days, 156-62
Spangenberg, Lester, 327
Spaulding, A. G., 226
Speakeasies, 370
Spectator sports (see also individual sports), in nineteenth century, 98, 136-47, 200-02, 223-28; in twentieth century, 344-45, 347-55, 396
Spencer, Herbert, quoted, 209
Sports (see also Spectator sports), in colonial period, 26, 31-37, 43; on frontier, 71-75; beginning of organization of, 182-99; in 1890's, 263-69; modern, 344-65; expenditures on, 364; commercialization of, 365
Sports car racing, 325
Sports sections of newspapers, 198, 201
Squash, 364
Stannard, Henry, runner, 144
Steamboat excursions, 164, 222
Stevens, Thomas, bicycler, 195
Stock companies (see also Theatre), 103, 213, 308-09
Stoole-ball, 13
Stoughton, William, quoted, 12
Stuart, James, quoted, 97, 152
Suburbs, 394
Sullivan, John L., 227-28, 352, 367
Sullivan, Mark, quoted, 277, 369

Sullivan, Yankee, prize-fighter, 145
Summer resorts, 64-65, 148-53, 202
Summer stock, 309
Swanson, Gloria, 297
Swimming (*see also* Bathing), 33, 52, 355-56
Swing, 371

Table tennis (*see also* Ping-pong), 363
Talkies. *See* Moving pictures.
Tall tales, 79-80
Talmadge, Constance, 297
Talmadge, Norma, 294
Tarkington, Booth, quoted, 265
Tavern-sports, 6, 19, 36-37
Taverns, colonial, 16-17, 36 *ff.*
Taxi dance-halls, 370
Taylor, Bayard, 126
Taylor, Elizabeth, 305
Television, introduced, 336-37; development and programs, 338-41; social effects, 341-43
Temple, Shirley, 301
Tennis, in colonial period, 52; lawn game introduced, 182, 192-93, 202, 240, 265; professional game, 354-55; as modern sport, 359-60, 366
Thackeray, William Makepeace, 153
Theatre, in colonial period, 6, 14, 48-49, 53-57, 62-65; church attacks on, 89, 204-05; nineteenth century development, 100-21, 213-16, 219, 234-37, 260-63; in twentieth century, 307-09
Theatre Guild, 308
Thomas, Augustus, producer, 237
Thomas, Theodore, 238
Thompson, Denman, actor, 261
Thorpe, Jim, 350
Three Musketeers, The, 297
Tibbett, Lawrence, 301
Tilden, William T., 345, 360
Tilyou, George C., 223
Tocqueville, Alexis de, quoted, 63, 255

Tom shows, 173, 258, 262-63
Tourism. *See* Travel, foreign.
Tourist camps, 321
Towle, George Makepeace, quoted, 191-92, 231
Town-ball, 185-86, 188
Track and field events (*see also* Running), 182, 269, 355
Tracy, Spencer, 305
Trailers, automobile, 321
Training days (*see also* Militia musters), 26, 29, 30, 43
Trap-shooting, 364
Travel (*see also* Motoring), 148-49; costs of, 321-22, 391-92; foreign, 381-85
Traveling shows (*see also* Circus, Carnivals), 39-42, 132-33, 155-56, 161
Treasure hunts, 367
Tristano, Lennie, 372
Trolley excursions, 221-22
Trollope, Frances, quoted, 67, 87, 98, 105
Trotting races, 141, 147, 226, 269, 279-80
Tunney, Gene, 345, 352, 353
Twain, Mark, quoted, 73-74, 169-70, 191
Twist, the, 371
Two-step, 254
Tyler, Royall, 29, 56

Union Square Theatre (New York), 234
Urban amusements. *See* Dance halls, Minstrel shows, Moving pictures, Society, Spectator sports, Theatre, Vaudeville.

Vacation travel. *See* Travel.
Vacations (*see also* Holidays), 204, 307, 320
Valentino, Rudolph, 305
Vallee, Rudy, 331
Vanderbilt, Mrs. William K., 231
Van Doren, Charles, 341
Variety shows, 98, 119-20, 217-18

Vaudeville, 119, 218-19, 307
Veblen, Thorstein, quoted, 230
Virginia, colonial amusements, 5, 8, 30, 34, 35, 58 *ff.*
Virginia City (Nevada), 169-74, 231
Volley-ball, 363

Wagner, Honus, baseball player, 226
Wallack, James L., 236
Wallack's Theatre (New York), 234
Waltz, 151
Ward, Artemus, 173
Ward, Samuel Dexter, quoted, 164
Warren, William, Jr., actor, 109
Washburn, Leonard Dana, quoted, 225
Washington, George, 60, 61, 62
Water skiing, 364
Watkins, Harry, actor, 109, 114
Watson, Elkanah, 279
Weber and Fields, 218
Weddings, on frontier, 78-79
Whist, 48, 252, 374
White, Pearl, actress, 261
White, William Allen, quoted, 248, 261, 384
White Sulphur Springs, 149, 150
Whiteman, Paul, 369
Whitman, Walt, quoted, 120
Whitney, Caspar, quoted, 185, 245
Whittier, John Greenleaf, 227
Wilde, Oscar, 236
Willard, Jess, 352
Williams, Ted, 351
Williams, Tennessee, 308

Williamsburg, 61-62
Wills, Helen, tennis player, 360
Wilson, Woodrow, 313-14
Winslow, Edward, 3
Winthrop, John, quoted, 7, 17
Wise, John, aeronaut, 165
WJZ, broadcasting station, 329, 330
Women, and colonial amusements, 30, 46-47, 59; in early nineteenth century, 95-98, 151; at theatre, 104 *ff.;* ocean bathing, 152, 201-02, 356; take up sports, 191-93, 195-96; and bicyling, 266-67; role in twentieth century sports, 356, 360, 362, 363
Women's clubs, 256-57
Wood, William, quoted, 7
Woodruff, Hiram, sulky driver, 141
World Series, 225
Works Progress Administration, 346
Wrenn, Robert D., tennis player, 193
Wrestling, 26, 34, 73, 171
Wright, Frances, quoted, 95
Wright, Henry, baseball player, 187-88
Wycliffe, John, 8
Wynne, Ed, 338

Yachting, 142-43, 148, 239, 240
Yale College, 31, 197, 198
Young Men's Christian Association, 206
Ysaye, Eugene, musician, 237

Zedwitz, Herman, musician, 53